Native American Resilience

A STORY OF RACISM GENOCIDE AND SURVIVAL

P. S. STRENG

- ISBN Print-book: 979-8-9918700-0-9

Published by Author House 02/10/2021
- ISBN: 978-1-6655-1370-8 (sc)
- ISBN: 978-1-6655-1369-2 (e)

Library of Congress Control Number: 2021900851

Author photograph provided by Erin and Meredith Schneider.

This book is dedicated with appreciation and affection to

My daughter, Elizabeth, and son, David, and to the memory of my husband, Roger, and daughter, Rhonda.

All Native Americans past and present who have inspired this work.

Foreword

This endorsement is characterized by recognizing the persistence and dedication of the author, P. S. Streng. Over the years, she has demonstrated the courage and resilience that inspires those who would read her research and writing. It is imperative that we spend our time and energy learning about her research and this finished work to avoid history repeating itself.

After nearly a half century in mental health counseling, including two years working directly with the Navajo and the Zuni people, it was intriguing to find the information in this book. Witnessing firsthand the Native American feelings of hopelessness but at the same time the unexplainable resilience through their social and economic dilemma, I was faced with an unsettling confusion. I came to understand that Native Americans were not only proud of who they are but also display an underlying characteristic of hope and persistence that was unexplained.

Through this researched manuscript, my eyes were opened to the systemic annihilation and genocide of a proud and noble people. And, through the manuscript, it was discovered that through generation after generation, the Native American civilization was lied to, manipulated and systematically deceived – that the powerful, greedy and gluttonous of one generation, who even used God as a reason for the annihilation of a human race, could dehumanize an entire civilization to get their needs met. Add to this the understanding that their human rights were not only taken away from them by deception, but also that the promises and treaties made were constantly being broken outright by a culture which claimed to be more civilized and enlightened.

The deep underlying tragedy which has been hidden from the world is now being manifested through the research and fact-finding of this genuine author. It is more than concerning that the historical truth has been hidden by a systematic cover-up, and it gives rise to the replication of deceit in our modern day. If we do not honor our history as a people and turn it around, we will inevitably repeat the catastrophe again. The government and the rich and powerful openly used lies and deceit to again annihilate not only the Native American, but also those who are Americans now.

The full force of this book begins to focus on the reality that there will always be men and women who love power and greed more than human life. There is a need for the human society in America to rise up and fight for all Native Americans and give them back their rights. It is important to remember that a society that does not remember its past history is doomed to live that same history again. Native Americans need to be given their resources, rights and privileges, so they can come out of the darkness of racism and truly manifest themselves as the resilient people they are and the culture that defines them. Our heritage is to know the truth and to act responsibly and immediately to provide Native Americans the assistance and their God-given resources necessary to be able to fully actualize their existence.

Norman Haney, LCSW, MAC.

Preface

In 1992, as a nontraditional student in my last semester of college, several things happened that changed my life's interest forever. For a required history course, I selected American History, and that class opened my heart and mind to the real story of American and Indian relationships. And, I attended a luncheon for graduating nontraditional students where I learned, through discussions at my table, that the United States did not sign the 1948 United Nations General Assembly Resolution 260 against genocide because of the legal implications against the genocide inflicted on Native Americans. It was not until Reagan became president that the U.S. finally signed the resolution and only after it had been significantly altered.

These things prompted my decision to write *Native American Resilience*, and it has taken me almost 30 years to achieve that goal. In the meantime, I have read a plethora of books, magazine articles and periodicals, visited libraries in several states, as well as accessed them online as part of my research. I found that my eight years of experience in the 1990's doing both market and early computer connectivity research for defense products and military records served me well in this endeavor. At that time, technology was nowhere near the level it is now, and those advancements have enabled me to easily research with even greater depth of coverage. As you will see, this book is based on research, so I am very grateful for my work experience and the rate of technological advancements.

As life would have it, also during this time, my husband became very ill. But until his passing, he encouraged me in this pursuit, asked probing questions and traveled with me, visiting the Cherokee Museum and Cultural Center in Cherokee, North Carolina and Denver Public Library archives to expand my research. A voracious reader himself, he tore articles about Native Americans from magazines and newspapers, adding to my knowledge base. There was a common goal to discover the facts to support the story I intended to write, and his feedback and support was invaluable.

During these years, I continued working full-time, had my own health issues and cared for my husband through his lengthy fight with cancer. The idea of a book about Native Americans and the racism and genocide they have endured was temporarily put on hold, but the passion for the project and the research work never left me.

In 1995, I wrote to Wilma Mankiller who was Principal Chief of the Cherokee Nation at that time, telling her of my book idea. I still have the handwritten note of encouragement I received from her. Having the Cherokee Principal Chief, someone who personally experienced many of the government's programs to integrate the Indian into white society, who protested during the Alcatraz sit-in and learned the value of peaceful protest to educate people and who took those lessons back to Oklahoma, willingly give me her support in this endeavor was invaluable to me.

Back in the 1990s, as I drove from my younger daughter's home in Mississippi to our home in Kentucky, these words came to me as a way to express my feelings and reason for writing this book, "On a bright spring morning, I drove towards home traveling the roads of Mississippi, Alabama, Tennessee and Kentucky before arriving at my destination. Dogwoods and redbuds were in full bloom and the wildflowers in leafy array along the hills and roadways. The story I am about to tell lays heavy upon my heart, and I am compelled to write of the struggles and survival of the People of this land. The Cherokees were one of the Native peoples to originally inhabit much of this region."

For untold centuries, hundreds of Native peoples were born, lived and died in the Americas. The *"Yunwiya,"* meaning *"The Real People,"* and called Cherokee by outsiders, were one such group. My research has revealed that all Indians have a word in their language that identifies them as "The "Real People." The Cherokee developed a rich and beautiful culture handed down generation to generation by the storytellers entrusted with their oral history and taught to the *Yunwiya* through stories and rituals. This oral history and traditions permeated their everyday lives, helping them understand the spirits, defining the seven clans and the matriarchal structure of their society, showing them the proper way for a man and a woman to conduct themselves, determining what a baby was to be named, the time to hunt or to make war. In honoring the traditions, the Cherokees lived prosperous lives.

The lives and history of the Cherokee are powerful examples of a proud People, their struggles and their survival. Part I of this book tells about the struggles the Cherokees have endured against racism and genocide since the arrival of the Europeans. Their struggles exemplify the struggles of all Native Americans – their forced removal from their homelands and the outlawing of their languages, religions, cultures and governments. Part II examines the 20th and 21st century laws and regulations of the United States that have forever changed the lives of Indian people. Various programs have been tried by the government to integrate or assimilate them into white society in an attempt to take care of the "Indian problem." Native Americans are unconquered, and they continue working to overcome the years of racism and genocide. Some of the Indian tribes are thriving in the 21st century, while others live in abject poverty. This is their story.

First, I believe it will be helpful to provide a little backstory. When the Europeans first landed in the New World, they made contact with a few natives along the coast of islands and the landmasses that would become Central, South and North America. From these few, the diseases of the whites spread rapidly, and the native occupants of the land had no immunity to them. Many tribes were reduced by half or greater before the majority of natives ever saw the first white man. Those that disease did not kill, the whites made war against – robbing, raping, plundering, killing or enslaving those who stood in their path. In the whites' quest for expansion into a country occupied by over 500 Nations of Indians, the concept of "Manifest Destiny" (white belief that continuous expansion was God's will) was developed and given as logical reasoning for the destruction or exploitation of the Native peoples. The invaders became "We, the People" as wars were fought, treaties negotiated, lands taken and Native people moved. There were times in the late 19th Century and early 20th Century that the United States government tried programs of acculturation, assimilation or dispersion as a way to bring the Cherokee and all other Native peoples into mainstream America. In 1924, Natives were recognized as citizens of the United States but without a Bill of Rights. However, they were finally given the legal right to their own form of government.

The centuries since the first white man came to the Americas have been filled with disease, violence, racism and genocide for the Native peoples. In spite of this, their story is one of resilience and survival. Several great men made telling the early history and traditions of the Cherokee people possible through their diligent efforts at recording their observations, discussions with the elders and correspondence. James Adair, a trader who lived among the Indians in what is now the southeastern United States, provided a firsthand account in his *History of the Indians*. Adair chronicled his life among the Indians, specifically the Cherokee, starting in 1735 and covered a forty-year period. One of the most important, yet least accessible, works about Cherokee Indians in the late eighteenth and early nineteenth centuries is a collection of writings by John Howard Payne and Daniel S. Butrick, known as the Payne Butrick Papers. Understanding the unsettled times, as the United States government pushed the American Indians to give up their lands to move west of the Mississippi and the determination of the Indians to remain in their ancestral lands, Payne and Butrick feared that their history would be lost forever. Over several decades, the two men, individually and then collectively, sought to record information on the Cherokee culture and history by living with them, through conversations with elders and correspondence the leaders entrusted to them when emigration loomed.

Sequoyah, a Cherokee, developed their first syllabary in 1821, thus enabling the Cherokee people to record their history and beliefs while still living in their ancestral land. The Trail of Tears occurred in 1839, resulting in the majority of Cherokees being forced to immigrate to Indian Territory west of the Mississippi. Little was known or recorded about the Eastern Band of Cherokees until James Mooney came to North Carolina in 1888. Mooney, an ethnographer with the Smithsonian

Institution, lived and worked among the Cherokee periodically until his death in 1921. He learned their language and customs and, more importantly, earned their trust and respect. This resulted in Mooney's collected works, *History, Myths, and Sacred Formulas of the Cherokees.* Mooney was entrusted with approximately 600 formulas of various chiefs and medicine men which had been written utilizing Sequoyah's syllabary. Of these "...he transliterated, translated, and annotated about one hundred and fifty with Swimmer's [medicine man] assistance in 1888 and 1889. Twenty-eight of these were published..." The remainder were lost.[1] He worked with a number of Indian tribes west of the Mississippi, but "... after visiting the Indian Territory in Oklahoma [he concluded] that the bulk of Cherokee traditional knowledge and ritual remained in the East."[2] The work of these men is included within this history.

In my curiosity and desire to know more about the Cherokee people, which broadened in scope to include other Native peoples, my research and investigation have led me to compile and document my findings in this historical account to the best of my resources and information available. It is based on research done by many people over the past 275 years and taken from records even older and more numerous. Please know that at the end of each chapter, there is a brief commentary entitled Author's Thoughts where I express my opinion. It is clearly separated from the research, and my overall thoughts and commentary, Reflections, at the close of the book is as well.

Other books have focused in depth on a particular era or subject related to Native Americans. Through their efforts and my research, it is my hope that the reader will gain a more complete sense of the lives of the Cherokees and all Native Americans. Their story continues through time into the struggles of the 21st Century.

It is my passion and purpose to increase awareness of the centuries of struggles endured by Native Americans. Awareness enables thought and discussion, which will hopefully help to redress the wrongs and increase support for Native Americans as they continue to persevere against overwhelming obstacles.

All proceeds from this book will go to the American Indian College Fund in Denver, Colorado

---

Endnotes:
[1]   Mooney's History, Intro 20, 22.
[2]   Mooney's History, Intro 23.

Author's Notes

Treaties, government documents, newspapers and the public referred to the Indigenous people of the land newly discovered by Columbus as Indians, taken from the Spanish word "Indios." This later changed to Natives, then Native Americans. In the 21st Century, American Indians came to mean those individuals, bands or tribes who live in the 48 contiguous states of the United States.

Native American is a term for those groups served by the Bureau of Indian Affairs under various U.S. laws and regulations.

Native Americans include: Indians, Inuits and Aleuts; Native Hawaiians; American Samoans; Chamorros of Guam; Native peoples of the Commonwealth of the Northern Mariana Islands; and Native peoples of the Republic of Palau. ...[1]

For the purposes of this book, when the word "Native" is capitalized, it is referring to Native Americans of the U.S. only. When native is lowercase, it refers to the natives of the areas being discussed. Similarly, the use of "People" and "Indian" refer only to Native Americans of the U.S.

As the author, I have chosen to utilize the terminology prevalent for the time period being discussed and maintained strict adherence with quotes. The authenticity of the quotes, including spelling and punctuation of the source, although different from that of the 21st century, is maintained throughout.

I have also chosen to use the dreamcatcher on the front cover because it illustrates the importance of Native American legends in their culture. Good dreams know the way through the dreamcatcher, allowing them to slip through the center hole and slide down the feathers while bad dreams get caught in the web and perish at first light. By holding onto their dreams through all obstacles, the Native people have survived and proven their resilience.

All information, other than my analysis and opinion in Author's Thoughts at the end of the chapters and "Reflections" at the end of the book, are from the materials listed in the bibliography. Paraphrasing and direct quotes are individually cited, and the source for each is listed in the endnotes of each chapter.

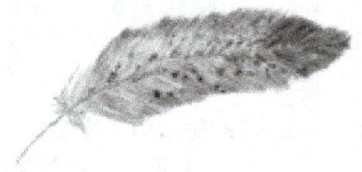

Endnote:

1   Utter, p. 31.

Table of Contents

Foreword.. i

Preface iii

Author's Notes ix

PART 1 - Cherokee Struggle and Survival

1 Cornerstones of Cherokee Culture
Oral Traditions from Earliest Time 1

2 The Confrontation 4th Century B.C.
Through Invasion of New World 21

3 Trade and Treaties From Early 1600s to 1830 39

4 Significant Leaders (1730 – 1850).. 59

5 Education, Religious and Cultural Change
1789 - 1990 When Rights Restored 71

6 Divergent Views on Removal
Early 1800s to 1872, No More Treaties 89

7 Removal and Settlement in "Indian Territory"
(1838 – 1889)... 109

8 Cherokee Embroiled in American Civil War
(1861 – 1865)... 129

9 Peace But at What Cost ?
(1785 to Oklahoma Statehood in 1907) 149

PART 2 - Native Americans within American Society

10 Ironies Abound (1897 to 1925).. 177

11 Perseverance through Endless Struggles
(1920s to 1950s) 197

12 One Nation – Many People (1961 to 1986)...........................221

13 Modern Era in Indian Relations (1981 to 2020) 249

14 Concerns Continue into the 21st Century 273

15 Promises versus Reality – In 2009 Government
   Is Held to Its 1899s Treaties 299

16 21st Century Court Cases Continue the Fight 323

17 Preserving Indian History – NAGPRA...........................345

Author's Reflections 368

Bibliography 378

Acknowledgments...404

Author Biography 405

PART I

Cherokee Struggle and Survival

| ONE |

Cornerstones of Cherokee Culture
Oral Traditions from Earliest Time

While stories and traditions vary from tribe to tribe, the Spirit remains the same, providing wisdom that guides the People throughout their lives. Stories go back to the beginning of time. They might be about the Spirit world or the creation of the ancestral land which provided everything necessary for their lives. Other times, the stories were of battles fought to retain the land, great love stories or ones about the many festivals. Called Cherokee by the outsiders who were to come, elders instilled within the people a deep and abiding faith in the Great Spirit and pride in the *Yunwiya,* meaning *The Real People.* The elders taught the People to revere the wisdom of the Great Spirit who provided guidance and nourishment throughout their lives. While all the stories can't be known, the ones that are illuminate the culture, beliefs and traditions necessary to understand the history and impact of events on the *Yunwiya.* They are all intertwined, thus making up the fabric of their lives, then and now.

James Mooney, a white man with a kind heart and an abiding interest in the culture and beliefs of native peoples, was an ethnologist who lived and worked among the Eastern Band of Cherokees in North Carolina in 1888 and 1889, returning in the early 1900s to continue his work. From Mooney's book, *History, Myths, and Sacred Formulas of the Cherokees*, one can learn the story of Selu and Kanati, which provides an important story about how and why the Cherokee believed sustenance for survival was provided. It is paraphrased below to provide an example of how these stories were part of, as well as influenced, the People's lives and cultures. According to the story:

1

As was customary, the people gathered around the evening fire in anticipation of the stories that would be shared. Tonight, they were again told a story they loved. It is an important story as it tells how and why the Cherokee believed sustenance for survival was provided. The story is about Selu, who was regarded as the first Cherokee woman, and her husband, Kanati, who was considered to be the first Cherokee man and patron of all hunters.

The couple had a son who loved to play along the river and another who, according to the legend, sprang from the blood of the deer that Selu washed in the river. The second son had magical powers and often led his brother into mischief. As the boys got older, they became curious about how Kanati was always able to bring game home from his hunting trips, so they decided to follow him. By observing him, they saw how to cut reeds and fit them with feathers to make arrows. Following their father as he climbed the mountain, they observed him move a rock and saw a deer jump forth. Now they knew why his hunts were successful and decided that they would try this in the future.

A few weeks passed and the boys saw an opportunity to try out their new knowledge. They stopped and collected some reeds and feathers to make some arrows. Then, continuing up the mountain, they arrived at the spot where Kanati had shot the deer. Removing the stone, first one deer jumped out and another and another. In their excitement, the boys forgot to replace the stone and finally, all the birds and animals had escaped down the mountain and into the forest.

The sound was so loud that Kanati, sitting at home, immediately knew what had happened. Furious, he climbed the mountain and found the boys still trying to figure out what to do. In his anger, Kanati overturned large jars containing the bugs of the world which proceeded to bite the boys. Not until they dropped to the ground in pain did Kanati take pity on them. He then explained that as a consequence of their actions, they would have to hunt throughout the forest for the game, and there would be times when they would find nothing.

Sending the boys home, Kanati went hunting hoping to find some game for their supper. The boys were tired and hungry when they arrived home, but Selu told them there was no meat, and she went to the storehouse to get corn and beans. Curious, the boys decided to follow, peeked through the logs of the storehouse and saw her rub her stomach and fill the basket half full of corn. Next, she rubbed her armpits and filled the basket with beans. Selu had always provided the family with corn and beans, but now the boys were suddenly afraid of their mother and decided she was a witch whom they should kill.

Selu knew they planned to kill her, but she did not want them to go hungry, so she carefully instructed them on what to do to ensure the corn would continue to grow and be plentiful. The boys were to clear the ground and drag her body around a large circle seven times. She told them that in order to have a plentiful corn crop, they would have to stay up and watch throughout the night. Not wanting to do everything Selu told them, the boys only cleared seven spots:

> This is the reason corn now grows only in a few places instead of over the whole world. They dragged the body of Selu around the circle, and wherever her blood fell on the ground the corn sprang up. But instead of dragging her body seven times across the ground, they dragged it over only twice, which is the reason the Indians still work their crop but twice a year. The two brothers sat up and watched their corn all night, and in the morning, it was full grown and ripe."[1]

Outsiders Invade Indian Land

While the stories endured, change came quickly to the American Indian, starting in the late 1600s. When the first Indians were discovered in North America, pictures, poems and stories depicted them as the "Nobel Savage" or the "Nobel Red Man," an image which gave way to a "Savage Red Man." By the time the ships arrived carrying settlers to the new world, their political, moral and religious mores determined their view of this new land and its inhabitants. The savage was to be conquered or destroyed. While many examples are documented among history books, specific instances documented in North America emphasize the reality of the impending disaster awaiting the Native people.

The invaders of the Indian lands were strong and plentiful and came into the Indian's land from every direction. Spain, Russia and England explored the California region in the 16th century, with Spain establishing missions during the 1770s. The French first positioned themselves in Canada and came into the midsection of America over land and via the waterways, extending to present-day Louisiana. Utilizing the Mississippi River and the numerous trading outposts established along its length, they gained access to the heart of the continent extending east. Although the French claimed the new land in America for their king, their principal purpose was trade, not settlement, and the Indians gladly traded pelts for guns, rifles, ammunition and other trade goods. Columbus laid claim to the lands of the Caribbean for the Spanish monarchy, with Spanish reach eventually extending into Florida and the Gulf Coast region. Spanish forces also laid claim to large swaths of land along the coast of present-day South Carolina.

England and Holland claimed the lands along the Atlantic coast. Spain, England and Holland planted colonies in the areas they claimed and from those colonies explored inland. A Cherokee tribal law required that a white man could only remain in their country if he married a Cherokee woman, at which time the man was given protection of the leaders, and the French traders were the primary ones to take advantage of this law. The explorations of the immigrants provided a picture of a bountiful land that was wide open to settlement.

There were scattered native towns and villages. However, in accordance with the beliefs of the Cherokee People, the vast lands were not owned by individuals but held in common by the Nation. Specific regions, Kentucky as an example, were reserved for hunting by many tribes. The immigrants refused to understand the Native viewpoints on the use of the land or to acknowledge their language, customs and traditions, insisting on bringing their own customs, laws and language instead.

Trade Brings Lifestyle Changes

Trading with any of the immigrants greatly changed the lives of the American Indian. The first metal weapons and cutting tools now replaced implements of stone and bone. Introduced about 1740, the horse quickly became popular, with large herds possessed by 1760, and each man owned from two to twelve mounts by 1775. The women prized the cotton fabrics and learned to sew. Many families raised sheep, and by 1770, it was popular to card wool, and those who could afford a spinning wheel and loom learned to use both.[2] In addition to corn, gardens provided an abundance of fresh vegetables, trees furnished fruits and nuts and cattle were domesticated.

Gender Roles: A Balance of Forces

In *Selu, Seeking the Corn-Mother's Wisdom,* Marilou Awiakta emphasized the importance of balance in Cherokee life:

> … traditionally, the Cherokee, like many other Native peoples, have applied the principle of gender balance to all levels of their society, from individual, family and community to ceremonies and government. Woman and man represent cardinal balances in nature. Among these balances are: the balance of forces – continuance in the midst of change; the balance of food – vegetables and meat; and the balance of relationships – taking and giving back with respect.
>
> Regardless of the era in which this ancient story of Selu is told, one of the unchanging elements is that a basic imbalance, a lack of respect, between genders disturbs the balance in the environment, just as imbalance in an individual invades the web of his or her life and affects all relationships… One of the most sustaining elements common to all Selu stories is healing. Even a break in the cardinal balance may be restored to wholeness and harmony … Hope strengthens the will to survive. Determination and work make survival possible.[3]

5

The All-Encompassing Great Spirit

The Great Spirit resided in all that was around the Cherokee – in the plants and animals, in the earth itself and the very air that was breathed. Many of the things the Great Spirit taught were essential to their understanding of life and survival. Throughout time, they drew upon sacred numbers to help guide their lives. The number seven was considered sacred and represented throughout their culture. The most significant were the seven-sided council house, seven great festivals, seven directions and seven matrilineal clans.

Government by Council

The council house was usually the first structure built in a new town. The seven sides were constructed of wood, with one door and one smoke hole and everything covered over with dirt to give the appearance of a mound from the outside. It was large enough to provide seating for all seven clans or approximately five hundred men. The center was lower, with a fire and seats to accommodate the chiefs, head men and Ghighau, which meant Beloved Woman or Beloved Mother. The seats for the others were raised to provide visibility for everyone in attendance. The women, other than Ghighau, had a separate council house.

The headmen, chiefs and Ghighau represented their towns in the National Council. The Beloved Woman participated in all town and national meetings whether for war or peace and led the local women's council. The council recommended what punishment prisoners received – even whether they lived or died, but it was Ghighau who had the final say on what punishment prisoners would receive. In addition, she prepared and served the sacred black drink used in rituals of the southeastern tribes in religious ceremonies and in state council ceremonies. Only those warriors who proved themselves in battle could partake of the drink, and those warriors had to be ritually purified.

Ceremonial and Individual Importance of Wampum

Wampum belts were originally used by the Iroquois and other members of the Five Nations along the upper east coast, with some of them dating back 4,500 years. The beads were made from shells, which was significant because of the connection the shell had with water and its life-giving properties. Though never worn as belts, wampum played an important role in the political and religious life of the Cherokees. In a speech given at Sweet Briar College, Virginia, on April 2, 1993, Chief Wilma Mankiller said that long before settlers organized themselves into colonies, the Cherokee had their own version of a constitution. "... our constitution was a wampum belt, and the color and the arrangements of the beads represented symbols of governance and principles by which we lived our lives, ..."[4] The beads were given great value due to the exacting and time-consuming work to produce them from the white of cylindrical seashells and purple from the quahog clam found in the North Atlantic. Messages contained in the wampum had to be memorized by the chosen carrier, so they could precisely recite the message contained in each belt. Wampum was a cultural link to their lives.

Wampum was exchanged when treaties or agreements were made. If a proffered belt was rejected, it meant the proposed treaty was not accepted. "They served as an oath before God."[5] The U.S. government did not understand the significance of the belts, thinking it was just some Native custom which would help get them what they wanted. The Natives "... believed the exchange of wampum's made an agreement sacred and binding to both sides."[6]

Seven belts had been preserved during the dark days of removal and secreted away after arrival in Indian Territory. When a group of traditional Cherokees formed the Keetoowah in the mid-1800s, the first order of business was to recover the belts. They are of various widths and lengths, and several are six feet long. The Keetoowah's "... believed the true interpretation of the symbols woven into them would reveal to them what they had lost."[7] These belts are still used in very special ceremonies in the life of the Keetoowah's in Oklahoma.

Another cultural aspect of wampum is that it was used in proposing marriage. A man would give wampum beads, on a single strand, to his representative to present to the family of the woman he wanted to marry. After the beads were given, the representative would retire to give the family an opportunity to discuss the proposed union. If the wampum was returned to the representative, the union was declined, and no further discussion would occur.

Seven Cherokee Clans, Seven Directions

In *The Cherokee People: The Story of the Cherokees from Earliest Origins to Contemporary Times,* Thomas Mails described the seven clans which included the Wolf Clan, which held the highest distinction, the Deer Clan, the Bird Clan, the Red Paint Clan, the Wild Potato Clan and the Long Hair Clan or Twister People. In ancient days, the Wolf Clan hunted like wolves, running after game and attacking in packs, while members of the Deer Clan were swift like the deer that they kept in captivity, observing the deer and training until skilled in hunting and killing them. The Bird Clan was fond of birds and often had captive crows and chicken hawks and was renowned for their expertise in hunting with snares and blowguns. Members of the Red Paint Clan ritually employed red iron-oxide paint to attract lovers and gain protection from witches and other harm, while the Wild Potato Clan gathered wild potatoes, which grew in swampy places along the rivers. The Long Hair Clan or Twister People obtained its name in one of two ways; within one group, the name evolved through the Cherokee word meaning one who twists, while the second version or long hair refers to the clan's love of personal adornment and elaborate hairstyles. The seventh was the Blue Clan that took its named after a bluish plant they gathered from swamps and used for food and medicine.[8]

Each person considered their clan the most important, and by tradition, their mother and grandmother determined their clan, so a newly married couple became part of the woman's clan. The husband came to live in his wife's house, and his authority over the children was restricted, while the mother's eldest brother had authority over the household.

It is also important to understand the significance of numbers in their lives and the symbolism of the colors associated with each. Four has a direct relationship to the four cardinal points: east, south, west and north with above, down and center completing the number seven. From the east, life begins with the rising sun. Its Spirit color is red and denotes power or war. From the south comes the Spirit color of white, which indicates peace. The west has the setting sun, and its Spirit color is black and means sickness and death. The north's Spirit color is blue and is symbolic for defeat or unsatisfied desire. Also significant is above where the heavenly bodies reside, down where evil lives and center meaning where the person is at present. From these seven comes the essence of all life.

Celebrating the New Year

The seven sacred festivals were based on the cycles of the moon, with the most important being the fall festival when the nuts and first new corn crops were ready, which signaled the beginning of the new year and a rebirth of their lives. It was a busy and exciting time of year when the homes and other buildings were cleaned and repaired inside and out. Clutter, including broken pottery, old broken furniture and unused items were discarded. The festival took place over many days so much food was prepared in anticipation. Finally, when all was ready, the fire of last year was extinguished and all fireplaces thoroughly cleaned. Then the People were led to the river with great anticipation to face the rising sun for the purification ritual. They celebrated the festival, and after the new fire was blessed, it was distributed to each home.

The People took pride in the many fine and varied crafts produced for both utilitarian and artistic purposes. Beautiful stone pipes, both large and small, depicting humans, birds and animals were carved and shaped with flint knives. Bows, arrows, blowguns and other weapons were all crafted with expert care. Pottery molded from native clay and baskets woven with intricate designs enabled them to gather and store a large variety and quantity of foodstuffs and other items. Well-crafted garments had decorations which not only enhanced them but displayed to visitors a well-organized group prepared for the challenges of the environment to such an extent that there were leisure hours enjoyed in such pursuits.

Cherokee Societal Structure

The Cherokee divided their settlements into geographically identified areas, as can be seen in histories of the region. The Upper Settlements were often called Overhills. The others were the Middle Towns, the Valley Settlements and the Lower Towns. While the Nation all spoke Cherokee, there were four different dialects. "The Middle and Valley Towns, different from the others, is predominant among the Qualla Indians of South Carolina today. The Lower Town dialect has practically disappeared. The Oklahoma Cherokee language has retained the Overhill sound."[9]

"The Cherokee form of government was a loosely knit union of seventy or eighty tribal towns."[10] Although each town operated independently, they worked together for mutual safety. In the distant past, the primary social units were the national capital, the town, the household and, finally, the clan. In Pat Alderman's 1978 book, *Nancy Ward & Dragging Canoe*, she wrote that each town served as the primary social unit, followed by the household and lastly, the clan. As few as four extended families but often two hundred or more houses made up the individual towns of the past with all seven clans typically represented within each town. The People selected a principal chief, a peace chief and a war chief based on merit. It is here that the Cherokee also saw a great disparity between themselves and the white man's civilization. Instead of merit, a white man could buy his office. They observed that justice was difficult for the poor white man to obtain; the rich were spared, but the rogue had to pay for his mistakes.

Matters of Justice

Refuge towns, sometimes known as "peace towns" or "white towns" existed among the Cherokee people, as well as the Creeks and other American Indians. The Cherokee set aside four towns designated as peace towns and their ancient capital, Echota, near the mouth of the Little Tennessee was such a town, which offered refuge to anyone who accidentally killed another. If they made it from the site of the killing to a peace town, friends or relatives of the victim could not enter the town to seek vengeance;

however, once the accused ventured outside the town, vengeance would be swiftly accorded.

Declared innocent until a court could be convened, judges examined the accused and witnesses knowledgeable of the circumstances surrounding the slaying. Testimony was preceded by a witness statement, which varied in degree depending upon the importance of the matter at hand. All of this spoke to the importance of the testimony and the strength of the People. In his book, Mails states:

> ... In affairs of great significance, the judge said to the witness, 'Have you now told me the real truth by the great and powerful name of the living God, which proclaims his existence without beginning or end, and by his self-existent and literal name in which I adjure you?' And the witness, assuming that he was properly fearful of God's chastisement of liars, would answer as strongly as possible, 'I have told you the naked truth, which I most solemnly swear by this adorable, great, divine, self-existent name, which we are not to profane, and I likewise attest to it, by his other beloved, unspeakable, sacred, essential name.'[11]

Once found guilty, the ancient law dictated several types of punishment which would not be considered in modern times. Although not condemned publicly, the accused might be placed in the forefront of battle to ensure a noble death. Responsibility for crimes of its members lay on the clan, so a brother would often dispose of the murderer to prevent a blood vengeance on the clan. Criminals who caused great harm might be stoned or taken to a high cliff where their elbows and knees were drawn up and tied, and they were then thrown onto the sharp rocks below. Depending upon the circumstances, an accidental killing might be satisfied by clan revenge or with a gift.[12]

Roles of Distinction

If a woman distinguished herself in battle, the chiefs could acclaim her as Ghighau -which was a lifetime honor and carried great respect and responsibility. A medicine man studied many years as an apprentice under the existing medicine man and then continued his studies throughout his life. *The Swimmer Manuscript,* published in 1932, provided information on the Cherokee medicine men, who were committed to preserving the faith, lore and customs of their people and led them in their many rituals and celebrations. "And with the disintegration of Cherokee material culture and social organization, the medicine man obtained a position of leadership which in many instances practically amounts to that of political head in another tribe."[13]

> Medicine men did not have special names, nor were they grouped in any society ... it is more customary to call them by a name which was more discriminating and descriptive of the specialty to which the medicine man referred to devoted himself.[14]

An individual medicine man could be called upon for his knowledge and expertise in one or many specialties. Some served as midwives, while others were skilled in rainmaking, in divination or incantations, with a few believed to have occult powers, but the principal reason for the people to turn to the medicine man was his ability to cure a disease. In the late 1800s, Mooney found the following:

> The overwhelming majority of the practitioners are men; sporadically there is yet a medicine woman to be found, but there are indications that lead us to believe that formerly there were far more of them than is now the case. An informant, when asked to account for the fact that there were so few female disease curers, as compared to males, told me that it was 'because women do not take so much interest in it (i.e., in the study of plants, of the formulas, etc.) as men do.' Apart from midwives there are now only two medicine women worth speaking of – one an old person of about 80 years old and Sally-Annie, the wife of Og.[15]

The Swimmer Manuscript: Cherokee Sacred Formulas by James Mooney and Frans Olbrecht documents the following:

> The brighter of the medicine men may truly be said to be

walking encyclopedias as far as their knowledge of aboriginal culture is concerned. Not only do they know all about disease and curing methods, but they are also invariably very competent botanist and naturalist ... [One] who worked with Mr. Mooney, knew at least 150 to 200 different plants, with all their peculiarities, their habitat, their time and period of blossoming, their properties and the lore pertaining to them.[16]

Early Documentation of Cherokee Life

The Cherokee had no written language until the 1830s. However, their stories and histories, like so many other Indian Nations, were diligently recorded by several men over disparate time periods, and their accounts will be included in the appropriate time frame. These were white men whose lives differed greatly, and although they faithfully recorded their observations and experiences living among the tribes, they were not often allowed to participate in the most important and profound ceremonies and councils. Observed from the outside, these men could not fully understand or appreciate the nuances of the lives and cultures they were writing about. However, they provided documentation that would otherwise have been lost to time.

Born about 1709, James Adair, a native of Ireland, came to North America in 1735 and became a trader among the Southeastern Indians. Although not an historian, his life among the Indians provided a unique perspective, as he was invited to participate in some of their festivals and experienced day-to-day living in his thirty-some years living chiefly among the Chikkasah [Chickasaw] Nation. He was encouraged by some intimate friends to record his life among the Indians, and Adair's experiences are captured in his book, *The History of the American Indians*, which was first published in 1775. Adair diligently recorded his life and practical knowledge of the Southeastern Indians, which, because of their acceptance and incorporation of many white social, cultural and legal mores into their culture, became known as the Five Civilized Tribes. These included the Katahba [Catawba], Cheerake [Cherokee], Muskohge [Creek], Choktah [Choctaw] and Chikkasah [Chickasaw].

Adair acknowledged that since origin histories had been lost to antiquity, it was impossible to definitely ascertain where the Indian people had originated; however, he postulated several possibilities. They might have come from China traveling across the northern land bridge available in ancient times or perhaps sailed across the Pacific Ocean, but he argued against this because of the differences between the two groups in their religion, laws and customs. He also considered that they could have migrated from the regions of Peru and Mexico but discounted this for a lack of evidence of the stately buildings known in the southern regions. His greatest belief was that all Indian people originated from a lost tribe of Israel, and he laid out twenty-three arguments to support his observations. John Howard Payne also postulated the lost tribe of Israel in his 1800s writings, but over time and lacking additional proof, anthropologists and other scientists set this hypothesis aside as they strove to answer the question – where did the American Indian originate? One general observation Adair made regarding the Indians of his acquaintance was that:

> The Indians are of a copper or red-clay colour – and they delight in everything, which they imagine may promote and increase it ... If we consider the common laws of nature and providence, we shall not be surprised at this custom; for everything loves best its own likeness and place in creation, and to ridicule its opposite ... All the Indians are so strongly attached to, and prejudiced in favour of, their own colour, that they think as meanly of the whites, as we possibly can do of them. The English traders among them, experience much of it, and are often very glad to be allowed to pass muster with the Indian chieftains, as fellow-brethren of the human species ... [17]

Adair continued with his observations of each of the five nations of Indians that he lived and worked among. For the Cherokee, he provided a description of their Appalachia Mountain lands complete with longitude and latitude. The ground between the mountain peaks received yearly snowmelt and was exceptionally fertile and situated as it was "... the severest cold is no detriment to their hunting."[18] The many crystal-clear rivers were used for purification, fishing, fowling and travel. He commented on various minerals, including whetstones, loadstones with silver deposits and crystalline stones. A February 1838 military intelligence report provided a survey of the Cherokee country and substantiated much of Adair's observations of the mid-1700s.

Gold had been discovered in North Carolina in 1799, but a second discovery in the mountains of Georgia in 1828 brought an influx of white people to Cherokee land, hastening the state of Georgia's resolve to incorporate Cherokee land into that state. During the 1830s, over 300 ounces of gold were produced per day, enough that in 1838 the Dahlonega Mint was established as a separate branch of the United States Mint to handle the Georgia gold. Consider that on September 16, 2020, one ounce of gold sold for $1,940.00, so 300 ounces would equal $582,000 a day. This brings the total value for one year to over $212 million. Georgia held lottery drawings from October 1832 to May 1833, which gave the winners 40 acres to work and brought an estimated 10,000 men to seek the riches of Northern Georgia. None of this money was shared with the Cherokee people.

Adair's reflection on the smallpox epidemic among the Cherokee provides numbers that are difficult to assimilate. He estimated there had been 64 well-populated towns with women and children and at least 6,000 fighting men; however, after a span of a few years, the epidemic and several wars had reduced the number of warriors to around 2,300. Adair concluded his writings with "General Observations on the North American Indians,"[19] which covers everything from conduct of domestic life, love of country and their form of government.

In addition to the Adair history, *The Payne – Butrick Papers: Volumes One, Two, Three,* edited and annotated by William L. Anderson, Jane L. Brown and Anne F. Rogers, are excellent resources of Cherokee lives. James Mooney, an ethnologist working for the Smithsonian Institute arrived in western North Carolina with an assignment "to collect information for comparison of religious practices, customs, and arts"[20] and to catalog linguistic traits of the Cherokee. He was invited to live with the Eastern Band in the secluded mountains of North Carolina. Later, after a brief time spent with the Western Band in Oklahoma, Mooney commented that he believed the Eastern Band adhered more closely to the old ways.

Mooney worked periodically from 1880 to 1920 interviewing the Cherokee chiefs and medicine men of North Carolina. He gained the trust of these men and, with them being of great age, they entrusted Mooney with their original written records of over 600 formulas. These records make up part of the Cherokee history maintained by the American Bureau of Ethnology. Twenty-eight were later published, but the rest remained in the Cherokee syllabary, and many of those were subsequently lost. The oral stories and traditions, as told to them by their fathers and grandfathers, were also shared with Mooney. These were published in *History, Myths, and Sacred Formulas of the Cherokees* and *The Swimmer Manuscript: Cherokee Sacred Formulas and Medicinal Prescriptions* by James Mooney and Frans M. Olbrechts.

By the mid-to-late 1800s, it was too late for many of their traditions to be preserved in writing. Time was against them; however, eighty-one notable Cherokee manuscripts were preserved, which included everything from letters, folklore and fragments of prose to deathbed remembrances.

A medicine man named Swimmer was Mooney's main informant on the history, mythology and, later especially, on the medicine and botany of the Cherokee. With Swimmer's passing in 1899, none were left with his skills and knowledge. It was through the painstaking attention to detail that Swimmer, Mooney and Olbrechts, another ethnologist, recorded significant aspects of the Cherokee medicine man's life. The task required multiple steps to bring the manuscript into a format that can be understood and appreciated. First, Mooney's transliteration was read aloud to prominent medicine men, who then wrote the text in the Sequoyah syllabary. The Sequoyah text was read aloud by the medicine man and taken down phonetically by Olbrechts. The final work resulted in a three-hundred-sixty-eight-page manuscript published in 1932.[21]

Contemporary Documentation of Cherokee Life

A contemporary book *Eastern Cherokee Stories: A Living Oral Tradition and Its Cultural Continuance* by Sandra Isaacs was published in 2019. Isaacs, a Cherokee herself, explores the work of James Mooney and numerous others, as she considers the Cherokee beliefs through time – providing an understanding of their continued tradition and beliefs. She was somewhat critical of Mooney's early work, as it reflected his Eurocentric viewpoint when he recounted the stories, myths and medicinal practices of the Cherokee during the late 1800s and early 1900s. Issacs saw the growth of Mooney's understanding as he spent more time with, and came to appreciate, what he learned from his Cherokee benefactors. For hundreds, if not thousands, of years, the Cherokee and other Native People who have been allowed to maintain their culture and beliefs, have believed in the Great Spirit or Creator. Issacs' life and research reflect the belief that nonhumans have spirits and that they talk to one another.[22] The Cherokee oral beliefs cover all aspects of creation. Where they differ from the Bible is their continued appreciation of the nonhuman: trees, plants, birds and animals, as well as rocks, water, air and things that many might ignore, not understanding their significance"… as they give their lives so that the People can eat, be strong, and heal themselves."[23] Cherokee hunters always gave thanks to the spirit of the deer when they slew it for sustenance and most likely some Cherokee hunters still do this. They understood that without the deer, they and their families might go hungry and without clothing and numerous other important items the deer provided by the giving of its life. This was not taken lightly.

Earlier, gender roles and the importance of maintaining a balance of forces was discussed. The contemporary Cherokees on the Qualla Boundary in North Carolina continue to maintain two important beliefs – that of people coming together to work for a common goal and of the individual walking the right path. It is equally important that a balance be kept between humans and nonhuman forces. The imbalance can be seen now as nature plays havoc in our weather.

Author's Thoughts

Guided by their belief in the Great Spirit, the Cherokee developed a culture rooted in the sacredness of the earth and the balance between the earth and man. A harmonious balance existed between a woman and man and between the human and nonhuman, with each respecting the other.

If the newcomers had learned to appreciate the culture of the Native Americans, perhaps several centuries of wrongs and countless deaths of both the newcomers and Native Americans could have been avoided. Beginning in the 1700s through present time, fear based upon Eurocentric beliefs with no knowledge of the Native cultures still influences the laws written by the U.S. Congress that govern Native American lives with little or no input from the people governed by those laws.

A number of Indian-led organizations have been established in the last half of the 20th century to help Native Americans achieve representation of their people and tribal governments. The Native American Rights Fund founded in 1970 is one of those organizations with a goal to "… provide legal assistance to Indian tribes, organizations, and individuals nationwide … and has achieved significant results in such critical areas as tribal sovereignty, treaty rights, natural resource protection, and Indian education."[24]

This was late in coming, but at least it was a start. The world is different now and the Yunwiya must adapt. They must bring the best of their traditions and the best of other cultures to create a new whole. We must all adapt and help one another in this ever-changing world.

Endnotes:

[1] Mooney, James. *History, Myths, and Sacred Formulas of the Cherokees*. Bright Mountain Books, Asheville, NC. 1992. pp. 244-245.

[2] Mailes, Thomas E. *The Cherokee People: The Story of the Cherokees from Earliest Origins to Contemporary Times*. Marlowe & Co., 1992. p. 192

[3] Awiakta, Marilou. *Selu, Seeking the Corn-Mother's Wisdom*. Fulcrum Publishing, 1993, p. 25-26.

[4] Mankiller, Wilma. "Rebuilding the Cherokee Nation." Speech at Sweet Brian College, VA. 2 Apr 1993. http://gos.sbc.edu/m/mankiller.html.

[5] Hendrix, Janey B. "Redbird Smith and the Nighthawk Keetoowahs." *Journal of Cherokee Studies, Volume VIII, No. 2, Fall 1983*, p 77.

[6] Hendrix. p. 78.

[7] Hendrix. p 77.

[8] Mails, Thomas E. *The Cherokee People: The Story of the Cherokees from Earliest Origins to Contemporary Times*. Marlowe & Co., 1992. pp. 79-81.

[9] Alderman., Pat. *Nancy Ward / Dragging Canoe: Cherokee Chieftainess/Cherokee Chickamauga War Chief*. 2nd ed., Overmountain Press, 1978. p. 4.

[10] Alderman, p. 3.

[11] Mails, Thomas E. *The Cherokee People: The Story of the Cherokees from Earliest Origins to Contemporary Times*. Marlowe & Co., 1992. p. 98.

[12] Mails. p. 98.

[13] Mooney, James and Frans M. Olbrechts. *The Swimmer Manuscript: Cherokee Sacred Formulas and Medicinal Prescriptions*. United States Government Printing Office, 1932, pp. 83-84.

[14] Mooney, Olbrechts. pp. 83-84.

[15] Mooney, Olbrechts. p. 84.

[16] Mooney, Olbrechts. p. 88.

17 Adair, James. *The History of The American Indians*. Pantianos Classics, First published in 1775, p. 8.

18 Adair, p. 105.

19 Adair. p. 169.

20 Mooney, James. *History, Myths, and Sacred Formulas of the Cherokees.* Bright Mountain Books, 1992. Intro, p. 10.

21 Mooney, James and Frans M. Olbrechts. *The Swimmer Manuscript: Cherokee Sacred Formulas and Medicinal Prescriptions*. United States Government Printing Office, 1932, p 99.

22 Isaacs, Sandra Muse. *Eastern Cherokee Stories: A Living Oral Tradition and Its Cultural Continuance*. U of Oklahoma P, 2019. p. 84.

23 Isaacs. p. 26.

24 "About Us." *Native American Rights Fund*, https://www.narf.org. Accessed. 21 Aug 2019.

| TWO |

The Confrontation
4th Century B.C. Through Invasion of New World

"Often I have been compelled to ask myself, 'Who is the civilized and who the savage is?'"

Rev William H. Goode, Methodist missionary, 1843.
Missouri Life, September 2018[1]

If the coming clash of ideology and mores between the American Indians and the invaders from Europe, including the religion of each, is to be understood beyond the histories taught to school children, there is a need to dig deep into all aspects surrounding that confrontation because it was a *confrontation* which drastically changed the lives of all the People forever.

The story of the Native peoples began on a distant shore. School children in the U.S. are taught that Columbus discovered the New World in 1492, but it was his letter dated March 4th, 1493 to His Majesties of Spain expounding upon the beauty and riches of the land that sowed the genesis of interest throughout Europe. Because of Gutenberg's invention of the printing press in 1440, a printed version of Columbus' letter published in Barcelona circulated throughout the city in less than a month. A month after that, a translated edition circulated in Rome, and within five years after Columbus's return, no less than seventeen translations had been distributed throughout Europe. The letter sparked the imagination of rulers, noblemen, the wealthy and the poor alike. To many who heard of Columbus' letter, hope flickered and, to some, became a dream.

Columbus left behind a land of violence, squalor, treachery and intolerance. Although looking for and believing he had found a route to the Indies, he happened upon islands, later called the Bahamas, that when combined with the Western Hemisphere covers over a quarter of the landmass of the earth. While scholarly debate will always remain, what is clear from archaeological evidence is that the New World had a rich and varied native population going back at least 19,000 years in North America and 13,000 years in South America. There are some highly respected scholars who put the figure for entry into the hemisphere as early as 70,000 B.C. Some cultures rose, made their mark on the world and disappeared, leaving evidence of their culture to be discovered. Many people are familiar with the major cultural centers, which include the Aztec and Mayan in Mexico, the Inca in South America and Adena or Hopewell Culture in North America. The Adena culture, centered in present-day Ohio, had settlements as far away as Vermont and south to West Virginia prior to the time that Rome took control of ancient Greece.

The Confrontation Begins

As the crews of the Nina, the Pinta and the Santa Maria came ashore to claim this new land in the name of the Spanish monarchs, Ferdinand and Isabella, gold featured foremost on the explorers' minds, but other riches were also required to maintain the high standard of living the European nobility enjoyed. This included slaves, which Columbus, the ex-African slave trader, proved willing and able to provide with the natives of the New World. Thus began the exploitation of the land and the People. At the same time, the European poor, who constituted the majority, lived in abject poverty where pestilence and death were daily occurrences.

A firestorm of contagion and purposeful genocide was unleashed upon the Peoples of America from the arrival of the first Europeans. History has shown that there is danger in forgetting the destructive forces behind invasions because great danger lies in forgetting. "Forgetting, however, will not affect only the dead. Should it triumph, the ashes of yesterday will cover our hopes for tomorrow."[2] To understand this phenomenon and the factors culminating in the genocide of the Natives of America, it is necessary to examine the cultural, physical, political and religious environment of the Old World, which resulted, and continues to result, in Eurocentric contempt for the Native people of America and those of Africa. This contempt reflected in scholarly writings is expressed in three Eurocentric viewpoints: racial, historical and geographic, which have long been accepted as the societal norms.

Examining the History of Racism

As the background to the history behind racism begins, because it covers more than North America, please be reminded from the Author's Notes at the beginning of the book that when the word "Native" is capitalized, it is referring to Native Americans of the U.S. only. When native is lowercase, it refers to the natives of the areas being discussed. Similarly, the use of "People" and "Indian" refer only to Native Americans of the U.S.

Historians of ancient Greece noted that racism was evident in the writings of Hippocrates in fourth century B.C. Greece when he wrote that different races existed on different continents, which, because of a variety of factors such as diet, climate and hereditary factors, resulted in a racial character unique to that country or region. During the Golden Age of the eighth century B.C., artistic and literary license prevailed, giving rise to depictions of sexual behavior that was, by the late 15th century, viewed as belonging to a previous time unless other, displaced remnants were found in distant unexplored places.

> To differentiate America from Africa and Asia, artists relied chiefly on her partial or complete nudity. Asia was always fully clothed, often sumptuously so. Africa, attired in sometimes revealing but always elegant dress, was supposed to look Moorish, since Europeans were most familiar with the Mediterranean area. America alone was a savage.[3]

Gradually, the concept that beasts or subhuman creatures with physical and biological characteristics that varied from European ideals came into the conscience beliefs of the people involved, and the racial Eurocentric concept was born. Once seen as "beasts," the people of the Americas were portrayed as demonic in appearance with heavy body hair or dark skin, sexually deprived, ungoverned and having strange speech. The next step was to declare all these beasts to be animals – animals to be eradicated and replaced by the chosen people of Europe, where human life was centered.

Historical Eurocentrism denoted a barbaric wasteland ready for civilization as ordained by God. The clergy believed that the New World was an opportunity to introduce the natives to the glory of God's grace. The Old Testament provided justification for extermination in Deuteronomy 20:16-17: "Of the cities ... which the Lord thy God doth give thee for an inheritance, thou shalt save alive nothing that breatheth ... But thou shalt utterly destroy them."[4] In David E. Stannard's book, *American Holocaust: The Conquest of the New World*, he quotes from Frederick H. Russell's book, *The Just War in the Middle Ages,* who summarized St. Augustine's – an early theologian and philosopher – views:

> Any violations of God's laws, and by easy extension, any violation of Christian doctrine, could be seen as an injustice warranting unlimited violent punishment. Further, the ... guilt of the enemy merited punishment of the enemy population without regard to the distinction between soldiers and civilians. Motivated by righteous wrath, the just warriors could kill with impunity even those who were morally innocent.[5]

During the eleventh, twelfth and thirteenth centuries, Europe experienced the Crusades and Inquisition. During the mid-fourteenth century, the Black Death wiped out a large portion of the European population in a matter of months. The fleas of black rats that traveled aboard ships from Asia and China caused the disease.

> Epidemic outbreaks of plague and smallpox, along with routine attacks of measles, influenza, diphtheria, typhus, typhoid fever, and more, frequently swept European cities and towns clean of ten to twenty percent of their populations at a single stroke.[6]

People came from the countryside hoping for a better life in the towns and cities and met with the reality of life there. The living could not manage the large number of human and animal deaths, so bodies were left untended or, at best, thrown in a large open pit inside the town. Human waste and garbage thrown in the streets resulted in a stench that could not be escaped. There were no public latrines and no clean drinking water, which resulted in water being gathered from gutters to drink and cook. With no concept of personal hygiene, many people did not bathe their entire lives. Every twenty to twenty-five years the cycle perpetuated itself. Only in the fifteenth century did living conditions begin to slowly change.

Religious Influences Grow

The Holy Wars inflicted death and torture in the name of God and combined with flood, pestilence, drought and famine, provided evidence for the peasantry of the Second Coming. As the conquistadors explored the lands of the New World, they initially remarked on the beauty and cleanliness of the people and their cities. The contrast between their homelands and the Incas in South America and the Aztec in Mexico, among others, was significant. Both cultures were highly developed for centuries prior to European discovery. They built magnificent cities with extensive roads and clean water systems. To systematically enslave and eradicate the people, the conquistadors dehumanized them by pointing to their differences in looks, language, culture and religion. In other words, they emphasized the Eurocentric superiority in all things. "Whether Greeks, Romans, or medieval Christians, moreover, the Europeans of all eras considered themselves to be 'chosen' people, the inhabitants of the center and most civil domain of human life."[7]

As the Protestants gained prominence during the Reformation, Martin Luther postulated "… that the possession of private property was an essential difference between men and beasts."[8] Church leaders throughout Europe espoused the doctrine that property must be productive, emphasizing the necessity for man to work. To be entitled to the land, one must work it. Those who did not would be looked down upon as something less than human, and settlers justified their actions because that is what God had ordained. In 1634, the Massachusetts Bay Colony Governor John Winthrop summarized the beliefs of the Puritans when he wrote that in the last two years, the four thousand Puritan settlers had suffered the deaths of three adults and three children by smallpox; however, since the majority of the natives died of the smallpox, it was the Lord's special providence to clear title to whatever land they possessed.[9] Similarly, when battles resulted in great loss of life for the Natives and only a few settlers, God's will had been determined.

Manifest Destiny and Eurocentric Attitudes

The doctrine of Manifest Destiny came into being in the nineteenth century to justify the inevitable expansion of the U.S. In the 2001 *2nd Edition of the American Indians: Answers to Today's Questions*, Jack Utter wrote:

> With regard to the actual meaning of *Manifest Destiny*, many people mistakenly take the view that it is a two-word noun. In fact, the *'manifest'* part of the term is merely an adjective (meaning "self-evident") for the noun *destiny*. The term came from a growing sense of nationalism in the early and mid-1840s when many U.S. politicians were saber rattling to go to war with Mexico and perhaps Great Britain, and to claim all the land between the Mississippi and the Pacific – which they felt it was America's divinely ordained destiny to have. As they saw it, the natural providence of the U.S. was to expand westward to the Pacific. Thus, when land was taken from the Indians or others who were in the way, it was merely a manifestation, or self-evident fulfillment, of American destiny."[10]

Utter continued, "Thus the American belief in Manifest Destiny was openly hostile to Indians and unsympathetic to their culture and their interests."[11]

The third and one of the most glaring of the Eurocentric attitudes and mores was reflected in world maps, which purposefully reduced the size of Africa based on the famous

Mercator projection introduced by a Flemish geographer and cartographer during the sixteenth century. The new geographic depiction increased the distance between the latitudinal lines as one moves away from the equator and closer to the Polar Regions, thus distorting the cartographic representations of the landmasses. This resulted in Africa, with over 2,000,000 more square miles, appearing to be much smaller than North America. In his 1962 book, *American Holocaust: The Conquest of the New World*, David E. Stannard wrote, "… the historical distortions that systematically reduce in demographic and cultural and moral significance the native peoples of the Americas are part of a very old and enduring political design."[12] Over the centuries, there have been a variety of world maps. However, in 1855, James Gall drew an early compromise that reflected a more logical representation by a true sizing of the landmasses and dividing the maps in the Pacific Ocean instead of dividing the eastern landmasses.

Disease, Brutality and Genocide

Historians and medical researchers now agree that based on the detailed written reports of men who participated in the campaigns of destruction, military and clergy alike, that the initial cause of so many deaths in the lands they explored resulted from swine flu. Columbus introduced pigs, along with other domesticated animals, to the islands when he brought them from the Canary Islands on his second trip to the New World. Researchers considered and set aside many other diseases because of the rapidity and great numbers of natives who fell ill and died. Even though the explorers had been exposed to all the pestilence of Europe, some of them still fell to the diseases. The natives of these islands had no previous exposure to these diseases, therefore no natural resistance. Once stricken, tens of thousands succumbed within days. According to Stannard, during the Spanish campaign of terror known as pacification, "… as horrific as the bloodbaths were in Vietnam, in sheer magnitude they were as nothing compared with what happened on the single island of Hispaniola five hundred years ago …"[13] Between the diseases that preceded the Europeans and the merciless slaughter of men, women and children, between one-third to one-half of the eight million people there had been wiped out between Columbus's arrival and the end of 1496. Within a normal lifetime, the native population who had resided for thousands of years on their home islands had been exterminated. This occurred throughout the islands and continued in Mesoamerica, South America and North America.

> ... the Spaniards' mammoth destruction of whole societies generally was a by-product of conquest and native enslavement, a genocidal means to an economic end, not an end in itself. And therein lies the central difference between the genocide committed by the Spanish and that of the Anglo-Americans: in British America extermination *was* the primary goal, and it was so precisely because it made economic sense.[14]

Dogs well trained from previous experience in Europe against Muslins, Jews and other ethnic groups traveled with the conquistadores. Like their masters, the wolfhounds and mastiffs wore protective armor and were used both to entertain the troops and to hunt humans. Raised on a diet of human flesh, they would fall upon their victims, ripping them apart, disemboweling and otherwise dismembering them. Detailed Spanish reports tell of babies torn from their mother's arms and thrown to the dogs, which seemed to favor the young ones. Few natives had ever seen dogs, and they were terrorized by the viciousness, making them easy prey for the conquistadores' dogging tactics.

A 1971 translation of *History of the Indies* by Andre Collard stated that Bartolome' de Las Casas reported more than 7,000 babies died within a three-month period in part because of the dogs but also because the mothers, overworked and malnourished, had no milk, while others were so desperate that they often aborted or drowned their babies. Husbands and young boys, removed to a different location, were lowered into the mines and not brought to the surface for long periods of time. Grueling work came with constant beatings, kicks, blows and inadequate food. The overlords were not motivated to feed them sufficiently, as they believed plenty more natives would take their place – or so they thought. The increased death rate, along with no time or energy to sustain the birthrate, became so significant that "This land which was so great, so powerful and fertile, though so unfortunate, was depopulated."[15] Forced labor in the mines and fields of Peru resulted in a life expectancy of three or four months – "about the same as that of someone working at slave labor in the synthetic rubber manufacturing plant at Auschwitz in the 1940s."[16]

Contrasting Ideologies of War

Historical records show that throughout the Western Hemisphere, natives announced their intentions to wage war and stated their reasons so all was clear before launching an attack. The ideological differences between the natives and the invaders could not have been more pronounced. The natives believed that war was ritualized, and few people died in battle. Centuries of crusades had solidified the European belief in a holy war, one where war devastated both people and property. Thus, Montezuma welcomed Cortes to his city, Tenochtitlan, in Central Mexico. Cortes clearly stated that he came as an ambassador of peace, and the Aztec ruler accepted him at his word, showing the Spanish through the great city – the magnificent palaces and public buildings and the marketplaces with all manner of fruits, vegetables, flowers and crafts. Beautiful birds from all over filled the aviaries. The city, built in the Lake of the Moons, was reached by causeways lined with gorgeous parks, homes and boulevards. When the singing and dancing began, Cortes' men set upon the citizens of this beautiful paradise killing everyone: men women, children, young and old. The Spanish noted that the Aztec made human sacrifices, which they believed justified the brutality they dispensed to the inhabitants. However, they slaughtered more than forty thousand in the first day of the attack, which was twice the twenty thousand warriors, never women and children, the Aztec were recorded sacrificing in a year. The rampage continued, again aided by the introduction of smallpox.

"The metropolis (Tenochtitlan) that the Spanish had just months earlier described as the most beautiful city on earth, so dazzling and beguiling in its exotic and brilliant variety, became a monotonous pile of rubble, a place of dust and flame and death."[17] Now the city lay in ruins, and those who survived were enslaved. The traditional method of razing a town did not work because the city was built on canals. Fire set to individual buildings would not spread across the bridges, so the structures were razed and dumped into the canals hoping to contaminate the freshwater supply of the lake. The residents tried to clear the debris but could not keep up with the onslaught. More than the destruction of the city occurred as, "The Christians searched all the refugees, they even opened the women's skirts and blouses and felt everywhere: their ears, their breasts, and their hair."[18] "Lastly, they burned the precious books salvaged by surviving Aztec priests and then fed the priests to Spanish dogs of war."[19]

> Through prior arrangement with his king, Cortes' share of the loot was one-fifth. In gold and jewelry and artwork, that was a fortune, probably more than $10,000,000 in 1990 American currency. In terms of slaves, it meant at least 3,000 human beings for his personal and private use, not counting about 23,000 Indian 'vassals' for the Crown.[20]

The rationale used by Montezuma is similar to that quoted by Thomas Budd when a seventeenth-century Lenape Indian explained in a discussion with a British colonist:

> We are minded to live at Peace: If we intend at any time to make War upon you, we will let you know of it, and the Reasons why we make War with you; and if you make us satisfaction for the Injury done us, for which the War is intended, then we will not make War on you. And if you intend at any time to make War on us, we would have you let us know of it, and the Reasons for which you make War on us, and then if we do not make satisfaction for the Injury done unto you, then you may make War on us, otherwise you ought not to do it.[21]

From numerous writings, it is apparent that the native peoples believed that war was not waged to eradicate their enemies as the invaders consistently did, but rather to avenge some personal wrong or individual acts of violence. Their code of honor traditionally spared women and children, while the invaders made a practice of killing everyone. The natives had no frame of reference for such conduct.

The "Savage Red Man" Was to Be Destroyed

As a reminder, the ships that arrived in the New World brought more than settlers; they brought the settler's views – one of which went from seeing the natives as the noble savage to the savage red man, a foreboding sign of things to come.

In 1521, the Spanish laid claim to large coastal areas of present-day South Carolina, primarily to capture and bring as many slaves as possible to the Bahamas to replace the millions of natives who had perished. This expedition introduced viral and bacterial diseases to the Natives who had no natural resistance, and the traditional medicine man had no concept of how to treat the diseases:

> The circles of life are mysterious. In 1620, when the Pilgrims arrived in Plymouth, Mass, American Indians met them and offered corn and stories. The Pilgrims took the corn. 'In the belly of the story,' the Indians said, 'is life for the people, a way to live in harmony with this land.' But the newcomers didn't want such stories. They had plans for the land – and for the Indians ... [22]

War soon consumed everyone, eradicating all hope of peace with fierce fighting on both sides. The English used deliberate attacks on noncombatants to terrorize the enemy. One of these was the mass murder of seven hundred Indian men, women and children who were celebrating their Green Corn Ceremony – their own Thanksgiving – in a place called Mystic Fort in what is now known as Groton, Connecticut. Finding the Indians gathered in their own meeting house, the soldiers ordered them from the building and shot them as they came out. Those who remained inside were burned alive. To commemorate this "victory over the enemy," the governor of Massachusetts Bay Colony in 1637 proclaimed the first official "Thanksgiving Day," which was celebrated for the next one hundred years.

Proof that he did so remained buried in archives for over three centuries, and history rarely mentioned this massacre. But the memory of the People is long. They did not forget the 700. In the 1970s, William Newell, a contemporary Penobscot Indian and professor with degrees from the University of Pennsylvania and Syracuse, went in search of the missing proof. He found it in documents stored in Holland libraries, as well as in letters, log reports, journals and other documents written during the mid-1600s.[23] *United Press International* newswire released a story about his findings on November 24, 1977. This was the "Thanksgiving of the Corn Borers" – a celebration of the burgeoning concept of manifest destiny:"[24]

> The European habit of indiscriminately killing women and children when engaged in hostilities with the natives of the Americas was more than atrocity. It was flatly and intentionally genocidal. For no population can survive if its women and children are destroyed.[25]

Many colonial leaders had been military men serving in the Irish wars. While the English considered the Irish a wild race, lessons learned in dealing with them helped significantly when they turned their attention to the American Indians. Washington told his generals in 1779, and again in 1783, that the war was a war of extermination. The Indians were considered mere beasts, something to get rid of to the last man, woman and child. With this accomplished, the troops proceeded to burn their houses and destroy all the crops, whether stored or in the field. No moral outrage was expressed when the victorious troops skinned the Indians like wild beasts. The colonial conquerors tanned the Indians' skin to make boots or leggings. Sometime later, the same concept was applied to a group of peaceful Mangoe Indians in the Ohio River Valley.

For many years prior to and after George Washington became president in 1783, there were major skirmishes and battles with the American Indians along the eastern seaboard and into the interior beyond the Appalachian Mountains as the settlers pushed into the Ohio River Valley. From the many historical documents of the time including letters, court testimonies and military records, Allan Eckert pieced together an account reported in his book, *A Dark & Bloody River: Chronicles of the Ohio River Valley,* which provides insights into the strife between the Native peoples of the region as they sought to retain the land of their birth and protect their way of life, as well as the settlers as they pushed into the wilderness looking for free land and the opportunity to establish a new life for themselves and their families.

Brutality Reigns

Eckert writes that after several instances with whites and Indians being killed and scalped or taken captive, a group of 33 men, led by Jacob Greathouse, took matters in their own hands. Intent on killing and collecting scalps, the group invited a group of Mangoe Indians from Chief Logan's town to come across the Ohio River to Kentucky on Saturday, April 30, 1774 for a sporting contest. If the Indians won, they would receive a jug of whiskey, and if the Greathouse party won, they would get beaver skins. Ten came across the next morning, including seven warriors, two women with one, Koonay, almost full-term in her pregnancy and carrying another on a cradleboard.

A second group of fourteen warriors, several women and teenage boys remained with their two canoes on the other side of the river. Twenty-six of the Greathouse group positioned themselves in hiding, while seven, including Greathouse, warmly welcomed the Indian party. The whites challenged the Indians to a shooting contest, and after the whites emptied their rifles at the target, the Indians relaxed and did the same, whereupon those in hiding rose and fired a barrage killing all seven warriors. The first woman was killed instantly. Koonay tried to run away but was tackled to the ground. The baby in the cradleboard was thrown clear while Koonay managed to scream, alerting the group across the river. One man grabbed the baby and covered her mouth, so her cries would not be heard.

The Greathouse party reloaded their rifles and waited for the second group of Indians to make it across the river. All but four were killed outright. Of those, two died of rifle fire after diving into the river, and two made it back across to safety, alternately diving and swimming to dodge the barrage of bullets. Coming back to Koonay, Greathouse stated his intent of getting the youngest Injun scalp every taken. Then Koonay, still alive, hung with her arms outstretched between two trees, had her stomach slit open and the baby pulled from her, whereupon both were scalped. The party set about scalping both groups they had killed. Koonay was the sister of Chief Logan and the wife of Major John Gibson of Carlisle, PA, an Indian trader. The rescued child, a girl, was delivered to him to raise. Chief Logan, who had always been at peace with the settlers, vowed vengeance on all whites from that day forward.

The men broke into small groups, moving swiftly from the site of the killings up the Ohio to more settled areas. Word of their misdeeds spread rapidly, and they were met with hostility in the general population, as these barbaric acts were too much even for them. The army readied their volunteers and alerted the people to move to the safety of the forts.[26]

In *Selu: Seeking the Corn-Mother's Wisdom*, Marilou Awiakta quotes from Howard Zinn's book, *A People's History of the United States*:

> As the Pilgrims grew stronger, however, they expanded their territory, and attitudes began to change, especially after 1830, with the coming of the Puritans, who were more rapacious and less tolerant. To justify taking Indian land, the governor of Massachusetts Bay Colony, John Winthrop, invoked secular English laws of property, which were contrary to the Indians' sacred law of communal use. He said the Indians had not 'subdued' the land and therefore had only a 'natural right' to it, but not a 'civil right.' 'Natural right' had no legal standing. The Puritans claimed biblical justification: Psalms 2:8, 'Ask of me, and I shall give thee the heathen for thine inheritance, and the uttermost parts of the earth for thy possession.' And to justify the use of force, they cited Romans 13:2 'Whosoever, therefore, resisteth, resisteth the ordinance of God: and they that resist shall receive to themselves damnation.'[27]

Genocide of the Indians Admitted

Genocide against various ethnic groups has been prevalent throughout history, but the unspeakable horrors perpetrated during World War II was a pivotal event in the history of mankind that coalesced the body politic in their resolve to define genocide. As a result, 133 member countries of the General Assembly of the United Nations came together to frame Resolution 260 titled "Convention on the Prevention and Punishment of the Crime of Genocide," which was adopted on December 9, 1948 making "... genocide a crime under international law, contrary to the spirit and aims of the United Nations, and condemned by the civilized world."[28] In *American Holocaust: The Conquest of the New World*, David Stannard summarized the resolution with the following observation, "... it is impossible to know what transpired in the Americas during the sixteenth, seventeenth, eighteenth, and nineteenth centuries and not conclude that it was genocide."[29]

The resolution will be discussed in Chapter 11, along with other laws and events that define the effects of genocide on the Native Americans of the U.S. It should be noted at this time that the U.S. did not join the world body in signing the resolution until November 4, 1988. That day, President Reagan signed the resolution into law during a brief stopover in Chicago.

Author's Thoughts

Columbus and those who came after him did not wage war with the natives. Rather, it was *systematic annihilation*. The natives were enslaved, starved and worked to death in the mines, fields and many other endeavors in support of the Spanish conquistadors and subsequent European powers. Many were fed to the dogs. Women were raped and murdered. Atrocities were done in the name of Christ as the priests, sanctioned by His Majesties of Spain, strived to save the heathens' souls. The natives did not understand Spanish nor the mysteries of the Catholic religion. Under threat of their lives, many converted and were killed anyway.

Annihilation occurred in Mystic Fort (now Groton, Connecticut) when 700 Indians were murdered. Soldiers shot the Indians as they exited their meetinghouse, while those remaining inside were burned alive. This first official "Thanksgiving Day" of 1637, marked by the governor of Massachusetts Bay Colony, is in stark contrast to the idyllic picture we have been taught of Thanksgiving celebrated by Native Americans and the colonists. History does not forget events; however, it often takes years, or as in this case, three centuries, before the events were revealed – buried in Holland's libraries.

Endnotes:

1. Soodalter, Ron. *Missouri Life Magazine*. "The Tribes of Missouri Part 2: Things Fall Apart." Quote by Rev William H. Goode, Methodist missionary, 1843, p. 16.

2. Rothchild, Sylvia, editor, *Voices from the Holocaust.* New American Library, 1982, p. 4.

3. West, Delno C. and August King, translation and commentary. *Libro de las Profecias of Christopher Columbus.* U of Florida, 1991, p.109.

4. Stannard, David E. *American Holocaust: The Conquest of the New World.* Oxford UP, 1992, p. 177; see Russell, Frederick H. *The Just War in the Middles Ages*. Cambridge UP, 1975, pp. 19-20; see Little, *'Holy War' Appeals and Western Christianity*, p. 126.

5. Stannard. p. 177.

6. Stannard. p. 57.

7. Stannard. p. 167.

8. Hanke, Lewis. *Aristotle and the American Indians*. Henry Regnery, 1959. And by Indiana University Press, 1975, p. 47. Also, Keith Thomas. *Man and the Natural World: Changing Attitudes in England 1500-1800*. Penguin Books, 1983, p. 31.

9. "John Winthrop describes life in Boston, 1634." *The Gilder Lehrman Institute of American History.* https://bit.ly/2GAl0wO

10. Utter, Jack. *American Indians: Answers to Today's Questions* 2nd *Ed. Revised and Enlarged.* U of Oklahoma P, 2001, p 125.

11. Utter. p. 127.

12. Stannard, David E. *American Holocaust: The Conquest of the New World.* Oxford UP. 1992, pp. 11-12.

13. Stannard. p. 72

14. Stannard. p. 221.

15. de Las Casas, Bartolome. *History of the Indies.* translated and edited by Andree Collard. Harper & Row, 1971, p. 94.

16. Hilberg, Paul. *The Destruction of the European Jews.* Quadrangle Books, 1961, p. 596.

17. Stannard, David E. *American Holocaust: The Conquest of the New World.* Oxford UP, 1992, p. 78.

18. Hilberg, Paul. *The Destruction of the European Jews.* Quadrangle Books, 1961, p. 596.

19. Stannard. David E. *American Holocaust: The Conquest of the New World.* Oxford UP, 1992, p. 80.

20. Stannard. p. 80.

21. Budd, Thomas. *Good Order Established in Pennsylvania & New Jersey in America, Being a True Account of the Country; With its Produce and Commodities There Made in the Year 1685.* London, 1685, p. 33.

22. Awiakta, Marilou. *Selu, Seeking the Corn-Mother's Wisdom.* Fulcrum Publishing, 1993, p. 155.

23. *Commercial Appeal, November 24, 1977.* (a quote from Awaikta) Note 49, p. 313.

24. Awaikta, Marilou. *Selu, Seeking the Corn-Mother's Wisdom.* Fulcrum Publishing, 1993, p. 313.

25. Stannard, David E. *American Holocaust: The Conquest of the New World.* Oxford UP, 1992, pp. 118-229.

26. Eckert, Allan W. *A Dark & Bloody River: Chronicles of the Ohio river Walley.* Bantam Books, 1995, pp. 55-59.

27. Zinn, Howard. *A People's History of the United States.* Harper and Row, 1980, p. 14.

28. United Nations, General Assembly. Convention on the Prevention and Punishment of the Crime Of Genocide. Resolution 260 A (III) 9 Dec 1948. https://bit.ly/3ddr6ie.

29. Stannard, David E. *American Holocaust: The Conquest of*

the New World. Oxford UP, 1992, p. 281.

| THREE |

Trade and Treaties
From Early 1600s to 1830

As long as the moon shall rise,
As long as the rivers shall flow,
As long as the sun shall shine,
As long as the grass shall grow.

Common expression for terms of treaties with
Native Americans
Wilma Mankiller, *"Mankiller: A Chief and Her People"*[1]

The blunt fact, however, is that an Indian tribe is
sovereign to the extent that the U.S. permits it to be
sovereign.

Federal District Judge Russell Smith,
*United States v. Blackfeet Tribe of Blackfeet Ind. Res.,
364 F. Supp. 192 (D. Mont. 1973)*[2]

The words "treaty" and "nation" are words of our own
language, selected in our diplomatic and legislative
proceedings, by ourselves, having each a definite and
well understood meaning. We have applied them to
the other nations of the earth. They are applied to all
in the same sense.

Chief Justice John Marshall of the U.S. Supreme
Court
Worcester v. Georgia (1832)[3]

Treaties form the backdrop of the past, confirm rights
of the present, and provide the basic definitions for the
evolving future.

Kickingbird et al. (1980.)[4]

When Sharlotte Neely wrote *Snowbird Cherokees: People of
Persistence* in 1991, it was estimated that Natives had lived
in the southern Appalachian region for at least 4,000 years. The
Cherokee, the largest Indian Nation in North America north of
Mexico, had a population of approximately 225,000 people and a
territory that now makes up parts of seven states: North Carolina,
South Carolina, Alabama, Georgia, Mississippi, Tennessee and
Kentucky. They were masters of their environment on a rich and
diverse continent, which became a staging ground for European
conquest through invasion, enslavement, disease, genocide,
destruction and colonization. By 1991, there were 127 Indian
languages still spoken in the U.S., and the Cherokee language,
part of the Iroquoian language family, ranked seventh in number
of speakers among American languages north of Mexico.[5] When
first encountering the Europeans, the Cherokee Nation claimed an
area encompassing 124,000 square miles; however, by 1819, they
held only 17,000 square miles of the original tract.[6]

The Onset of Disease

The lives of all the Indigenous people of what is now the
United States changed dramatically and forever when, during
1738-1739, a slave ship arrived in the harbor of Charles Town
(Charleston, South Carolina) and unloaded not only slaves but an
epidemic of smallpox which ravaged the Cherokee Nation.
Smallpox spread through contact with bodily fluids or a
contaminated object and produced a high fever with vomiting. The
medicine men had never experienced anything like it and at first
told the People that the Great Spirit was punishing them for
something terrible.

As the smallpox spread, the medicine men resorted to
sweat baths, followed by a cold plunge in the river, the very worst
things that could have been recommended. Thirty percent of those
infected usually died within two weeks. It was worse for the

Cherokee and when it finally abated, more than half that population had died – estimated between nine to ten thousand men, women and children. Many who lived were often blinded or severely pockmarked. Some of the surviving warriors committed suicide, not wanting to live disfigured or worse – unable to hunt and care for themselves and their families.

While the 1738-1739 epidemic appears to have been an accident, there are recorded incidences of intentional exposure of the Indians to the smallpox by various military officials including purposeful exposure to the Delaware Indian delegation by the British officers of Fort Pitt in 1763. General Amherst used the garrison's smallpox breakout to his advantage and is quoted in a letter to Colonel Bouquet, "Could it not be contrived to send the smallpox among the disaffected tribes of Indians? We must on this occasion use every stratagem in our power to reduce them."[5] They provided the Delaware delegates with two blankets, a silk handkerchief and linens from the smallpox hospital:

> When smallpox was introduced among Cree Indians in Canada as late as the eighteenth century, one native witnessing the horrifying epidemic that destroyed his people explained, 'We had no belief that one man could give it to another, any more than a wounded man could give his wound to another.'[7]

Treaties Abound

In the 170 years prior to the first treaties concluded between the fledgling U.S. government and the Indian tribes, there were approximately 175 treaties negotiated between the British colonial government and the Indian tribes. Under the influence of the French and British policy of dealing with the Indians as individual sovereign nations, the U.S. continued this policy after the Revolutionary War, and these early treaties established the format used between the U.S. and the Indian Nations in all future treaties. Under "Section C: Treaties and Agreements," Jack Utter wrote:

> ... There is no set form for treaties. Most, however, including Indian-U.S. treaties, usually contain five

elements: (1) a preamble, (2) terms and conditions, (3) provisos (special conditions, usually referring to sometime in the future), (4) consideration (the exchange of something of value), and (5) signatures, seals, and marks.[8]

All nations understood that treaties were governed by the rule of law and were the instrument used between two sovereign nations, each giving and receiving mutually and beneficially to one another: peace, return of prisoners, punishment for crimes committed by citizens of one nation against the other, trade, boundaries agreed upon with punishment for those infringing upon the lands of the Indians, considerations (usually in money or goods) for ceded lands, justice for The Indians' interests and the right to send a representative to Congress. The Indian representative, whether selected by the Indians or chosen by the government, had no voice or vote in the proceedings.

Signed in 1785 and ratified by Congress in 1791, the Treaty of Hopewell was the first treaty between the Cherokee Nation and the nascent government. The treaty sought to maintain peace and prevent crimes inflicted by and on both nations and set boundaries. It ended with Article XIII, which states, "The hatchet shall be forever buried, and peace given by the United States ..." A total of 22 treaties between the U.S. and the Cherokee were ratified between 1785 and June 6, 1868 when the final treaty was ratified. Two treaties in 1828 and 1833 were ratified with the Western Band of Cherokee. All remaining land rights east of the Mississippi were ceded to the federal government at that time, except for a reservation in North Carolina claimed by the Eastern Band of Cherokee.

Jack Utter wrote *American Indians: Answers to Today's Questions* in 2001, which presented several noteworthy answers that need to be studied for their full implications of treaty law. The treaty provisions were not abrogated just because the Congress declared the Indian Nations were no longer considered to be independent nations and ceased entering into treaties in the late 1880s. A brief quote from the milestone Supreme Court case of *United States v. Winans* (1905) summarizes the overall point:

'[T]he treaty was not a grant of rights to the Indians, but a grant of rights from them' The frequently heard term 'treaty rights' thus refers to rights explicitly and implicitly retained by the tribe and not to rights granted by the U.S. government. It also refers to those obligations which the government owed the tribe in exchange for its lands as well as other consideration received from the federal government.[9]

When asked, "What is the present status of the Indian–U.S. treaties?" Utter wrote the following:

Those people who question their validity solely because of the treaties' age are also, indirectly, questioning the validity of our 200-year-old Constitution, which not only pre-dates them but authorizes their negotiation and ratification. [10]

Early Influence of the Founding Fathers

George Washington's family was involved with the Ohio Land Company as early as 1748. As he surveyed extensive tracts of land in the Ohio River region, Washington and his agents laid claim to vast areas because he understood that Americans would soon want to occupy the region. Washington's early interest in surveying and his ability to recognize the potential led him to make wise investments "... even though he was reputedly the richest man in America at this point."[11] He believed the settlers would find the land to their liking and too good an opportunity to pass up. Further, the settlers would make excellent militia against the Indians and protect the interests of the country.

Even as the Americans spread out beyond the Alleghenies, Benjamin Franklin and Thomas Jefferson, along with many of the Founding Fathers and other Europeans, were studying the Iroquois Great Law of Peace. Established between 1390 and 1500, the League of the Iroquois, made up of a confederacy of Six Indian Nations – Mohawk, Oneida, Onondaga, Cayuga, Seneca and Tuscarora – had their seat of government in Syracuse, New York. In 1754, Franklin submitted a draft of the Albany Plan of Union for a representative government based on the Iroquois Great Law of Peace, which laid the foundation for the Union. The Articles of Confederation approved in 1777 became effective in 1781.

After the Revolutionary War in 1783, the British ceded their claims to territory within the U.S. that was not theirs to cede. The Indians retained ownership of territory while granting the British, as well as the French, rights to trap and establish outposts in the territory. Fully aware of that fact, the government representatives were nevertheless eager to accept British claims to the territory and negotiated the terms to mean that the U.S. was "... now and forever after sole owners of the vast Northwestern Territory."[12] The ebbs and flows of the consequences of presidential policy can be seen from the very first treaties. At that time, it was to the benefit of the economically strapped union to negotiate treaties with the Indians, thus providing a period of peace in which they could get the country on a solid footing.

Continental Congress Adds to the Injustice

"Under the direction of the Continental Congress of 1775, a Committee on Indian Affairs was organized in an attempt to assert a collective influence among the Indians. Upon this committee's recommendation, three departments were established ..."[13] This divided the responsibility for the Native Nations into three geographical regions; the southern department included the Cherokees. The attitudes of leaders of the time are reflected in Washington's letter to James Duane on September 7th, 1783 when he compared Indians with wolves, "... both being beasts of prey, tho' they differ in shape."[14]

One early task facing the Continental Congress included reading correspondence from George Washington in which he recommended the dispersal of American Indian groups living in the Ohio Valley and others in general. "He suggested, in order to 'induce them to relinquish [our] territories and remove to the illimitable regions of the West,' that the Indians be maneuvered into positions where they had little choice but to sell their lands."[15] Washington took the oath of office in April 1789 and swore to serve the people of the republic "... to the best of my Ability, preserve, protect and defend the Constitution of the United States."[16] The American Indians were not included as Washington led policies that forced them to move, took their land, limited their freedom and waged unrelenting war against them. As president, Washington took care to ensure that the U.S. Constitution was fully upheld as he negotiated the first Indian treaties.

Next Steps: Good Intentions, Poor Execution

Henry Knox became Secretary of War by an Ordinance of August 7, 1789, which made him responsible for Indian affairs. The previous June, he wrote to Washington, expressing the policy he felt the government should follow "... in acquiring title to Indian land: The Indians being the prior occupants, possess the right of the soil. It cannot be taken from them unless by their free consent, or by the right of conquest in case of a just war ...[17]

> On August 22, 1789, he [President Washington] visited the Senate chamber in the company of Secretary Knox to confer with the Senate in regard to the southern tribes. He quickly reached the central issue in the Indian problem when he stated, 'The treaty with the Cherokees has been entirely violated by the disorderly white people on the frontiers of North Carolina.'[18]

Knox had the primary task of formulating Indian policy from this point on, and he felt that it was important to secure the trust of both the Indians and the settlers by implementing the terms of the treaties. This meant the government should restrain settlers from moving into Indian Territory and assist Indians in learning care of domestic animals and cultivating crops as stipulated in the various treaties.[19]

Stipulations within the treaties outlined the importance of preventing hunting or settling on any Indian grounds, with the military authorized to remove those who disobeyed the treaty stipulations. The government required passports to travel within the Indian Territory, and this requirement was generally upheld by traders; however, others largely ignored the treaty stipulations because they felt that they had the right to live and hunt within the territory. The military oversaw such a large territory that it made it extremely difficult to prevent the incursions. Regular army and volunteers attempted to keep the Indians within the confines of their territory but did not feel compelled to keep the whites out.

As Trade Expands, Native Americans Lose

Long before the Revolutionary War, the British made a practice of settling Indian debts incurred in their trade with the British by land cessions. From the earliest contact between the Indians and the Europeans, trade was established. The northern regions produced the highest quality beaver pelts that the European consumer demanded for men's hats fashionable at that time. The demand reached a peak of about 19,000 beaver pelts in 1720. Records kept by the English from 1699 to 1759 show the decimation of the deer population throughout the region east of the Mississippi River. The average number of deerskins shipped to England in the early years was 54,000; however, that increased to well over one and a half million shipped from Charles Town yearly. By the time the practice of settling the Cherokee debts through trade was made permanent in Washington's administration, the deer population was hardly sufficient to sustain the needs of the Indian population, which made land cession their next course of action.

Washington's administration established the Trade and Intercourse Act of 1790, which provided strategic locations for government trading houses in Indian Territory and placed their oversight in the hands of the president. The act included several provisions directing the interaction with the various Indian tribes, including promotion of civilization, establishing a licensed trade to ensure honesty of employees and restricting the flow of liquor to the Indians. One such government-operated factory was established at Tellico, Tennessee. By operating and maintaining the trading houses, the government meant to undersell their rivals: Britain, France and Spain. The French were of greatest concern because their goods were acknowledged to be better than what the government offered. The ultimate goals were to make the Indians dependent on American trade goods and to place them in debt to the government such that they would be required to give up more territory in the next treaty. The 1790s acts were temporary laws;

however, a permanent law was enacted in 1802, and "... remain[ed] in force as the 'basic law governing Indian relations,' with additions from time to time as necessary, until the new codification of Indian policy in 1834."[20] The one policy retained for a longer period required the Indian traders to maintain their license, and they were closely supervised.

Jefferson and Others Promote Indian Containment

The lust for land, seen as unoccupied and, therefore, not belonging to anyone, pushed explorers and settlers ever farther away from the coastline, across the mountains and into the frontier of America. They came up against the Native people who resisted the invasion of their lands, resulting in strife and conflict and costing lives on both sides. This incessant quest for land was documented in the following:

> President Washington issued a Proclamation on December 12, 1792 wherein he stated that the State of Georgia was responsible for destroying a Cherokee town and killing several members of the Cherokee Nation even though the Cherokee People had a friendly relationship with the United States. Further he offered a Five Hundred Dollar reward for persons suspected of perpetrating these crimes who were apprehended and brought to trial.[21]

While the idea of a separate "Indian Country" was first promulgated after the French and Indian War ended in 1760, the purchase of Louisiana in 1803 provided President Jefferson, who served from 1801 to 1809, the answer he sought. A number of the country's presidents earned the fear of the American Indians, and Jefferson fit into that category. In 1807, he wrote to the Secretary of War expressing his opinion that resistance by any Indians to American expansion would be met with war, a war in which some Americans would undoubtedly die, but the intent would be to destroy the Indians. Other leaders before and after Jefferson often stated that it was best for the Indians to remove themselves before the military forced them to move – something that occurred repeatedly.[22]

Had these same words been enunciated by a German leader in 1939 and directed at European Jews, they would be engraved in modern memory. Since they were uttered by one of America's founding fathers, however, the most widely admired of the South's slaveholding philosophers of freedom, they conveniently have become lost to most historians in their insistent celebration of Jefferson's wisdom and humanity.[23]

The country now owned the lands between the mighty Mississippi River and the Rocky Mountains, from the Canadian border to the Gulf of Mexico, and the government positioned itself to force the migration of all the Indian Nations to the west of the Mississippi, stating that it was best for the Indians to remove themselves from the influence of the whites. Jefferson drafted a constitutional amendment that allowed the exchange of land that the tribes held in the east, specifically Georgia, for other lands west of the Mississippi, which vindicated Jefferson's purchase of the Louisiana Country and answered the question of what to do with the Indians. Congress never gave serious consideration to the amendment; however, they did authorize him,

"... to 'stipulate with any Indian tribes owning lands on the east side of the Mississippi, and residing thereon, for an exchange of lands, the property of the United States, on the west side of the Mississippi, in case the said tribes shall remove and settle thereon.'"[24]

As noted earlier, the British and then the U.S. government, by the establishment of the Trade and Intercourse Act of 1790, provided a means to obtain Indian lands without war. President Jefferson wrote in a letter to Indiana Territory governor William Henry Harrison that a "policy of getting Indians in debt so they would have to give up land" was to be established. The following is an excerpt from that letter:

Our system is to live in perpetual peace with the Indians, to cultivate an affectionate attachment for them by everything just and liberal which we can do for them within the bounds of reason and by giving them effectual protection against the wrongs from our own people. When they withdraw themselves to the culture of a small piece of land, they will perceive how useless to them are the extensive forests and will be willing to pare them off in exchange for necessaries for their farms and families. To promote this, we shall push our trading houses, and be glad to see the good and influential individuals among them in debt because we observe when these debts go beyond what the individual can pay, they become willing to lop them off by a cession of lands. But should any tribe refuse the preferred hand and take up the hatchet, it will be driven across the Mississippi and the whole of its lands confiscated.[25]

Explorers View Native Americans as "In Their Way"

Shortly after the consummation of the Louisiana Purchase, President Jefferson commissioned Meriwether Lewis and George Rogers Clark to explore and map out the newly purchased territory, to:

> ... find a practical route across the western half of the continent, and to establish an American presence in this territory before Britain and other European powers tried to claim it. The campaign's secondary objectives were scientific and economic: to study the area's plants, animal life, and geography, and to establish trade with local American Indian tribes.[26]

During Lewis and Clark's exploration of the NW Passage, they carried a vial of smallpox to ensure their safety. Nick Estes writes in his book *Our History is The Future* quoting from *The Travels of Capts, Lewis & Clarke* that they understood the fear Native Americans had of smallpox and the very threat of using it provoked fear. Wintering with the Sioux in 1805, Lewis documents their safety concerns, believing that the Sioux planned to murder them. A threat of releasing the smallpox among the Indians prevented the attack, allowing them to proceed with their exploration in the spring.[27]

When the immigrants arrived from the Old Country, they

had preconceived views of Indians as first obtained from Columbus and augmented with each new report and the popular books written which idealized the Indians. Respect changed as settlers came to view the Indians as simply part of the frontier and an impediment to expansion. Religious leaders emphasized that God not only desired, but required man, to work the land. Land was coveted and the Indians did not adhere to God's laws, thus they must submit to "... subjugation, exploitation, and ultimate elimination."[28]

The Land Grab Continues

Three years after leaving office and again the following year, Jefferson expressed his belief that it was necessary to drive the Indians from their eastern homelands when he wrote, "... the American government had no other choice before it than 'to pursue [the Indians] to extermination, or drive them to new seats beyond our reach.'"[29]

The wording of successive treaties always built on the wording of prior treaties, which was particularly important in two treaties ratified by President Monroe in 1817 and 1819. Through these two treaties:

> ... permanent arrangements were made for the Cherokee nation on their present territory; and into the last of these treaties the intercourse law of the United States was ingrafted; thus affording a pledge, that the power of the national government should always be exerted to preserve the territory of the Cherokees inviolate.[30]

In Article 5 of The Treaty of the Cherokee Agency of 1817, the federal government proposes for the first time that lands ceded east of the Mississippi would be exchanged acre for acre on the Arkansas and White rivers "... and shall be done soon after the ratification of this treaty ..."[31] Article 6 continues with the U.S. promising specific articles for those warriors who willingly immigrated to Indian Territory. These items were considered "... full compensation for the improvements which they may leave ..."[32] While many left little behind in the east, they had even less when they arrived in Indian territory. Promised a rifle and ammunition, blanket and brass kettle, they still had no ax to fell trees for a fire or to build a cabin, no hoe to work the land and no food to get them through the first months in their new surroundings.

Over protests of those wishing to remain in the east, approximately 1,500 to 2,000 Cherokee elected to move west in 1817, joining a small number of emigrants known as the Old Settlers who had drifted west at the turn of the century. Those who remained were offered an experiment in citizenship whereby they could apply for a 640-acre reserve of the lands ceded and citizenship. The states fought the experiment and were slow to survey the reserves, which allowed war veterans and others to move onto the land, thereby ending any possibility of Indian assimilation.

Specific Cherokees Become Citizens and Given Land

In the treaty of February 27, 1819, the majority of the Cherokee east of the Mississippi stated their desire to remain on their ancestral lands. The treaty ceded almost four million acres, which they hoped would leave them in peace and end further efforts to remove them from their lands. The treaty stipulated an annuity, which was to be divided by population with two-thirds paid to the Cherokees east of the Mississippi and one-third to the Cherokees west of that river.[33] Improvements made by individuals to the lands ceded were to be paid for by the national government. The 1819 treaty also stipulated that lands previously used by the Cherokee Nation for schools were to be sold and the money placed in trust for the Cherokee Nation. As in the 1817 treaty, the new treaty specified that reservations of 640 acres were to be set aside in fee simple (a permanent and absolute tenure of an estate in land with freedom to dispose of it at will) for specified Cherokee individuals who chose to remain on their ancestral lands and become U.S. citizens.

Congress Ignores Protests of Cherokee Council

The men that signed the land cessions of 1817-1819 were not officials authorized to represent the Cherokee Nation;

therefore, their actions were considered illegal. The federal government chose to ratify the sessions, and to make the situation worse, Congress ignored a memorial signed by 67 chiefs in official council action and submitted to Congress in protest. "During the fall session of 1820 the Cherokee Council voted, by special decree, [that] ... it was made an act of treason, punishable by death, for any individual to negotiate the sale of Cherokee lands to whites without consent of the national council."[34] As a result of continuing problems, the Cherokee General Council passed the Cherokee Blood Law on October 24, 1829 which clarified the 1820 vote and further stated: "... citizens of this Nation, may kill him or them so offending, in any manner most convenient, within the limits of this Nation, and shall not be held accountable for the same."[35] This law later resulted in the deaths of three Treaty Party leaders and subsequent turmoil between the Old Settlers, the Treaty Party and the Ross Party as they tried to unify the groups into one Cherokee Nation in Indian Territory.

In 1823, a lawsuit, *Johnson v. McIntosh* (21 U.S. 543), was presented to the Supreme Court to determine whether Indians had the right to sell land to a private citizen or could only sell to the federal government. Jack Utter explained in his book, *American Indians: Answers to Today's Questions,* that Chief Justice John Marshall wrote the Court's opinion based on the "Discovery Doctrine," which originated with the British when they took legal title to the land from the Indians by rights of discovery:

> This culturally racist 'superior culture and superior religion' conception of the Discovery Doctrine can be clearly traced all the way back to the first Crusade of 1095, and even further back to the equally arrogant ideas of Aristotle's *Politics*, written in the 4th century B.C.[36]

In writing the opinion of the Supreme Court, Marshall confirmed that the British believed that in bringing civilization and Christianity to the Indians, they had been compensated for the lands. Both the British and the United States believed that this right was transferred to the U.S. government at the successful conclusion of the American Revolution. From this point on, it was determined that the Indians had the right of occupancy to the lands, but only the U.S. government could purchase or sell the land.[37] Utter continued by stating:

> The Discovery Doctrine provides the foundational principles of modern federal Indian law. It also provides some of the justification for Congressional 'plenary' (or near absolute) power over Indian affairs. And, it has always been in the background of such federal policies as assimilation, removal, allotment, forced education, the reservation system, partial termination (e.g., Public Law 280), termination, and relocation.[38]

More Treaties – More Land Lost

Georgia was one of the thirteen colonies to sign the Declaration of Independence and in 1788 became the fourth state to ratify the U.S. Constitution. By doing so, Georgia agreed that treaty-making powers resided within the federal government and that they would abide by all existing treaties. In 1802, Georgia relinquished its claim on the lands extending to the Mississippi River that they had claimed since their adoption of the Constitution. The proviso being that "... the United States should 'at their own expense, extinguish, for the use of Georgia, as early as the same can be peaceably obtained, on reasonable terms,' Indian title to that area included in the State boundaries."[39]

The U.S. was obligated to Georgia, but the territory had always been held by the Cherokee, and the federal government had treaties with the Cherokee, which, like Georgia, guaranteed title to their lands in return for land cession.

In the 1820s, the states, most prominently Georgia, were advancing state's rights and wanted legal control over all territory within the borders they claimed. Numerous treaties, confirmed and ratified, ceded large portions of Indian Territory of which Georgia received about twenty million acres. The Cherokee territory contained about five million acres when in 1827, Georgia announced that the territory was theirs by right of discovery and that the Indians were mere occupants. It was further stated that the federal government had failed to clear title to the lands by either negotiation or force and that Georgia meant to rectify the situation. Effective June 1, 1830, all laws and ordinances, including the Cherokee Constitution adopted on July 26, 1827, were declared null and void by Georgia.

As a conquered people, the Georgia legislation stated that the Cherokee had no right to self-government, no right to their property and no legal standing in the local or state courts, therefore no recourse against white aggression and no recourse through the law to harm against their persons. The untenable and all–encompassing situation of the Cherokees under the Georgia law was described by Jeremiah Evarts when he wrote:

> If the cattle of a Cherokee are driven away in his presence; if his fences are thrown down and his crops destroyed, if his children are beaten, and his domestic sanctuary invaded; – whatever outrage and whatever injury he may experience, he cannot even seek a legal remedy. He can neither be a party, nor a witness ... Even the slaves of his new neighbors are defended by the self-interest of their masters. But he has not even this consolation ...[40]

The legislators meant to extinguish Cherokee claims to their lands, as well as extend the authority of Georgia's laws over the Cherokee, which included acts considered both oppressive and tyrannical. The intent of the legislation was to force all American Indians within the state limits to remove themselves or to pledge allegiance to Georgia. Cherokee lands were ultimately disposed of through a public lottery.

Author's Thoughts

As unrelenting as the ocean tide pulling the sand out from under our feet was the wave of humanity arriving in the new country previously inhabited solely by the Native Americans. The immigrants came to claim free land upon which to build their dreams. First, numerous European powers sought treaties with the Indians; then the grand experiment in democracy called the United States made treaties with the different tribes to set the economically strapped country on a solid footing.

Where the Indians resisted, there were wars or subterfuge, as in the examples of the trading houses purposefully getting the Indians into debt, then magnanimously canceling the debt in exchange for great areas of land. Another deception of the whites was the time they conspired to provide items infected with smallpox to silently kill off the Indians and clear the way to claim the land.

Benjamin Franklin and the other Founding Fathers drafted the U.S. representative government based on the Iroquois Great Law of Peace. Ironically, when the Cherokee, an independent Nation, based their representative government on that of the U.S., President Jackson chided them for establishing a government within a government.

In good faith, the Cherokees relinquished thousands of acres of land, believing the federal government when it stipulated that the treaties would be honored *As Long as the Moon Shall Rise and As Long as the Rivers Shall Flow.*[41] As it turned out, all the Indian Nations learned to their detriment that the treaties lasted only as long as their lands were not coveted by the federal government – yet another assault on their lives.

Endnotes:

1. Mankiller, Wilma and Michael Wallis. *Mankiller: A Chief and Her People*. St Martin's Press, 1993, p. 118.
2. United State District Court, District of Montana, *United States v. Blackfeet Tribe of the Blackfeet Indian Reservation,* 364 F. Supp. 192, 10 Oct 1973. https://law.justia.com/cases/federal/district-courts/FSupp/364/192/2259045/
3. United States, Supreme Court. *Worcester v. Georgia,* 31 U.S.

515.1832.https://supreme.justia.com/cases/federal/us/31/515/

4. Kickingbird et al. (1980 p. 45). Utter, Jack. *American Indians: Answers to Today's Questions 2nd Ed. Revised and Enlarged.* U of Oklahoma P, 2001. p. 87.

5. Neely, Sharlotte. *Snowbird Cherokees: People of Persistence.* U of Georgia, 1991, p. 15.

6. Anderson, William L, editor. *Cherokee Removal: Before and After.* Brown Thrasher Books, U of Georgia P, 1991, p. vii-viii.

7. Stannard, David E. *American Holocaust: The Conquest of the New World.* Oxford UP, 1992, p. 53.

8. Utter, Jack. *"American Indians: Answers to Today's Questions 2nd Ed. Revised and Enlarged.* U of Oklahoma P, 2001. p. 79.

9. Utter. p. 85.

10. Utter. p. 87.

11. Eckert, Allan W. *A Dark and Bloody River: Chronicles of the Ohio River Valley.* Bantam Books, 1995, p. 440.

12. Eckert. p. 437.

13. Tyler, S. Lyman. *A History of Indian Policy.* U.S. Department of the Interior, Bureau of Indian Affairs, 1973, p. 33.

14. Washington, George. "Letter to James Duane, 7 September 1783." *National Archives.* https://bit.ly/2TUzD0X. Accessed 19 Jul 2019.

15. Eckert, Allan W. *A Dark and Bloody River: Chronicles of the Ohio River Valley.* Bantam Books, 1995, p. 440.

16. "Presidential Oath of Office." ArtII.S1.C8. *constitution.congress.gov.* https://bit.ly/32fR00J.

17. Tyler, S. Lyman. *A History of Indian Policy.* U.S. Department of the Interior, Bureau of Indian Affairs, 1973. p. 35.

18. Tyler. pp. 38-39.

19. Tyler. pp. 38-39.

20. Tyler. p. 42.

21. King, Duane H. and E. Raymond Evans. "Washington Attempts to Bring Justice to the Cherokees." *Journal of Cherokee Studies, Vol. IV, No. 2, Spring 1979.* Printed in *The Connecticut* Courant, Jan. 7, 1793. p 59.

22. Stannard, David E. *American Holocaust: The Conquest of the New World.* Oxford UP, 1962, p. 120

23. Stannard. p. 120.

24. Tyler, S. Lyman, *A History of Indian Policy.* U.S. Department of the Interior, Bureau of Indian Affairs, 1973, pp. 54, 71.

25. Eckert, Allan W. *A Dark & Bloody River: Chronicles of the Ohio River Valley.* Bantam Books, 1995, Frontispiece: Excerpts from a letter written by President Thomas Jefferson.

26. "Lewis and Clark Expedition." *Wikipedia: The Free Encyclopedia*, Wikimedia Foundation, https://bit.ly/2SdkpmL. Accessed 21 Jul 2019.

27. Estes, Nick. *The History is The Future: Standing Rock vs the Dakota Access Pipeline, and the Long Tradition of Indigenous Resistance"* Verso, 2019, p. 86.

28. Christianson, James R. "Removal: A Foundation for the Formation of Federal Indian Policy" *Journal of Cherokee Studies, Vol. X, No. 2, Fall 1985*, p 224.

29. Stannard, David E. *American Holocaust: The Conquest of the New World.* Oxford UP, 1962, p. 120.

30. Evarts, Jeremiah. *Cherokee Removal: The "William Penn" Essays and Other Writings.* Edited and with an introduction by Francis Paul Prucha, The U of Tennessee P, 1981, p. 221.

31. Kappler, Charles J compiled and edited. *Indian Treaties, 1778-1883.* Amereon House, 1972, p. 142.

32. Kappler. p. 143.

33. Kappler. p. 179.

34. Alderman, Pat. *Nancy Ward / Dragging Canoe: Cherokee Chieftainess/Cherokee-Chickamauga War Chief.* 2nd ed., Overmountain Press, 1978, p. 81.

35. "The Cherokee Blood Law." https://bit.ly/33if2t2. Accessed 1 Feb 2017 and 30 Jul 2019.

36. Utter, Jack. *American Indians: Answers to Today's Questions 2nd Ed. Revised and Enlarged.* U of Oklahoma P, 2001, pp. 17-18.

37. Utter. p. 17.

38. Utter. p. 18.

39. United States, Supreme Court. *Worcester v. Georgia,* 31 U.S. 515. 1832.

https://supreme.justia.com/cases/federal/us/31/515/

40. Evarts, Jeremiah. *Cherokee Removal: The "William Penn" Essays and Other Writings*. Edited and with an Introduction by Francis Paul Prucha, The U of Tennessee P, 1981, p. 174.

41. Mankiller, Wilma and Michael Wallis. *Mankiller: A Chief and Her People*. St Martin's Press, 1993, p. 118.

| FOUR |

Significant Leaders (1730 – 1850)

While there were many leaders who made a difference in the lives of the Cherokee during the eighteenth and nineteenth century, there were four who made far-reaching contributions to their Nation in the areas of peace, war and literacy. The four leaders were Attakullahulla, Tsi.yu Gansi.ni, Nan-ye-hi and Sequoyah.

Native Americans typically have several names during their lifetime. The first name is given to the child and the second name, which replaces the first, is given later in life when the child does something that distinguishes him or herself. The story of Attakullahulla – whose narrative follows – was a second name for Chuconnunta, who later became known to the Americans as The Little Carpenter. Tsi.su Gansi. ni, who earns the name Dragging Canoe, is another example.

Chuconnunta ➤ Attakullahulla ➤ The Little Carpenter

The story of The Little Carpenter begins in 1730 when an Englishman, Sir Alexander Cuming, visited Cherokee country. Several written accounts have been given of Cuming's exploits. One account says that he was sent on a secret mission to smooth over grievances the Cherokee had with the English and prevent their alliance with the French. Another account stated that Cuming wanted to establish a name for himself and had worked out a plan to take several warriors back to London to meet the king. Whatever the reason, Cuming, with the help of a young warrior friend, was finally able to convince Chuconnunta (later known as Attakullahulla) that the distance to London was not so great and that he would be back home by the end of summer or early fall. Although hesitant and a little fearful about making such a long journey, Chuconnunta, finally agreed. Six others also volunteered to make a trip. The arrival of seven Cherokee men in London caused quite a stir and made a great impression on the English people, as well as on the Cherokee. Wined and dined by King George II, the king paid their expenses for an extended stay, gifts were exchanged and mutual pledges given. "The Cherokee promised that no other white people would be allowed to settle in their country and that they would trade with no one else but King George's representatives."[1] Attakullahulla saw man-of-war ships, experienced big guns being fired, enjoyed the pageantry of the king's throne room and knew without a doubt that the British were very powerful. All this had the intended effect on the men. Before their return home, they pledged to be allies with the British in exchange for gifts brought home to the Cherokee. "They also promised to aid Great Britain in time of war ... The Cherokee had gained a Great White Father but had mortgaged their freedom."[2]

On May 11, 1731, almost a year after they left, they arrived back in their homeland. This trip had made a lasting impression on Chuconnunta, molding the young brave who later served as a great Cherokee Peace Chief and became known to his People as well as the whites as The Little Carpenter. He played a prominent role in history, utilizing his diplomacy skills to work for peace in dealing with the British. It is said that the name Little Carpenter came from his ability to carve treaty stipulations wanted by both and merge them to make a treaty agreeable to both nations.

Imagine the young People listening to the stories of The Little Carpenter. Children listened to the history and took away aspects that were important to their lives. In this manner, Tsi.yu Gansi.ni (Dragging Canoe) heard his father, The Little Carpenter, tell him about the might of Britain, and he understood that it would be necessary to fight to retain Cherokee ancestral lands. When Dragging Canoe was forty, he became the last Great Cherokee War Chief. In contrast, Nan-ye-yi (Nancy Ward), cousin to Dragging Canoe, listened to the stories of her uncle's trip to England and believed that it was imperative that the two nations learn from one another and work together for the benefit of everyone. She became a Beloved Woman and an advocate for peace.

Tsi.yu Gansi.ni ➤ Dragging Canoe

The second significant leader, Tsi.yu Gansi.ni, the son of The Little Carpenter, was born around 1732. He was approximately seven years of age when he contracted smallpox. Although Tsi.yu Gansi.ni lived through the ravages of the disease, he was badly pockmarked. While still quite young, his father refused Tsi.yu Gansi.ni's request to accompany a war party to battle the Shawnee, but the boy left the village ahead of the war party and made his way to the dugouts they would use. When discovered, The Little Carpenter demanded the boy return to the village but then relented, telling his son that if he could carry the canoe over the portage, he would be allowed to join them. Encouraged by the warriors' shouts, Tri.yu Gansi.ni grabbed the end of a canoe and started dragging it, earning him the name Dragging Canoe.

Dragging Canoe adhered to his father's wishes for many years as The Little Carpenter endeavored to maintain peace between the whites and the Cherokees. But in March 1775, a council meeting was held in Sycamore Shoals, Tennessee with Richard Henderson of the Transylvania Company, wherein it was proposed that in exchange for several wagonloads of supplies and trinkets, the Cherokee would sign over approximately twenty million acres located in Kentucky and Tennessee.

After speeches were given in favor of the new treaty, including one by his father, Dragging Canoe gave an impassioned speech, emphasizing the fact that every time they made a treaty with the white people, the whites came back for more land, more concessions, and now was the time to take a stand. This tract was the last of their remaining ancestral hunting lands, and they were dependent upon it for meat. Now over forty, tall and strong, Dragging Canoe spoke to the hearts and minds of the braves of his generation. They watched as the older chiefs signed the treaty, but when Henderson immediately said "I have more goods, guns, and ammunition that you have not seen. There is land between where we stand and Kaintuckee. I do not like to walk over the land of my brothers; I want to buy from you the Road to Kaintuckee,"[3] Dragging Canoe, and those braves who felt the same as he did, immediately broke away from the main body of the Cherokee, and he became the last Great Cherokee War Chief.

This group of young leaders and their families, who left the central body of Cherokees because they did not believe in the promises of the whites, later became the Chickamauga. Their pledge to continue to wage war ultimately cost the Cherokee Nation over five million acres of land before the signing of the 1776 treaty. Dragging Canoe lead a bloody war against the whites until his death in 1792. Although the treaty was later declared illegal because it was with an individual, Henderson, who entered into the treaty instead of the government, the seeds of destruction were sown, making it easier for the U.S. government to approach the Cherokee for land concessions after the Revolutionary War.

Wild Rose ➤ Nan-ye-hi ➤ Ghighau ➤Beloved Mother ➤ Nancy Ward

Dragging Canoe's cousin, Nan-ye-hi, had a leadership role as well. Although the specific dates she lived are unknown, it is believed it was from 1738 to 1822, a period which proved very challenging for all American Indians, as the whites kept pushing onto and demanding great pieces of land. Nan-ye-hi is not only remembered as an important figure to the Cherokee People but is also considered an early pioneer for women in American politics, as she advocated for a woman's voice during a turbulent period in her tribe's history.

As a child, Nan-ye-hi was called Wild Rose. Her mother was Tame Doe of the Wolf Clan and a sister to Attakullahulla, the Peace Chief. Wild Rose's birthplace and home was the town of Chota, considered both a major town and a Peace Town. The Cherokee were a matriarchal society, so Wild Rose, through her mother and grandmother, became a member of one of the most distinguished clans which gave her "... as strong a claim to royal blood as Cherokee culture afforded."[4] Later named Nan-ye-hi (one who is with the Nunnehi, the Spirit People), she married Kingfisher, a Cherokee warrior, and they had two children, Catherine and Five Killer.

Nan-ye-hi was in her teens when she accompanied Kingfisher during a battle between the Cherokee and Creeks over territory disputed since 1715. When Kingfisher was killed, she took up his weapons and shouted a war cry, which encouraged the Cherokee warriors to continue the fight. The decisive victory over the Creeks ended with many prisoners and cleared Cherokee title to Northern Georgia. Upon returning to their village, the warriors held meetings to confer honors on those earned during battle which included naming Nan-ye-hi "Ghighau," the lifetime honor of Beloved Woman or Beloved Mother:

> [It was a]... lifetime distinction bestowed as an extreme mark of valorous merit. During State Council meetings in the Town House at Chota, Nancy, in her role of *Ghighau*, sat with the Peace Chief and War Chief in the holy area near the ceremonial fire. As head of the Woman's Council, she could speak out and let their opinions be heard. The Female Council did not hesitate to vote to oppose the decisions made by the ruling Headmen if they thought the welfare of the Tribe was at stake.[5]

While young for such an honor, the lessons learned from The Little Carpenter became a part of Nan-ye-hi's life as she matured in her leadership role becoming an advocate for peace.

One of the important functions of Ghighau was the preparation of the black drink which was used in significant council ceremonies and festivals. Only those who had proven themselves as brave warriors and had undergone the purification rituals were allowed to partake of the drink. Ghighau also prepared the black drink for those participating in the councils within the Nation and for councils with the white leaders. She and the other women had a voice in those councils as well. Understanding the importance of women was a significant part of the Cherokee matriarchal society, again bringing the harmonious balance between the male and female. The Cherokee women were not only famous in war but also held power in council, and Attaullakilla included them among his delegation:

> Their presence also has ceremonial significance: it is meant to show honor to the other delegation. But that delegation is composed of males only; to them the

absence of women is irrelevant, a trivial consideration.[6]

In September 1756, Nan-ye-hi, who the whites called Nancy because it was easier to pronounce, married Bryant Ward, a British trader who lived among the Cherokee. She and Bryant had a daughter, Elizabeth, whom they called Betsy. She and Nancy's other two children were members of the Wolf Clan and afforded all the honors and responsibilities associated with the clan. Throughout her life, Nancy advocated peace with the whites and saved many from death or severe punishment, returning a number to their families. "One of Nancy's most common sayings was, 'The white men are our brothers. The same house shelters us, and the same sky covers us all.' Her cry was *ALL FOR PEACE*."[7]

In her position as Beloved Mother, Nancy rescued Lydia Bean, a white woman who had been captured during an attack on Fort Watauga in 1776. She took Lydia into her home and nursed her back to health. They formed a friendship, with each giving and teaching about their lives. Nancy learned to weave, which ultimately changed the Cherokee clothing from being made predominately of hides. Now they were no longer dependent upon cloth solely purchased from traders. When The Little Carpenter, Peace Chief and uncle to Nancy, escorted Lydia Bean home, she gave him two dairy cattle, which Nancy eagerly accepted and learned the benefits of having dairy products for her family.

George Gist ➤ Sequoyah

The fourth leader was Sequoyah, known as George Gist as a child, and his contributions proved to be long-lasting, with references and honors in his name still visible today. He was born around 1775 to a Cherokee mother, a woman from a high-ranking clan, and a white father who abandoned them. George never attended school, but from a young age, he was curious about the world around him. He constructed small stick houses, later using that knowledge to improve the building over the spring where the milk from his mother's cows was kept cold. He developed a method of enticing the colts with salt licks in felled trees, which made them easier to train, and he became a proficient rider. His mother extended credit for items sold to the hunters, and George went with them on hunting trips to bring meat and hides back on extra horses. In this way, he learned to hunt and added to the family's resources.

He taught himself to work silver and fashioned ornaments with various designs that the Cherokee of the time liked to wear. Wanting the People to recognize his work, he learned to engrave his name on the pieces, adding detailed pictures of humans and animals into his designs. He was fascinated with the white man's "Talking Leaves," wondering how the white man could read the books and writings of someone from another place and time and know what was meant. This interest and curiosity about the written word remained throughout his life.

George (now known as Sequoyah) joined other Cherokees to assist General Andrew Jackson in the campaign against the Creek in 1813 and 1814. He returned partially disabled and walked with a limp thereafter. No longer able to participate in strenuous activities, he spent his time and mind pursuing his passion in developing a written Cherokee syllabary, which took him twelve long years to complete but was then destroyed in a fire. There are several stories about the fire. One was that after several years of spending so much time dedicated to developing the syllabary and ignoring the family, his wife, in desperation, set all his work on fire. Another story was that the People were afraid of his work and looked upon it as a sort of witchcraft. Whatever the true reason for the fire, it turned out to be a good thing because when George started over, he decided on a different methodology of developing characters for sounds instead of individual words, ultimately creating a Cherokee syllabary of 85 letters and combinations. His first student was his daughter, Ah-yo-ka, and she easily learned and demonstrated to the skeptics among the People that they could learn as well.

During this time, Sequoyah took an interest in politics and was one of 331 Cherokees who migrated to Arkansas country as a result of the 1817 treaty. In the early 1820s, he returned to his homeland for a visit and demonstrated his work by reading letters from family and friends in Indian Territory. Initially doubtful because the People did not understand the advantage of the "talking leaves," this demonstration of hearing letters read from friends and family they thought never to hear from again helped them appreciate how writing would enable them to keep in touch with one another.

The American Board of Commissioners for Foreign Missions was formed in 1810, which was shortly after the U.S. government started providing money for missions to be established in the Cherokee Nation. Samuel Austin Worcester was a missionary and linguist with the Foreign Missions and spent his career with the Cherokee first in their eastern homeland and then voluntarily participating in the Trail of Tears which took him and his family to Indian Territory. Determined to bring Sequoyah's syllabary to the general Cherokee population, Reverend Worcester hired a traveling Native speaker who met with great success often having classes of "... seventy to eighty students raging in ages from six to eighty. In spite of the size of the classes and range of ages of the students, the classes met in order and with dignity."[8] Marilou Awaikta writes in her book, *Selu: Seeking the Corn-Mother's Wisdom,* that with Sequoyah's gift, anyone who spoke Cherokee fluently (though many of the People did not because of the settlers' language influence) learned to read and write Cherokee, and "Within two years the whole nation, east and west, was literate, and shortly a newspaper was published, *The Cherokee Phoenix.*"[9]

The next 20 years saw many changes brought about through the ability to read and write. The Cherokee shifted to "... a centralized government and in 1827 adopted a written constitution modeled after the U. S. Constitution,"[10] along with significant development of laws governing property. Two separate types of property were established: the land itself was owned by the Cherokee Nation, not an individual, but any improvements to the property belonged to the individual. "The Cherokee hoped that these changes would make peaceful coexistence possible, and the government would allow them to remain on their ancestral lands. None of these adaptations saved the Nation."[11]

The federal government completed the Louisiana Purchase, ratified the Indian Removal Act and brokered a treaty with a group of Cherokee who were not official representatives of the Nation but were more closely aligned with the aspirations of the federal government. Although over 17,000 men signed a petition to have the treaty set aside, it suited the U.S. government to ignore their petition and maintain the validity of the treaty as written. The provisions of the treaty were enforced in 1838 when the Cherokee were compelled to move to Indian Territory.

Sequoyah's syllabary enabled the Cherokee to make a written record of much of their history and beliefs. It was almost too late, but the urgency and necessity to ensure that the children knew of their heritage encouraged everyone to learn. Many great leaders, knowledgeable in the oral traditions, were already with the Great Spirit or of great age. Because of the insight and efforts of some whites who came as friends to live and work among the People, much of the oral history, both spiritual and historical, was put to paper and later translated into English. In 1836, Sequoyah's work was recognized by Albert Gallatin in *Synopsis of the Indian Tribes, in Trans. A. Antiq. Soc. II:*

> In the various schemes of symbolic thought representation… the English system, although not yet perfect, stands at the head of the list, the result of three thousand years of development by Egyptian, Phoenician, and Greek. Sequoyah's syllabary, the unaided work of an uneducated Indian reared amid semi-savage surrounds, stands second.[12]

Three diverse honors illustrate Sequoyah's place in the history of the Cherokee and also of the United States. First, in 1847, the giant redwoods of California were designated Sequoia gigantean or Sequoia by an Austrian biologist. Two separate honors were conferred in Washington, D.C. when a statue of Sequoyah, the first of a Native American to gain such an honor, was installed in the United States Capitol Building in 1917 and a bronze panel featuring Sequoyah was placed in the John Adams Building of the Library of Congress in 1939. Sequoyah's achievements earned him a great legacy in the cultural and historical monuments of the United States.

In the 21st century, Indian People of all Nations are being encouraged to bring back their cultures, beliefs and languages, and the Cherokee continue to make great use of Sequoyah's gift of the syllabary.

Author's Thoughts

Even with the many years of work by these leaders to safeguard the Cherokee and their way of life, the pressure by the whites resulted in the Cherokee sacrificing large areas of their homeland. They believed the treaties would ensure their ancestral lands where their religion, traditions and culture were rooted. At the same time, Sequoyah's syllabary allowed them to develop a government and laws structured like that of the U.S. No change, no sacrifice was great enough, and eventually they were forced to immigrate west.

Ultimately, the U.S. government could not suppress the indomitable Cherokee spirit. The many challenges these leaders faced in the early 1800s proved their religion, traditions and culture were well grounded. This enabled them to re-establish a government with executive, legislative and judicial branches, and their schools and businesses flourished once again in Indian Territory as they had in their lands east of the Mississippi. Many changes have been imposed on all Indian Nations since their first encounter with the Europeans and, as of 2019, there are 567 federally recognized tribes in the United States with 39 of them residing in Oklahoma – a tribute to their strength and perseverance.

Endnotes:

1. Alderman, Pat. *Nancy Ward / Dragging Canoe Cherokee Chieftainess/Cherokee-Chickamauga War Chief.* 2nd ed., Overmountain Press, 1978, p. 9.
2. Alderman. pp. 9-10
3. Alderman. p. 40.
4. Alderman. p. 10.
5. Alderman. p. 3.
6. Awiakta, Marilou. *Selu, Seeking the Corn-Mother's Wisdom.* Fulcrum Publishing, 1993, p. 92.
7. Alderman, Pat. *Nancy Ward / Dragging Canoe Cherokee Chieftainess/Cherokee-Chickamauga War Chief.* 2nd ed., Overmountain Press, 1978, p. 44.
8. Monteith. "Literacy Among the Cherokee in the Early Nineteenth Century," *Journal of Cherokee Studies, Vol. IX, No. 2, Fall 1984, p. 61.*
9. Awiakta, Marilou. *"Selu, Seeking the Corn-Mother's Wisdom.* Fulcrum Publishing, 1993, p. 288.
10. Awiakta. p. 288.
11. Awiakta. p. 288.
12. Gallatin, Albert. "A Synopsis of the Indian Tribes Within the United States East of the Rocky Mountains, and in the British and Russian Possessions in North America." *Transactions And Collections of the American Antiquarian Society Vol II,* Cambridge, 1836. p. 220.

| FIVE |

Education, Religious and Cultural Change 1789 to 1990 When Rights Restored

The cornerstones of Cherokee culture, as described in the first chapter, were literally under assault before many of the Native peoplesencountered the first newcomers with infectious diseases, killing record numbers or completely eradicating some tribes. In the case of the Cherokees, records indicate that the 1738-1739 smallpox epidemic disseminated their People, killing between nine to ten thousand or more than half of the estimated population, which caused significant change in the social and cultural structures as some villages were abandoned and others formed. There were three primary groups that further altered the foundation of their culture. The traders and missionary groups effected change largely through example, while the U.S. government effected change through purposeful policies.

At the end of the 18th century, more whites pushed onto Indian lands, and with their increased numbers came new ideas that the mixed bloods, those with Indian mothers and white fathers, accepted more readily. Many Indians clung to their traditional ways, honoring the matriarchal society, the Great Spirit and celebrating their festivals. At the same time, long-established traditions were challenged as religion was introduced and commerce was established between the traders and the Indians. Social and cultural changes occurred as they began cultivating crops and attending to domesticated animals. The newcomers represented many countries, but over time they coalesced around a new democratic form of government that put the American Indians at a distinct disadvantage. The Indians were independent nations, and it wasn't until late in their dealings with the newcomers that there was some recognition on their part that an alliance between their nations was in their best interest. However, by then it was too late.

Whites Seek to Acculturate the Indians

Many whites believed the Indians could be acculturated to the ideal Eurocentric civilization of farming and domestic work through church worship and Christian education. To that end, President Washington's Secretary of War, Henry Knox, recommended as early as 1789 that federal funds be provided for Indian education through the efforts of the missionary societies. It wasn't until 1819 that "Congress created the Civilization Fund, an annual sum of $10,000 that was used to support Indian education."[1] Because of the diversified curriculum of the missionary schools, they required items from the traditional school supplies of books and paper to the agrarian items of tools and plows. Due to their position within the Indian communities, the missionaries were able to lead by example, helping the adults understand the benefits of utilizing the various tools and plows. By extension, the hope was that the adults would see the benefit of an education for their children and learn through word of mouth about the missionaries' God, which brought converts to Christianity.

Traders were agents of change as they introduced new products to the Indians, including guns and ammunition, tools, cloth and household goods and numerous other items. These products made the lives of the Indian easier and made him or her beholden to the trader as they trapped and exchanged furs and pelts for the increasingly necessary items. At the same time, the Indians learned by example as they watched the traders clear land to provide crops for their families and introduce livestock.

In his essay "Cherokee Land Use in Georgia before Removal," Douglas C. Wilms identified the missionary societies as the third group working as agents of change in Indian country as they led by example. However, the missionaries were assisted by the U.S. Government as it carried out its purpose of intentionally changing the broader Native society.

The federal government gave livestock and implements to the natives and appointed agents to demonstrate their use. In addition, financial assistance was given to missionary societies for establishing schools in the nation. Here, formal and vocational education, they hoped, would encourage civilization and help bring about other desirable changes in the Cherokee society and economy.[2]

Thomas Mails wrote that "The missionaries wanted to convert the 'Heathens' and save their souls, but the Cherokees wanted to read and write, so as to better compete in the white man's world."[3] The mission schools were open to all the children, and many of their sons, especially mixed bloods, went on to school in the east. The Cornwall, Connecticut school established by the American Board of Commissioners for Foreign Missions provided a classical education with a curriculum similar to those attending Harvard or Yale at that time, which included the arts, science, math, philosophy and the foreign languages intended to broaden their experiences and viewpoints, along with gaining an education:

> Over the next thirty years, the Cherokee nation would undergo changes that, because they moved the tribe closer to what whites considered to be civilization, were for mixed bloods welcome and good. On the other hand, because they moved the nation away from traditional life, the full bloods considered the changes to be unwelcome and bad.[4]

Sequoyah's Syllabary Used for Conversion

Five different Protestant missionary groups lived and worked within the Cherokee homeland. Realizing the significance of Sequoyah's syllabary and seeking to utilize it to the fullest extent, the "American Board of Commissioners for Foreign Missions had the first five verses of the book of Genesis written in the syllabary to be reproduced in their magazine, the *Missionary Herald*. With assistance from the Foreign Missions, a printing press was set up:

... the efforts of many individuals resulted in the printing of the first American Indian newspaper (titled *Cherokee Phoenix* and printed partly in Cherokee and partly in English) on February 21, 1828 at New Echota, Georgia (near present-day Calhoun, Georgia) capital of the Cherokee Nation.[5]

WPA Implements Documentation Efforts

There is an old adage which goes something like: There is no great harm without a little bit of good. With that in mind, without the depression and the Works Project Administration (WPA), it is unlikely a survey would have been undertaken, and the historical record of the lives of former slaves and Native Americans would be incomplete. Like interviews done in the 21st century to capture the memories of the WWII soldiers, the slaves and Indians had lived through a momentous time in American history, but little was known of their lives. Collections of letters and remembrances of the educated are preserved, but those interviewed in the survey could not read or write, and time was of the upmost importance in preserving their memories.

As one of the projects established during the Great Depression to employ some of the millions of job seekers, the WPA was instrumental in documenting the lives of the nations' poor and illiterate into the Historical Records Survey. In the introduction to Theda Perdue's book, *Nations Remembered: An Oral History,* she explained:

> In conjunction with the University of Oklahoma and the Oklahoma Historical Society, the [WPA] employed between eighty and one hundred individuals to send questionnaires to and conduct interviews with Oklahoma citizens who were knowledgeable about the days before statehood. Grant Foreman, the well-known Oklahoma historian, supervised the collection and compilation of the information, which ultimately filled 112 volumes.[6]

Many sources exist from which to create a picture, a glimpse, into significant aspects of Cherokee life from the mid-to-late 1800s. Through this documentation, a sense of the daily life, as well as the struggles they encountered can be brought to light.

Beginning with family structure, the matriarchal society which governed Cherokee life since the beginning of their history had been on the wane due to increasing association with white society. There were seven clans represented in each village and after marrying, the matriarchal society governed the marriage of a Cherokee woman to a white man, which made him a member of his wife's clan, but by the late 1800s, there were white woman marrying Cherokee men. Laws had to be adapted to cover a marriage where the wife had no clan, as well as how to recognize children born to their union. Men increasingly assumed a prominent position in the life of the tribe, further undermining the gender balance in all levels of their society. When Wilma Mankiller ran as Deputy Chief of the Cherokee Nation in 1983, many men questioned the ability of a woman to hold such a position – the gender balance had been forsaken. She served as Principal Chief from 1985 to 1995, proving that not only that a woman did have the ability to serve as Chief, but she worked tirelessly to improve the image of Native Americans. Chief Mankiller opened the eyes of many to an essential element that was missing from their heritage.

Changes were also evident through the way Cherokee children learned. The first male and female Cherokee seminaries opened in the early 1850s. Lack of funding and the Civil War caused them to close at various periods. The school for the girls reopened in 1881 but burned in 1887. A new school built of brick with steam heat and an inside toilet opened in 1889. Two-hundred-fifty Cherokee girls attended the new school in north Tahlequah, Oklahoma. Spencer Stephens, the recently hired superintendent, was a firm believer that the girls needed the best to complete their education. Accordingly, "... [he] went to St. Louis, and, among other things, he selected real linen tablecloths and napkins, and silver dishes and knives and forks for the fourteen long tables in the dining room."[7] Some complained at the amount of money that was spent, but he held firm to his beliefs that the girls needed the best education.

The *Journal of Cherokee Studies* provided the 1899 curriculum for the Female Seminary in their spring 1985 edition. It is very comprehensive, and the curriculum was better than many of the schools non-Indians were attending:

Freshman
First Semester – English, United States History, Physiology, Arithmetic
Second Semester – English, Latin, Botany, Algebra

Sophomore
First Semester – Latin, English, General History, Algebra
Second Semester – Latin, English, General History, Algebra

Junior
First Semester – Latin, English, Physics, Algebra
Second Semester – Latin, English, Physics, Geometry

Senior
First Semester – Latin, Civics, English, Chemistry, Geometry
Second Semester – Latin, Civics, English, Chemistry, Geometry[8]

Oklahoma purchased the building, land and equipment of the Cherokee Female Seminary March 6, 1909. Northeastern State Normal School opened the next academic year and later became Northeastern State University. "Seminary Hall is the oldest building on NSU's campus and in 1994 the building was completely restored ... At the main entrance of the building is featured three Indian murals painted in the 1930s as a WPA project ..."[9]

There also emerged a story regarding how the Cherokee would go about clearing land, called tree girdling. It had been practiced by Native Americans, as well as other people, for centuries and was described in the WPA interviews. When the moon was a certain stage in the month of August, an axe was used to cut a ring around a tree, which deprived the flow of sap to the branches. The nutriments from the sun and rain could not flow to the roots. Thus, over a year's time, the tree, and the roots died, which made it easier to clear the land for farming or to maintain a forest by thinning the trees. After a year, the dead tree could easily be pushed over and cut for firewood or hauled away. It was observed that many white men cut the trees down, leaving a stump to plow around which broke their plows.[10]

With the land cleared, the Cherokees planted trees that would be of use to them. They liked to plant fruit trees on the inside corner of their fences, which helped them in several ways. First, the trees were protected when teams or plows were used to cultivate their fields. A second benefit was "... the native hogs would smell the ripe fruit and they would come up and eat the fruit, root up the ground, and lay under the shade of the trees. . . In this way they kept the vegetation down all around the field for quite a space."[11]

The Cherokee joined outside organizations in order to better their economics and create a way to have a voice. One was the Masonic Lodge, which began in 1852 in Tahlequah. After the Civil War, a number of fraternal organizations flourished throughout the U.S. The veterans' organizations had a wide appeal for the Indians and were well attended for a number of years. However, as the years passed, their numbers dwindled with age and deaths and did not become viable again until after WWI.

The progressives in Indian Territory utilized these organizations to expand into politics, commercial and business ventures. They typically met in commercial centers and were meant to "... attract whites with money to spend or capital to invest..."[12] Out of these efforts came the International Indian Fair which began in 1875 with horse racing, a particular favorite of the Indians, and various events and holidays were initiated to attract a large number of people and help the area economy.

Despite these economic gains and efforts, after the Civil War, a number of laws were passed that were, for a time, detrimental to the Indians. In 1870, Congress expanded upon the lands given the railroads during the negotiations at the end of the war now providing for "… every other section of land on each side of the railroad track" to be given to the rail companies: [13]

> The Cherokees protested this act of Congress giving so much acreage to the railroad, and after many heated court battles carried finally into the Supreme Court of the United States, the Cherokee Nation won on the ground that Congress had no authority to sell or give away lands patented or deeded to this Nation.[14]

Government Education in Indian Territories

The beginnings of the Bureau of Indian Affairs (BIA) can be traced back to the Continental Congress, making it the oldest of the federal agencies. The BIA is charged with carrying out the goals established by Congress and the various federal agencies. Its mission has been wide-reaching and varied as administrations change. Until very recently in the history of the country, Eurocentric ideals determined what was best for the Native Americans without consulting them. Goals as diversified as subjugating the Indians, assimilating them into the overall American society and/or providing means for them to achieve self-determination have been tried at various times, but throughout, education was primary starting with the mission schools in the early 1800s.

As the Cherokees established themselves in Indian Territory, they utilized funds appropriated by the treaties to pay for the public-school system. "By 1843 there were eighteen public schools in operation, and in 1851 two seminaries for higher learning were opened to Cherokee students — a National Female Seminary … and a National Male Seminary…"[15] All of these were overseen by a national superintendent. In fact, the Cherokee had "… the first institute of higher learning for women west of the Mississippi."[16] Much of what was established in this period was destroyed during the Civil War. And, as in other parts of the country, the Cherokee had to start over, establishing their homes, farms, schools, businesses and reconstructing the infrastructure and their lives.

During the time called the reservation period and before the allotment policy went into effect in 1887, there was a serious attempt by the federal government to improve the educational program made available to the Indians. By that year, "...there was a reported enrollment of 14,333, with an average attendance of 10,520 in 227 schools."[17] In all ways, teachers were to impress upon their students the opportunities the government was providing, that they should strive to achieve much in their lives and be appreciative for the benefits they received.[18] In 1889, the House of Representatives required American influences be instilled to promote patriotism in Indian students to prepare them for citizenship. Some stipulations included:

> ... erect a flagstaff, from which should float constantly, in suitable weather, the American flag... Patriotic songs should be taught, National holidays – Washington's Birthday, Decoration Day, Fourth of July, Thanksgiving, and Christmas – should be observed with appropriate exercises in all Indian schools.[19]

Under the direction of President Theodore Roosevelt's administration, the Indian Bureau took over responsibility for schooling the children of the Five Civilized Tribes. Parents were never consulted; the BIA agents simply took children from their families, literally scooping them up without the parents' permission. This was another aspect of genocide – forced indoctrination through "Forcibly transferring children of the group to another group."[20] This definition was later defined by the United Nations Resolution on the Crime of Genocide and will be further discussed in Chapter 11.

They then traveled hundreds of miles to bring the children to the BIA boarding schools, where their braids were cut, and they were forced to wear white mans' clothing and shoes. Only English could be spoken, and if they forgot and spoke their Native language, they were punished. Their religion, which made up the core of their lives, was outlawed. Identities were systematically stripped away to create new ones. Because of the distance from these schools to their homes, most of the children never or seldom saw their families. The many years of indoctrination were little more than brainwashing. This isolation was meant to make them forget their culture, language and heritage. For many, it was a lonely existence, and if they ever returned to their families, they no longer fit in. Often scarred both in body and soul, many were neither Indian nor white.

Bureau of Indian Affairs Eventually Adds Heritage to Education

In the 1960s, the BIA hoped that by involving the parents they would be interested in the education their children were obtaining and become active participants in the content of the programs thus making the parents "… entirely responsible for their school program."[21] This was followed in 1972 with the Ethnic Heritage Program, which was a major step forward for all ethnic groups within the United States. Up to that time, programs were meant to eradicate the ethnic culture, specifically that of the Native American. The new program was established to "… assist children and adults in the United States 'to learn about the differing and unique contributions to the national heritage made by each ethnic group,' and to learn about the nature of their own cultural heritage."[22] Languages and cultural identities are now being taught in public schools. In many situations, only the elders speak the Native language, so they are being called upon to teach the language before it dies out completely. Schools are now utilizing enrichment programs, and students are given the information to enable embracing their cultural identities and taking pride in their history.

Native Rituals, Dances and Feasts Banned

In an effort to civilize the Indians, their purification rituals, dances and feasts were outlawed by the U.S. government and, if continued, the People were punished. Dances for religious or social occasions were different across the tribes, but there were dances and celebrations common across linguistically related tribes. Some dances, most famously the Sioux Sun Dance, involved the ritual piercing of the skin. Not understanding the religious significance of their dances, whites considered them as barbaric rituals, and attempts were made to suppress the dances, which resulted in them being performed in secret. Records show that flagellation and other types of religious rites have been practiced by many people throughout history, so the Native Americans' dances were not new but were disturbing to the whites who knew about or witnessed them.

> "With the issuance of the 'Indian Religious Freedom and Indian Culture' circular in 1934; however, the right to practice Native religions and to observe cultural traditions was guaranteed ... It also acknowledges the prior violation of that right." [23]

Cherokee Religious Beliefs Important Throughout Time

This is one of many Cherokee stories that documents their beliefs, which have been handed down for generations and provide a glimpse into their religious practices – the importance and strength they provide to the People:

> While the Cherokees were migrating in earliest times, Hasi told us to make an ark of the covenant in which to carry the sacred fire and other holy things. This ark would represent the everlasting bond between the Creator and the Cherokees, and the army that carried the ark before it when it went to war would be invincible.[24] The ark was described as a square tightly woven basket – 'perhaps twenty inches in length, fifteen inches broad, and fifteen inches high.[25] Only the purification ritual allowed the priest and his right-hand man to touch the ark and no enemy would dare to touch it. It was said that the priest who carried the ark could follow the enemy at night as well as anyone else could in the day.[26]

Religious Freedom Becomes Official

Until 1978, people of the United States except American Indians were protected by the Third Article of the Bill of Rights to practice their religion of choice. The 1934 circular was finally codified in The American Indian Religious Freedom Act (AIRFA):

enacted to return basic civil liberties to Native Americans, Eskimos, Aleuts, and Native Hawaiians, and to allow them to practice, protect and preserve their inherent right of freedom to believe, express, and exercise their traditional religious rights, and spiritual and cultural practices. These rights include, but are not limited to, access to sacred sites, freedom to worship through ceremonial and traditional rites, and use and possession of objects traditionally considered sacred by their cultures.[27]

Many aspects of Native American religions such as their sacred ceremonies had been prohibited by law prior to AIRFA. This act allows the American Indian to practice his or her religion, but it took many long years before that freedom was theirs to enjoy. In Sandra Isaacs' book, *Eastern Cherokee Stories,* she compares the ancient or traditional beliefs with the contemporary beliefs of all Cherokees, east and west, as she relates their beliefs and compares them with the earlier works of ethnologist James Mooney. Isaacs discusses the nonhuman creatures of their universe that worked together to create the wondrous land of mountains and valleys that make up the ancient Cherokee homeland, which helps to explain why Cherokees have such a strong attachment to the earth. In Chapter 2, Isaacs covers "'those who are to be avoided; dreadful; wondrous things' and Witches"[28] and follows in Chapter 3 with stories of "Those who fill us with wonder."[29] She quotes Donald Fixico who suggests, "[t]he spirituality of any entity is timeless, such that a story is reawakened and moved through linear time … (thus) becomes a part of the present, and the past and present is projected into the future."[30] Understanding Cherokee beliefs through time provides a greater understanding of their traditions and beliefs.

In the 21st century, powwows can be considered an exercise of Native American religious freedom. With the goals to entertain and educate, as well as financially support the tribe, many Indian tribes throughout the country have museums, outdoor displays and hold annual celebrations including a powwow which "… is a Native American gathering focused on dance, song and family celebration. Powwows celebrate the connections to tradition and spirituality, to the Earth and to one another in a social, personal and spiritual meeting."[31] For many years, the powwow was forbidden – another example of the white man "knowing" what was best for the Indian People of this nation.

The education programs for American Indians were thoroughly examined during the 1960s, but Indian powerlessness was still prevalent at the end of the decade, and no discernable changes were made. But some things had become clearer:

> It is not just the Indian who has learned from us, there is much to be learned from him – the values inherent in group identity: respect for nature; the right of men to participate in the institutions that affect their lives; and that no policy or program, regardless of how well intended will succeed without his approval.[32]

BIA Implements Cultural Rights

In addition to the religious freedoms given by AIRFA, cultural changes came about with the passing of the Indian Arts and Crafts Act of 1990. The U.S. Department of the Interior had established the Indian Arts and Crafts Board in 1934 which "... serves the Indian, Eskimo, and Aluet communities, and the general public, as an informational, promotional, and advisory clearinghouse for all matters pertaining to the development of authentic Native arts and crafts of the U.S."[33] The board also has the responsibility for overseeing the implementation of the 1990 act. Many Indian tribes are noted for their exquisite craftsmanship (an example being the finely woven Navajo rugs and blankets), but the number of items being produced and offered for sale by non-natives as authentic Native American arts and crafts had been a growing problem until the passing of the 1990 act "... which covers all Indian and Indian-style traditional and contemporary arts and crafts produced after 1934."[34] Just like so many internationally recognized companies that are copied today, so too are the Native American arts and crafts copied internationally and sold in the U.S. and overseas to unsuspecting customers.

Each craft item (painting, pottery, jewelry, baskets, figures, etc.) must have a tag with the name and tribal affiliation of the artist and must be certified by the Indian Arts and Crafts Board, U.S. Department of Interior. These pieces are handmade, requiring much more creativity and attention to detail than those done by non-Indians, thus commanding a higher price for the artist. Numerous pieces can be found in private collections and in museums.

Prior to the act, pieces were often manufactured en mass either nationally or internationally. There are now civil and criminal penalties for individuals or businesses, including fines, prison or both for those found guilty of violating the 1990 act.

Author's Thoughts

For too long, the lives of the American Indians have been determined by the federal government without any say on the part of the Indians. Senator Henry L. Dawes made one visit to the Cherokee in the early 1880s prior to Oklahoma becoming a state in 1907. This was one more visit than made by many members of Congress, making him somewhat of an authority on the subject of Indians. Dawes was a sympathetic supporter of the American Indians and he, along with a number of like-minded individuals in and out of government, worked to establish programs they felt would benefit the Indians. As a result of his trip and with hopes to improve the lives of the Indians came the Dawes Act of 1887. Dawes and the others felt that the tribal leaders were encouraging the People to maintain their culture and religion, thus suppressing their efforts to move into the 19th century and adopt the white culture, which, in their minds, would make Indian lives better. They believed that they could make more progress by breaking up the reservations, bypassing tribal leaders and working with individuals instead. Even if well-intentioned, this was yet another attempt to replace tribal culture with white culture and open lands to the immigrants.

Never were the Indians asked for their opinion of proposed programs, which explains why the majority of the programs not only failed to produce the desired results but often resulted in making the lives of Native Americans worse. The endeavor to recreate the Indian in the image of the prevalent white population was detrimental to their education, religion and culture. Education was fashioned on white precepts, so upon entering school, they were forced to dress like white students in non-Indian schools. Prohibited from speaking their language, they were punished if they spoke their language even on the first day of school when they had no knowledge of the white language.

Native religions, including their sacred practices and dances, were not understood by the whites, hence feared. The U.S. government outlawed their religions and much of their culture and those caught participating in any of these forbidden elements were punished. The Native American Religious Freedom Act acknowledges the prior violation of the right of Native Americans to practice their religions – a right enjoyed by other Americans under the First Amendment of the United States Bill of Rights. A 1994 amendment to the act expanded those freedoms; however, because Native religions do not fit the prevalent Anglo-American religious beliefs, Native Americans are still required to fight for and educate the public on their beliefs. Clearly, the Americentric attitude definitely does not fit all people. It is morally wrong to force one group to accept the culture or religion of another group and hurts inclusivity, which is a great benefit to our country.

The Ethnic Heritage Program of 1972, the American Indian Religious Freedom Act of 1978 and its amendment and the Indian Arts and Crafts Act of 1990, along with other laws and opportunities, did provide the American Indians hope, hope in the continued revitalization of their cultures and religions, hope in their tribal self-government and their individual sovereignty and self-determination. Hope is an essential element in life and hope had been missing from theirs for a very long time.

Endnotes:

1. Wilms, Douglas C. "Cherokee Land Use in Georgia Before Removal." *Cherokee Removal: Before and After*, edited by William L. Anderson, U of Georgia P, 1991. pp. 4-5.
2. Wilms. p. 4.
3. Mails, Thomas E. *The Cherokee People: The Story of the Cherokees from Earliest Origins to Contemporary Times.* Marlowe & Co., 1992, p. 194.
4. Mails. p. 194-195.
5. Monteith, Carmeleta L. "Literacy Among the Cherokee in the Early Nineteenth Century." *Journal of Cherokee Studies, Volume IX, No.2, Fall 1984*, pp. 59-62.
6. Perdue, Theda. *Nations Remembered: An Oral History of the Cherokees, Chickasaws, Choctaws, Creeks, and Seminoles in Oklahoma, 1865-1907.* U of Oklahoma P, 1993, p. xvii.
7. Perdue. pp. 134-135.
8. King, Duane H., editor. "An Illustrated Souvenir Catalog of The Cherokee National Female Seminary." *Journal of Cherokee Studies, Volume X, No. 1, Spring 1985.* "An Illustrated Souvenir Catalog of The Cherokee National Female Seminary, Tahlequah, Indian Territory 1850 to 1906," Arranged and Printed at the Indian Print Shop, p. 140.
9. Courtney, Gary. "Seminary Hall, at Northeastern State University." 20 Mar 2016. https://www.deviantart.com/garycourtneyauthor/art/Seminary-Hall-at-Northeastern-State-University-597847310
10. Perdue, Theda. *Nations Remembered: An Oral History of the Cherokees, Chickasaws, Choctaws, Creeks, and Seminoles in Oklahoma, 1865-1907.* U of Oklahoma P, 1993. p. 47.
11. Perdue. p. 47.
12. Perdue. p. 68.
13. Perdue. p. 153.
14. Perdue. p. 153.
15. Mails, Thomas E. *The Cherokee People: The Story of the Cherokees from Earliest Origins to Contemporary Times.* Marlowe & Co., 1992, p. 269.

16. "Cherokee Nation." *Oklahoma Indian Country Guide: One State – Many Nations,*" p. 25.

17. Tyler, S. Lyman. *"A History of Indian Policy."* U.S. Department of the Interior, Bureau of Indian Affairs, 1973. p. 88.

18. House Executive Document no. 1, 51st Cong., 2d sess., serial 2841, p. clxvii.

19. Prucha, Francis Paul, editor. *Documents of United States Indian Policy"* 2nd *Ed.* U of Nebraska P, 1990, p. 181.

20. United Nations Office on Genocide Prevention and the Responsibility to Protect. "Genocide." https://bit.ly/2Hg6nwa.

21. Tyler, L. Lyman. *A History of Indian Policy.* U.S. Department of the Interior, Bureau of Indian Affairs, 1973, p. 278.

22. Tyler. p. 278.

23. Library of Congress, "Sioux Song and Dance. *Loc.gov.* https://bit.ly/3mZnV2e. Accessed 15 Jul 2019.

24. Mailes, Thomas E. *The Cherokee People: The Story of the Cherokees from Earliest Origins to Contemporary Times.* Marlowe & Co., 1992, p. 151.

25. Mailes. p. 112.

26. Mailes. p. 100.

27. Public Law No. 95-341, The American Indian Religious Freedom Act, 92 Stat. 469, August 11, 1978, 42 U.S.C. § 1996. https://bit.ly/3kNPF8L. Accessed 1 Nov 2020.

28. Isaacs, Sandra Muse. *Eastern Cherokee Stories: A Living Oral Tradition and Its Cultural Continuance.* U of Oklahoma P, 2019, pp. 86-113.

29. Isaacs. pp. 114-156.

30. Isaacs. p. 93.

31. St Joseph's Indian School. "Wachípi -powwow — a Native American tradition." *St. Joseph's Indian School.* https://bit.ly/3cMU092. Accessed 16 Jul 2019.

32. Tyler, L. Lyman. *A History of Indian Policy.* U.S. Department of the Interior, Bureau of Indian Affairs. 1973, p. 227.

33. Utter, Jack. *American Indians: Answers to Today's Questions. 2ⁿᵈ Ed. Rev. and Enlarged.* U Oklahoma P. 2001. p. 325.

34. Indian Arts and Crafts Act of 1990." *U.S. Department of the Interior*, https://on.doi.gov/3jlQ29Q. Accessed 14 Jul 2019.

| SIX |

Divergent Views on Removal
Early 1800s to 1872, No More Treaties

Once while all the warriors of a certain Cherokee town were off on a hunt or attending a dance in another settlement, an old man who has been left behind was chopping wood on the side of a ridge.

Suddenly a party of enemy warriors from some other tribe came upon him. The old man threw his hatchet at the nearest one, and then he turned and ran for the house to get his gun and defend the village as best as he could. When he came out of the house with the gun, he was surprised to find a large body of strange warriors driving back the enemy. There was no time for questions, and taking his place with the others, the old man fought hard until the enemy was pressed back up the creek. Finally, they broke and retreated across the mountain.

When it was all over and there was time to breathe again, the old man turned to thank his new friends, but found that he was all alone. They had disappeared as though the mountain had swallowed them. Then he knew that they were the Nuñnehi, the Immortals, who had come to help their friends the Cherokees.[1]

Like Chief Mankiller, James Mooney recorded stories of the Immortals. They were the "… spirit people who lived in the highlands of the old Cherokee country"[2] and helped the People. The *Nuñnehi* were invisible unless they wanted to be seen, and then they looked and sounded like all the other People. Mooney recorded a story "… about the way they assisted the Cherokee people before removal by 'warning them of wars and misfortunes which the future held in store.'"[3] Help from the Immortals was indeed needed as the Cherokee faced their uncertain future.

Great political drama created fractures within the Cherokees in the early 1800s, and as in any policy debate, the views of the People were divergent and not always along the lines that might be expected. As settlers moved beyond the areas between the Atlantic Ocean and the Alleghany Mountains, Indian tribes were forced to withdraw or fight for their lands. Many whites and Indians believed that it was best for the Indians to remain on their ancestral lands, while others believed it was in the best interest of both the white people and the Indians for them to move to lands beyond the influence of the whites. Both groups were eloquent in their memorials presented to Congress and published in the newspapers of many cities. Lawsuits worked their way through the courts, with the U.S. Supreme Court often having the final judgment. As these played out in the court of public opinion, other important factors entered into the debate.

Public Debate on Removal: Pretense vs. Reality

During the period of May 1831 to February 1832, the Frenchman, Alexis de Tocqueville, visited the United States. From his travels and observations of the young republic, de Tocqueville wrote *Democracy in America*, which was published in 1835, and again in 1840, and remains a preeminent tract on democracy that is studied today. Ronald N. Satz quoted from de Tocqueville in his essay "Rhetoric Versus Reality:"

> Alexis de Tocqueville poignantly observed that Jacksonian Indian policy was designed to evict the eastern tribes 'with wonderful ease, quietly, legally, and philanthropically, without spilling blood and without violating a single one of the great principles of morality in the eyes of the world.' According to Tocqueville, although American treaty commissioners, 'inspired by the most chaste affection for legal formalities' used the treaty making process and noble rhetoric to emphasize American justice in dealing with

the Indians, the substance of American policy revealed manipulation and coercion ...[4]

In reality, the treatment of the American Indians was being played out on the world stage for others to judge the workings of democracy. "... the War Department blatantly violated tribal sovereignty by encouraging the American treaty commissioners to *select* the particular chief or faction of a tribe with whom the United States would deal ..."[5] The commissioners would exploit any perceived tribal division, and they would negotiate with the party that was willing to cede land for money and or emigration, no matter the wishes for the majority of that tribe. Frances Prucha wrote in his preface to Evarts' *Cherokee Removal: The William Penn Essays and Other Writings:*

> Although the American Indians and their rights and welfare for long periods of time received little attention from the dominant white society in the United States, on occasion they burst into the public consciousness as political or moral issues of great magnitude. One such occasion was the removal of eastern Indians to the regions west of the Mississippi in the 1830s ... The removal policy affected Indians both north and south, but the public agitation was focused on the removal of the Five Civilized Tribes of the southeastern United States – the Cherokees, Creeks, Choctaws, Chickasaws, and Seminoles. And, of these, the Cherokees were the center of attention because of the aggressive drive of Georgia to force them out of the state.[6]

Evarts' writings reminded the citizens that this was a nation that conformed to the "rule of law" and that from the first treaty of 1783 entered into by the Confederated States, to "... the adoption of the Federal Constitution, all treaties were confirmed and ratified, not by the nation merely, as a whole, but by each State, as it performed the solemn act of coming into the Union."[7]

Many notable white men, including Senators Theodore Frelinghuysen and Henry Clay, as well as representatives Abrose

Spencer and David Crocket, along with Daniel Webster, Edward Henry Wise and Jeremiah Evarts fought not a physical battle, but a tougher battle in the United States Congress and in the court of public opinion through the press and meeting with people in support of the American Indians, specifically the Cherokees. They fought long and hard to prevent the removal of the Indians from their homeland, but the economic and environmental pressures of the U.S. government for removal were greater. As Henry R. Schoolcraft succinctly stated in *Personal Memoirs of a Residence of Thirty Years with the Indian Tribes on the American Frontiers*:

> In terms of our relations with whites, the real problem confronting the Indians between 1829 and 1837 was not simply the presence of Jackson in the White House, but that, as one astute contemporary put it, 'the whole Indian race' was not, 'in the political scales, worth one white man's vote.'[8]

Controversy among the Cherokee on Best Path Forward

After a substantial amount of controversy among the People, the Cherokee National Council voted in the early 1800s to approve a system of roads to be built first north and south, then later east and west. Doublehead, a Cherokee warrior, argued that opening Cherokee lands to roads would allow greater access to "'… many people of all descriptions' to dispossess them of their land."[9] James Vann, a Cherokee businessman, wanted to expand his ability to move goods, which would offer a wider profit potential. Both men were proven correct, as opening the Cherokee lands provided benefits to the People, but also allowed the newcomers greater access to the lands, not just as a way through but with a greater knowledge of the bounty of the land, thus encouraging them to take the land as Doublehead had predicted. The roads provided safe passage for the post and passengers, opened the area to commerce with businesses and taverns along the routes and the *Cherokee Phoenix* – a Cherokee language newspaper – was more rapidly distributed. Missionaries and teachers opened churches and schools. The Cherokee leaders established a formal government modeled on that of the United States with three branches of government and written laws.

Originally written in English, it was later translated into Cherokee, which could be read and understood by the majority of the People. All this contributed to a higher standard of living for the Cherokee and encouraged the newcomers as they looked desirously on lands considered ideal to settle.

Consequences of Georgia Legislation

When Georgia passed legislation extending the authority of its government over the Cherokee Nation effective June 1, 1830, not only were problems created by this declaration between the Cherokee, the United States Government and Georgia, an additional obstacle arose between the federal government and the new laws of Georgia concerning the work of the American Board of Commissions for Foreign Missions among the Cherokee. The Secretary of War, William H. Crawford (Aug. 1, 1815 – Oct. 22, 1816) authorized the American Board of Commissioners for Foreign Missions to provide teachers and missionaries to live and work among the Cherokee as stipulated in the treaties. Successive U.S. presidents and secretaries of war received annual reports from the board specifying the work being done and how money appropriated by Congress was utilized. In opposition to the United States Constitution, when Georgia exerted its authority over the Cherokee in 1830, it required a license or permit from the governor, plus an oath of allegiance to the State of Georgia of any white persons living within the Cherokee Nation. This included the teachers and missionaries, and those who did not comply were arrested and imprisoned.[10]

Jackson Campaigns to Remove Indians

After campaigning to remove all Indians from the East, which won him strong support in the South, Andrew Jackson was sworn in as the seventh president of the United States on March 4, 1829. The mood of the nation at that time was such that if Jackson did not uphold Georgia's claims, it could have caused a split in the Union. However, no mention of the campaign promise appeared in his first inaugural speech when he simply stated:

> It will be my sincere and constant desire to observe toward the Indian tribes within our limits a just and

liberal policy, and to give that humane and considerate attention to their rights and their wants which is consistent with the habits of our Government and the feelings of our people.[11]

Jackson was born in Waxhaw Settlement between North Carolina and South Carolina but spent much of his adult life west of the Blue Ridge Mountains waging military campaigns against various Indian tribes. He retired to his home in Nashville, Tennessee after leaving the presidency in 1837, so he was intimately familiar with the Five Civilized Tribes and the advancements of the Cherokees. Writings covering Jackson as a man, a military leader and a president cast him as both a devil and an angel. Jackson's history with the Southeastern Tribes was very often bloody and always callous. On March 27, 1814, following the Battle of Horseshoe Bend, [General] Andrew Jackson oversaw not only the stripping away of dead Indians' flesh for manufacture into bridle reins, but he saw to it that souvenirs from the corpses were distributed "... to the ladies of Tennessee."[12]

Jackson's convictions had been reinforced over the years, and he expressed them on numerous occasions, stating that the Indians lacked the intelligence and industry to change their lives and that they must not continue living surrounded by the increasing number of white people. The Indian must either emigrate away from the whites who were surrounding their settlements or their race would succumb and disappear before the advancing superior race.[13]

In 1829, Jackson participated in a specular debate in Congress that resembled a miniature civil war when, "He stressed the impossibility of maintaining two sovereignties within a State and suggested removal as a means of allowing the Indians to continue to govern themselves."[14]

Greatly debated among the citizens of the country and in Congress, the Indian Removal Act was finally passed on May 28, 1830. Then, in 1833, Jackson appointed the Rev. Mr. Schermerhorn as commissioner to negotiate a treaty with the Cherokees. Attempting to find a Cherokee name that fit their perception of the person, Rev. Schermerhorn became known as Skáynooyáunah, or literally the "devil's horn," for his work against the Cherokee. This made the People laugh in the midst of a very serious situation.[15]

For their part, the Cherokees claimed that their participation in the Battle of Horseshoe Bend saved General Jackson's army from defeat. Chief Junaluska, revered among the Quala Boundary Indians of western North Carolina, remarked years later after participating in the battle that "If I had known that Andrew Jackson would later drive us from our homes, I would have killed him."[16]

North Carolina Cherokee Get Assistance and Recognition

The major Cherokee groups discussed during this period are the Treaty Party and the Ross Party. However, in John Finger's essay "The Impact of Removal on the North Carolina Cherokees," he identified a third group of Cherokees who worked with their chief, Yonaguska, in an effort to remain on their land. Among the group was "… a local white merchant William Holland Thomas [who] had been adopted into the tribe while a boy and by the early 1830s had become their trusted adviser."[17] Many of these individuals:

> … had taken advantage of clauses in the treaties of 1817 and 1819 allowing certain individuals and their families to separate from the nation and occupy private reservations on lands ceded to the United States. They claimed to be citizens of North Carolina, but their precise status was in fact uncertain.[18]

"The North Carolina reservations consisted of forty-nine life estates and two fee simple reserves"[19] in the initial allotted reservations. Over the years, Thomas represented the interests of the Quallatown Cherokees in Washington, D.C., defended their status as citizens, worked with the white members of the community to emphasize the peaceful nature of the Indians to prevent their removal, bought up available land to increase their reservations and purchased supplies. In an effort to protect the land of the Quallatown Cherokee that Thomas purchased, he set up a corporation in 1845 and transferred the title to that company. Thomas' help over the years is corroborated in John Finger's writings:

> In 1868 the federal government agreed to recognize the North Carolina Cherokees as a distinct tribe and to assume responsibility for them. During the next decade, through a series of complicated maneuverings, the government acquired in their behalf much of the land that Thomas had held for them, as well as other scattered tracts. The tribe organized its own government and in 1889 incorporated as the Eastern Band of Cherokee Indians.[20]

From this meager beginning to their recognition and into current time, the group has maintained much of their traditional life, while incorporating aspects of the whites, which benefitted Cherokee lives and economic well-being. At the same time that the North Carolina Cherokee were working to maintain their lands, politics continued to play out on the national front.

Indians Suffer Multiple Removals

Jackson's administration oversaw this tumultuous time in American history, which ultimately resulted in 46,000 Indians being removed from lands in the East. A number of supposed benefits included, "… free them from the alleged evils of close contact with whites … Indians could pursue self-rule in the West … the federal government would promote the 'civilization' of the Indians in the West."[21] Small remnants of once-great tribes ultimately remained on their ancestral lands or they moved from those lands to another territory while remaining east of the Mississippi. The Indians, who made the Great Plains their home and hunting grounds, were forced onto reservations, thus allowing Jackson to open lands in the West as well – over one-hundred million acres total.

The administration's failure to establish long-range planning was evident to Native Americans. Many of the northern Indians suffered the hardship of removal more than once. "Although spoken at a later time, the words of Sioux Chief Spotted Tail summarized the reality facing Winnebago and Potawatomi emigrants: 'Why does not the Great Father put his red children on wheels, so he can move them as he will?'"[22] The Chickasaw and Choctaw were two tribes who had lands in Mississippi and Alabama that Jackson was anxious to open to settlement, and both tribes were being resettled in Indian Territory. Even as the Choctaw were making their way west in 1831, Jackson sent negotiators to meet with the emigrants.[23] He wanted them to give up a portion of the lands recently assigned to them in Indian Territory so it could be given to the Chickasaws. Kappler wrote in *Indian Affairs:*

> One of the Choctaws who met with the American treaty negotiators to discuss Jackson's proposal reflected the views of many others when he suggested the president should at least allow the Indians to step on the soil of their new tribal domain before asking them to sell a part of it.[24]

Diverse Views and Broken Promises

The Cherokee had factions arguing for and against removal and, as with any other group of people, the arguments were not always straightforward, with the People changing sides as the U.S. government and the Cherokee aristocracy brought forth different proposals. Much has been written about the Treaty Party made up of Major Ridge, John Ridge, Elias Boudinot and Stand Watie who signed the 1835 Treaty, ultimately resulting in the Cherokees being removed to Indian territory west of the Mississippi and those against removal, called the Ross Party, that consisted of the brothers, John and Lewis Ross, John Martin and Joseph Vann.

Theda Perdue wrote in her essay, "The Conflict Within," that there were underlying forces that ultimately mandated the removal. As the Cherokee prepared for a constitutional convention in 1827, Perdue wrote that a rebellion of a segment under White Path's leadership came out in support of the "common Indians."[25] The common Indians were mainly subsistence farmers living in small log cabins who wanted to stay on the ancestral lands. The Cherokee leaders were well-educated, mixed bloods with a white father and a Cherokee mother who had numerous commercial enterprises within the Nation. These men lived in large homes with slaves to help maintain their lives, businesses and agricultural endeavors. Additionally, many of the elite had been given "reservations" of land by the U.S. after previous treaties were ratified by the U.S. Congress. Reservations were lands within the ceded treaty areas that became their personal property and contributed to their growing accumulation of wealth. This was in opposition to the Cherokee Constitution, which stated that all land was held in common for the entire People; however, any improvements, buildings, etc., belonged to the individual. The values of the two groups were divergent, but their core goal to retain their ancestral ground united them.

Treaty Party Argues for Cherokees to Immigrate

The Treaty Party was part of the "rising middle class;"[26] however, they did not have the financial resources nor the political connections to reap the rewards they saw realized by the political elite. Additionally, these men were deeply in debt to the elite they wanted to replace. Perdue wrote:

> But perhaps equally important was the analogy that Jackson made between Cherokee society and his own, and he saw in the Cherokee middle class people similar to those who had elected him. Furthermore, their complaints against the aristocracy resembled his own objections to the privileged elite in the United States.[27]

These same men had led some people west in the early 1800s, but they returned to live in the East, hoping to convince the Cherokee people that immigration was their only recourse. Other Cherokees drifted to Indian Territory over the next 30 years; however, reports coming back from what became known as

"Oklahoma Territory" said the land was not good, and there was also no good water or wood source. Of greater concern, the land was already occupied by other groups of American Indians who had no interest in parting with it. The U.S. government stipulated in the 1828 Treaty with the Cherokee that $50,000 would be paid to the Cherokees who emigrated west of the Mississippi, but after two years the government had still not disbursed the funds to the Indian agents.[28] The money was desperately needed to pay for food, clothing and other necessities, as well as hoes and axes to build houses, chop firewood and to cultivate the ground, thus providing sustenance to stave off starvation.

When, in 1835, the Cherokee adhered to their 1820 law to not sell any more land, the federal commissioners turned to those who headed the unauthorized faction known as the Treaty Party. These men favored the idea of immigration because they believed that regardless of what concessions the Cherokee made and how their culture advanced, they would ultimately be forced from their ancestral lands by the ever-encroaching white population, and it was better to move in their own time – and time ultimately proved them right.

The Treaty Party understood that battles were being waged on behalf of the Cherokee in the federal courts but believed those battles could not be won, so they fought a battle for the minds and hearts of the Cherokee to make them understand it was essential to make the best treaty possible and emigrate to Indian Territory. These men also knew they were jeopardizing their lives in signing the 1835 Treaty, as the Cherokee Blood Law against selling land could be applied to them, but they believed it was a risk worth taking. The time was appropriate to sign a treaty to obtain the best outcome to accomplish the move west to Indian Territory. The government promised money to replace homes, tools and animals left behind, money to help with the move itself, and the Cherokee were promised land where they could live in peace under their own laws and government, along with the promised annuity. But this financial promise was not fulfilled as "… the five million dollars promised in the Treaty of 1835 proved to be worthless. The government simply appropriated it in exchange for relocation costs and the land the nation had received in Indian Territory."[29]

Although John Ross denied any knowledge or duplicity of the events, the Treaty Party's concerns about jeopardizing their lives were justified because "The assassinations of Major Ridge, John Ridge and Elias Boudinot by Ross supporters on June 22, 1839 marked the beginning of internal hostilities which would last for generations."[30]

Ross Party Takes a Stand to Remain in Ancestral Land

The second faction, known as the Ross Party, had no intention of the Cherokee ever immigrating to the west, and the reports from their brothers who had gone west solidified their resolve. This group went about their daily lives with the conviction that their legal cases before the U.S. Supreme Court and the support of many influential white men would work in their defense. "In spite of a petition from over 15,000 Cherokees protesting the treaty, the United States Senate ratified the Treaty of New Echota in May 1836."[31] The treaty compelled all the People to remove to the West by May 1838; however, a lawsuit before the Supreme Court and many memorials written to members of Congress and printed in various newspapers throughout the country in support of setting aside the Treaty of New Echota gave the Ross Party hope that they would remain in their ancestral lands. Firmly believing they would prevail, they went about their everyday lives, overseeing commercial enterprises, cultivating farmlands, planting crops and constructing houses and outbuildings. Like the roads north-south and east-west that were approved and built by the Cherokees in the early 1820s, the ferries they had operated for years provided easier travel for them but also provided greater access for the settlers. These improvements were clearly desired by the whites as they moved deeper into the ancestral land and ultimately took it over as their own.

A "Memorial of the Cherokee Nation to the United States Congress, September 28, 1836," presented at the Red Clay Council Ground, Cherokee Nation East (C.N.E), clearly stated the Cherokee concern for the impending removal west of the Mississippi. Principal Chief John Ross, along with a list of other chiefs, "… thirty-one members of the National Committee and

National Council and 2,174 others. ..."[32] signed the Memorial, which included the following:

> In truth, our cause is your own. It is the cause of liberty and justice. It is based on your own principles which we have learned from yourselves; for we have gloried to count your Washington and your Jefferson our great teachers. We have practiced the same precepts with success and the result is manifest. The wilderness of forest gave place to comfortable dwellings and cultivated fields.... We have learned your religion also. We have read your sacred books. Hundreds of our people have embraced their doctrines, practiced the virtue they teach, cherished the hopes they awaken ... But we speak to the representatives of a Christian country; the friends of justice; the patrons of the oppressed; and our hopes revive, and our prospects brighten, as we indulge the thought. On your sentence our fate is suspended. Prosperity or desolation depends on your word. ... On your kindness, on your humanity, on your compassion, on your benevolence, we rest our hopes.[33]

Cherokees Judged by Americentrism

The Cherokee people incorporated the good they saw in the white culture to make their lives better, while maintaining their own beliefs and culture. However, they were still judged by the belief in the preeminence of the American culture.

There were many Americans who wanted the Cherokee to be more like the white man. They didn't understand why the Cherokee needed large tracts of land and why the Cherokee saw no value in toiling on a piece of ground, raising crops and animals. Many ways of the white man were learned; the Cherokee syllabary allowed a constitution to be written fashioned on the U.S. Constitution, laws were written and attorneys trained to represent the People before the U.S. Congress. Ultimately, Supreme Court Justice John Marshall agreed with the Cherokee in his 1832 *Worcester v. Georgia* opinion stating that the relationship between the Indian Nations and the United States is that of nations;

therefore, Georgia had no jurisdiction over the Cherokee Nation. The Court did not have federal marshals enforce the law, and President Jackson did not listen to John Marshall's opinion. Forced removal became a fact in June 1838.

The first treaty written between the United States and the Cherokees in 1785 set the boundaries, and Article V stipulated that, "No citizen of the United States was to settle on Indian lands."[34] As became the norm in treaty language, Article XIII states, "The hatchet shall be forever buried, and the peace given by the United States, and friendship re-established between said states on the one part, and all the Cherokees on the other, shall be universal ..."[35] This treaty, like those to follow, promised peace and friendship perpetually – or until the next time when the white people wanted the fertile lands, the gold discovered in Georgia or later still, when oil was discovered in Indian Territory.

Cherokee Government Relocated: Advances Made

In 1825, the Cherokee seat of government relocated to New Echota in what became the state of Georgia. A federal court building and a legislative building were constructed to house the national council, consisting of a senate and council, along with a home for the presiding chief. New Echota was home to the *Cherokee Phoenix*, a bilingual newspaper, where the newspaper, official pamphlets and other government documents were printed. Advances put much of Cherokee cultural and social development on a par with the white settlements. Businesses, including stores, mills and taverns, were built. Churches flourished with many Cherokee converting to Christianity. A great number of the People lived in the traditional log cabin, but some of the Cherokee lived in beautifully furnished homes constructed on large farms with extensive crops and large herds of livestock.

Change in Federal Government Policy

External forces had far-reaching effects on American Indians, as seen in treaties ratified by Congress with nations outside the continent. In 1850, the Clayton-Bulwer Treaty between the United States and England prevented England from expanding its dominion in South America by building a canal. This, in turn, called into question the United States' concept of Manifest Destiny, with many prominent men supporting the idea of expansionism beyond the continental United States. Numerous people believed that the white civilization was ordained to spread out across the continent, tame it and make it into a new land, but there were those who thought the government was too imperialistic in its expansionistic goals.

Treaties agreed upon between the United States and American Indians as two sovereign nations were now called into dispute, with Manifest Destiny providing the rational explanation for white expansion. From 1791 to 1866, the Cherokee and federal government signed and ratified fourteen treaties. When there was no "chief" elected or appointed by the Cherokee people, a U.S. official "selected" a chief for the Cherokee. These men were usually chosen because they could be bribed into signing a treaty favorable to the United States in keeping with its policy of Manifest Destiny.

As the 1828 Georgia legislation prevailed, the Cherokee government and elected officials were not just ignored, they were declared null and void. Access to their capitol, New Echota, was denied and subsequently destroyed by the Georgia militia. The 1835 treaty signed by the Treaty Party replaced the eastern homelands with lands foreign to them in Oklahoma territory – lands occupied by other tribes. In 1871, Congress declared the Indians within the boundaries of the United States to no longer be independent nations, thus treaties were no longer required. Congress could simply write a law that the Indians would be required to honor.

Author's Thoughts

At the conclusion of each treaty, the Cherokee went away believing the articles written into the treaties by the white secretary that said the "remaining" lands were guaranteed to them in perpetuity. They learned, to their detriment that the whites meant the lands were theirs until the next time – the next time when they were asked, then forced, to give up whole blocks of their lands so vast that it represented what became entire states. The 1835 treaty signed by the Treaty Party provided the Cherokee with seven-million acres in Indian Territory, and they were also guaranteed a perpetual outlet west which gave them access to lands west belonging to the United States. Many Cherokee were rightfully wary of the government promises of a new territory protected from intrusion of the whites. History proved them right.

Because Martin Luther King, Jr. spoke out and was subsequently assassinated in 1968 to advance the Civil Rights movement, more people are aware of the struggles of minority people; however, that has very rarely included an awareness of the struggles of Native Americans. Kept on the fringe of society, it has taken organizations like the American Indian Movement (AIM), the Native American Rights Funds (NARF) and Indian Defense Association (IDA) among others who work daily to gain or maintain rights that the majority of Americans take for granted. Two of the many important cases NARF is currently working on at the time of this publication are the Keystone XL Pipeline that crosses through the Great Sioux Nation, impacting their water supply, as well as traversing much of the sacred ground of their reservation, and the North Dakota Voter ID Law, which is discriminatory in that it requires an individual to have a current residential street address to qualify to vote. To date, the U.S. Postal Service does not provide residential delivery in some rural Indian communities, which requires members to use a post office box. A post office box is not accepted for voter identification.

In America, we hear snippets of news as we go about our busy day. But we are bombarded with so much on TV and social media that unless it is something particularly bad or surprisingly uplifting, we often do not give the news any great thought. At the same time, tribal governments and the various Native American organizations continue the struggle against racism, poverty and violence. We need to do better – to listen, to really hear what is being said and done, recognize the depth of their struggles and help all people overcome racism and inequality.

Endnotes:

1   Mankiller, Wilma and Michael Wallis. *Mankiller: A Chief and Her People*. St Martin's Press, 1993, p. 143.

2   Mooney, James. *History, Myths, and Sacred Formulas of the Cherokees.* Bright Mountain Books, 1992, p. 330.

3   Mooney. pp. 330-332.

4   Satz, Ronald N. "Rhetoric Versus Reality: The Indian Policy of Andrew Jackson," *Cherokee Removal: Before and After*, edited by William L. Anderson, U of Georgia P, 1991, p 34.

5   Satz. p. 34-35.

6   Evarts, Jeremiah. *Cherokee Removal: The 'William Penn Essays and Other Writings,* edited and with Introduction by Francis Paul Prucha, The U of Tennessee P, 1981, Preface, v.

7   Evarts. pp. 264-265.

8   Schoolcraft, Henry R. *Personal Memoirs of a Residence of Thirty Years with the Indian Tribes on the American Frontiers.* Lippincott, Grambo, 1851, pp. 318-319.

9   Evans, E. Raymond. "Highways to Progress: Nineteenth Century Roads in The Cherokee Nation." *Journal of Cherokee Studies, Volume II, No. 4, Fall 1977*, p. 400.

10 King, Duane H., editor and E. Raymond Evans, consultant editorial. "The New York Spectator (New York, N.Y.)" *Journal of Cherokee Studies, Vol. IV, No. 2, Spring 1979.*

January 3, 1832 from *The Boston Courier of Wednesday* reported on the Cherokee Missionaries. pp. 86-88.

[11] "First Inaugural Address of Andrew Jackson" Wednesday, March 4, 1829. para 9. avalon.law.yale.edu.

[12] Takaki, Ronald T. *Iron Cages: Race and Culture in 19th-Century America and Empire-Building.* U of Minnesota P, 1980, pp. 448-449.

[13] nativenewsonline.net, Wed, December 14, 2016 & "The Addresses and Messages of the Presidents of the United States, Jackson's Fifth Annual Message, edited by Edwin Williams, Vol 2, p 839, google.com/books

[14] Tyler, S. Lyman. *A History of Indian Policy.* U.S. Department of the Interior, Bureau of Indian Affairs, 1973, p. 6.

[15] Rozema. Vicki. editor. "Voices from The Trail of Tears" John F. Blair, Winston-Salem, NC, 2003. pp. 74-75

[16] Mooney, James. *History, Myths, and Sacred Formulas of the Cherokees.* Da Capo Press Inc., 1995, p. 164.

[17] Finger, John R. "The Impact of Removal on the North Carolina Cherokees," *Cherokee Removal: Before and After,* edited by William L. Anderson. U of Georgia P, 1991, p. 97

[18] Finger. p. 97.

[19] Finger. note 2, p. 109.

[20] Finger, John R. "The North Carolina Cherokees, 1838-1866: Traditionalism, Progressivism, and The Affirmation of State Citizenship." *Journal of Cherokee Studies, Vol. V, No. 1, Spring 1980,* pp. 21, 25.

[21] Satz, Ronald N. "Rhetoric Versus Reality: The Indian Policy of Andrew Jackson," *Cherokee Removal: Before and After.* William L. Anderson, editor, U of Georgia P, 1991, pp. 39-40

[22] Satz, Ronald N. "Rhetoric Versus Reality: The Indian Policy of Andrew Jackson," *Cherokee Removal: Before and After.* William L. Anderson, editor, U of Georgia P, 1991, p 39.

[23] Satz. p.38

[24] Statutes at Large 4:411-12; Kappler, Charles J. compiler and editor. *Indian Affairs,* 2:310-11

[25] Perdue, Theda, "The Conflict Within: Cherokees and Removal," *Cherokee Removal: Before and After.* William L. Anderson, editor, The U of Georgia P, 1991, p 62.

[26] Perdue. p. 66.

[27] Perdue. p. 68.

[28] King, Duane H., editor and E. Raymond Evans, consultant editorial. "Cherokees Oppressed in Georgia." *Journal of Cherokee Studies, Vol. IV, No. 2, Spring 1979.* Printed in *The Saturday Bulletin*, Philadelphia, PA, June 19, 1830. p. 76.

[29] Mails, Thomas E. *The Cherokee People: The Story of the Cherokees from Earliest Origins to Contemporary Times.* Marlowe & Co., 1992, p. 269.

[30] King, Duane H., editor and E. Raymond Evans, consultant editorial. "The Murder of John Ridge." *Journal of Cherokee Studies, Vol. IV, No. 2, Spring 1979.* Printed in *The Daily Albany Argus* (Albany, N.Y.) Aug. 2. 1939. p 109.

[31] Anderson, William L., editor. "Cherokee Removal: Before and After." Brown Thrasher Books, The U of Georgia P, 1991, Introduction, p. xii. p xii

[32] American Indian Nonfiction: An Anthology of Writings, 1760-1930s. "To the Senate and House of Representatives. John Ross et al (1836) Southeast and Indian Territory." File Copy, National Archives, RG 233, 25th Cong. U of Oklahoma P. 2007. p. 140.

[33] "Treaty of Hopewell, 1785." Article XIII. https://bit.ly/2Jxrm0O.

[34] Kappler, Charles J., compiler and editor. *Indian Treaties, 1778-1883.* Amereon House, 1972, p. 9.

[35] Kappler. pp. 10-11.

| SEVEN |

Removal and Settlement in "Indian Territory" (1838 – 1889)

Many thousands of years ago, before the earth existed, the animals lived in the area above the sky vault with only water beneath them. They enjoyed life but as their numbers increased, they became increasingly crowded. They held council meetings to discuss what should be done. The little Water-Beetle offered to learn what the depths of water held. Darting about in every direction and finding no resting place, he dove to the bottom returning with some soft mud which began to grow and spread until it became an island. Suspended by cords at the four corners – east, south, west, and north – above the great ocean, the island remained very flat, soft and wet. Many different birds ventured forth to find dry land, but all of them returned unsuccessful and exhausted. After some time, the Great Buzzard volunteered to fly over the land; however, he also found it too soft. After flying a great distance, he grew tired and flew ever lower, flapping his wings from time to time which caused valleys and mountains to form. The other animals became concerned that the entire earth would be mountainous, so they called the Great Buzzard back to the sky vault. This wonderful land created by the Great Buzzard contained stands of forests with evergreens, trees and shrubs with rushing streams and clear water. Numerous other plants provided beauty and medicines as well as food if one was wise enough to understand the bounty of nature. The Spirit entrusted this country to the Cherokee, to care for even as it nourished their bodies and souls. This became Cherokee country.[1]

The country entrusted to the Cherokees by the Great Spirit was their heart and soul. Their lives were benefitted by and focused around the land, the plants and the animals contained within. Their festivals celebrated the cycles of the land. But the United States government had another plan for the Cherokees, and it meant taking their land.

The 1838 forced removal of the Cherokee from the Eastern United States resulted in two independent groups who, out of necessity and despite sharing a common history until the trials of removal, developed different cultures based on that history but unique to each group. The first group lives in North Carolina and today is known as The Eastern Band of Cherokee Indians, and the second group immigrated to Indian Territory, which later became Oklahoma. Today, this group is officially known as the Cherokee Nation. A third tribe, originally known as the Old Settlers, started migrating west of the Mississippi in the early 1800s, and others joined them periodically. These were, for the most part, full bloods who maintained their conservative lives – adhering to their belief in the Great Spirit and preserving their traditions and culture. Called Keetoowah since the mid-1800s, today they are recognized by the federal government as the United Keetoowah Band of Cherokee Indians. They too are located in Oklahoma.

President Jackson's handpicked successor, Martin Van Buren "made clear his determination to enforce the controversial Cherokee removal treaty of 1835."[2] He declared, "No state can achieve proper culture, civilization, and progress in safety as long as Indians are permitted to remain."[3] In June 1838, President Van Buren ordered the Army to initiate the forced removal of the Cherokee to lands west of the Mississippi. Anticipating resistance, the Army built three forts to hold the Indians as they were rounded up. The forts had walls that were sixteen-foot high with no floor or roof to afford protection from the elements to those imprisoned there.[4] An article on the "Fort Marr Blockhouse: The Last Evidence of America's First Concentration Camps" by E. Raymond Evans includes a picture of the Fort Marr Blockhouse, presently located off U.S. Highway 411 at Benton (Polk County) Tennessee, in which Evans states:

> No privacy was possible; according [to] missionaries present, the Cherokees were hearded [herded] like pigs in a sty.[5] There were no provisions for sanitation, and the water supply was inadequate and questionable. The prisoners received a daily ration of flour and salt pork, but few had cooking utensils. Eating the salt pork raw, or poorly cooked, made the shortage of water all the more apparent.[6]

Horrific Conditions During Removal

Missionary Elizur Butler reported that the conditions of the camps without adequate food, clothing, bedding or pots and cooking utensils and no shelter from the elements contributed to the deaths of "… at least two thousand people"[7] prior to even departing their ancestral lands. The added horror was parents seeing the traders induce their daughters to drink the illegal whiskey and then be passed from man to man as they stood helplessly by and watched.

In *Mankiller: A Chief and Her People,* Wilma Mankiller wrote, "The routes the federal soldiers forced our tribe to take were known as Nunna daul Tsunyi, which in Cherokee means literally, 'the trail where we cried.' In English, the removal became known as the Trail of Tears."[8] The march resulted in the outright death of 4,000 of the estimated 17,000 Cherokees at the start of the trek west. Much has been written about the Trail of Tears, which covered over 1,500 miles from Eastern Tennessee to Indian Territory. What many do not know is that this was primarily done on foot.

The original plan called for the People to be moved by riverboat down the Tennessee and Ohio Rivers, then across the Mississippi River where they were unloaded to walk the rest of the way to Indian Territory. Of the several thousand who made the river trip in June 1838, the oppressive summer heat and disease killed so many that John Ross and other leaders prevailed upon General Scott, the officer in charge, to allow the remaining

Cherokees, some 13,000, to wait until fall to begin the trip. Ross divided the People into 13 groups of 1,000 each. The first group left on August 23, 1838, arriving January 17, 1839. Ten groups left during September, with arrival dates spanning January 4 to March 14, 1839. The group that left on October 23 arrived on March 24, 1839. The last of the People departed on Dec 5 and arrived March 18, 1839. The overland trek went north through parts of Tennessee and Kentucky, then west from Illinois and across the Mississippi River. This included areas where cholera and other epidemic diseases were raging. Due to the time of year, the Mississippi River was often iced over, causing the detachments to wait long periods before it was safe for boats to take them across to Missouri where they continued the trek across that state into Arkansas, the beginning of Indian Territory, before finally reaching their destination. After this length of time, so many people had traveled the same route that the immigrants and soldiers were forced to range farther from the campsites before finding firewood or game. Some of the older and sick were permitted to ride, and occasional stretches of the journey were done by river.

During the whole of the journey, the rations were meager and often made up of rancid meat and spoiled flour. There was insufficient protection from the long, cold winter, as the People were forced from their homes without time to gather blankets and additional clothing to replace the threadbare clothing they wore as they trudged frozen or muddy trails without shoes. People who died along the trail were hastily buried, and the remainder forced to move along without rest.

> The policy of issuing contracts for food and transportation for emigrants to the lowest bidders contributed to the misery of Indians on their trek to the West more than anything else. Many unscrupulous contractors furnished the emigrants with scanty, even spoiled rations, thin blankets, and other shoddy items in order to reap a sizable profit from their contracts.[9]

This relocation of the Cherokees can be compared "... in

terms of mortality rate directly attributable to it, almost as destructive as the Bataan Death March of 1942, the most notorious Japanese atrocity in all of the Second World War."[10] Of the 10,000 or so Americans who were victims of the Bataan Death March, 4,000 survived to the end of the war, meaning that about 6,000, or sixty-percent, died on the march or during the subsequent three years of imprisonment. About 8,000 of the approximately 17,000 Cherokee who began that death march died on the Trail of Tears and in the immediate aftermath – about forty-seven percent. The comparison is incomplete, however, because unlike the Bataan march, no one knows how many Cherokee died during the next three years of reservation imprisonment, and also because, again unlike the Bataan Death March which was only men, the Cherokee death march included many thousands of women and children.

The number of people, Cherokee and slave, departing on the march and the number arriving in Indian Territory were kept by the military, John Ross and Dr. Elizur Butler (appointed by John Ross as medical doctor for one of the thirteen groups), as well as others who kept tally of the People, differed greatly. Butler, sympathetic to the Cherokees, was from Connecticut and had made his figures of the losses, which were greater than that of others, known to the eastern public. He wanted this horrific tragedy to be highlighted and the government to explain this egregious act.

John Ehle provides a background for the government's response in his book, *Trail of Tears: The Rise and Fall of the Cherokee Nation,* from a message to Congress by President Van Buren. Ehle quotes the words of the president:

> It affords me sincere pleasure to be able to apprise you of the entire removal of the Cherokee Nation of Indians to their new homes west of the Mississippi. The measures authorized by Congress with a view to the long-standing controversy with them have had the happiest effect, and they have emigrated without any apparent resistance.[11]

Slaves Play a Role in Removal

In pre-European contact, slavery was a component of Cherokee life. Seen as a failure of the individual's performance during battle, captives from other tribes taken in battle became slaves or could be adopted into the tribe. Some captives were killed in revenge of lives lost, with the Ghighau having the final say as to whether they lived or died.

After European contact, the Cherokee made use of African American slaves to do the physical labor required to support the agricultural endeavors of their farms and plantations. In addition to those who worked the fields, some worked at the Indian trading posts. There were also house servants, those who cared for the plantation owners' children, seamstresses and some skilled as blacksmiths. The slaves provided the labor required to sustain the plantation economy, as well as the subsistence farming done by some Cherokee families.

In a March 6, 2018 article, "How Native American Slaveholders Complicate the Trail of Tears Narrative," Ryan P. Smith wrote about the new Smithsonian exhibit "Americans." In an effort "… to provide the museum-going public with an unflinching history, even when doing so is painful … [museum curator Paul Chaat Smith (Comanche)] addressed the enslavement of blacks by prominent members of all five so-called 'Civilized Tribes.'"[12] Slaveholding was beneficial to the Native Americans economically, as it showed financial success, and culturally as "… ownership of black slaves came about as a way for Native Americans to illustrate their societal sophistication to white settlers."[13]

When the Cherokee were forced to immigrate in 1838, the African American slave population, estimated at 1,500, immigrated with them and performed much of the physical labor during the removal. They were also a source of labor used to rebuild the nation in Indian Territory.

The Ruthless Removal

As the Cherokee people were marched to Indian Territory, they died of hunger, exposure, exhaustion and disease. Those who lived suffered those things as well as the pain of losing friends and loved one. In the *Myths of the Cherokee: Historical Sketch of the Cherokee,* James Mooney interviewed participants in the removal who described the scene:

> Under [General] Scott's orders the troops were disposed at various points throughout the Cherokee country, where stockade forts were erected for gathering in and holding the Indians preparatory to removal. From these, squads of troops were sent to search out with rifle and bayonet every small cabin hidden away in the coves or by the sides of mountain streams, to seize and bring in as prisoners all the occupants, however or wherever they might be found. Families at dinner were startled by the sudden gleam of bayonets in the doorway and rose to be driven with blows and oaths along the weary miles of trail that led to the stockade. Men were seized in their fields or going along the road, women were taken from their wheels and children from their play. In many cases, on turning for one last look as they crossed the ridge, they saw their homes in flames, fired by the lawless rabble that followed on the heels of the soldiers to loot and pillage. So keen were these outlaws on the scent that in some instances they were driving off the cattle and other stock of the Indians almost before the soldiers had fairly started their owners in the other direction. Systematic hunts were made by the same men for Indian graves to rob them of silver pendants and other valuables deposited with the dead. A Georgia volunteer, afterward a colonel in the Confederate service, said: 'I fought through the civil war and have seen men shot to pieces and slaughtered by thousands, but the Cherokee removal was the cruelest work I ever knew.'[14]

Some North Carolina Cherokees Escape Removal

According to the 1840 census, 247 Cherokee families, consisting of 999 individuals, were able to avoid removal. A group of a little over 300 were Oconaluftee Citizen Indians living in

North Carolina, and they claimed exemption under the Treaty of New Echota and petitioned the state and federal government to remain. In January of 1837, the North Carolina General Assembly, while refraining from acknowledging the Cherokee as citizens, tacitly allowed them to stay.[15] "Besides the 1,100 or so Cherokees remaining in North Carolina, there were perhaps 300 in nearby parts of Georgia, Alabama, and Tennessee, making a total of about 1,400 who avoided removal...."[16]

A Tale of Cherokee Heroes

Tsali and his family were part of the fugitives trying to escape the Army's roundup in North Carolina by hiding in caves in the Smoky Mountains during the day and coming out at night in search of food. The stories surrounding Tsali have grown since 1838, illustrating an act of heroism that is now depicted in the tribal pageant, *Unto These Hills*, which is enacted each tourist season in Cherokee, North Carolina, and has been seen by millions of visitors from all over the world. The pageant portrays Tsali's act of bravery when he killed two soldiers who, he said, abused his ailing wife. Tsali, his brother and two sons escaped into the mountain wilderness. According to conflicting accounts, General Scott sent word that he would allow the North Carolina Cherokees to remain if Tsali and his men surrendered for their crimes, which they did to protect and ultimately save those in hiding. To prove a point, the Army required the Cherokee themselves to perform the executions, which made Tsali a martyr and the father of his People.[17]

The story surrounding Tsali has grown over the years, and the pageant depicts the story as it is now known. However, the research done by The Cherokee Historical Association in an endeavor to bring the facts surrounding the deaths of the two soldiers and the capture and execution of Tsali and the other men to the public through the military records of the 1838 event[18] was published in the Fall 1979 *Journal of Cherokee Studies*. Though somewhat different from the pageant story, the facts are nonetheless interesting and emphasize the love of country and desire to stay in their homeland.

In early August, General Scott ordered mounted troops and Indian runners into the mountains to capture a group of about 300 fugitives, including Tsali, his wife, Nancy, and ten other family members. Trying to elude the army roundup of the North Carolina Cherokee, Tsali and his family were finally captured on October 30, 1838. They managed to escape on November 1, but two soldiers were killed and another wounded. Concerned that the actions of Tsali and his family could jeopardize the petition of the Cherokees to remain in North Carolina, the Oconolufty Cherokee under Chief Euchella were granted permission to assist the Army in the search. Euchella and his band were faced with the difficult task of bringing their own countrymen in to face the U.S. military for the unwarranted murder of the two soldiers. Striving to live in the changing world, Euchella demonstrated his love for the People he sought to protect, while endeavoring to ensure they could remain in their homeland.

On November 19, four of the men were captured. A board of inquiry was convened on November 21, and three of the four were executed on November 23. The fourth was spared because of his youth. Tsali was captured and executed on November 25.[19] It should be noted that on November 24, 1838, Colonel W. S. Foster, commander of the North Carolina forces, wrote a final report to General Scott providing details of Euchella's assistance. Colonel Foster stated:

> All the objects of your instructions have been fully complied with. … This band and their chief from the first have behaved nobly, himself, his brothers, and Wahchee sha and brother are the only men of this band, in all about forty strong. I have given them in writing my permission (in consequence of their friendship in defaticable, & untiring industry, in the late pursuit apprehension and punishment of the murderers), to remain in this country as long as they conduct themselves as peacible citizens of North Carolina subject to the final decision of the government.[20]

Tsali and his family demonstrated the depth of their determination to remain in their homeland no matter what the cost. Their plight and that of numerous other Cherokees, as they sought to avoid the Army roundup and subsequent forced removal to Indian Territory, vary in the details but provides a greater understanding of the strong ties of Native Americans to their homes and land.

That original group of about 1,100 has grown to nearly 13,000 members in the ensuing years and has been officially recognized by the United States Government as the Eastern Band of the Cherokee Nation headquartered in Cherokee, North Carolina which encompasses over 68,000 acres. Their home is called the Land of Blue Smoke.[21]

Over the years, individuals from the Eastern Cherokee visited the Western Cherokee and vice versa. A reunion of the two groups occurred in 1984 when the Eastern and Western Cherokee came together as one people, if only for awhile, at Cleveland, Tennessee. The last council before removal was held at Red Clay in 1837 near the place of the 1984 reunion.

Early Cherokee Settlement in Indian Territory

There were those among the Cherokee who recognized that their way of life was being threatened by the influx of the white traders, military forts and settlers. These Cherokee did not want to leave their ancestral lands, but their greater concern was in maintaining their traditional way of life. Made up primarily of full-blood Cherokee, they migrated first to Arkansas, then to lands designated as Indian Territory in the early 1800s. Others joined them over the next 20 to 30 years. Initially known as the Old Settlers, they formed the Keetoowah Society as a political organization about 1859, pledging to follow the old or traditional way of life, favoring revival of the old religion and placing greater emphasis upon the establishment and use of dance or medicine grounds.

The Oklahoma Indian Country Guide: One State – Many Nations provides some background on the Keetoowah:

> Keetoowah Cherokee people believe that 'Kituwah' or 'Keetoowah' is the true name of the Cherokee people given to them by the Creator atop a mountain peak known as Kuwahi. This site today is referred to as

Clingman's Dome and straddles the borders of North Carolina and Tennessee in the Great Smoky Mountains. The Keetoowah Cherokees also received their laws and sacred fire in their ancestral homelands ... [They] still see themselves as the guardians of traditional Cherokee ways today.[22]

Often maligned for their traditional ways, it is informative to read a quote taken from a lengthy letter written to Federal Judge Joseph A. Gill, in Muskogee, Indian Territory on May 16, 1903 which refutes that charge. "The Letter tells us a great deal about the nature of the society, and its eloquence has the additional significance of revealing the high educational level of those who wrote it:"[23]

> ... The Keetoowahs have been so vilified, and lied about, that we appreciate how hard it will be to put us right in the minds of the people. We are charged with the responsibility for a failure on the part of the full bloods to enroll, because they do not rush to the land office and take their allotment. The full-blood Indian, as is well known by those familiar with the Indian character, is timid and suspicious, because he is not acquainted with the ways of the whites, who has so often been the victim of cheats and frauds who take advantage of his ignorance. He is deliberate in all of his business dealings, and becomes confused when hurried, yet he is abused because he does not come to the land office and take his allotment in low grade public lands while there are many more intelligent citizens unlawfully in possession of thousands of acres of the best land, to the exclusion of would-be allottees.[24]
> ...

The Old Settlers were well established when the first group of immigrants led by John Ridge arrived in Indian Territory around 1820, followed by a second group known as The Treaty Party lead by Ridge-Boudinot, who immigrated after the signing of the 1835 Treaty.

Conflict Threatens Cherokee Unity

Conflict simmered between the Cherokee factions from the time the Eastern Cherokees led by Chief John Ross arrived in Indian Territory in 1838-1839. While still in their homeland, the Ross contingent had voted to maintain their form of government, which included having John Ross continue as chief. All of these people had come from the same ancient culture with strong clan identification and belief in the Great Spirit; however, they had all suffered the loss of their homeland, endured immigration and the deaths of many of their people. They were the same people, yet they were different, and each group had established its own laws and way of life that differed somewhat from the others, and each group believed its way should be adopted by the others.

A convention to merge the groups was originally scheduled for June 1839; however, civil war broke out between the groups when the 1829 "Cherokee Blood Law" was enacted, resulting in the murder of Major Ridge, John Ridge and Elias Boudinot the evening prior to the convention. Stand Waite, another leader of the Treaty Party, was able to escape and later served as a general in the Confederate Army. Blamed for the murders, the Ross party claimed their innocence, nothing was ever proved, and the matter was dropped but not forgotten. This event prompted a period of lawlessness within the Nation, including revenge murders, arson and theft much like "... a distorted version of the old clan revenge system."[25]

On September 6, 1839, Sequoyah served as president of the Constitutional Convention and saw the Cherokees formally united. The unification was on paper but not in the hearts, minds and actions of the People, as they endured continued bad feelings and retaliatory assassinations. It wasn't until 1846 when the federal government required the factions to sign a treaty unifying the Nation that some modicum of peace was obtained. "Even then, bitter partisans nursed hatreds that would erupt again when the Cherokees were drawn into the American Civil War."[26]

Slave Revolt in Indian Territory

On November 15, 1842, a revolt of African Americans

occurred in the Cherokee Nation when 20 slaves escaped. After raiding a local store for supplies and weapons, they made their way toward Mexico where slavery had been abolished in 1836. Another group of 15 slaves, who had escaped from the Creek Nation, was headed south and joined them. These fugitives were pursued by some Cherokee and Creek men, and the encounter between the groups resulted in 14 slaves either killed or captured and returned to their respective Nations. The remaining 21 continued south while the Cherokee National Council "… raise (d) a company of 100 citizens to 'pursue, arrest, and deliver the African Slaves to Fort Gibson.'"[27]

While all this was going on, two slave catchers intercepted a family of two adults and three children heading west. The southbound group killed the two slave catchers, and the party continued south. "The pursuing company caught up with the slave group seven miles north of the Red River on November 28. The tired fugitives, weak from hunger, offered no resistance."[28] Five were later executed for the murder of the slave catchers; however, their actions inspired others to revolt so that "By 1851, a total of nearly 300 blacks had tried to escape from Indian Territory."[29]

Although the pro-Union segment of the Cherokee government had abolished slavery prior to the Civil War, it is estimated that "… When the Civil War erupted in 1861, more than eight thousand blacks were enslaved in Indian Territory. They comprised 14 percent of the population. …"[30] The treaties with the U.S. government at the end of the war required all tribes to designate the slaves as freedmen, and the Emancipation Proclamation in 1863 granted citizenship to all freedmen in the Confederate States, including those in Indian Territory. "The U.S. government required that they free their slaves and offer full Cherokee citizenship to those who wanted to stay with the nation."[31]

Revival of the Cherokee Nation

The Strickland's identified a period of revival from 1849 to 1860 for the Cherokee Nation in their essay "Beyond the Trail of Tears: One Hundred Fifty Years of Cherokee Survival." This

"Golden Age of the Cherokees"[32] is a period where the People finally worked together, building on the success they had made prior to removal.

The bilingual newspaper, the *Cherokee Advocate*, published books and kept the People informed on everyday news, as well as developments between the Cherokee and the U.S. government. "The tribe established college-level education and 126 public schools, graduating men and women of talent and competency."[33] The traditional Cherokee, as well as the mixed bloods, enjoyed a level of prosperity greater than their white neighbors of the surrounding states. "Thus, without any aid from the United States, the Cherokees built a nation that was often described as the 'Athens of the West.'"[34]

Religion, not politics, formed the basis of ancient Cherokee life; however, in 1840, the trend began to change from a matriarchal-led society to one that gave the father more authority. Increasingly, a shift of the Cherokee political system took them from the clan-tribal unit towards a republican form of government. The Cherokee laws and government were again in place, which meant that the land was held in common for all the People. Poverty was practically unknown. No one had to wait until they had the money to buy property; they could utilize the land and make improvements to support their family, farm or business. The improvements were theirs, and they could enjoy the use of the common land.

When the 1835 treaty was signed, the Cherokee lands in the east were exchanged for seven-million acres of assigned lands in Indian Territory, as well as an outlet that was supposed to provide them "a perpetual outlet west, and a free and unmolested use of all the country west ... as far west as the sovereignty of the United States" extended.[35]

A surveying error of the outlet occurred, which resulted in the addition of the Cherokee Strip that was two-miles wide along the northern border (present day Oklahoma-Kansas) of the outlet, and both came to be commonly called the Cherokee Outlet. This land proved to be a great economic benefit to the Nation in the coming years; however, it was also a source of consternation between the Cherokee people and the federal government, as the People sought to retain ownership, and the government strived to eradicate their title through various means. Underlying all this was the "… agricultural crisis in a decade when droughts, sharply declining agricultural prices, and the Panic of 1893 bankrupted many farmers."[36] The goal of the U.S. government was to make the land available to white settlers who were on the verge of starvation.[37] This was finally achieved through allotment and a succession of seven land runs. The most famous run occurred on April 22, 1889, when nearly two million acres of unassigned land was opened to white settlement. Again, the needs of the settlers took precedence over the needs of the Native Americans and the treaty obligations of the U.S. government.

Author's Thoughts

At the time of removal, the Cherokee were the most acculturated of the Native peoples, having accepted and incorporated many American beliefs and practices into their lives. Changes were made for many reasons, but all the practices they embraced improved their lives in one fashion or another and were best for the People. However, none of their adaptations made a difference to their eventual fate. Manifest Destiny was the cry of the public and elected officials – the land was required for other purposes, and the People stood in the way. Assimilation was no longer an option. As inconceivable as it was, they had to submit, give up the lands provided to them by the Great Spirit, the lands of their ancestors and immigrate to lands foreign to them.

The factions within the Cherokee people due to removal caused many years of internal strife. Once the factions were forced by the U.S. to sign a treaty of unification in 1846, their differences were set aside, if not entirely forgotten, and great strides were made in many areas including education, business, agriculture and government. But in many minds were the lingering thoughts – when was the government going to want their new lands? It is difficult to trust once promises are repeatedly broken, as evidenced by the many treaties contravened by the United States government.

Things were bad in Indian Territory, as well as the rest of the nation, during the Civil War. But not long after the conclusion of the war, the government proved the doubts of the Cherokee to be accurate. After trying a number of government programs in the late 1800s, including the General Allotment Act, intended to separate the Indians from their lands, two new programs (relocation and tribal termination) designed to assimilate the Indians were undertaken in the 1930s to late 1950s. Although relocation was important in achieving the government's goal of assimilation, the primary goal was the disintegration of the tribal government and its influence on the People – another type of termination.

Very few economic opportunities were available on the reservations. With that in mind, the Bureau of Indian Affairs developed a job-placement service to encourage individuals and families to seek opportunities away from the reservations. The relocation program was voluntary, but the decision to move was predicated on information the BIA provided highlighting good jobs and homes. The program saw many Indians move to cities along the West Coast, while others were sent to Chicago, Denver, Salt Lake City and other large cities, primarily in the Midwest and West Coast regions. Again, Native Americans were being placed in an environment entirely foreign to them creating a sense of detachment from their home that their ancestors felt when they relocated to Indian Territory. In this case, they had to learn to navigate in a city, how to get to jobs and schools, set up bank accounts, buy groceries and, in some cases, learn to use a telephone for the first time.

Soap – it's such an everyday necessity that most Americans give it little or no thought. It is just there when we need it. However, a basic necessity like soap played a significant part in the policy decisions of the U.S. government. John Ehle writes that when soap was added to the Cherokee list of provisions needed for their immigration to Indian Territory, the government pushed back. The appropriated figures for the move were already high, and officials questioned the added expense. "Would not the travelers have their own soap?"[38] Really? People who are taken from their homes, fields and businesses with a rifle pointed at them do not think of soap – there are so many more important things to consider. This intentional decision to deny a basic need is just one example of the government's lack of empathy and cruel treatment of the Indians during this forced immigration. While soap is not a cause we rally around, it is indicative of a greater problem. We should be willing to provide for basic human needs – illustrating our humanity and exemplifying that "We are all created equal."[39]

In spite of all this, Native Americans answered the call to serve during WWI, WWII and all military actions since, fighting on the front lines, as well as volunteering to fill many critical functions at home. After all, America was their country long before the arrival of the immigrants from Europe and other foreign countries. Love of country is the reason so many American military personnel, including Native Americans, have given their lives to ensure the freedom provided in the Declaration of Independence.

When the Twin Towers came down on 9/11, construction workers, including Native American iron workers, were immediately there to assist with the rescue and cleanup. They were among those who built the Twin Towers and now helped in the aftermath of the disaster. Native People were evacuated from the offices of the National Museum of the American Indian just five blocks from the site of the attack. Because of the potential for attack at that time, they were among those forced from their government offices and agencies in Washington, D.C. Collectively they donated "… over $2 million to the relief effort by week's end."[40] The gift was given freely by "… the most economically impoverished segment of society. …"[41]

When there is a need in our country Native Americans are among those to answer the call. They, along with other groups including first responders and the military, deserve our recognition, support and undying gratitude.

Thank you.

Endnotes:

1. Mooney, James. *History, Myths, and Sacred Formulas of the Cherokees.* Bright Mountain Books, 1992, story 1, pp. 239-242.
2. Satz, Ronald N. "Rhetoric Versus Reality: The Indian Policy of Andrew Jackson." *Cherokee Removal: Before and After,* edited by William L. Anderson, U of Georgia P, 1991. p 43.
3. Mankiller, Wilma and Michael Wallis. *Mankiller: A Chief and Her People.* St Martin's Press, 1993, p. 93.
4. Evans, E. Raymond. "Fort Marr Blockhouse: The Last Evidence of America's First Concentration Camps." *Journal of Cherokee Studies, Vol. II, No. 2, Spring 1977,* p. 258.
5. Evans. p. 258-259.
6. Evans. p. 258.
7. Evans. p. 259.
8. Mankiller, Wilma and Michael Wallis. *Mankiller: A Chief and Her People.* St Martin's Press, 1993, p. 46.
9. Satz, Ronald N. "Rhetoric Versus Reality: The Indian Policy of Andrew Jackson." *Cherokee Removal: Before and After,* edited by William L. Anderson, U of Georgia P, 1991, p 41.
10. Knox, Donald. *Death March: The Survivors of Bataan.* Harcourt Brace Jovanovich, 1981, Ch 4, quote 101.
11. Ehle, John. *Trail of Tears: The Rise and Fall of the Cherokee Nation.* Anchor Books, Doubleday, 1988, p. 392.
12. Smith, Ryan P. "How Native American Slaveholders Complicate the Trail of Tears Narrative." *Smithsonian Magazine,* 6 Mar 2018. https://bit.ly/3cP2Jrg. Accessed 15 Oct 2019.
13. Smith, Ryan P.

14. Mooney, James. *Myths of the Cherokee: Historical Sketch of the Cherokee, The Removal – 1838-1839,* Bright Mountain Books, 1992. p 130.

15. Finger, John. "The North Carolina Cherokees, 1838-1866: Traditionalism, Progressivism, and The Affirmation of State Citizenship," *Journal of Cherokee Studies, Vol. V, No. 1, Spring 1980,* pp. 17-29

16. Finger, John R. "The Impact of Removal on the North Carolina Cherokees." *Cherokee Removal: Before and After,* edited by William L. Anderson, U of Georgia P, 1991, pp. 105-106.

17. Finger. pp. 103-104.

18. King, Duane and E. Raymond Evans. "Tsali: The Man Behind the Legend." *Journal of Cherokee Studies, Vol. IV, No. 4, Fall 1979,* pp. 197-199.

19. King and Evans. pp. 197-199.

20. "Colonel W. S. Foster to Gen. W. Scott, Nov. 24. 1838." *Journal of Cherokee Studies, Vol. IV, No. 4, Fall 1979,* p. 226.

21. "About the Eastern Band of Cherokee Indians." *cherokeepreservation.org.* https://bit.ly/2IbWcMj. Accessed 31 Jan 2017.

22. "United Keetoowah Bank of Cherokee Indians." *Oklahoma Indian Country Guide: One State – Many Nations* p 61.

23. Mails, Thomas E. *The Cherokee People: The Story of the Cherokees from Earliest Origins to Contemporary Times.* Marlowe & Co., 1992, p. 282.

24. Mails. para 10, p. 283.

25. Strickland, Rennard and William M. Strickland. "Beyond the Trail of Tears: One Hundred Fifty Years of Cherokee Survival." *Cherokee Removal: Before and After,* edited by William L. Anderson, U of Georgia P, 1991, p. 113-114.

26. Strickland. p. 114.

27. "1842 Slave Revolt in the Cherokee Nation." https://bit.ly/355vblf. Accessed 28 Aug 2019.

28. https://bit.ly/355vblf.

29. https://bit.ly/355vblf.

30. Krauthamer, Barbara. "The Encyclopedia of Oklahoma History and Culture – Slavery." *Oklahoma Historical Society,* https://bit.ly/3ihjHiU.

31. McLoughlin, William G. *After the Trail of Tears: The Cherokee's Struggle for Sovereignty 1839-1880.* U of North Carolina P, 1994, pp. 681, 690, 699.

32. Strickland, Rennard and William M. Strickland. "Beyond the Trail of Tears: One Hundred Fifty Years of Cherokee Survival." *Cherokee Removal: Before and After*, edited by William L. Anderson, U of Georgia P, 1991, p. 114.

33. Strickland. p. 114.

34. Strickland. p. 115.

35. Kappler, Charles J., compiler and editor. *Indian Treaties 1778-1883*. "Treaty with the Cherokee, 1835, Article *2*," p. 441, Amereon House, 1972.

36. Turner, Alvin O. "Cherokee Outlet Opening." *Oklahoma Historical Society*, https://bit.ly/3cN9OZh.

37. Turner. para. 5.

38. Ehle, John. *Trail of Tears: The Rise and Fall of the Cherokee Nation*. Anchor Books, Doubleday, 1988, p. 349.

39. "Declaration of Independence, 1776." *America's Founding Documents*. https://bit.ly/3lNQ6jl.

40. Harjo, Suzan Shown. "The week of 9/11 – Native Peoples in the Society of Sorrow and Justice." *Indian Country Today*, 11 Sep 2018, https://bit.ly/34gQn78.

41. Harjo.

| EIGHT |

Cherokee Embroiled in American Civil War (1861 to 1865)

We old Indians believe in the one Creator, who governs the affairs of the Universe & whose place is in the center of the sky, directly over-head.

In the beginning, we think certain lines were settled upon to go in certain directions and which directions it was determined should be called by the names which in English express the points of the compass. . .

These lines being settled, human beings were formed and sent from each direction to each point upon the earth, each of the four beings differing in color from the other.

First came the Red Man – he was sent from the East. The Blue Man, from the North, came next, and then from the West, the region of the setting sun, there came the Black Man ... and, last of all, from the South was sent the White Man, [1]

The growing division between the slaveholding south and the antislavery north caused great concern across the country. President Taylor, "A firm believer in national supremacy,"[2] came into office in March 1849. The discovery of gold in California in 1848 caused an influx of over 80,000 settlers in a year. Taylor considered it vital that California formulate a constitution and be admitted to the Union as a free state; however, that would upset the north-south balance, which neither Congress nor the president was eager to do. At this time there were thirty states in the Union with an equal number of slaveholding and antislavery states. He did not involve himself in the slavery debates in Congress where tensions ran high, as the issue was passionately debated with threats of secession from southerners. "… President Taylor told a group of southern leaders that he would hang anyone who tried to disrupt the union by force or by conspiracy."[3] With Taylor's admonition hovering over them, a group of senators brokered a series of five separate bills:

> The Compromise of 1850 contained the following provisions: (1) California was admitted to the Union as a free state; (2) the remainder of the Mexican cession was divided into the two territories of New Mexico and Utah and organized without mention of slavery; (3) the claim of Texas to a portion of New Mexico was satisfied by a payment of $10 million; (4) new legislation (the Fugitive Slave Act) was passed to apprehend runaway slaves and return them to their masters; and (5) the buying and selling of slaves (but not slavery) was abolished in the District of Columbia.[4]

Taylor died in July 1850, and the Compromise was signed into law by President Fillmore in September 1850, which allowed the controversy to pass – at least for the time being.

Country Embroiled in Civil War

Eleven years later, the issue had to be dealt with by President Lincoln, but long before the Civil War began, the heightened political discourse within the United States regarding slavery and secession affected Indian Territory. The 1835 census taken of the Cherokee Nation while still in Georgia showed, "Of the total population, 8,936 were Cherokees, 776 were slaves, and 68 were intermarried whites."[5] During the removal in 1839, slaves made the arduous trek along with their Cherokee owners, and as the Cherokee settled their new land, agriculture became increasingly important, along with the use of slaves. Although much progress had been made to establish new businesses, a government structure and buildings, schools and churches, along with other supporting facets of life, the tensions created between the Treaty Party and John Ross's Party always existed. Although the Western Cherokees had officially abolished slavery in 1863, at the time the Western Cherokees entered the Civil War, whether for the Confederacy or the Union, slaves were held by both sides. Only a war that tore the republic apart would eventually "settle" the issue throughout the nation.

Lincoln became president with sweeping support of the North but little support of the South. Even before he took office on March 4, 1861, he faced the growing sentiments of slavery and secession. Realizing compromise between the various factions within the Republican and Democratic parties was impossible, seven southern slave states withdrew from the Union, establishing the Confederate States of America. When the Confederates attacked Fort Sumter on April 12, 1861, the United States officially divided with the North solidly behind Lincoln.

Eastern Cherokees Serve in Civil War

William Thomas, who served the Eastern Cherokee ably during and after the removal, was again able to serve them during the Civil War. Thomas, a North Carolina state senator, was on his seventh term when asked to be a delegate to the Confederate convention, where he cast a vote for the southern cause and immediately resigned from the Senate. He intended to raise funds and supplies to support the Confederate cause and discouraged the Indians from joining with the Confederates as active participants, rather planning for them to be scouts and home guards. His plans were thwarted when an agent came among the Cherokee and aroused their war spirit. Thereupon, Thomas accepted a commission as colonel and commanded the "Thomas Legion," which became legendary during the war. Of the approximately 400 able-bodied Cherokee men, all enlisted to serve under Thomas, initially bringing his contingent to 2,800 men.

"The Cherokee troops that fought under Thomas became increasingly feared by their enemies. They were famous for their skill and persistence in tracking escapees and bushwhackers."[6] Their exploits became almost mystic, but their loyalty was more for Thomas than the Confederate cause.

Upon enlisting, the Cherokee sought out their priests, who recited the war prayer formulas for four nights before they set out to meet the enemy. They "... also consulted a medicine man who had a divining stone. Interestingly enough, only two or three were wounded in actual battle, and none was killed."[7] A few did succumb to the diseases of the other combatants.

It was not until 1866 that North Carolina gave the federal government assurances they would grant state citizenship to the Cherokees. Desperately needed money from the 1848 removal fund had not been paid out to them during this period. It was not until 1875, almost 30 years later, that money was made available by the U.S. government to "… purchase lands and the quieting of titles for the benefit of the Indians."[8]

Indians Penalized as Annuities Are Withheld

Concerned about funds falling into enemy hands, the United States refused to pay annuities to the Cherokee as stipulated in the 1835 treaty. Depending heavily upon the annuities to support their government, police and schools, tribal leaders questioned the validity of a government that did not honor payments guaranteed by treaty. The South played on this concern, pointing out that a large amount of the investment of tribal funds was in southern state bonds. If the South lost the war, the bonds would be forfeited, causing further financial hardship on all the tribes. It can be helpful to understand the congressional budget process and how withholding payments of annuities or, in current times, closing down the federal government over an impasse between legislators, can devastate individuals and families, as well as Indian tribes. On *nationalpriorities.org* there is an article titled "Budget Process: Federal Budget 101" and it states, "The vision of democracy is that the federal budget – and all activities of the federal government – reflect the values of a majority of Americans."[9]

In addition to withholding annuities, the United States pulled the military from forts in Indian Territory in early 1861. To the consternation of the Indian tribes, the Texans, with whom the tribes had a history of violent relations, had proved willing to cross into Indian Territory to man the forts, as did Arkansans who also expressed willingness to help defend the forts. The incompetence of the United States caused concern for the tribes and many decided it was better to be with the Confederacy, which included the men from Texas and Arkansas, that:

> ... understood the importance of securing its western border and was willing to promise money, political participation and sovereignty. . . . Sovereignty included the right to determine citizenship, restrict residence within the nations, reject allotment and statehood, and control trade. The Confederacy also offered Indian delegate's participation in its legislature, a privilege the United States had never conferred.[10]

Civil War Devastated Indian Territory

When they finally signed a treaty with the Confederates, the Cherokee and Choctaw took advantage of the privilege to have a legislative delegate. Having a voice was extremely important, and that delegate kept the Confederate legislature informed as to the situation within Indian Territory, often expressing dissatisfaction with the lack of support from the South.

When the Western Cherokees entered the Civil War, they exemplified the precepts held within the United States. "The Civil War in Indian Territory followed a similar path; the outbreak of war followed decades of tensions and transition. Residents of the Cherokee Nation had split over issues in the past and would do so again."[11] The actions of the Cherokee were bound by their family and clan identities, their belief systems and how firmly they believed in the terms of existing treaties. Their position in the war was determined as an individual but even greater was tribal survival. "We do not wish our soil to become the battleground between the states and our homes to be rendered desolate and miserable by the horrors of civil war," he [Chief John Ross] wrote to one Confederate officer."[12] Ross spent the early part of 1861 maintaining Cherokee neutrality and striving to keep the Nation unified, which became increasingly difficult as events and people worked to divide them. Stand Waite, a leader of the Treaty Party, organized his followers into an armed unit aligned with the South and ready to defend themselves.

The effects of the unrest heightened as representatives from the Confederate government sought to include the Native peoples on their side. A Bureau of Indian Affairs had been organized by the new government in Richmond, and officials came to negotiate treaties, establish alliances and recruit soldiers. People from western Arkansas and Texas came to influence the Five Nations' decision, but the politics of the Cherokees, Chickasaws, Choctaws, Creek (Muscogee) and Seminole were as divergent as the tribes themselves. Chief Ross's goal was to maintain the autonomy of the Cherokee Nation and protect its borders, but the lack of support from the federal government, combined with the increasing number of alliances with the Confederates between members of the Treaty Party as well as other tribes, persuaded Ross that an alliance with the South made sense. Four thousand males attended the Cherokee council called by Ross in August 1861. He concluded his speech by urging them to align with the Confederates, which they did unanimously. The Five Nations, along with the Seneca's, Osages and Shawnees signed a treaty with the Confederates on October 7, 1861.

Russell Thornton, a sociologist and a Cherokee, wrote a scholarly essay titled "Demography of the Trail of Tears" which is included in *Cherokee Removal: Before and After,* and provides a description of the dire circumstances the Cherokees faced during and after the Civil War:

> Cherokees in Indian Territory formally sided with the Confederacy in the Civil War. However, the Cherokees were factionalized, and individual Cherokee fought on both sides in the war. The result was disastrous for them. Charles C. Royce describes the effects of the Civil War on the Cherokees: 'Raided and sacked alternately, not only the Confederate and Union forces, but by the vindictive ferocity and hate of their own factional divisions, their country became a blackened and desolate waste. Driven from comfortable homes, exposed to want, misery, and the elements, they perished like sheep in a snow storm. Their houses, fences, and other improvements were burned, their orchards destroyed, their flocks and herds slaughtered

or driven off, their schools broken up, and their schoolhouses given to the flames, and their churches and public buildings subjected to a similar fate, and that entire portion of their country which had been occupied by their settlements was distinguishable from the virgin prairie only by the scorched and blackened chimneys and the plowed but now neglected fields'.[13]

Impoverishment Rampant Throughout Indian Territory

A field report dated February 1862 by Army surgeon A. B Campbell reported on the conditions in the Indian refugee camps of the Civil War:

> It is impossible for me to depict the wretchedness of their condition. The only protection from the snow upon which they lie is prairie grass, and from the wind and weather scraps and rags which did not conceal their nakedness, and I saw 7 varying in age from 3-15 years without a thread upon their bodies ... They greatly need medical assistance, many have their toes frozen off, other's feet are wounded by sharp ice or branches of trees lying on the snow ...[14]

Many have written about the losses suffered by the Natives during the Civil War; however, Clarissa W. Confer gave a succinct appraisal when she wrote in *The Cherokee Nation in the Civil War:*

> Although much could be repaired, structures rebuilt, and farms replanted, some damage proved to be permanent. The disappearance of cattle as a result of widespread rustling ranked high among the most obvious long-term losses. Estimates place the number of cattle run out of Indian Territory into Kansas at 300,000 head, worth $4 million. ... Fraud at the expense of the Natives would continue to be a hallmark of the government, but the immediate consequence of the cattle raids for the Indians was the loss of a critical food supply and personal wealth that would never be recovered.[15]

As with many wars fought on home ground, families were not spared. Women remained to care for and defend the children and home. Raiders from the neighboring states and territories, as well as bushwhackers, practiced a type of guerrilla warfare, striking families and individuals in rural areas. Subsistence farming was done only to have the crops, as well as homes, destroyed, leaving people starving and destitute. The villages were not spared, as demonstrated in the ransacking, looting and burning of the leaders' homes. Thousands of civilian Indian refugees poured into Kansas for any protection, food and clothing the Union forces could afford them. Native soldiers returned home as often as possible to assist their families, but they had a difficult time just maintaining themselves, as they had to provide their own horses, rations, clothing and blankets – items that were supplied by the government to the white soldiers.

White soldiers received military training and muskets, while the Indian soldiers received plain muzzle-loading rifles and no training by the Union or Confederate military. During the four-year war, "Nearly 18,000 Indian soldiers served in the ever-shifting contest, fighting for both the Union and Confederacy and occasionally switching sides."[16] Stand Watie's Treaty Party regiment was trained and ready to fight, with the goal of ultimately breaking free of the Ross power structure. As soon as the council voted to join the Confederates, the Cherokee Executive Committee organized a "mounted regiment for Confederate service."[17]

Stand Watie's wife, Sarah, and their children, along with other prominent Confederate families, were forced to evacuate the Cherokee Nation, moving south into Chickasaw and Choctaw territory or, in Sarah's case, to the safety of relatives in Texas. "Chief Ross's own family lost homes and belongings amid indiscriminate violence. It seemed that everyone bore the ravages of the war."[18] Diaries and letters preserved from that period provide information on the lives and difficulties endured by soldiers and civilians. This is not, however, a realistic picture of the trials endured by the poor and uneducated who were known to be unable to evacuate to safer surroundings and had no means of recording the hardships they endured.

By 1862, Chief Ross believed that the Confederate forces had been ineffective in providing for and protecting the Cherokee Nation and its allies. As Ross was wavering in his support of the Confederacy, Missionary Evan Jones delivered a letter from the Superintendent of Indian Affairs, which reaffirmed the Union's treaty obligations. "Ross's pledge to the Confederacy had been made in good faith and was not lightly broken. His ultimate loyalty, however, was to the Cherokee people, who now seemed better served by the strengthening Union forces on their doorstep."[19] The Army commander solved Ross's dilemma when the chief, his family and supporters were arrested and immediately paroled on July 15, 1862. The group was then provided an Army escort to Union territory. "The Cherokee Nation was officially divided."[20]

Negotiations Illustrate U.S. Resolve to Punish Indians

President Lincoln was assassinated on April 15, 1865, and the Civil War ended by proclamation on May 9, 1865. The hard-won results celebrated in the East included Union victory, slavery officially abolished by the 13th Amendment five months earlier in January, preservation of territorial integrity, dissolution of the Confederate States and the beginning of the Reconstruction Era. It also meant another round of treaty negotiations for the Indian people:

> Federal commissioners met the representatives of the Five Nations at Fort Smith, Arkansas, in September 1865... This group traveled to Arkansas, as it turned out, not only to deal with the Indian Nations. They also met with lobbyists and politicians from Kansas who clamored for the opportunity to solve their 'Indian problem' by relocating unwanted tribes to Indian Territory.[21]

Stand Watie firmly believed that the two Cherokee factions could not coexist and wanted the country divided. John Ross did not agree, arguing that the Cherokee Nation must remain united. The negotiations failed, and new negotiations were moved to Washington, D.C. with a date set for January 1866.

Ross' first wife, Quatie, died of pneumonia early February 1839, as they traveled the Trail of Tears. Mary Brian Stapler became his second wife in 1844, and it was to the safety of her family in Philadelphia that they now moved. From here, Ross endeavored to represent his people in Washington, D.C. Mary died July 20, 1865, his beloved home in Tahlequah was destroyed and his health was failing. The task before him was arduous, but he was determined to hold the Nation together. The Union gained a formidable opponent in Ross as they, the victors, sought onerous stipulations in new treaties with the Indians. Commissioner of Indian Affairs Dennis Cooley led a campaign to brand Ross a traitor for leading his People in rebellion against the United States and signing with the Confederate States. By discrediting Chief Ross, the commissioner sought to gain the leverage needed to break up the Cherokee Nation. "Cooley published his charges in a pamphlet titled "The Cherokee Question," forcing Ross, in the last days of his life, to endure scathing attacks on his character and leadership ..."[22]

The requirement for negotiations to be held in Washington, D.C placed hardships on the Indian Nations, causing concerns about the expense to tribal representatives when the money could best be used to alleviate the suffering and starvation of the Native people who were struggling to rebuild their lives and their country from the ravages of war. In her book, *Cherokee Nation in the Civil War,* Clarissa Confer states "It also deprived the nations of their strongest leaders in an extremely difficult period of adjustment after the war,"[23] Referencing January 1866, she stated:

> Refusing to be passive victims, the Five Nations had representatives and legal counsel in Washington who acted on their behalf. The Choctaws and Chickasaws struck the best deal with the government, gaining a settlement deemed by scholars to be the 'least reconstructive' of all the treaties. The Creeks and Seminoles lost a great deal of land in their treaties but managed to reunite their societies after the divisions of the war.[24]

Factionalism Reignited

The factionalism that plagued the Cherokees from the early 1830s and resulted in the removal treaty of 1835 again manifested itself in the divisions during the Civil War and brought the parties representing the Watie and Ross factions to the negotiations in Washington. Watie and Ross each had visions for the future of the Cherokee Nation, but how they proposed accomplishing those visions varied greatly, which put them at odds when negotiating a treaty at the end of the war. The U.S. negotiators argued that the Cherokee people had entered the war on the side of the Confederacy, even though many members had fought, died or suffered privation in support of the Union. The goal of the negotiators was to reduce the land holdings, withhold annuities and punish the tribes. Cooley took advantage of the situation to play one against the other and worked with Watie to sign a treaty advantageous to the United States, which required the Cherokee to give up considerable territory in exchange for some money and, most important to Watie, the division of the Cherokee Nation. He maintained that the divisiveness within the Nation resulting from the 1835 Treaty, the removal and the internal strife since arriving in Indian Territory, coupled with the fractures from the Civil War, was sufficient to warrant this division.

Chief John Ross Prevails

Ross exerted his considerable diplomatic skills to make sure that the Cherokee Nation remained as one unified Nation. Accordingly, he met with President Johnson to protest Cooley's attempts to discredit him. On February 15, 1866, the Ross delegation met with President Johnson, Secretary [of the Interior] Harlan and Commissioner Cooley where documents of the Fort Smith negotiations were presented, and Ross clarified some information, and, in fact, provided information that Cooley had not included in his report:[25]

> ... [Ross] refused to yield to a division of his Cherokee Nation and fought hard to counteract Cooley's decision by lobbying Congress and the President to refuse ratification. He worked behind the scenes with Radical Republicans predisposed to distrust

Confederates and rallied public opinion to his side from the editorial pages of the *New York Tribune*. The treaty was rejected.[26]

Despite his failing health, which required working from his hotel room, Ross masterfully directed the work to obtain the best possible outcome for the Cherokee:

> Proceeding as a strong ally of the United States, the Ross delegation presented a treaty predicated on the fact that all previous treaties between the parties were still in effect, pointedly repudiating Cooley's position that the Cherokees had forfeited their rights. While the loyalist Cherokees generously granted protection of rights and property to their southern brethren, they also asserted control over railroad land grants, criminal and civil jurisdiction in the nation, and the access of other tribes to the Cherokee' excess lands.[27]

Ross died on August 1 but not before he learned that the government had recognized both his loyalty and leadership of the Cherokee Nation. The final treaty ratified by the Senate and proclaimed on August 11, 1866, "… conceded much but retained what Ross had fought for most of his life to achieve – a single western Cherokee Nation:"[28]

> The treaty enabled the sale of the Cherokee Neutral Lands, settlement of the Kansas Indians on unoccupied Cherokee lands, and specified a two-hundred-foot right-of-way for railroads, considerably less than lobbyists had expected. … No southern states were forced to surrender land to the federal government, but it was a predetermined fact to the negotiations with Indians. The Cherokee Nation gave up territory, so the government could pursue its goal of concentrating all unwanted Native people in Indian Territory. In a requirement that both paralleled and exceeded demands made on former Confederate slave owners, Indian slaves had to be adopted into the tribes or given land with their new freedom. … The government even forced them to admit members of

other tribes to citizenship."[29]

Freedmen

Article 9 of the 1866 treaty specifies the abolishment of slavery; however, in 1863, the Cherokee national council had already voluntarily abolished slavery. At the same time, the council abolished involuntary servitude within the Nation unless as a punishment of a crime. The 1866 treaty stipulated all freedmen and their descendants who resided in the Nation at that time or who returned within six months would have all the rights of Native Cherokees. Every Cherokee and freedmen were given the rights to 160 acres east of the Creek reservation.

Citizenship of the freedmen has been contested over the years, beginning with enrollment of tribal members required by the Dawes Commission in the late 1800s. "In the early 1980s, the Cherokee Nation administration amended citizenship rules to require direct descent from an ancestor listed on the 'Cherokee By Blood' section of the Dawes Rolls."[30] The proviso had been contested in the Cherokee Supreme Court, and the citizenship rules have changed several times since then. In 2017, "… the U.S. District Court ruled in favor of the Freedmen descendants … and the Cherokee Nation has accepted this decision…"[31] Some of the freedmen descendants have stated that after several decades of struggle to maintain their Cherokee citizenship, they are ambivalent about their ties.

The Civil War pitted "brother against brother" across the United States, yet when the war was over, the Union did not require the South to provide lands to the emancipated slaves. It was, however, a foregone conclusion that the Indian tribes would be required to surrender lands. This was in recognition of their support of the Confederacy, which provided a further benefit to the Union as it freed more lands for white settlement. Additionally, Article 15 of the treaty stipulated that the Cherokee would provide lands to other Indian tribes. This was done so that "The United States may settle any civilized Indians, friendly with the Cherokees and adjacent tribes, within the Cherokee country, on unoccupied lands east of 96°…"[32]

Counting Lives Lost

Regarding the war, in *Mankiller: A Chief and Her People,*
Wilma Mankiller stated "… at least one-quarter of the tribal
population had lost their lives. So many of our people died that one
of the main priorities became the construction of an orphanage."[33]
Russell Thornton's essay summarizes the U.S. census of 1894, the
writings of James Mooney in 1900 and that of Stearn & Stearn in
1945 as illustrative of the situation:

> … [These sources] asserted that the Cherokee
> population figures in Indian Territory declined by
> 7,000 as a result of the five-year Civil War – from
> 21,000 to 14,000 – and that the war left 'their whole
> country in ashes.' Smallpox also continued to infect the
> Cherokees, particularly in 1865-1866, immediately
> after the Civil War, and in 1899-1900.[34]

Smallpox again played a significant role in the deaths
recorded; however, during the Civil War, it indiscriminately
affected all soldiers – whites, Blacks and Natives alike.

> Smallpox was just one note in a symphony of terrifying
> diseases that killed more Civil War soldiers than
> bullets, cannon balls and bayonets ever did. Although
> estimates vary on the number of soldiers who died during
> the war, even the most recent holds that about two of
> every three men who died were slain by disease.[35]

Struggle to Obtain Benefits

Charles J. Kappler's compilation of treaties provides this
information on the 1866 treaty. Article 25 stipulated:

> A large number of the Cherokees who served in the
> Army of the United States having died, leaving no heirs
> entitled to receive bounties and arrears of pay on
> account of such service, it is agreed that all bounties
> and arrears for service in the regiments of Indian United
> States volunteers which shall remain unclaimed by any
> person legally entitled to receive the same for two years
> from the ratification of this treaty, shall be paid as the

national council may direct, to be applied to the foundation and support of an asylum for the education of orphan children, which asylum shall be under the control of the national council, or of such benevolent society as said council may designate, subject to the approval of the Secretary of the Interior.[36]

Thousands of Cherokee soldiers were loyal to the Union, many of whom died or were severely wounded. However, it was at the discretion of the Secretary of the Interior whether to forward their accrued pay for the benefit of the Cherokee tribe. Even prior to Lincoln's assassination, the United States was hostile towards the tribe, an attitude that strengthened in President Andrew Johnson's administration. The Cherokee Nation was guaranteed lands with fee-title status (granted full interest in real property) in the 1835 treaty which required their removal to the West. The hostile attitude of the government enabled Congress to pass laws stripping the fee-title status, which facilitated the government's negotiations of the 1866 treaty. The new struggles of the Cherokee Nation produced costs as devastating as the removal of 1839 with stipulations which "… required [they] surrender land, open their territory to railroads, and begin the process that would ultimately produce statehood."[37] Thus ended the treaty era.

Author's Thoughts

The end of the Civil War marked another round of aggressive endeavors by the public and government officials to acquire Indian lands. This was done through a series of laws put in place to solve the "Indian problem" and open land to white settlement. As usual, Native Americans were not consulted but informed after the fact about what they were required to do.

Yes, the treaty era ended, but what many may not know is that those treaties are in *full force and effect* until amended by a vote of the House of Representatives and Senate and signed by the president. Unless amended as stated by law, the treaties still govern the relations between the various tribes and the federal government with many still in effect in the 21st century. Monies owed to the Indian tribes are held in trust by the United States

Treasury to be paid out at the direction of the Bureau of Indian Affairs under the purview of the Department of the Interior. The government has not upheld its fiduciary obligations, admitting to destroying documents, while other papers have been lost, making it difficult to achieve an accurate accounting. Annuities promised and not yet paid are still owed to either the tribe or individuals as stipulated.

The Five Civilized Tribes of Indian Territory: Creeks, Choctaws, Chickasaws, Seminole and Cherokee are autonomous tribes, and the government negotiated individual treaties with the tribes at the conclusion of the Civil War. The negotiators forced the tribes to surrender land to the government, which was to be used to settle other Indian tribes from the central United States – perpetually shrinking the lands occupied by Native Americans to benefit the ever-growing sea of immigrants.

In addition to the lands lost, negotiations included admitting the freedmen into the individual tribes, and the government stipulated in the treaties with the Cherokees, Creeks and Seminoles that the former slaves should be granted full citizenship. There was pushback from the Choctaws and Chickasaws resulting in "… an optional provision in their peace treaty [whereby] the United States agreed to remove the freedmen within two years and colonize them elsewhere if the Indians should decide against adoption. …"[38] Both tribes were quick to vote against the adoption of the freedmen; however, the U.S. never fulfilled its promise to remove the freedmen, and the Choctaws and Chickasaws had to address the issue in later years.

Ironically, several additional, onerous stipulations were included in the Native American treaties. First, "The government forced them to admit members of other tribes to citizenship,"[39] and second, where the Indians were required to give land to the freedmen, the same was not required of the Confederate slaveholders. The government did differentiate between what it believed were "wild' and "not-so-wild" Indians when they required the Cherokee to accept the not-so-wild Delaware and Shawnee Indians into citizenship. The irony is that neither the Cherokee nor the Delaware and Shawnee had a choice in the government's decision. And, this edict cleared a portion of Kansas for settlement – the ultimate goal. Given the arbitrary historical pronouncements of the U.S. government, it is clear that the Natives never had a choice or voice and that continues as is seen in many of the adjudications in the 21st Century.

Endnotes:

1   Anderson, William L., Jane L. Brown & Anne F. Rogers, edited & annotated by. *The Payne-Butrick Papers: Volumes 1, 2, 3.* U of Nebraska P, 2010, pp. 129-130.

2   Holt, Michael. "Zachary Taylor: Domestic Affairs." *U of Virginia, Miller Center.* https://bit.ly/2H9b8u7

3   Holt.

4   "The Compromise of 1850." *Anchor: A North Carolina History Online Resource. https:*//bit.ly/31eThsF.

5   Wilms, Douglas C. "Cherokee Land Use in Georgia Before Removal." *Cherokee Removal: Before and After,* edited by William L. Anderson, U of Georgia P, 1991, p. 13.

6   "Civil War Era NC." https://cwnc.omeka.chass.ncsu.edu. Accessed 2 Sep 2019.

7   Mails, Thomas E. *The Cherokee People, The Story of the Cherokees from Earliest Origins to Contemporary Times.* Marlowe & Co., 1992, p 102.

8   Mooney, James. *History, Myths, and Sacred Formulas of the Cherokee.* Bright Mountain Books, 1992, p 168.

9   "Fighting for a U.S. federal budget that priorities peace, economic security and shared prosperity — Budget Process: Federal Budget 101." *National Priorities Project.* https://bit.ly/3673kkQ. Accessed 7 Nov 2020.

10 Confer, Clarissa W. *The Cherokee Nation in the Civil War.* U of Oklahoma P, 2007, p. 47.

11 Confer. p. 17.

[12] Confer. p. 43.

[13] Thornton, Russell. "The Demography of the Trail of Tears Period: A New Estimate of Cherokee Population Losses." *Cherokee Removal: Before and After*, edited by William L. Anderson, U of Georgia P, 1991, note 3, p. 93.

[14] Confer, Clarissa W. *The Cherokee Nation in the Civil War."* U of Oklahoma P, 2007, pp. 118-119.

[15] Confer. 145-147

[16] Confer. p. 52.

[17] Confer. p. 55.

[18] Confer. p. 81.

[19] Confer. p. 79.

[20] Confer. p. 79.

[21] Confer. pp. 148-149.

[22] Confer. p. 153.

[23] Confer. p. 151.

[24] Confer. pp. 151-153.

[25] Confer. pp. 154-155.

[26] Confer. p. 155.

[27] Confer. p. 154.

[28] Confer. p. 155.

[29] Confer. p. 156.

[30] "Cherokee freedmen controversy." https://bit.ly/37ta9zR. Accessed 2 Sep 2019.

[31] Chow, Katt, reporter. "Judge Rules That Cherokee Freedmen Have Right to Tribal Citizenship." August 31, 2017. https://n.pr/3m0F3mP.

[32] Kappler, Charles J. compiler and editor. *Indian Treaties 1778-1883*. Amereon House, 1972, Article 15, p. 946.

[33] Mankiller, Wilma and Michael Wallis. *Mankiller: A Chief and Her People*.
St Martin's Press, 1993. p. 128.

[34] Thornton, Russell. "The Demography of the Trail of Tears Period: A New Estimate of Cherokee Population Losses." *Cherokee Removal: Before and After*, edited by William L. Anderson, U of Georgia P, 1991, note 3, p. 94.

[35] Eschner, Kat. "Fearing a Smallpox Epidemic, Civil War Troops Tried to Self-Vaccinate." 1 May 2017. https://bit.ly/3dyK8A1.

36 Kappler, Charles J. compiler and editor. *Indian Treaties, 1778-1883*. Amereon House, 1972, p. 949.

37 Strickland Rennard and William M. Strickland, "Beyond the Trail of Tears: One Hundred Fifty Years of Cherokee Survival." *Cherokee Removal: Before and After*, edited by William L. Anderson, U of Georgia P, 1991, pp. 116-117.

38 Angie Debo. *And Still the Waters Run: The Betrayal of the Five Civilized Tribes*. Princeton UP, 1940. p. 10.

39 Confer, Clarissa W. *The Cherokee Nation in the Civil War*. U of Oklahoma P, 2007, p. 156.

| NINE |

Peace But at What Cost ?
1785 to Oklahoma Statehood in 1907

With the surrender of General Robert E. Lee, the American Civil War was over, and the nation was once again united, although the country had suffered great losses of family members, homes, businesses and property. The government assessed those losses and prioritized them to affect the reconstruction process. However, while the Civil War occupied the nation, a number of internal factors were in play across the country, as well as external forces which would significantly impact specific groups of people, including Native Americans.

Land Ordinance of 1785

The wave of humanity continually arriving on the shores of the new republic was a benefit to the growing expansionist plans of government and religious leaders, as well as the American people in general. Accordingly, the Land Ordinance of 1785 was established by the U.S. Congress of the Confederation and created a system to survey and plot out townships on the lands purchased from the Indians. The legislation provided a mechanism to subdivide the townships for resale, which enabled the settlers to purchase farmland surrounding the townships as settlements progressed west. Recognizing the need for schools, the sale of township lots and farmland provided funding that the young country used to establish public education. As the nation expanded west, the states added ordinances to the Land Ordinance, which covered religion, inspired civic duty and provided a framework for spreading democratic ideals. The new arrivals pushed across Indian lands, with some traveling all the way to California.

149

Many elected to go to homestead lands specifically set aside by treaty between an Indian nation and the federal government regarding these homesteads. Article 3 of the 1835 treaty states, "… they shall also be protected against interruption and intrusion from citizens of the United States, who may attempt to settle in the country without their consent; and all such persons shall be removed from the same by order of the President of the United States. …"[1] Outsiders came into Cherokee Territory and settled on the choice lands – put up their cabins and fenced the ground, growing livestock and crops. The Cherokee had no legal recourse to keep the settlers out nor did they have legal recourse to evict the ones who were there. And the U.S., although obligated by treaty, refused to take action against the settlers. Rather, the government facilitated the white expansion by not doing so.

Two other pieces of legislation that impacted the entire West and the Native Americans living there were "… the 1862 Homestead Act [which] encouraged agricultural settlement on dry western lands unsuitable for settler farming techniques developed in the east … the Desert Land Act [1877] amended the Homestead Act and provided federal money for western irrigation projects."[2] The results of these two acts can be seen in the 21st century as water becomes a scare resource.

Wagon Trains and Settlers

The Cherokee were occupied with the rebuilding of their Nation and did not feel the immediate effects of the settlers and their wagon trains, as Cherokee land was south and east of the main trails; however, the railroad made great inroads, bisecting Cherokee country north to south and east to west. Article 15 of the 1866 Treaty at the end of the Civil War was yet to be enacted which allowed the United States to "… settle any civilized Indians, friendly with the Cherokees and adjacent tribes, within the Cherokee Country…"[3] but that time was coming.

Traveling mainly by wagon train, the settlers started in Kansas City, Missouri, and the trails fanned out in a radius from there. The major trails included the Oregon Trail into Portland, Oregon and the Santa Fe Trail to Santa Fe, New Mexico, there joining the Old Spanish Trail to Los Angeles, California. The Indians watched as their land was crisscrossed by a sea of wagon trains, with multitudes of people killing the game, cutting trees for firewood and leaving behind litter – early environmental concerns. Gold discoveries caused further movement, as the men went from one discovery to another hoping to strike it rich. The first was California in 1848, then Colorado in 1849, Montana in 1860s and on to Alaska in 1899. The Bozeman Trail took gold seekers northwest into Montana starting in 1863, and from there, they could join the Oregon Trail.

Pony Express, Telegraph and Railroads

Pony Express riders rode through Missouri, Kansas, Nebraska, Wyoming, Utah and Nevada, finally arriving in California. They were the early lifeblood of the country, providing written communications east to west and west to east for private citizens, businesses and government. On their heels came the telegraph lines which allowed businesses and the government to communicate instantaneously. Because of the cost, few people sent telegrams, but the telegraph lines were installed close to the rail lines and provided support for the railroad industry.[4] The telegraph helped the government in its westward expansion as it allowed military orders to be transmitted quickly down the chain of command. This enabled local governments to stay in touch with territorial governments, making it easier to govern as the nation expanded west.

A third component to the westward expansion was the completion of the transcontinental railroad in 1869; however, it also "… escalated conflicts between Native American tribes and settlers who now had easier access to new territories."[5] Towns sprung up at rail termini, which provided for transportation of passengers, cattle and produce to and from these points, all supporting the development of land outside of the towns. With the passing of the Homestead Act and Desert Land Act, The Northern Pacific Railway "… opened colonization offices in Germany, Sweden, Denmark, Norway, and England to entice European immigrants to settle the Northern Plains and, therefore, to create a demand for railroad transportation."[6]

The transcontinental railroad included spurs to remote areas of the country, which allowed the Army and others quick access to areas previously difficult to reach. The bison herds, which provided meat for the men building the railroads, as well as the mainstay of life for the Plains Indians, disappeared. Shot from trains for sport, the hides were sent back east and the bison, which had provided the Indians with food, as well as hides for clothing and shelter for generations, were left to rot. With this economic base gone, the Indian leaders lost their political autonomy and were forced to rely on the Bureau of Indians Affairs. The U.S. authorities wanted the Indians to settle down, and the loss of the bison helped caused that to happen and also deepened their reliance on the annuities.

Peaceful Cheyenne Camp Attacked

The cost of peace proved high for a group of 600 Cheyenne camped at Sand Creek not far from Denver, Colorado. In 1865, Col. John Chivington led an attack of 700 heavily armed soldiers on the Cheyenne who were camped under a white flag and an American flag to show they were not hostile. That did not prevent the soldiers from killing and mutilating the vast majority with only a few escaping to tell of the horrific tragedy. When President Theodore Roosevelt became president in 1901, he is quoted as saying the massacre was ". . . as righteous and beneficial a deed as ever took place on the frontier."[7]

> I saw some Indians that had been scalped, and the ears were cut off of the body of White Antelope. One Indian who had been scalped had also his skull all smashed in, and I heard that the privates of White Antelope had been cut off to make a tobacco bag out of. I heard some men say that the privates of one of the squaws had been cut out and put on a stick. — Captain L. Wilson, First Colorado Cavalry[8]

> Damn any man who sympathizes with Indians! ... I have come to kill Indians, and believe it is right and honorable to use any means under God's heaven to kill Indians. Kill and scalp all, big and little; nits make

lice. —Col. John Milton Chivington[9]

The Indian Peace Commission created by Congress in 1867 provided recommendations for dealing with the Indians which were meant to make it safer for persons moving westward. When President Ulysses S. Grant came into office in 1869, The Peace Commission made a good background for his proposed peace policy, which he presented in his first annual message to the Congress in December 1869. Some of the recommendations included the following: supervision of Indian affairs would not be turned over to the War Department, the Office of Indian Affairs be made an independent establishment, all superintendents and agents to be removed and the competent and faithful reappointed, the laws governing trade be revised, the states and territories forbidden to call out troops to wage war against Indians and adequate provision be made for removing trespassers on Indian land.[10]

The Army believed it was best positioned to force the Indians to work, and General Sherman and others fought to bring about acculturation of the Indians at "the point of the bayonet..."[11] The peace policy prompted President Grant to put several religious organizations to work with the Indians, as their mission work would be the most humanitarian and enable them to provide religious training as well. The history of the Bureau of Indian Affairs (BIA) is rooted in the Continental Congress, and in 1824, the BIA came under the administration of the Secretary of War. It was subsequently transferred to the U.S. Department of Interior in 1849, where it has remained. Because of its early history, military personnel were often selected to be Indian agents. With the institution of the peace policy, civil offices could not be filled by military personnel. Now, Indian agents were appointed by the president and confirmed by the Senate, and the president often used recommendations of the religious organizations in selecting agents.[12]

Fight for Survival Shifts to Halls of Congress

"Treaty making had been abandoned in 1871; however, agreements continued to be made subject to the approval of both the Senate and the House of Representatives before they became law."[13]

"Thus, in 1871,the fights for survival shifted from the open fields of treaty negotiation to the closed legislative halls of Congress."[14] Even today it is necessary for Native groups to have paid staff in Washington, D.C. to represent their interests when Congress is in session. The 1800s were no different, and over $30,000 was spent by the Cherokees in 1876 maintaining a delegation to fight "… attempts to break down the treaty barriers which keep the speculators and railroad land grabbers off our possessions."[15] Bills would be introduced, fought against and dropped, only to be reintroduced with slightly different wording, but with the same intent, in the next session of Congress. The financial cost of these fights, which included travel to Washington, D.C. and associated expenses, prevented the money from being used for the well-being of the Cherokee people, including education, healthcare, protecting orphans, and infrastructure and land improvements.

Cherokee Lewis Downing served as a Lt. Col. in the Union Army during the Civil War and directed his efforts to serving the Cherokee Nation after the war. In 1871, during his second term as the elected Principal Chief of the Cherokee, he turned his attention to uniting the Cherokee into one Nation, which required bringing the divergent interests of the Old Settlers (now the Keetoowah), the Treaty Party and Ross Party together. They were one Nation on paper but not in the hearts and minds of the People. The National Council adopted the seal of the Cherokee Nation, and it was approved in 1871 to commemorate the unification council Sequoyah had presided over in 1839 – rebuilding had begun.

Cherokee Laws Ignored Amid Westward Expansion

As westward expansion continued, outsiders ignored the laws of the Cherokee people and continued to rob and steal, sneaking onto the land to take timber. Simultaneously, outsiders again broke Cherokee law, as squatters laid claim to the most desirable portions of their land – something that concerned the Cherokee even as they were forced from their lands in the east.

The seven-million acres and the outlet guaranteed to the Cherokee in the 1835 Treaty were further solidified by a land patent, the highest evidence of title to a defined area, which was signed by the president and dated December 31, 1839. "A land patent is a supreme title to land which was originally acquired within the United States of America by a treaty. It grants the rights to ... the individual person named on the patent and to their heirs and their assigns forever."[16] Holders of land patents also have the rights to the mineral resources, and the Cherokee land of Oklahoma is rich in raw materials, which should have benefitted the Cherokee people. However, it took the federal government until the 21st century to pay the Cherokee on these resources guaranteed to them in the mid-1800s and that was only after an extended court battle.

After the Civil War, the Cherokee took greater advantage of the grazing lands of the Cherokee Outlet when cattle were increasingly driven along the Chisholm Trail from Texas to the railhead in Abilene, Kansas. The outlet proved a good stopping point for the cattle to graze and fatten for the northern market, and cattle interests aspired to lease it. In 1880, the Cherokee Strip Livestock Association leased the Cherokee Outlet for five-years for $100,000 a year, and it was renewed for another five years at $200,000 annually. The land was held in common, so the money was utilized for the common good of the People to "... build public facilities including schools and government offices."[17]

The Cherokee Outlet leases were seen by the federal government as an excuse to force the Cherokee and other tribes to cede those lands that the government saw as excess and not needed by the Indians. "Congress nullified the arrangement in March 1889 and authorized purchasing the region for $1.25 per acre."[18] This was far below the $3.00 per acre offered by the cattlemen. When the Cherokee protested, all grazing was forbidden by the government, and the Cherokee lost the annual grazing money. Without the financial resources provided by the Outlet lease, they lost their ability to continue building and making improvements. Forced to near bankruptcy, the Cherokee lacked the resources to fight the enactments perpetrated by Congress, which resulted in several long-term consequences. "The government forced the Cherokee to sell their Outlet lands for $1.25 per acre [and] in 1893, the Cherokee Outlet was opened to non-Indian settlement."[19] The U.S. did not pay the 1893 claim until 1964 and then only after protracted legal appeals. The compensation for the land only, not the natural resources, was as follows:

> The settlement brought approximately $14.7 million to the original allottees or their heirs. While officials performed the legal work required to disburse the payments, the principal earned nearly $2 million in interest, which the Cherokee Nation designated for programs to benefit the tribe as a whole.[20]

During the Civil War, the Keetoowah supported nationalistic aims, favored abolition of Black slavery and claimed loyalty to the Union. They continued their resistance after the Dawes Commission began forcing the transfer of Oklahoma tribal lands in the Indian Territory to individual ownership in the 1890. Individual allotments would mean the end of the Cherokee reservation that was held in common for all the People. Allotments of specific acreage depended on the sex and age of the recipient, with the ultimate goal of the government being to open up land not allotted for settlement by the whites. "After years of discussion … the Keetoowah Society decided to act to retrieve and retain in land and religion what either had been lost or was in danger of being lost. In 1896 … a committee was appointed to accomplish these ends."[21]

> During Redbird's visits to the Creeks, the Four Mother's Society was formed and became the instrument that united into one resistance organization the majority of the full bloods of four of the Five Civilized Tribes … In makeup, it resembled the old intertribal councils, and it retained lawyers and sent delegates to Washington to argue its cases.[22]

Greater Government Experimentation with Indian Policy

Over the years, Congress has passed acts that proved detrimental to the American Indians. The major one to consider is the Indian Intercourse Act of 1834, which was intended to concentrate the Indians west of the Mississippi and is exemplified by the removal of the Cherokees during the Trail of Tears, although there have been numerous other removals endured by every tribe at one or more times in the history of the United States.

The Indian Appropriations Act of 1871 established Indian reservations specifically forcing the Western Indians onto lands that previously belonged to the Five Civilized Tribes. As victors of the Civil War, the federal government rewrote the treaties, forcing the tribes to relinquish large swaths of land. Europeans considered lands designated for reservations as less desirable for settlement, and it was only when natural resources such as oil were discovered that the lands were coveted by the same people who previously believed it was not good enough for them but was good enough for the Indians.

Of equal importance, by the 1871 Indian Appropriations Act, Congress declared that the Indians were no longer free, independent nations but now were legally designated "wards" of the federal government. No longer independent nations "... the statute also declared no obligation of any treaty lawfully made and ratified with any such Indian nation or tribe prior to March 3, 1871, shall be hereby invalidated or impaired."[23] Although the act declared the Indians wards of the government, it also stipulated that the government was legally obligated to uphold all treaties that had been ratified. Unless amended, these same treaties are still in force in the 21st century and are the basis of numerous lawsuits against the U.S. government.

This act sparked conflicts known as the Indian Wars as Natives resisted being forced onto reservations, but the superior weapons and numbers of the Army ultimately compelled the Indians to surrender their independence and live on reservations dependent on government annuities – food, clothing and other essentials provided under contract from the lowest bidder. In addition to the inferior foods, moldy flour, poor quality meats and grains given to them, other foods that were typical of the settlers (an example being sugar) were introduced into the Indian diet. The Indians were also given poor quality tools and household goods. Required to relinquish their weapons, they could no longer hunt for the little game that remained on the reservations. Starvation was common, and disease spread rapidly among people who were used to living in open spaces but were now compelled to live in close quarters.

Rutherford B. Hayes came to the presidency during a time when greater experimentation with Indian policy was being advocated.

By way of recommendations for policy in the administration of Indian affairs, Commissioner Ezra Hayt itemized seven suggestions in 1877:

1. A code of laws for reservations and means for dispensing justice;
2. Indian police under white officers;
3. the promotion of agriculture and the division of land '. . . into farms of convenient size, the title to which shall be vested in individuals and inalienable for 20 years';
4. the establishment of a compulsory common school system, including industrial schools;
5. free access to Indians of missionaries;
6. insistence on labor in return for food and clothing; and
7. a steady concentration of the smaller bands on larger reservations.[24]

Lands Taken Under the Dawes General Allotment Act

When the Allotment Act became law on February 8, 1887, it did not include the Five Civilized Tribes; however, that changed in 1893 when the act's provisions were extended to include them. Individuals with each tribe were expected to enroll on the Dawes rolls. "This process assisted the BIA and the secretary of the interior in determining the eligibility of individual members for land distribution."[25] The full bloods (conservatives) were very suspicious of the government, as the government had proved time after time to be capricious and arbitrary. Wanting to maintain their way of life, the full bloods retreated to the hills and woods, refusing to enroll per the government's edict.

Not all of the government's actions were focused on gaining land as there were well-meaning individuals, like Senator Henry Dawes of Massachusetts, who felt they were working in the best interests of the Indians and put forward some of these acts.

However, without a true understanding of the culture and history of the different tribes, the acts were doomed to failure and caused more harm than good. In addition:

> The refusal of the government to adequately protect Indians in their rights against non-Indians played an important part in the failure of the *concentration* policy, the *reservation* policy, and the *allotment* policy. During each of the three periods mentioned, the Congress, time after time, responded to local non-Indian voters to the detriment of the Indians. Policies that failed to achieve the goals of civilization and assimilation set for the Indians often succeeded in securing the land or other resources as planned for the non-Indians.[26]

S. Lyman Tyler's book, *A History of Indian Policy,* stated the four primary goals of the Dawes Act. First and most important, the government believed that the Native Americans would be much better off with a white lifestyle and culture; therefore, the objective of the act was to eradicate tribal culture and replace it with the superior white civilization. The railroads, many predatory individuals and even the government coveted Indian lands, but the second goal of the Dawes Act was meant to protect the individual Indian from the grasp of those individuals and organizations. Though well intended, the act did not protect the Indians from the avaricious intent of those determined to obtain Indian lands. If the land was held by an individual Indian (allotment) instead of collectively by the tribe, it would be easier to acquire the land for expansion. It has been documented that a number of Indians were cheated out of their land while others sold outright. The third and fourth provisions were insidious in the continued efforts to separate the Native American from the land desired by the white government. Those provisions read:

> Since white individualism seemed to result in more rapid progress than tribal community life, it seemed desirable to break up tribal groups. ... Since allotment seemed to be a shortcut method for securing assimilation, this seemed to be a way to save the Government further expense in its relations with the

Indians.[27]

Simply stated, the Dawes Act "... tended to encourage Government officials to deal with individual Indians and Indian families, and to bypass tribal leaders and to sometimes ignore the tribal groupings."[28] Senator Dawes and the commission believed that the act would eliminate the reservations by breaking up the land and allotting it to individual Indians. The government was convinced that with title to their land, this would encourage the Indians to be farmers – to have domesticated animals and grow crops, eliminating the need to hunt and gather.

The reservation system was a program that the government ultimately wanted to bring to an end, but this did not happen:[29]

> The land allotted to the Indians included desert or near-desert lands unsuitable for farming. In addition, the techniques of self-sufficient farming were much different from their tribal way of life. Many Indians did not want to take up agriculture, and those who did want to farm could not afford the tools, animals, seed, and other supplies necessary to get started. There were also problems with inheritance. Often young children inherited allotments that they could not farm because they had been sent away to boarding schools. Multiple heirs also caused a problem; when several people inherited an allotment, the size of the holdings became too small for efficient farming.[30]

In 1887, American Indian land totaled more than 138,000,000 acres. Less than fifty years later, when the allotment policy was finally abandoned, only 48,000,000 acres remained in the hands of Native people. It was one of the most massive thefts in American history and created many landless and destitute Indians.[31]

> The land base of the Creeks, Choctaws, Seminoles, and Chickasaws was destroyed. The lands of the Five Tribes at the beginning of the allotment era constituted a total of 19,525,966 acres; 15,794,400 of those acres

were allotted to the Indian tribal citizens. The balance of 4 million acres included 309 town sites and segregated coal and timber lands, as well as other allotted lands that were sold at public auction.[32]

Even as these events took place, hope was held that it would be possible to establish two states from the territory. It was postulated that "The lands of the Five Tribes, known as the Indian Territory, would enter the Union as the state of Sequoyah; the Oklahoma Territory would join the Union as Oklahoma."[33] This symbolic struggle for statehood came to an end when Oklahoma became the 46th state admitted to the union on November 16, 1907 and encompassed all the lands, including those of the various Indian tribes.

Breaking up the land previously held in common for the entire tribe and dispersing it to individual Indian landholders proved disastrous for the Indians in several ways. The Indians had no concept for individually owned land and proved to be an easy target for the fraud and corruption of unscrupulous persons trying to purchase or cheat the Indians out of their land. Additionally, once the land was broken up and given to individual allottees, the secretary of the interior purchased the unassigned surplus land and opened it for public sale. The money gained from the sale of the land was to be held in trust by the secretary of the interior and provide for the "education, welfare, and civilization"[34] of tribal members as appropriated by the Congress. As will be shown in Chapter 13, lawsuits of the late 20th century and early 21st century proved the trust fund to be mismanaged through the years; therefore, no accurate financial audit can be provided. The law did, however, provide for Indians who received allotments to become United States citizens. Over the years, other laws declared Indians to be citizens under certain circumstances, but it wasn't until 1924 that Congress declared all Indians to be citizens – citizens without benefit of the Bill of Rights guaranteed to every other citizen of the United States.

Land Runs in Indian Territory

Originally thought to be unsuitable for white occupation, the almost two million acres of Indian Territory were opened by

Congress through a series of land runs. The first land run occurred on April 22, 1889, just six weeks after Benjamin Harrison became president. The land classified as unassigned was opened to settlers at high noon that day on a first-come basis. Funds from these runs were distributed to the various tribes by the Land Office. Oklahoma Territory was created in 1890. The Land Run of September 16, 1893, known as the Cherokee Strip Land Run, was the largest land run in U.S. history. It opened 8,144,682.91 acres (12,726 square miles) to settlement.

Where the Dawes Act tried and failed through negotiation with the Indian nations, the 1898 Curtis Act proved to be a significant legislative victory for the government, as it applied to all Indian nations. In a concerted effort to break up the territory or reservation held for the common good of all tribal members, the lands were surveyed, and a predetermined acreage set aside for town sites, schools, churches, charitable institutions, public buildings and graveyards. Once the sites specified by the government were determined, without input from the Cherokee, the surface of the remaining lands were allotted to individuals on the rolls: husband, wife, children and individuals:

> Another Cherokee treaty was introduced into Congress giving each Cherokee surface rights to eighty acres of land. This Chief Buffington bitterly opposed, declaring, 'Our enrollment is not yet complete, but it has reached the stage where we, our people, number only about 30,000 Cherokees and freedmen, and we own nearly 5 million acres of land. To offer of us only eighty acres is an outrage.'[35]

Curtis Act Reserves Mineral Rights

The Curtis Act of 1898 stipulated that the title of all mineral rights on the allotted land – oil, coal, asphalt, etc. – were reserved to the tribes. The money was to be deposited in a trust fund maintained by the secretary of the interior and paid directly to individuals. Previously, money from treaties or agreements between the government and tribes was paid to the tribe and used for the benefit of the entire tribe. In addition, without asking or receiving consent from the Indians involved, the Curtis Act effectively destroyed tribal governments through allotments and by abolishing the tribal courts. As of 1889, all civil and criminal trials previously handled by the tribal courts were transferred to the United States courts for that area.

Just as there was a difference of opinion between the progressives and the conservatives in their reaction to the 1835 treaty, which required the Cherokee to migrate west, the difference existed between the two groups as they faced the destructive forces of the Dawes Act and the Curtis Act. The progressives favored accepting allotment, the loss of the excess lands after allotment was accomplished and the very real possibility of statehood. The conservatives wanted to maintain their lands for the benefit of all and withdrew into their ancient ceremonies, seeking to retain their traditional culture and values.[36] In *Nations Remembered: An Oral History of the Cherokees, Chickasaws, Choctaws, Creeks, and Seminoles in Oklahoma, 1865-1907*, Theda Perdue states:

> A survey of the Indian Territory in 1900 disclosed that there was 101,000 Indians of all tribes, as compared to over 396,000 whites. The Indians' count naturally took in all men enrolled in the tribes, many of whom were entirely white but who had intermarried. ... Many white men, not members of Indian families, had been adopted by various tribes and thus given right of citizenship. ... The white man was rapidly taking possession of the country given by treaty to the Indian as his as long as grass grows and water flows.[37]

Treaty Period Ends

Treaties between the American Indian nations and the United States government can be broken into three distinct periods as delineated in the document, *Native American Heritage: American Indian Treaties* in the National Archives:

> From 1774 until about 1832, treaties between individual sovereign American Indian nations were negotiated to establish borders and prescribe conditions of behavior

between the parties.... From 1832 until 1871, American Indian nations were considered to be domestic, dependent tribes. Negotiated treaties between tribes and the U.S. had to be approved by the U.S. Congress. ... In 1871, the House of Representatives ceased recognition of individual tribes within the U.S. as independent nations with whom the United States could contract by treaty.[38]

When Charles J. Kappler's *Indian Treaties: 1778-1883* was reissued in 1972, Brantley Blue, Indian Claims Commissioner, wrote a new forward where he voiced the finality of the situation for Native Americans when he stated, "Thus, the period of Indian treaties closed. As the American nation became stronger, the Indians had declined. The old equality was over."[39]

When Congress declared the tribes to no longer be independent nations, events were set in motion as identified by Rennard and William Strickland in their essay "Beyond the Trail of Tears: One Hundred Fifty Years of Cherokee Survival." They identified the many struggles and challenges endured by Native American tribes in The Post Treaty Era (1871 – 1948), which were broken into two significant time frames. The first was from 1872 to 1906 when the tribes disputed efforts of "Tribal Dissolution," and the second was from 1907 to 1946 as they fought to preserve their "Tribal Identity."[40]

A series of laws were subsequently passed that were meant to replace tribal culture with white culture: protect the individual Indian allottee from the grasping hands of whites, the railroads and the government itself, break up tribal groups and secure assimilation for the individual Indian.[41]

It is easy for us to look back on the Allotment Act of 1887 and call it a failure, but to friends of the Indian groups, almost unanimously, it had seemed the solution to the Indian problem, *before it was tried*. Perhaps we should find in this a warning of the difficulties that surround attempts by one people, even in sincerity and friendship, to decide what is best for another.[42]

Presidents State Their Opinions on Indians

President Cleveland stated that he intended "… to have the Allotment Act applied slowly to a reservation at a time as each was properly prepared."[43] However, when Congress included a clause in the act that allowed the secretary of the interior to purchase surplus lands and open them for sale, the president's idea became moot. Consequently "…. Indian landholdings had shrunk from 155,632,312 acres in 1881 to 77,865,373 acres in 1900."[44]

Elected in 1904 as president, Theodore Roosevelt was always outspoken. He is quoted as having said, "I don't go so far as to think that the only good Indians are dead Indians, but I believe nine out of ten are, and I shouldn't like to inquire too closely into the case of the tenth."[45] G. Stanley Hall, an American psychologist and educator, concluded that the western exploration should eradicate all lower races as "weeds in the human garden:"[46]

> … Theodore Roosevelt, added his opinion that the extermination of the American Indians and the expropriation of their lands 'was as ultimately beneficial as it was inevitable. Such conquests,' he continued, 'are sure to come when a masterful people, still in its raw barbarian prime, finds itself face to face with the weaker and wholly alien race which holds a coveted prize in its feeble grasp.'[47]

Wilma Mankiller further expounded on Hall's thoughts when she wrote in *Mankiller: A Chief and Her People:*

> … even though Theodore Roosevelt called the Dawes Act 'a mighty pulverizing engine to break up the tribal mass,' the act failed because the American Indians considered land not as a possession but as a physical and spiritual domain shared by all living things.[48]

The distain of the United States government and the public at large was exemplified in the continual erosion of the treaty stipulations. Progress, though unwanted by the Indian people, came to their territory. Telephone companies secured the right to string wires across reservations in 1899, and electric power across reservations was granted in 1901. Even as railroad building continued across Indian country, Congress authorized public roads through Indian lands in 1901, and with the increased production of low-cost automobiles, the open lands and roads of Indian Territory brought the intrusions closer to Indian homes, bringing with it a new way of life. Then, on July 3, 1902, the secretary of the interior made the first oil and gas lease on Indian lands within the present boundaries of the state of Oklahoma. Within six years, oil development expanded at a remarkable rate, prompting about 22,000 additional leases. The money from these leases was to be held in trust by the Department of Interior for the benefit of the individual Indians.[49]

> The history of oil development in Oklahoma is intimately related to the alienation of Indian lands in the area occupied by the Five Civilized Tribes. It was oil, not agriculture, that was the prime incentive for exploitation, and that resulted in the separation of thousands of Oklahoma Indians from their lands and money.[50]

Between the end of the Civil War and Oklahoma becoming a state in 1907, the Cherokee marked many firsts within the Nation. Chief Mankiller included the establishment of the first free and compulsory public education system, the installation of the first telephone west of the Mississippi and the graduation of more students from college than in Texas and Arkansas combined.[51] These events did not impress everyone, particularly the military and the politicians. Many continued to look down on the Indians with little regard for them or their situation. The promises made in the 1835 treaty, which were legally binding on the United States government as well as the Cherokee, provided an exchange of the ancestral homeland for land in Indian Territory, where they would forever be left alone. Once again, Indians mourned the loss of land and homes as others celebrated with fancy parties and barbecues on November 16, 1907 when

President Roosevelt proclaimed that Oklahoma had been admitted as the forty-sixth state in the Union.

During Roosevelt's time in office, he made a concerted effort, in the name of conservation, to secure title to certain forest lands held by various western tribes. During his last two days in office, he signed eight executive orders which were designed to bring two and a half million acres of Indian reservation forest land within the bounds of contiguous national forests. "It was later determined that the action taken by President Roosevelt was beyond the power of the Executive. The lands were, therefore, returned to their former status."[52]

Author's Thoughts

The lofty goal that was stated by various presidents and legislators when arguing the merits and finally passing the Indian Removal Act indicated that lands would be set aside, lands where the Indians would be insulated from the white population – which again turned out to be just words. This became a moot point as Indian Territory was looked upon with desire by those same people. The white population was expanding throughout the country, and they wanted land. To satisfy the demand, the government sponsored seven land runs which brought thousands of people determined to establish homesteads on the free land that was offered to them. New towns sprang up with all the corresponding infrastructure of banks, barber shops, salons, mercantile interests, telegraph and land offices, schools, churches and railroads, along with the stagecoaches and other miscellaneous businesses. Breaking up the land for individual ownership is contrary to the Indian belief of holding the land in common for the use of all members of the tribe. The Indians were now interspersed with the white farms and businesses, further eroding the Native culture and values.

As other tribes in the Midwest from the Canadian border to the Mexican border were displaced, Congress sought land to force the consolidation of those tribes. Large expanses of the Cherokee territory were taken to accommodate the 39 (including the Cherokee Nation) tribes now living in Oklahoma. A 2012 USDA report on the land holdings within the Lakota and

Dakota reservations states:

> Non-Natives collect 84.5 percent of all agricultural income, controlling nearly 60 percent of the agricultural lands and 65 percent of all reservation-based farms. This includes the white billionaire and media tycoon Ted Turner, who owns more than a million acres of ranchland across the globe and more than 200,000 acres of Oceti Sakowin treaty land in western South Dakota. The radical scholar Cedric Robinson identified this system, in which a single white man owns more wealth and land then entire Indigenous nations, as racial capitalism."[53]

This situation is indicative of the legal and moral battles that Native Americans must continuously wage to obtain what is theirs. *All* treaties, even those ratified in the 1700s and 1800s, are still "in full force and effect" unless changed by law in the intervening years from the 1700s to now (2021).

By the stroke of a pen, Congress enacted the Indian Appropriations Act in 1871 that declared all Indians wards of the federal government. As wards they had no say in their lives, where they could live, how their children were educated, what they could do or even believe as their cultures were outlawed – again by the stroke of a congressional pen. Their chiefs and principal people were appointed by the president. In 2020, there are 573 federally recognized Indian Nations in the United States with approximately 230 of these Nations located in Alaska.

"However, over 80 indigenous tribes disappeared between 1900 and 1957, and of a population of over one million during this period, 80% had been killed through deculturalization, disease or murder."[54] All these contributed to the resultant genocide perpetrated on the Native population since the first encounters with the Europeans and continued through the stipulations of the Indians Appropriations Act and other federal laws. Then there was the massive loss of life wrought by the diseases imported from

Europe that decimated a people with no immune system to fight them. As a nation, we have a long way to go as we work together to recognize our First Citizens. Recent federal laws have recognized past problems, and from the mid-1950s to present day, the federal government has finally made attempts, often as a result of lawsuits by various Indian nations, to be more responsive to the needs of the individual Indian and the Indian nations.

After many years when their cultures and governments were denied to them, Native Americans have tribal governments that are responsible for all aspects of "... governmental activities on tribal lands. ..."[55] These rights have been hard won, also often as a result of lawsuits which required the government to relinquish control. Think about this – the Native Americans had to fight for the rights that should have been theirs all along. It's inexcusable, and anything unfairly taken should be returned, rights or otherwise.

In a long and pervasive pattern of reneged promises, the federal government has failed Native Americans; however, an indomitable will is seen in the over 370,000 citizens of the Cherokee Nation. Many of them live and work internationally, striving to maintain and grow their culture and increase the number of people fluent in the Cherokee language. While growing as individuals, they continue to work together to benefit their communities and, as they have for centuries, they take into consideration their actions of today and what effect it will have on the next seven generations – the time frame Cherokees use as opposed to a number of years.

As a country, we need to recognize our social and moral obligations to Native Americans and stand by our treaty obligations – not just when it benefits us, but always.

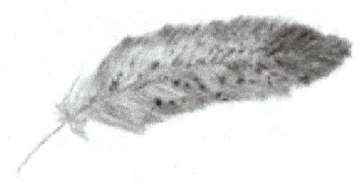

Endnotes:

[1] Kappler, Charles J., compiler and editor. *Indian Treaties: 1778-1883. "Treaty with the Cherokee 1835."* Amereon House, 1972, p 441.

[2] Estes, Nick. *Our History is the Future: Standing Rock vs the Dakota Access Pipeline, and the Long Tradition of Indigenous Resistance.* Verso, 2019, p. 148

[3] Kappler, Charles J., compiler and editor. *Indian Treaties 1778-1883.* "Treaty with the Cherokee, 1866." Amereon House, 1972, Article 15, p. 946.

[4] Nonnenmacher, Tomas. "History of the U.S. Telegraph Industry." *Economic History Association.* https://bit.ly/3mRJYHa. Acessed. 8 Sep 2019.

[5] "Transcontinental Railroad." *History.com* editors. https://bit.ly/38f7ycY. Original: 20 Apr 2010; updated 11 Sep 2019.

[6] Estes, Nick. *Our History is the Future*: *Standing Rock vs the Dakota Access Pipeline, and the Long Tradition of Indigenous Resistance.* Verso, 2019, p. 148.

[7] Dyer, Thomas G. *Theodore Roosevelt and the Idea of Race.* Louisiana State U P, 1980, p. 79.

[8] Stannnard, David E. *American Holocaust: The Conquest of the New World.* Oxford UP, 1992. p. 133.

[9] Brown, Dee Alexander. *Bury My Heart at Hounded Knee: An Indian History of the American West.* Hampton Sides, 2009, p. 104.

[10] Tyler, S. Lyman. *A History of Indian Policy.* U.S. Department of the Interior, Bureau of Indian Affairs, 1973, pp. 77-78.

11 Tyler. p. 80.

12 Tyler. pp. 78-80.

13 Tyler. p. 84.

14 Strickland Rennard and William M. Strickland, "Beyond the Trail of Tears: One Hundred Fifty Years of Cherokee Survival." *Cherokee Removal: Before and After*, edited by William L. Anderson, Brown Thrasher Books, U of Georgia P, 1991, p. 117.

15 Cherokee Nation, Oklahoma. *Protest of the Cherokee Nation Against a Territorial Government.* Washington: Cunningham & McIntosh, printers, 1871. p. 9.

16 "Land Patent Law and Legal Definition." *US Legal.* https://bit.ly/38RQHNO. Accessed 14 Jan 2020.

17 Strickland Rennard and William M. Strickland, "Beyond the Trail of Tears: One Hundred Fifty Years of Cherokee Survival." *Cherokee Removal: Before and After*, edited by William L. Anderson, Brown Thrasher Books, U of Georgia P, 1991, p. 121.

18 Turner, Alvin O. "Cherokee Outlet Opening," *Oklahoma Historical Society.* https://bit.ly/3cN9OZh. Accessed 20 Nov 2019.

19 nativeamericannetroots.net>diary, original date Mar 24, 2014, accessed Jan 15, 2020.

20 Lowe, Marjorie. 'Let's Make it Happen" W.W. Keeler and Cherokee Renewal. Originally published in *The Chronicles of Oklahoma.* Summer 1996. https://bit.ly/346c3Tm. Accessed 2 Aug 2019.

21 Mails, Thomas E. *The Cherokee People: The Story of the Cherokees from Earliest Origins to Contemporary Times.* Marlowe & Co., 1992, pp. 278-279.

22 Mails. p. 279.

23 Subchapter I – Treaties. 25 USC Chapter 3 – Agreements with Indians. https://bit.ly/3k53wX5. Archived from the original March 17, 2012.

24 Tyler, S. Lyman. *A History of Indian Policy*. U.S. Department of the Interior, Bureau of Indian Affairs, Washington, D.C., 1973, pp. 85-86.

25 "Dawes Act (1887)." https://bit.ly/3kbAq8w Accessed 19 Dec 2019.

26 Perdue, Theda. *Nations Remembered: An Oral History of the Cherokees, Chickasaws, Choctaws, Creeks, and Seminoles in Oklahoma, 1865-1907*. U of Oklahoma P, 1993. p. 181

27 Tyler, S. Lyman. *A History of Indian Policy*. U.S. Department of the Interior, Bureau of Indian Affairs, Washington, D.C., 1973, pp. 96-97.

28 Tyler. p. 95.

29 Tyler. p. 95.

30 "Dawes Act (1887)." https://bit.ly/3kbAq8w. Accessed 19 Dec 2019.

31 Mankiller, Wilma and Michael Wallis. *Mankiller: A Chief and Her People*. St Martin's Press, 1993, p. 135.

32 Strickland, Rennard and William M. Strickland, "Beyond the Trail of Tears: One Hundred Fifty Years of Cherokee Survival." *Cherokee Removal: Before and After*, edited by William L. Anderson, Brown Thrasher Books, U of Georgia P, 1991, p. 124.

33 Strickland, Rennard and William M. Strickland, p. 124.

34 Tyler, S. Lyman. *A History of Indian Policy*. U.S. Department of the Interior, Bureau of Indian Affairs, Washington, D.C., 1973, p. 7.

35 Tyler. p. 86.

36 Perdue. *Nations Remembered: An Oral History of the Cherokees, Chickasaws, Choctaws, Creeks, and Seminoles in Oklahoma, 1865-1907*. U of Oklahoma P, 1993, p. 177.

37 Perdue. p.180.

38 archives.gov. Native American Heritage: American Indian Treaties.

39 Kappler, Charles J., compiled and edited. *Indian Treaties, 1778-1883*. Amereon House, 1972. Quote in forward by Brantley Blue, Indian Claims Commissioner, Washington, DC, 1972.

40 Strickland Rennard and William M. Strickland, "Beyond the Trail of Tears: One Hundred Fifty Years of Cherokee Survival." *Cherokee Removal: Before and After*, edited by William L. Anderson, Brown Thrasher Books, U of Georgia P, 1991, pp. 118-128.

[41] Tyler, S. Lyman. *A History of Indian Policy*. U.S. Department of the Interior, Bureau of Indian Affairs, Washington, D.C., 1973, p. 98.

[42] Tyler. p. 98.

[43] Tyler, p. 97.

[44] Tyler. p. 97.

[45] Williams, Edwin, compiler. "Jackson's Fifth Annual Message." *The Addresses and Messages of the Presidents of the United States, Inaugural, Annual, and Special, from 1789 to 1846 Vol. II."* Edward Walker, 1849. p. 839. google.com/books.

[46] Hall, G. Stanley. *Adolescence: Its Psychology and Its Relations to Physiology, Anthropology, Sociology, Sex, Crime, Religion, and Education, Vol. Two.* Appleton and Company, 1904, p. 651; Stannard, David E. *American Holocaust: The Conquest of the New World.* Oxford UP, 1962, p. 245. Note 145, p. 336.

[47] Stannard, David E. *American Holocaust: The Conquest of the New World."* Oxford UP, 1962, p. 245.

[48] Mankiller, Wilma and Michael Wallis. *Mankiller: A Chief and Her People.* St Martin's Press, 1993, pp. 5-6

[49] Tyler, S. Lyman. *A History of Indian Policy.* U.S. Department of the Interior, Bureau of Indian Affairs, Washington, D.C., 1973, p. 106.

[50] Tyler. pp. 106-107.

[51] Mankiller, Wilma and Michael Wallis. *Mankiller: A Chief and Her People.* St Martin's Press, 1993, p. 133.

[52] Tyler, S. Lyman. *A History of Indian Policy.* U.S. Department of the Interior, Bureau of Indian Affairs, Washington, D.C., 1973, p. 105.

[53] Estes, Nick. *Our History is The Future: Standing Rock vs the Dakota Access Pipeline, and the Long Tradition of Indigenous Resistance.* Verso, 2019, note 9, p 28; Also see Ted Turner Enterprises, "Ted Turner Ranches FAQ," Ted Turner official website, *tedturner.com*

[54] "Genocide of indigenous peoples." https://bit.ly/2TXk88o. Accessed 8 Jan 2020.

[55] *"Tribal Nations & the United States: An Introduction."* *National Congress of American Indians.* www.ncai.org/about-tribes. Accessed 8 May 2019.

PART II

Native Americans within American Society

| TEN |

Ironies Abound (1897 to 1925)

> ... all of our people all over the country – except the pure-blooded Indians – are immigrants or descendants of immigrants, including even those who came over here on the Mayflower.
>
> President Franklin D. Roosevelt on November 4, 1944
> Fenway Park in Boston, Massachusetts[1]

Roosevelt's statement symbolizes the attitude and approach of many towards the Indian at the start of the 20th century. As this century began, the work of the Dawes Commission was in full swing. The Dawes Act required the enrollment of all Native tribes, except the Five Civilized Tribes, and appraisal of the land. However, in 1898, Congress passed the Curtis Act, which amended the Dawes Act to incorporate the Five Civilized Tribes, the Cherokee, Chickasaw, Choctaw, Seminoles and Creek (or Muskogee), which were autonomous Indian republics each having its own government. Each tribe sent representatives to Congress to voice their concerns with the Dawes Commission requirements to enroll their People. Finally, however, they realized that the white man, whether through the government or as individuals, was going to get "his" way. Once again, a scheme had been devised to take away Indian land. The first step was to enroll by name each man, woman and child to determine how many People belonged to each tribe. The full bloods refused and withdrew to their homes, which meant that Dawes agents had to search each one out – often with the help of other tribal members.

Another unit of the commission was tasked with appraising the land. Among the types of land given considerations were bottom, forest, prairie and mountain, and these were subsequently valued in three classes which "… were valued at $5.00, $2.50 and $1.25 an acre."[2] In an effort to make sure every person got an allotment from each type of land, the agents came up with a formula that they believed would distribute the land with no one receiving only good or only poor land. Realizing People would be reluctant to leave their homesteads, the land and homestead where each person resided was part of their allotment. This was as equitable a formula as they could devise in this monumental task.

Requirements of the Dawes and Curtis Acts

The Curtis Act required the recertification of the Dawes rolls and superseded all previous rolls. While all this was going on, problems arose with the enrollment when more than 250,000 people applied for membership. Among those eligible for enrollment included citizens by blood, citizens by marriage, freedmen and members of the Delaware and Shawnee tribes admitted to the Cherokee tribe as stipulated by the federal government after the Civil War. The non-native census takers introduced the idea of blood quantum during the enrollment process. The Act of May 27, 1908 defined blood quantum and delineated the legal encumbrances on the land for a particular set of Indians. These categories are defined as follows:

> All lands, including homesteads, of said allottees enrolled as intermarried whites, as freedmen, and as mixed-blood Indians having less than half Indian blood including minors shall be free from all restrictions.

> All lands, except homesteads, of said allottees enrolled as mixed-blood Indians having half or more than half and less than three-quarters Indian blood shall be free from all restrictions.

> All homesteads of said allottees enrolled as mixed-blood Indians having half or more than half Indian blood, including minors of such degrees of blood, and all allotted lands of enrolled full-bloods, and enrolled mixed-bloods of three-quarters or more

Indian blood, including minors of such degrees of blood, shall not be subject to alienation, contract to sell, power of attorney, or any other incumbrance prior to April twenty-sixth, nineteen hundred and thirty-one, except that the Secretary of the Interior may remove such restrictions, wholly or in part, under such rules and regulations concerning terms of sale and disposal of the proceeds for the benefit of the respective Indians as he may prescribe.

The Secretary of the Interior shall not be prohibited by this Act from continuing to remove restrictions as heretofore ... [3]

It did not seem significant to the Five Tribes at the time, but in the 20th and 21st centuries, federally recognized Indian Nations still require certification of their enrollees utilizing the blood quantum defined in the Act of 1908. In her book, *And Still the Waters Run: The Betrayal of the Five Civilized Tribes,* Angie Debo stated, "While the Cherokees were resisting enrollment, thousands of white applicants carried their claims to the United States Supreme Court. Their case was decided in 1906, and the Cherokee citizenship laws were upheld in every particular. White people who had intermarried with Cherokees after 1877 were denied any share of the tribal property."[4]

Another example of the numbers put to the citizenship test is also provided by Debo when she wrote that only 286 of the 3,627 claimants who had intermarried before 1877 were admitted.[5] Challenges have been made over the last 100 years that involve the Freedmen and the validity of the blood quantum required to obtain membership into the individual tribes. While membership no longer provides any opportunities for land, there are other benefits to being recognized as a member.

These benefits include free healthcare at tribal-run clinics and hospitals, which are funded through the Indian Health Services – part of the federal Department of Health and Human Services. This benefit includes prescription drugs and eyeglasses. The level of care depends upon the personnel administering the program and the federal funding during any given year – much like the Veterans Administration. Because of the Cherokee-owned casinos and associated hospitality industries, Cherokee students wanting to study hospitality administration can apply for scholarships in those fields. Additionally, citizens of the Cherokee Nation are considered first for jobs within the Nation and can vote in tribal elections.

The adventurous were immigrating to the area in staggering numbers, as shown by the census. The number of white people grew from 109,393 in 1890 to 339,500 in 1900 and increased again to 538,512 in 1907, as speculation grew prior to statehood. During this same period "... the Indian population remained stationary.[6] The sheer number of people moving into the area and onto their land overwhelmed the Indians.

Major Events in Oklahoma Territory

In quick succession, a number of major events occurred in the lives of the People of Oklahoma Territory. "On July 3, 1902, the secretary of the interior made the first oil and gas lease on Indian lands within the present boundaries of the State of Oklahoma."[7] With the proliferation of laws, acts and supplements passed to protect the Indians, plus the requisite House and Senate hearings, it was difficult for those versed in law to keep up with events, and it was virtually impossible for the Indians as individuals or tribal governments to keep up. The oil and gas leases alone caused thousands of Indians to lose their lands and money as the cupidity of the non-Indians abounded. And some of the acts and supplemental bills required to fix unanticipated problems that arose from the original laws caused additional problems which opened the Indians to more fraud and abuse.

In 1903, the Indian Appropriations Act "... remove[d] restrictions from much of the allotted lands held by the Five Civilized Tribes, and non-Indians began to systematically separate the Indians from their land."[8] This was followed by the Curtis Act, which was a triumph for non-Indians as it rendered tribal governments ineffectual by abolishing all tribal laws and tribal courts as of March 6, 1906. An estimated 90 million acres of land formerly reserved for Native Americans were removed from their control.[9] The Dawes rolls officially closed on March 4, 1907; however, several corrections required the rolls be reopened. The corrections were made, and the rolls immediately closed. The Cherokee roll was reopened in 1914 to add the names of minor children, and it was immediately closed. The rolls reflected the blood quantum of the different groups of Indians determining whether they were eligible for land allotments and, if so, how long they were required to keep their allotment. These events were culminated by Oklahoma being admitted as the forty-sixth state on November 16, 1907.

Some Allottees Protected

There were some conscientious federal employees supervising the work of the Dawes and Curtis Acts, plus amendments and supplements. These individuals came to realize that the majority of the Indians, particularly the full bloods, had no concept of private land ownership and that there were many white people ready to take advantage of the Indian to gain the allotted land for themselves. With the goal of safeguarding the Indians and protecting their homesteads from intrusion, the McCumber Amendment was passed which "... extended the inalienability of the entire allotment of full bloods, for twenty-five years from the passage of the law, and provided that these restrictions could be removed only by act of Congress."[10] The amendment protected the entire allotment, not just the homestead, as being inalienable, which meant the land title was nontransferable for 25 years. This provided some protection for the Indians by preventing the land from going into the hands of those trying to acquire it by whatever means available. However, loopholes in the laws were seen as opportunities for exploitation.

The full bloods suffered greatly during this process because most of them spoke only Cherokee and were distrustful of the government and the changes that were being perpetrated against the Indians. "The unassimilated Indians, bewildered and disheartened, withdrew in fear and silence from the alien society that had displaced the old simple order in which they had proudly borne their part."[11] When allotment certificates were delivered, they went unopened or even refused. They did not understand that their homestead was part of their allotment and did not register them. Consequently, many homesteads were lost:

> ... the Indian grieved deeply as a man without a country; he cared nothing for the few paltry acres in his own name that had replaced the wide sweep of mountain and prairie, the winding rivers, and the deep forests that had all been his. Shy and distrustful as any wild thing, he hid from the enrolment parties, and returned his allotment certificate to the Agency.[12]

The non-natives of Oklahoma territory worked vigorously to convince the federal government that they were capable of caring for all the people of the territory, including the Indians. Once Oklahoma became a state, the clamor became incessant. Taxes could be levied on private property, which provided the Oklahoma citizens and legislature alike an increased incentive to move the land into the hands of individual Indians, whites and freedmen. Without inquiring into the capability of the new state, the U.S. government relinquished most of its oversight of Indian property and People. In May 1908, the Oklahoma legislature enacted a bill which was to remain in place for twenty years with the following caveat:

> All these restrictions were to remain in effect until April 26, 1931, unless removed by the Secretary ... Restricted allottees might give agricultural leases of their surplus land for five years, and their homesteads for one year without supervision; but agricultural leases for longer periods and all mineral leases were subject to the approval of the Secretary."[13]

Plight of Child Allottees

While the grafters were hard at work extorting land from the Indians, another type of schemer was equally hard at work to the detriment of many Native children. These people conspired to get themselves appointed administrator for orphans or even children with parents – sometimes 150 or more children. As legal guardians, they then sold the child's allotted land and made off with the money, leaving them destitute and without any means of support. "Approximately sixty thousand minors with land valued at $130,000,000 besides an oil valuation of $25,000,000, were placed under the jurisdiction of forty county judges."[14] Kate Barnard worked extensively in charitable organizations of Oklahoma City and was determined to make the public aware of the plight of the Native children.[15] It was through her efforts that "... the office of Commissioner of Charities and Corrections had been created by the Constitutional Convention, and at the first state election she herself had been elected to the position by an overwhelming majority."[16]

Barnard heard about the circumstances surrounding three small children that illustrated the situation many children found themselves in. It took her awhile to locate the children, and it was reported that "She found three small Indians sleeping in the hallow of an old tree, drinking from a stream, and securing food from neighboring farmhouses. ..."[17] After some investigation, Barnard determined "... that their parents were dead, that they owned valuable oil land, and the guardian had been collecting their royalties and charging them exorbitant prices for their education and support. He had fifty-one other children under his protection."[18]

It was not until June 9, 1911 that Barnard was able to get Oklahoma to authorize limited protection of orphans. The sheer number of children affected was well beyond the capabilities of Barnard and her limited staff, but they worked diligently and made great inroads. Working with a public defender in her department, they prosecuted the wrongs done to orphan children. By October 1st, the public defender had won 207 cases in 25 counties, "... and had recovered $187,991.94 for orphan minors who had been defrauded."[19]

Grafters – Dealers in Indian Lands

By the Act of May 27, 1908, sometimes referred to as the "Crime of 1908," thousands of mixed bloods, freedmen and other allottees were given their lands without restrictions. Nearly 90 percent of the allottees had disposed of these lands to non-Indians and spent the proceeds, leaving them with neither land, homestead nor a way of supporting themselves.[20] As that day in May loomed, the potential of getting rich quick on real estate appropriated from the Indians was the goal of the "grafter" which was a term "… applied as a matter of course to dealers in Indian land, …"[21] Today there are any number of scams perpetuated upon people, and the grafters were an earlier version of scammers. Their goal was to relieve the Indians of their land, and they were very good at it – utilizing different methods on each of the Five Tribes. These grafters, some even educated Indians who wanted to get their portion of the riches, also included "Enterprising scouts [who] went into the fullblood settlements, gathered up the Indians, loaded them on trains and brought them in, and sold them [the rights to work with the Indians] to the highest bidder among the real estate dealers."[22] The dealers instructed the Indians on making their land selections, handled all the paperwork of the sale and got them to the head of the line at the land office to register the deeds, which were turned over to the dealers.

A number of factors played a part in the Indians accepting the help of the grafters. In addition to their lack of knowledge and general bewilderment of the allotment process, the trip to the land office was often a distance that required several days travel. That, along with the cost of food while they waited, the vast number of Indians waiting to register their deeds, plus the actual expense of registering the deeds, all placed financial restrictions on the ability of the Indians to register their allotment. The Indians were willing to accept the assistance of the grafters, not realizing the ultimate cost for them. In return for all this "help," the dealers paid the Indians a fraction of the land's value. The Indian received little money, and the dealer went on to the next target:

> In the excitement of discovering oil fields, building cities, and placing rich land under the plow, personal greed and public spirit were almost inextricably joined. If they [the newcomers] could build their personal fortunes and create a great state by destroying

the Indian, they would destroy him in the name of all that was selfish and all that was holy.[23]

Restrictions Removed by Special Acts of Congress

Restrictions were removed by special acts of Congress without the Indians' knowledge in a targeted method of securing oil property, townsites and other land desired by the grafters.[24] "Most of the victims were fullbloods, and the restrictions were usually removed from both homestead and surplus. The legislation was in the form of 'riders' to Indian appropriation bills."[25]

Unfortunately, the opportunities for fraud and the promises of riches tempted federal employees as well. In August 1903, charges were made of employees speculating in Indian land. Two investigations followed which found some guilty of owning stock in land companies, and others were listed as officers or directors of the companies, while many more owned shares. Once the land was sold or leased, the employees stood to make money. These opportunities were gained through their knowledge of the best agriculture or timber land, oil or coal deposits and potential town sites: "... the Indian Appropriation Act of 1904 contained a prohibition sufficiently comprehensive to cover all possible dealing in Indian property."[26]

Need of Medical Assistance Highlighted

Since 1873, efforts had been attempted to provide medical assistance to the Indians through the Bureau of Indian Affairs. Little money was available, and medical care was often left to missionary doctors who did good work under deplorable conditions. Finally, in 1911, a survey was conducted of the health and sanitation conditions in schools and on the reservations. President Taft startled the country in 1912 with his special message to Congress where he quoted from the survey and requested $253,000 specifically for medical relief for the Indians.[27]

In *A History of Indian Policy* prepared for the United States Department of the Interior, S. Lyman Tyler quotes excerpts from President Taft's message that presents "... a summary of the deplorable health conditions of Indians then under Federal supervision:"[28] In one of the few presidential messages dealing with Indians in the 20th century, Taft stated:

> In many parts of the Indian country infant mortality, tuberculosis and disastrous diseases generally prevail to an extent exceeded only in some of the most unsanitary of our white rural districts and in the worst slums of our large cities. The death rate of the Indian country is 35 per thousand as compares with 15 per thousand – the average death rate of the United States as a whole . . . Last year, of 42,000 Indians examined for disease, over 16 percent of them had trachoma, a contagious disease of the eye, frequently resulting in blindness, and so easily spread that it threatens both the Indian communities and all their white neighbors . . . Of the 40,000 Indians examined, 6,000 had tuberculosis . . . Few Indian homes anywhere have proper sanitary conditions, and in most instances the bad conditions of their domestic surroundings are almost beyond belief.
>
> As guardians of the welfare of the Indians, it is our immediate duty to give the race a fair chance of an unmaimed birth, healthy childhood, and a physically efficient maturity. The most vigorous campaign ever waged against diseases among the Indians is now under way. It began in 1909. Prior to that time little attention had been given to the hygiene and health of the Indians. In some reservations, equal in area to a State, there were not more than two physicians, frequently only one. In 1909 tens of thousands of Indians were substantially without any chance to reach a doctor.[29]

While Congress realized the significance of the situation, they only marginally increased the medical funding. However, as the public became aware of the shameful medical and healthcare on the reservations, Congress increased appropriations from

$40,000 in 1911 to $350,000 in 1918.

It should be noted here that the 21St century has not seen a significant change in Native healthcare. In September 2004, the U.S. Commission on Civil Rights stated:

> It has long been recognized that Native Americans are dying of diabetes, alcoholism, tuberculosis, suicide, and other health conditions at shocking rates. Beyond disturbingly high mortality rates, Native Americans also suffer a significantly lower health status and disproportionate rates of disease compared with all other Americans."[30]

Additionally, recent studies also point to rising rates of stroke,[31] heart disease[32] and diabetes[33] in the Native American population.

War and Native American Service

In 1913, Woodrow Wilson was elected president, the first Democrat elected to two consecutive terms since Andrew Jackson. War broke out in Europe, and the United States initially maintained a policy of neutrality in an effort to keep the country out of World War I; however, the U.S. declared war against Germany on April 4, 1917. Although not formally allied with Britain or France, the United States operated as an associated power, and the country raised an army through conscription. Native Americans fought in WWI and have served in all other conflicts the United States has been involved in since that time and continuing into the present.

Funding for many government agencies, including the Bureau of Indian Affairs, was severely curtailed in support of the war, resulting in deplorable conditions of Indian buildings, hospitals, schools and homes. Initially, Native Americans were required to register for the draft but were not considered for conscription since they were not regarded as citizens. This double standard caused the Indians "... confusion, resentment and even outright rebellion."[34] As the war took its toll, the draft included Indians with an estimated 12,000 throughout the United States serving in the military – 10,000 in the Army and 2,000 in the Navy with over 54% drafted and the remainder volunteering. While serving in the military helped their communities economically, it also provided an opportunity for Native Americans to display their strength and discipline as warriors.[35]

Acknowledged for bravery under fire, many Native Americans often volunteered for dangerous positions and suffered a higher percentage of deaths in combat. Their losses were "… about five percent compared to one percent for U.S. troops overall. [and] … Fourteen American Indian women served in the U.S. Army Nurse Corps."[36] The country was united in one cause – to support the Allies and defeat the Germans. On the home front, Native women worked with the Red Cross and relief organizations, and children bought Liberty bonds, while Indians overall "… purchased $25 million in war bonds, equal to $75 for every American Indian."[37]

From early in the history of the country, the U.S. had strived to eradicate all the Native languages, with punishment especially severe in the Indian boarding schools. Although discouraged throughout their lives from learning the language of their respective tribes, that knowledge served them well in the military and saved the lives of many American and Allied soldiers as well as civilians in the war-torn countries as the war progressed:

> … many American Indians were fluent in their native languages. Cherokee and Choctaw troops used their language to securely transmit communications that the Germans could not understand. These soldiers were the precursors to the better-known Code Talkers of World War II."[38]

During WWI, all methods of communication within the Allied powers, including carrier pigeons, proved ineffectual against the enemy, whereas the German's coded communications were in any number of European languages or mathematical progressions and extremely difficult to break. "As part of their service, many Native Americans of the 142nd Infantry, 36th

Division became the nation's first Code Talkers, sending messages encrypted in their Native languages over radio, telephone and telegraph lines, which were never broken by Germany." Colonel A.W. Bloor is quoted from an official report. "The enemy's complete surprise is evidence that he could not decipher the messages. The tide of battle turned within 24 hours, and within 72 hours the Allies were on full attack."[39] The 36th Division included 1,000 men, representing 26 tribes mainly from Texas and Oklahoma.

Then during World War II, an enigma machine was utilized by the Germans to relay orders, direct troop movements and the general conduct of the war. Because of the billions of ways the machine encoded messages, it proved incredibly difficult to break. The enigma permitted the Nazis to rain terror upon many countries, especially the blitzkrieg of London. It wasn't until 1941 that the British cryptologists broke the code.

Code talking employed by the Cherokee and Choctaw during WWI again played a major part in WWII. Military leaders of WWI heard the Native Americans speaking their own language to one another and understood the significance. The use and success of the Cherokee and Choctaw code talkers during WWI meant that Native Americans were actively recruited in WWII to serve as bilingual code talkers in the U.S. Marine Corps. These men from the Comanche, Meskwaki, Basque and Navajo brought their languages to provide a cryptographic code unbreakable by the enemies of the Allied forces.[40] The code talkers were a group so secret within the United States military that it was many years before their actions were declassified and ordinary citizens learned of them. The Navajo language was not understood by the Nazis and their spies, and their code proved unbreakable. The code talkers, many of whom were underaged but wanted to escape the enforced white schooling where they were not allowed to speak their Native languages or practice their Native customs, nonetheless ensured the safety and welfare of many of the American and Allied troops. "They [the Navajo] received congressional recognition for their exploits in 2000, whereas the remaining tribes had to wait eight more years until a bill passed praising them for their 'dedication and valor.'"[41]

Citizenship for Native Americans

Thousands of Native Americans fought and died alongside other Americans to protect democracy in WWI, WWII and subsequent conflicts. Many Native Americans felt that the Citizenship Act of 1924 came in recognition of those who volunteered during World War I. When President Calvin Coolidge signed the citizenship bill on June 2, 1924, there came a change for Native Americans as the bill "... granted full U.S. citizenship to the indigenous peoples of the United States."[42] The bill reads as follows:

> *Be it enacted by the Senate and House of Representatives of the United States of America in Congress assembled,* That all non-citizen Indians born within the territorial limits of the United States be, and they are hereby, declared to be citizens of the United States: *Provided,* That the granting of such citizenship shall not in any manner impair or otherwise affect the right of any Indian to tribal or other property.[43]

Prior to the 1924 Citizenship Act, the only way Indians could become citizens of the United States was by relinquishing their tribal citizenship, which some Cherokees did in order to remain in their ancestral homelands of the East. This was particularly prevalent during the 1820s to 1830s when Georgia required Native Americans to pledge allegiance to the state or move. The 1924 act provided for Indigenous people to hold dual citizenship.

The Fourteenth Amendment to the United States Constitution was adopted on July 9, 1868 and defines citizens as any persons born in the U.S. and subject to its jurisdiction to include descendants of African slaves. At that time the amendment was interpreted to not apply to Natives making them a "dependent" people. Native Americans granted citizenship rights under the 1924 Act did not have full citizenship and suffrage rights until 1948. According to a survey by the Department of the Interior, seven states still refused to grant Indians voting rights in 1938, and it wasn't until 1978 that the American Indian Religious Freedom Act afforded them the right and protection to practice their traditional religions. Tyler's *History of Indian Policy* tells that while citizenship had no immediate effect:

> ... later the fact that all Indians were citizens would be used by the national Government as a pressure on the States to treat Indians as other citizens, to grant them all the rights and privileges other citizens were allowed, and to give them all the services. It would be used on the Indians to accept the same duties and responsibilities that other citizens were heir to, including 'freedom' and taxes.[44]

The 1924 bill did not include all of the five major rights of a democratic country afforded to every other citizen at that time. These are "... freedom of speech, the right to a fair and public trial, the right to due process, the right to vote freely and the right to worship freely."[45]

Author's Thoughts

While Native Americans were glad to be recognized as citizens, they could not fathom why the people and government of the United States failed to acknowledge that they were the "first citizens." Imagine having to gain citizenship in a country that belonged to them long before others came to this land from England, France, Germany, Italy, Spain, Africa, China, Japan, India and other places too numerous to list – it is flat out wrong and the ultimate irony. Other ironies include:

- Allotments of the children and full bloods were supposed to be protected and yet: Schemers and grafters managed to abscond with millions of dollars of land.
- President Taft requested money for medical relief and yet: Deplorable health and sanitation conditions persisted in schools and on the reservations.
- Indians were considered wards of the United States and yet: They enlisted in the military and served with distinction.
- They were forbidden from speaking their native languages in school and yet: Their languages provided

a cryptographic code unbreakable by the enemies.

As Americans, and as we look back over the interactions between our country and Native Americans, are we comfortable with the knowledge of having taken land and resources guaranteed to them by treaties with the federal government? If we scrutinize our motives, are we comfortable with what we have learned? A number of authors have displayed courage with their willingness to hold the mirror up to the national consciousness. While many have done this, Angie Debo stands out.

Debo, a non-native, was born on January 30, 1890 in Kansas. At the age of nine, she and her family moved in a covered wagon to Oklahoma Territory where she lived most of her life. Debo earned an A.B. in history from the University of Oklahoma and a master's degree in international relations from the University of Chicago. Over the course of her life, Debo wrote 13 books and hundreds of articles about Native Americans and Oklahoma history.[46] One of her more controversial books, *And Still the Waters Run: The Betrayal of the Five Civilized Tribes*, is a quoted source for my writings, and for a time, this book resulted in Debo being barred from teaching in Oklahoma. "In the words of historian Ellen Fitzpatrick, Debo's book 'advanced a crushing analysis of the corruption, moral depravity, and criminal activity that underlay white administration and execution of the allotment policy."[47]

Debo's research and writing of that book challenged the American public when she presented the history of westward expansion as the exploitation of the Native Americans. Completed in 1936, her charges were so controversial that the University of Oklahoma withdrew as publisher. It was finally published by Princeton University Press in 1940. The book has become a classic and challenges both readers and writers of Native American history. Republished in 1972, she wrote an updated preface providing additional insights to her original work. It is through the dedicated work of individuals like Debo and others like Ellen Fitzpatrick, Oliver LaFarge and Vine Deloria, Jr. that we learn the true unvarnished history.

History is the mirror of our lives. It presents a true reflection of our deeds, and however much we may not like what we see, it is only by understanding the mistakes of our past that we have an opportunity to make a better future for Native Americans and, ultimately, all of us.

Endnotes:

[1] Roosevelt, Franklin D. "Speech at Fenway Park in Boston, MA." 4 Nov 1944. "US Presidents in Their Own Words Concerning American Indians." *Nativenewsonline.net*, edited by Levi Rickert. https://bit.ly/3cLS00L. Accessed 23 Jun 2018.

[2] Debo, Angie. *And Still the Waters Run: The Betrayal of the Five Civilized Tribes.* Princeton UP, 1940, p. 48.

[3] "Act of May 27, 1908: 35 Stat. 312, H.R. 151641." http://thorpe.ou.edu/treatises/statutes/Fct35.html.

[4] Debo, Angie. *And Still the Waters Run: The Betrayal of the Five Civilized Tribes.* Princeton UP, 1940, p. 46.

[5] Debo. p. 46.

[6] Debo, p. 93, note 1. "Population of Oklahoma and Indian Territory 1907, p. 9, Thirteenth Census of the United States, 1910, III, 464."

[7] Tyler, S. Lyman. *A History of Indian Policy.* U.S. Department of the Interior, Bureau of Indian Affairs, Washington, D.C., 1973, p. 106.

[8] Tyler. p. 105.

[9] "America 1900: The General Allotment Act." The American Experience, *National Public Radio.* https://www.pbs.org/wgbh/americanexperience/features/1900-allotment-act/

[10] Debo, Angie. *And Still the Waters Run: The Betrayal of the Five Civilized Tribes*. Princeton UP, 1940, p. 90.

[11] Debo. p. 126.

[12] Debo. p. 127.

[13] Debo. p. 179.

[14] Debo. p. 183.

[15] Debo. p. 184.

[16] Debo. p. 184.

[17] Debo. p. 185.

[18] Debo. p. 185.

[19] Debo. p. 187.

[20] Tyler, S. Lyman. *A History of Indian Policy*. U.S. Department of the Interior, Bureau of Indian Affairs, Washington, D.C., 1973, p. 105.

[21] Debo, Angie. *And Still the Waters Run: The Betrayal of the Five Civilized Tribes*. Princeton UP, 1940, p. 92.

[22] Debo. pp. 95-96.

[23] Debo, p. 93.

[24] Debo. p. 116.

[25] Debo. p. 116, note 49. "Select Committee, I, 304-41; Kappler, *Laws and Treaties*, III, 64, 213, 279, 482."

[26] Debo, Angie. *And Still the Waters Run: The Betrayal of the Five Civilized Tribes*. Princeton UP, 1940, p. 119.

[27] Tyler, S. Lyman. *A History of Indian Policy*. U.S. Department of the Interior, Bureau of Indian Affairs, Washington, D.C., 1973, p. 107.

[28] Tyler. pp. 107-108.

[29] Tyler. pp. 107-108.

[30] Latour, Mark Louis. *American Government and the Vision of the Democrats*. University Press of America. 2007. p. 313.

[31] Schieb, Linda J. "Trends and Disparities in Stroke Mortality by Region for American Indians and Alaska Natives." *American Journal of Public Health*. Supplement 3, 2014. Vol 104, No 33. https://bit.ly/38iL4If.

[32] Veazie, Mark. *"Trends and Disparities in Heart Disease Among American Indians/Alaska Natives, 1990-2009."* *American Journal Public Health*. Supplement 3, 2014, Vol 104, No S3: *S35967. https://bit.ly/3p6TEiY*.

33   Nuyujukian, D.S. (2017). "Sleep Duration and Diabetes Risk in American Indian and Alaska Native Participants of a Lifestyle Intervention Project." *Oxford Academic Sleep Research Society. Sleep,* Vol. 39, Issue 11, Nov 2016, Pages 1919-1926.

34   "1917: American Indians volunteer for WWI.*" The United States World War One Centennial Commission.* Accessed 20 Jan 2020. https://bit.ly/3l0BxZL.

35   "1917: American Indians volunteer for WWI." *The United States World War One Centennial Commission.* Accessed 20 Jan 2020. https://bit.ly/3l0BxZL.

36   "1917: American Indians volunteer for WWI." *The United States World War One Centennial Commission.* Accessed 20 Jan 2020. https://bit.ly/3l0BxZL.

37   "1917: American Indians volunteer for WWI." *The United States World War One Centennial Commission.* Accessed 20 Jan 2020. https://bit.ly/3l0BxZL.

38   Greenspan, Jesse. "How Native American Code Talkers Pioneered a New Type of Military Intelligence." Nov 5, 2019. https://bit.ly/35c3Ai9. Accessed 20 Jan 2020.

39   Bell, Danna. "Native Americans in the First World War and the Fight for Citizenship." April 5, 2018. https://bit.ly/31mBRud. Accessed 20 Jan 2020.

40   Tyler, S. Lyman. *A History of Indian Policy.* U.S. Department of the Interior, Bureau of Indian Affairs, Washington, D.C., 1973, p. 109.

41   Greenspan, Jesse. "How Native American Code Talkers Pioneered a New Type of Military Intelligence." Nov 5, 2019. https://bit.ly/35c3Ai9. Accessed 20 Jan 2020.

42   Shaping the Constitution: *Indian Citizenship Act*, June 2, 1924. http://edu.lva.Virginia.gov/.

43   Mankiller, Wilma and Michael Wallis. *Mankiller: A Chief and Her People.* St Martin's Press, 1993, pp. 173-174; "Act of June 2, 1924, Public Law 68-175 43 STAT 253, which authorized the Secretary of the Interior to issue certificates of citizenship to Indians." *archives.gov.* https://constitutioncenter.org/blog/on-this-day-in-1924-all-indians-made-united-states-citizens

44 Tyler, S. Lyman. *A History of Indian Policy*. U.S. Department of the Interior, Bureau of Indian Affairs, Washington, D.C., 1973, p. 115.

45 National Constitution Center Staff. "On this day, all Indians made United States citizens." *National Constitution Center*. 2 Jun 2020. https://bit.ly/3nyXLmm. Accessed 23 Jan 2020.

46 Debo, Angie. "Oklahoma Historian, 98" *The New York Times*, February 23, 1988.

47 Fitzpatrick, Ellen. *History's Memory: Writing Writing America's Past, 1880-1980.* Harvard UP, 2004, p. 133

| ELEVEN |

Perseverance through Endless Struggles (1920s to 1950s)

ARTICLE I.

The Contracting Parties confirm that genocide, whether committed in time of peace or in time of war, is a crime under international law which they undertake to prevent and to punish.

ARTICLE II.

In the present Convention, genocide means any of the following acts committed with intent to destroy, in whole or in part, a national, ethnical, racial or religious group, as such:

(a) Killing members of the group;

(b) Causing serious bodily or mental harm to members of the group;

(c) Deliberately inflicting on the group conditions of life calculated to bring about its physical destruction in whole or in part;

(d) Imposing measures intended to prevent births within the group;

(e) Forcibly transferring children of the group to another group.

United Nations Resolution 260
Convention on the Prevention and
Punishment of the Crime of Genocide
December 9, 1948

People throughout history have struggled to protect their lives and that of their families by providing sufficient food and land, worshiping their gods through various religious beliefs and festivals, developing a government structure and culture specific to their needs, as well as maintaining relationships with their neighbors. For Native Americans, these were systematically challenged with the arrival of the Europeans, to the extent that many tribes became extinct, while others were reduced by as much as 90% over the course of time. Indian lands were taken, and they were forced to move – some more than once or twice. Laws were written forbidding their religion, language and governments. Children were taken from their parents to be educated and "civilized" in the white man's schools. Documents show that some groups were intentionally exposed to smallpox and other infectious diseases. While the struggles the Native Americans faced fit within the definition of the UN Resolution 260 i.e., genocide, they have nonetheless persevered.

The Great Depression

Vice President Calvin Coolidge became President of the United States when Warren G. Harding passed away in August 1929, having served only 17 months in office. Coolidge inherited a stringent federal budget imposed by Harding in an effort to counter the inflation following World War I and subsequent Great Depression, which started in the United States in 1929 and spread throughout the world's economy before it improved in the late 1930s. All agencies were directed to economize federal expenditures and to increase efficiencies from the president's office on down. This, of course, drastically affected the services provided to the Indian people across the nation.

President Coolidge appointed Dr. Hubert Work, a former president of the American Medical Association from Colorado, to the office of secretary of the interior. Along with Charles H. Burke, commissioner of Indian affairs, the two men strived to accomplish the policy directive at a time when an increase in funding, rather than status quo, was needed to improve critical health and education services for the Indians.

Bureau of Indian Affairs Investigated and Changes Recommended

Secretary Work called upon a national advisory committee on Indian affairs called the Committee of One Hundred to investigate the Bureau of Indian Affairs and make recommendations. Completed in December 1923, the report titled "The Indian Program" was part of the congressional document in 1924.[1] Following that, Secretary Work issued a report in 1927 on Indian affairs "... headed by a seven page section called 'The Poverty of the Indian Service.'"[2] It began with this summary statement:

> The Indian Service has not kept pace with the progress elsewhere along health, educational, industrial, and social lines. ... The cumulative effect of many years of financial neglect has demanded even larger appropriations, if the Government may perform its full duty to the American Indian. Underrating the requirements of the Indian Service has continued so long that it has become a habit difficult to correct.[3]

As a result of these reports, it was recommended that a "non-government, disinterested organization, with a field force of experts"[4] be engaged to make a study. They suggested that such a study, properly done, "... would carry great weight not only with Congress but also with the general public." John D. Rockefeller, Jr. financed the survey, and Work received it on February 21, 1928. The eye-opening results of that exhaustive study of the social and economic conditions among Native people signaled the beginning of change in the federal government's thinking about American Indians. From this study came the Meriam Report, which detailed the poor conditions of tribal economies and the utter destitution in Indian country.

> Many changes identified in 1928 would not occur until the 1930s and 1940s. ... It [the Meriam Report] was a document that all who were interested in the Indian were able to rally behind: The Congress, the Bureau, the reformers, and the general public. It was to be a 'bible' for Indian administration.[6]

The Indian Reorganization Act, often referred to as the "Indian New Deal," followed in 1934. Government authorities finally recognized federal policies had failed the Native people. Several facts needed to be addressed. First, Indians were not a dying race, and instead of forcing assimilation into mainstream America, their societies should be strengthened. Second, the Indian programs were more complex than previously recognized and management of Indian assets should be returned to them, along with assistance in establishing a foundation for sound economic policy.

The Meriam Report did not present a revolutionary recommendation; however, it brought all the thoughts and ideas together and presented them as one cogent document. Further, it came from a private organization with no political agenda. President Herbert Hoover appointed a team of three highly respected men to carry out the recommendations.[7] Significant progress was made in irrigation and reclamation practices, agriculture, an improved health program and education through close cooperation with the Department of Interior, including vocational training and greater federal and state cooperation. However, within eight months after Hoover took office, he found himself dealing with the Great Depression. "The last two years of the Hoover administration were devoted largely to developing means of fighting the depression."[8] One program of importance to the Five Civilized Tribes of Oklahoma during the depression was the Works Progress Administration (WPA) that provided government jobs to individuals who sent out questionnaires and conducted interviews of Indians who had lived in the mid-1850s. This work would not have been done without the Depression, and the Cherokee historical record would have been incomplete.[9]

Native Advocate Named Commissioner of BIA

The Indian Defense Association (IDA) named John Collier as its secretary in 1923. An ardent advocate of Native rights, he had observed the detrimental effects of the 1800s Indian policy of assimilation. Collier got an opportunity to work for the betterment of American Indians when he was appointed as the commissioner for the Bureau of Indian Affairs (BIA), which enabled him to implement President Roosevelt's reformist policy. Collier served as commissioner from 1933 to 1945 and oversaw the Indian New Deal, thus changing the direction of Indian policy. The scope of the work to be done by Collier and the BIA personnel was realized by a thorough understanding of the Meriam Report:

> ... which detailed the poor conditions of tribal economies and the utter destitution in the Indian country. According to the report, the average national per capita income in 1920 was $1,350 while the average American Indian made only $100 a year. The Meriam Report implicated U.S. Indian policy in helping to create such poverty.[10]

Collier brought refreshing vigor to the office, and his enthusiasm spread to his staff. William F. Zimmerman, Jr., who was assistant commissioner under Collier is quoted in S. Tyler's *A History of Indian Policy:*

> In the evenings we sometimes met at Collier's apartment which was so sparsely furnished that some would sit on the floor and on a bright Sunday morning, the meetings might be on a grassy point in Potomac Park. There was zest and fun in those meetings, but also always a sense of urgency, of fighting time, of doing things now, before it should be too late; but there was always a feeling of accomplishment.[11]

Collier and his staff were very outspoken regarding issues they found within the Indian Office, flatly stating "... that the Indian Office ignored the Indians themselves and their views and rode roughshod over their rights."[12] As a result of their work, some significant changes were made, which included encouraging Native arts, having children attend community day schools and public schools instead of boarding schools, and the practice of Indian customs and religion previously forbidden were now recognized to be of cultural significance. Natives were encouraged to be bilingual, which provided another opportunity to safeguard Native languages. Collier continued and expanded the WPA practice of sending out questionnaires and interviewing

American Indians, thus recording the history and traditions which would otherwise have been lost.

The New Deal also specified that Indians were to be employed in the Indian Service, and "With President Franklin D. Roosevelt's approval 72 work camps in 15 western States were assigned to the Indians, to be administered by the Bureau."[13]

Positive Indian Legislation Passed

Appointed to the Department of Interior Solicitor's Office by President Roosevelt in 1933 and holding the position until 1947, Felix S. Cohen was in the vanguard of those working on legislation that not only affected existing Indian law and policy, but created new ones as well. Cohen worked to establish laws to fortify tribal governments and restrict federal interference in Indian tribes. Regarding two decades of unsettled Indian claims:

> Felix Cohen stated that by early 1945 some $37 million had been awarded to Indian tribes under the old system which required the Congress to enact special statutes allowing specific tribes to appear in the court of claims for stipulated injuries arising under treaties and agreements. He estimated that the cost to the United States in litigation and other procedural matters was greater than what the tribes had been awarded.[15]

As part of the "New Deal," the Wheeler-Howard Act, otherwise known as the Indian Reorganization Act (IRA), was passed on June 18, 1934. This was a significant piece of legislation affecting Indian lives, but for the first time in a positive way:

> It was recommended that the Indians themselves be allowed to express their opinion in relation to the proposed legislation, and that finally they should have the privilege of voting on whether they would choose to accept the legislation on behalf of their tribes or not. To make this possible a series of 'congresses of Indians' were held in areas where Indian population was concentrated.[16]

Finally, there was a legal process for the Indians to voice their opinions regarding policies that directly affected their lives. Land and asset management was restored, including rights to manage mineral resources. All the provisions were intended to place management of the Indian lands in their hands and on a sound economic footing. The IRA also provided for an:

> ... attack on problems of physical conservation: of land, soil, water, and vegetation. ... Acquisition of additional lands, irrigation works, checking of erosion, further use of Indian resources by Indians, new homes, schools, hospitals, roads, trails, and bridges. . . There were improved medical resources, a new attack on trachoma that by 1939 saw vast improvement of treatment, and by 1943 a virtual end to consideration of this disease as a major problem. The formation of the Arts and Crafts Board with its accomplishments, [to encourage the arts and crafts of native people which previously had been banned] the continuing and enlargement on cooperation with other Government agencies. [17]

Indians at Work, a monthly magazine published from the late 1930s until the early 1940s, had widespread circulation and highlighted the positive aspects of life on the American Indian reservations. Although serving as commissioner of the BIA, John Collier continued to make his voice heard as a regular contributor to the magazine. The Indian Reorganization Act was a significant accomplishment of Collier in that it reversed the assimilation policy of the allotment period. Long a proponent of federal policy change, the IRA encouraged Indian leaders to reestablish community life, including their arts, language, religion and tribal organizations.

The Great Depression provided an unexpected benefit to American Indians. There was no pressure by non-Indians to open more reservation lands for settlement during this period, so allotment programs were eliminated, and the BIA was able to restore some lands that had been lost through various government programs over the last century. The years between 1935 and 1937 saw reservation total acreage increase by 2,100,000 acres. The population on many reservations, including that of the Navajo, was increasing rapidly, and the increased land holdings became an essential part of the solution. Additional purchases were imperative, and the IRA addressed many of the pressing issues facing Indians and provided remedies to some of those issues.[18] Tribal reforms were encouraged wanting Native Americans to manage their own affairs, children left boarding schools to be educated in their local communities and tribal customs, language and religions previously outlawed were now revitalized.

Prisoner of War Camps Established in Oklahoma

As progress was being made through tribal reforms instituted by the BIA, America entered WWII with the bombing of Pearl Harbor. Then, in 1942, the Cherokees suffered another type of relocation, not on the scale of removal from the Southeastern United States in 1838, but just as devastating for the seventy families affected. With American involvement in WWII, prisoner-of-war (POW) camps were needed within the continental U.S. for those captured "… during campaigns in North Africa, Italy, France and other places where American troops fought Adolf Hitler's Nazis."[19] Over 22,000 POWs would eventually be housed in at least 26 counties in Oklahoma.

Previously allotted to Cherokee individuals and families in the early 1900s when the government broke up the tribal reservations and governments, the U.S. now condemned eighty tracts, more than thirty-two thousand acres, and the Cherokee families were given a forty-five-day notification to vacate their homes and move their belongings, including livestock if they could manage it, without any financial assistance.

With these condemned tracts, the Army expanded Camp Gruber outside of Muskogee, Oklahoma, opening it on May 29, 1943 as a base camp with a number of branch camps.[20] Utilized as an infantry, field artillery and tank destroyer training camp, it had a POW camp established within the grounds with a capacity of 5,750 prisoners. The maximum number of prisoners held at the camp at any given time was 4,702.

An article written by Will Chavez, Assistant Editor of the *Cherokee Phoenix*, in 2012 provided a firsthand account by Harold Summerlin, whose parents and five siblings were forced to move to make way for Camp Gruber. They only had a wagon to get everything moved, and he remembered, "By the time we got out of there, the Army was already moving in with heavy artillery, so it wasn't even safe to be close."[21] Although the corn wasn't ready to harvest, Summerlin said he made several trips back on horseback and brought what green corn he could in a gunnysack. The family couldn't eat it, but it was good to feed the hogs. Their new place was only a couple of miles away; however, the limited time forced them to leave behind simple things like firewood needed to heat their homes for the winter and to cook with, as well as leaving animals used for food. There was also a loss of community as they left schools and the family cemeteries. Improvements made by his family to the original 160 acres, included "... two houses, two ponds, one barn, a chicken house and an orchard" for which they were paid $1,200.00[22] which, even at that time, wasn't enough to rebuild and replace what was lost. Some families hired lawyers and were promised an additional $400.00, with the lawyer getting as much as half of whatever they received, but years later, numerous families still waited for the government to pay them.

Ironies abound in the story of Camp Gruber. First, the Summerlins were forced to move again about a year later because Tenkiller Dam was being built, and their new location would be under water once the dam was operational. They finally settled in Tahlequah, 10 miles north of their most recent home. Second, the approximately 5,000 prisoners of Camp Gruber, Germans and other enemy combatants, fared better than the Natives forced from their homes. The Geneva Convention dictated the treatment of prisoners, and American officials hoped that their humane treatment of the POWs would precipitate like treatment of American prisoners.

As the POWs were transported by train to various camps in the United States, they saw that contrary to the propaganda they had been told about American cities being bombed and the destitution of the people, the POWs realized this was not true. Additionally, their living conditions in the camps were better than many of their cold-water flats in Germany. They were paid American military wages, roughly $0.80 a day for enlisted soldiers, and many were allowed to work on the surrounding farms, which helped offset the shortage of labor of those men serving in the U.S. military.

A third irony concerns the 2019 status of the 63,920 acres acquired for Camp Gruber. Initially, the government indicated that the land would be returned to the Cherokee at the end of the war. However, Patti K. Locklear reported in 2006 that "In 1967 ... the Oklahoma Army National Guard acquired 23,515 acres to establish Camp Gruber ... as a training base for summer field exercises and for weekend training."[23] The remaining part of the 1942 reservation remains in federal hands.

President Truman Institutes the Termination Policy

Harry S. Truman became president upon the death of Franklin D. Roosevelt in April 1945. Truman's presidency marked the end of the IRA, otherwise known as the Indian New Deal begun under Roosevelt in 1934. In those years, the IRA had relaxed policies, providing the Indian tribes the opportunity to regenerate tribal governments, customs and traditions. While the IRA led to an era of hope, it was understood that allotment and the accompanying changes had taken heavy tolls on the Indian people.

As was customary, the incoming president had his own policies regarding the future of Native Americans. While President Truman had good intentions as he sought to encourage racial integration, his termination plan once again endeavored to assimilate Indians into the white society through "... termination policies [which] dismantled trust relationships, relocated Indians to urban centers and stripped tribes of land and sovereignty."[24]

> Rather than leading to the destruction of Native American sovereignty and culture, one of the legacies of termination was the rise of modern Native American activism. ... Truman would have appreciated 'the resolve demonstrated by Native

people, and their efforts toward realizing self-sufficiency and self-government.'[25]

Truman saw Indian people as individuals who should be accorded the same rights and freedoms of other citizens. However, his belief was formed without an understanding of tribal relations and the importance of tribal culture. Truman's policies resulted in the trust relationship between more than 100 tribes and the federal government being terminated in the first decade of the policy. While the government ceased most termination efforts by 1958, the program did not officially end until the Nixon administration in 1970. Its effects "... forever altered the dynamics between tribes and the federal government."[26] In 1949, Truman stated, "The United States, which would live on Christian principles with all of the peoples of the world, cannot omit a fair deal for its own Indian citizens."[27]

One year later, in 1950, Truman appointed Dillon Myer as commissioner of the BIA. Myer headed the War Relocation Authority during World War II and oversaw the internment camps of the Japanese Americans. For this work, Truman awarded him the Medal for Merit giving the Indian tribes hope that under Myer's leadership they would receive more assistance and less paternalism. The opposite proved to be true, as he became a proponent of and accelerated the federal termination policy begun in the 1940s.

Myer's expanded the termination policies with the urban relocation program – another attempt to integrate Indians into the white society when individuals and families were encouraged to relocate to major cities like Chicago, Los Angeles and San Francisco to attend school or to seek employment. The relocation disrupted their close ties, and many returned to their tribal homes, some right away, while for others it was years. Nations saw the return of individuals and extended families who wanted to see relatives, strengthen family ties and teach the new generation their cultural values, religion and language.

While Truman's dealings with Native Americans were complicated, it is also evident that in some areas, he was sympathetic towards their situation, doing what he could to extend their equal rights. One example of this was a relief effort:

> In 1949, Truman authorized Operation Snowbound, a large-scale relief effort that delivered food and supplies for people and livestock affected by severe snowstorms in the Dakotas, Montana, Wyoming and Nebraska. [and] In response to a letter from former first lady Eleanor Roosevelt, Truman in 1950, signed the Navajo-Hopi Rehabilitation Act, which appropriated $88 million for schools, hospitals and roads.[28]

Native American Activism

The activism which resulted from termination can be seen when in November 1944, fifty tribes with delegates from 27 states met in Denver, Colorado to organize the National Congress of American Indians. The purpose of the new organization was ". . . to enlighten the public, preserve Indian cultural values, seek an equitable adjustment of tribal affairs, and secure and preserve their rights under treaties."[29] Recognizing that few members of Congress had the time or the interest in studying the needs of Indians, the National Congress of American Indians sought to keep the members of Congress informed on any Indian legislation before them. It became the lobbying group that addressed Indian needs, concerns and interests.[30]

In 1949, "... the responsibility of helping the Indian Bureau 'to work itself out of a job'"[31] was seen as the primary goal of the National Congress of American Indians. Theodore H. Haas, Chief Counsel United States Indian Service, addressed those in attendance at the meeting, stating:

> ... we have frequently said that one of the Bureau's objectives is the termination of Federal supervision and control special to Indians, and the progressive transfer of tribal property and tribal enterprises to Indian-owned and controlled Federal corporations. I believe that you have passed resolutions to the same general effect. Yet only two tribes numbering together about 1,000 members ... have voted under

their constitutions and charters to end the supervision of the Department of the Interior over several types of their leases and contracts[32]

United Nations Resolution260

World War II affected the global population in many dramatic ways and required much of people as the rebuilding process began. There had been some inkling of the problems in the Nazi-held countries, but the full scope of the atrocities committed against the population, specifically Jews, was only fully understood after the Allies gained access to the death camps. As a result, the United Nations world body accepted Resolution 260 titled Convention on the Prevention and Punishment of the Crime of Genocide, which was formally adopted on December 9, 1948 making "… genocide a crime under international law, contrary to the spirit and aims of the United Nations, and condemned by the civilized world."[33]

Resolution 260 was meant to address the genocide perpetrated during WWII but is a reflection of what has happened to the Native Americans since the first intrusion from the east. (Aspects and results of Resolution 260 will be expanded in future chapters.) The majority of the body politic signed the resolution in late 1940s and early 1950s. Although President Truman signed the resolution, the Senate refused to ratify it until almost 40 years later. The country could not officially recognize the atrocity of genocide because of the legal implications against the United States by its Indigenous peoples.

President Eisenhower Elected in 1953

When Dwight D. Eisenhower became the 34th President of the United States in January 1953, men of the military were returning from World War II and stepping into jobs that had been done by women who had answered the call to fill factory and other traditionally male jobs. People tried to fit into the newly developing society as changes resulted in a building boom of new homes, businesses and highways. The country enjoyed economic prosperity, but the American Indians who served the war effort returned to their land to find major changes, including massive unemployment caused by the termination policy. These men and their families were encouraged to relocate to the cities. Native peoples were being moved from their homes by various government programs which, in theory, were meant to integrate them into the mainstream of American life. They were dispersed from their homeland (the 1835 territory given to them in what became the states of Oklahoma, Arkansas, Texas and Kansas) to various cities throughout the United States.

Wilma Mankiller, who served as Principal Chief of the Cherokee Nation from 1985 to 1995, provided personal reflections into the "voluntary" termination policy in her 1993 autobiography, *Mankiller: A Chief and Her People*:

> It was part of the national Indian policy of the 1950s. The government wanted to break up tribal communities and 'mainstream' Indians, so it relocated rural families to urban areas. One day I was living in a rural Cherokee community, and a few days later I was living in California and trying to deal with the mysteries of television, neon lights, and elevators. It was total culture shock.[34]

The termination policy pursued by Dillon Myer earned him the following distinction in Francis Paul Prucha's 1984 book, *The Great Father: The United States Government and the American Indians,* in which he quoted "Harold Ickes, former Secretary of State, [who] called Myer 'a Hitler and Mussolini rolled into one,'"[35] for his vigorous pursuits of the termination policy. Those opposing the policy included the National Congress of American Indians, the American Civil Liberties Union, the Association on American Indian Affairs and numerous other nationally recognized organizations including many members of the American Bar Association. The controversy was finally laid to rest when Secretary of the Interior Oscar L. Chapman abandoned Myer's regulation. When President Eisenhower came into office in 1953, he accepted Myer's resignation as a part of the administration's transition.

Glenn L. Emmons was then appointed by President Eisenhower and served as the commissioner of the BIA throughout Eisenhower's eight years in office. Emmons had four main goals for the BIA to accomplish:

1) Efforts were made to improve Indian health programs and to bring health standards for Indian communities up to the same standard as the surrounding communities.

2) A strenuous effort was made to see that all eligible Indian children were able to attend either Federal or public schools. There was a special drive to meet the needs of Navajo young people.

3) Economic development programs sought to improve resources on the reservations and to attract industry to locate plants on or immediately adjacent to reservations to furnish employment to Indians.

4) Through assistance in connection with relocation services and by providing vocational training Indians were enabled to leave the reservation and find employment in non-Indian communities.[36]

Indian Health Service Established

The present-day Indian Health Service had its genesis in the government-to-government relationship, which "... established in 1787, is based on Article 1, Section 8 of the Constitution, and has been given form and substance by numerous treaties, laws, Supreme Court decisions, and Executive Orders."[37] From that beginning came the Indian Health Transfer Act, signed by President Eisenhower in 1954, which provided for the transfer of responsibility for Indian healthcare from the BIA to the Public Health Service and created the Indian Health Service (IHS).[38]

Then in 1980, the IHS was moved under the auspices of the newly formed Department of Health and Human Services. The agency overview states, "The IHS is the principal federal health care provider and health advocate for Indian people, and its goal is to raise their health status to the highest possible level."[39]

On November 19, 2019, Chief Chuck Hoskin Jr. of the Cherokee Nation of Oklahoma announced the recent opening of a 470,000 square-foot tribal outpatient health facility in Tahlequah, the capital city of the Cherokee Nation. The new facility was built through a joint venture between the IHS and the Cherokee Nation and provides "more than 240 exam rooms, two MRI machines, an ambulatory surgery center, 34 dental chairs, full-service optometry and many specialty health services ... The facility also symbolizes the fulfillment of a long-standing promise."[40]

> Enshrined in treaties, set forth in statues, and embodied in court decisions is a solemn promise that, as reparation for the hardship and dispossession borne by our ancestors at the hand of the United States, this country would provide for the health and welfare of tribal citizens in perpetuity. We, as Indian nations, have struggled for decades with the United States' failures to adequately fulfill that obligation.[41]

The federal government had shut down the very successful joint venture construction program between the IHS and Native tribes, and it was only through the lobbying efforts of several interested congressional representatives that the program was re-established. By then the U.S. was "... more than $2 billion behind in building new health facilities in Indian Country, including Cherokee Nation."[42] On February 26, 2016, the IHS signed a new joint venture agreement with the Cherokee Nation whereby the Nation agreed to construct the health facility, and the IHS would request funding from Congress to cover staff, operations and maintenance of the facility for the next 20 years.

The new facility will provide healthcare for American Indians in the service area, as well as the residents of NE Oklahoma providing them access to better healthcare. With over 850 healthcare and support staff, the facility will also provide a significant economic impact to the NE Oklahoma area.

Bureau of Indian Affairs Mission

Much like previous mission statements of the BIA, the 2019 mission is to enhance the quality of life, to promote economic opportunity and to carry out the responsibility to protect and improve trust assets of American Indians, Indian tribes, and Alaska Natives.[43] This is often difficult to accomplish in light of congressional oversight of the BIA. Congress conducted two studies in 1944, 1947 and a third in 1952, which included a survey, to determine what tribes were ready for termination of government oversight partially or in full. With the tribes slow to act, the House of Representatives wrote the Commissioner of Indian Affairs in 1952 requesting a complete report on a number of propositions. The first was to determine how qualified the 293 tribes, identified by the BIA, were to manage their own affairs. This was a measure used to terminate supervision of the federal government. Of these tribes, 187 indicated an immediate readiness to handle their own affairs and 19 were ready with conditions; however, 78 tribes did not qualify, and three were questionable.

The remaining propositions dealt with the bureau's management of the Indian Trust Account, and three of those are of great importance on a later lawsuit filed against the Department of Interior and include:

> ... (2) The manner in which the Bureau of Indian Affairs has fulfilled its obligations of trust as the agency of the Federal Government charged with the guardianship of Indian property; (3) The adequacy of law and regulations as assure the faithful performance of trust in the exchange, lease, or sale of surface or subsurface interests in or title to real property or disposition of personal property of Indian wards; ... (9) Findings concerning transactions involving the exchange, lease, or sale of lands belonging to Indian wards. ...[44]

The bureau's response to the propositions appeared in a 1,594-page House of Representatives Report. Published in 1953, the report contained 157 maps, along with numerous tables to aid in determining which tribes were ready for termination of government oversight.[45] Commissioner Emmons was quoted in Tyler's *A History of Indian Policy*:

> ... H. Con. Res. 108 [House Concurrent Resolution

108] is basically a notification to the Indian people that 'some day they are going to reach the age of 21' and that they should start planning, thinking and preparing themselves for the responsibilities that necessarily go with full freedom and unrestricted ownership of their individual and tribal properties. ...[46]

Slowly, the government understood that instead of dictating how the Native people were to run their lives, they needed to be consulted and make their own decisions. An effort was made to improve health standards within the Indian community to match those standards of the surrounding communities. Instead of only training people for jobs outside the reservation, industries were encouraged to locate on or near the reservations and to train and utilize the Indian people to fill those positions, thus creating a self-sustaining employment environment. Indian self-government was encouraged in communities where there were tribal leaders ready to step into governing roles. A cultural and religious revival started as the bureau stepped back and allowed the People to express themselves.

Author's Thoughts

By the time the Europeans came to the new world intent upon conquering the land and the people and making it their own, the Indigenous people had lived in the western hemisphere for many centuries. Archaeologists have found evidence that people had lived in some areas for millennium. There were Native people who developed thriving cultures but subsequently died out leaving clues for us to find their civilizations. The centuries-old, oral traditions and subsequent written records of the Cherokees indicate they had a prosperous culture, traded with their neighbors and, at times, waged war on them, but the land the Europeans sought to conquer provided what the Cherokee and other Natives needed to survive and thrive. Everything changed for these people from their first contact with the Europeans. Their struggles to survive have since been unrelenting.

Born on June 24, 1900 in what is now Belarus, Raphael

Lemkin came to the United States in 1941, joining the law faculty at Duke University. As a teenager, he read about millions of innocent Armenian men, women and children being killed by the Turks who ruled the Ottoman Empire at that time. His law professor explained that the prevailing power had the absolute sovereignty within its borders to do with and to the people as they chose. Lemkin was not satisfied with the idea that people could be killed with no accountability. After numerous attempts to construct a word to convey the atrocity of such acts, he coined the term "genocide" and later drafted the Convention on the Prevention and Punishment of the Crime of Genocide, which became UN Resolution 260. Many people associate genocide to events like the death camps in WWII, the death of Muslims during the Bosnian War or, more recently, the deaths in Syria. However, the term genocide is much more far reaching as seen in the Articles of UN Resolution 260, and the United States is guilty of all items (a) through (e) of Article II:

> According to Lemkin, colonization was in itself 'intrinsically genocidal.' He saw this genocide as a two-stage process, the first being the destruction of the indigenous population's way of life. In the second stage, the newcomers impose their way of life on the indigenous group. ... [Lemkin] argued that cultural genocide, sometimes called ethnocide, should also be recognized. A people may continue to exist, but if they are prevented from perpetuating their group identity by prohibitions against cultural and religious practices that are the basis of that identity, this may also be considered a form of genocide.[47]

As we look back over the history of the United States and its dealings with the American Indians, we see a pattern that fits Lemkin's definition of genocide with the termination policy of the 1940s and 1950s being just one example. Termination included relocating Native groups to urban locations in an attempt to integrate Indians into white society and eliminate their Native identity.

An era of Native activism resulted from the termination

policy and all the government policies that preceded it. From this emerged the formation of national groups to strengthen the Native voice in areas affecting them. The largest impact was in the political arena, including currently having Native Americans as elected members of Congress. With a unified voice, Native Americans are being heard in the halls of Congress.

There is yet much to be done, but there is great hope.

Endnotes:

1. Tyler, S. Lyman. A History of Indian Policy. U.S. Department of the Interior, Bureau of Indian Affairs, Washington, D.C., 1973. p. 113.
2. Prucha, Francis Paul. The Great Father. The United States Government and the American Indians. Vol II, pg. 792.
3. Prucha, Francia Paul. "The Great Father" The United States Government and the American Indians. Vol II, pg. 792-793. And CIA Report, 1927, p. I.
4. Tyler, S. Lyman. A History of Indian Policy. U.S. Department of the Interior, Bureau of Indian Affairs, Washington, D.C., 1973. p. 113.
5. Tyler. p. 113.
6. Tyler. p. 116.
7. Tyler. p. 116.
8. Tyler. p. 125.
9. Perdue, Theda. Nations Remembered: An Oral History of the Cherokees, Chickasaws, Choctaws, Creeks, and Seminoles in Oklahoma, 1865-1907." U of Oklahoma P, 1993, p. xvii.
10. Rhodes, Eric. "Indian New Deal." National Archives Pieces of History. 20 November 2015.https://bit.ly/3ifmtVT.
11. Tyler, S. Lyman. A History of Indian Policy. U.S. Department of the Interior, Bureau of Indian Affairs, Washington, D.C., 1973, p. 127.

12 Prucha, Francis Paul. The Great Father: The United States Government and the American Indians. U of Nebraska P, 1984. p. 806.

13 Tyler, S. Lyman. A History of Indian Policy. U.S. Department of the Interior, Bureau of Indian Affairs, Washington, D.C., 1973. p. 128.

14 Tyler. p. 128.

15 Tyler. pp. 149-150.

16 Tyler. pp. 129-130.

17 Tyler. p. 135.

18 Tyler. p. 135.

19 Curtis, Gene. "Only in Oklahoma: State housed German POWs during WWII." 10 Feb 2007, updated 24 Feb 2019. tulsanews.com. https://bit.ly/36aIhy7. Accessed 22 Aug 2019.

20 Locklear, Patti K. "Corbett presents history of Oklahoma WWII Prison Camps." woodwardnews.net. 26 Feb 2006. https://bit.ly/35457YC.

21 Chavez, Will, Assistant Editor, Cherokee Phoenix. "Camp Gruber Forced 2nd Removal for Cherokees." https://bit.ly/35WI3KP, 22 Oct 2012.

22 Chavez, Will.

23 Locklear, Patti K. "Corbett presents history of Oklahoma WWII Prison Camps." woodwardnews.com, 26 Feb 2006. https://bit.ly/35457YC. Accessed 22 Aug 2019.

24 Laundry, Alysa. "Harry S. Truman: Beginning of Indian Termination Era." Indian Country Today, 16 Aug 2016. https://bit.ly/2U1MoHa

25 Hosmer, Brian. "Native Americans and the Legacy of Harry S. Truman." Truman State UP, January 1, 2010, Introduction.

26 Laundry, Alysa. "Harry S. Truman: Beginning of Indian Termination Era." Indian Country Today, 16 Aug 2016. https://bit.ly/2U1MoHa

27 "Problems of the American Indian: Status of the Indian in American Life" CQ Researcher, 13 Apr 1949. https://bit.ly/3kBhnVj.

28 Laundry, Alysa. "Harry S. Truman: Beginning of Indian Termination Era." Indian Country Today, 16 Aug 2016. https://bit.ly/2U1MoHa.

29 Tyler, S. Lyman. A History of Indian Policy. U.S. Department of the Interior, Bureau of Indian Affairs, Washington, D.C., 1973. p. 145; "The Founding Meeting of NCAI: Preamble, adopted Nov 16, 1944." The National Congress of American Indians. https://bit.ly/38U6JGJ.

30 Tyler, S. Lyman. A History of Indian Policy. U.S. Department of the Interior, Bureau of Indian Affairs, Washington, D.C., 1973. pp. 145-146.

31 Tyler. p. 167.

32 Tyler. p. 167.

33 United Nations, General Assembly. Convention on the Prevention and Punishment of the Crime Of Genocide. Resolution 260 A (III) 9 Dec 1948. https://bit.ly/3ddr6ie.

34 Mankiller, Wilma and Michael Wallis. Mankiller: A Chief and Her People. St Martin's Press, 1993. p. xx.

35 Prucha, Francis Paul. The Great Father: The United States Government and the American Indians. U of Nebraska P, 1984. p. 1030.

36 Tyler, S. Lyman. A History of Indian Policy. U.S. Department of the Interior, Bureau of Indian Affairs, Washington, D.C., 1973. p. 179.

37 "Indian Health Service, Agency Overview." U.S. Department of Health and Human Services. 20 Feb 2020. https://www.ihs.gov/aboutihs/overview.

38 "Timeline 1954: President Eisenhower establishes the Indian Health Service." Native Voices. https://www.nlm.nih.gov/nativevoices/timeline/490.html"Ind

39 "Indian Health Service, Agency Overview," U.S. Department of Health and Human Services. 20 Feb 2020. https://www.ihs.gov/aboutihs/overview.

40 Hoskin, Chuck Jr. "New Cherokee Health Center will transform health care for generations." Chief Chat, 19 Nov 2019. newsletters@cherokee.org.

41 Hoskin, Chief Chat, 19 Nov 2019.

42 Hoskin, Chief Chat, 19 Nov 2019.

43 "Bureau of Indian Affairs 2019 Mission Statement." U.S. Department of the Interior, Indian Affairs. https://www.bia.gov. Accessed 12 July 2019.

44 Tyler, S. Lyman. A History of Indian Policy. U.S. Department of the Interior, Bureau of Indian Affairs, Washington, D.C., 1973. pp. 168-169.

45 Tyler. p. 169; Note 26: House Report No 2503, the 82nd Congress, second session. pp. 2-3.

46 Tyler, S. Lyman. A History of Indian Policy. U.S. Department of the Interior, Bureau of Indian Affairs, Washington, D.C., 1973. p. 178.

47 Union of International Associations. "Genocide of indigenous peoples." http:// encyclopedia.uia.org/en/problem/157395

| TWELVE |

One Nation – Many People (1961 to 1986)

With the inauguration of John F. Kennedy on January 20, 1961, the country gained a young, charismatic leader who issued a challenge to the nation during his inaugural speech stating, "… my fellow Americans: ask not what your country can do for you – ask what you can do for your country."[1] With those words, he challenged society to contribute to the public good.

In June of that year, Native Americans held a meeting with a goal to present a unified voice to the Kennedy administration on "… economic development, health, welfare, housing, education, law, and other topics."[2] At that time, "… more than four hundred Indians from sixty-seven tribes met at the University of Chicago to discuss all aspects of Indian affairs."[3] In light of the 1948 United Nations Resolution against genocide, it is important to consider the American Indian Pledge and Creed from the June 1961 conference in their entirety:

The American Indian Pledge

1) We are steadfast, as all other true Americans, in our absolute faith in the wisdom and justice of our American system of Government.
2) We join with all other loyal citizens of our beloved country in offering our lives, our property and our sacred honor in the defense of this country and of its institutions.
3) We renounce in emphatic terms the efforts of the promoters of any alien form.

Creed

We believe in the inherent right of all people to retain spiritual and cultural values, and that the free exercise of these values is necessary to the normal development of any people. Indians exercised this inherent right to live their own lives for thousands of years before the white man came and took their lands. It is a more complex world in which Indians live today, but the Indian people who first settled the New World and built the great civilizations which only now are being dug out of the past, long ago demonstrated that they could master complexity.

We Believe that the history and development of America shows that the Indian has been subjected to duress, stifling influence, unwarranted pressures, and self-destroying policies which have produced uncertainty, frustration, and despair. Only when the public understands these conditions and is moved to take action toward the formulation and adoption of sound and consistent policies and programs will these destroying factors be removed and the Indian resume his normal growth and make his maximum contribution to modern society.

We Believe in the future of a greater America, an America which we were the first to love, where life, liberty, and the pursuit of happiness will be a reality. In such a future, with Indians and all other Americans cooperating, a cultural climate will be created in which the Indian people will grow and develop as members of a free society.[4]

The Forgotten American

Lyndon B. Johnson became the 37th President of the United States when John F. Kennedy was assassinated on November 22, 1963. Johnson completed the partial term, won a full term and when he left office on January 20, 1969, there was a solid domestic policy in place designated as the "Great Society" with emphasis on his "War on Poverty." His policies highlighted urban and rural problems, as well as the plight of the American Indian. Johnson stated:

> The American Indian, once proud and free, is torn now between White and tribal values; between the politics and language of the White man and his own historic culture. His problems, sharpened by years of defeat and exploitation, neglect and inadequate effort, will take many years to overcome.[5]

Johnson delivered his Special Message to the Congress on the Problems of the American Indian: "The Forgotten American" on March 6, 1968. In the message, he "… called for an end to discussion of tribal termination and proposed a 'new goal' for the government's Indian programs …:" [6]

> A goal that ends the old debate about "termination" of Indian programs and stresses self-determination; a goal that erases old attitudes of paternalism and promotes partnership.

Our goal must be:

- A standard of living for the Indian equal to that of the country as a whole.
- Freedom of Choice: An opportunity to remain in their homelands, if they choose, without surrendering their dignity; an opportunity to move to the towns and cities of America, if they choose, equipped with the skills to live in equality and dignity.
- Full participation in the life of modern America, with a full share of economic opportunity and social justice.[7]

In September 1968, Democratic Senator George McGovern spearheaded a resolution through the Senate which put Johnson's proposed goals into policy. A poem written by an Indian student expressed the hope the policy embodied:

We shall learn all these devices the white man has.
We shall handle his tools for ourselves.
We shall master his machinery and his inventions,
> his skills, his medicine, his planning;
Butwe'llretainour beauty
And still be Indian.[8]

Robert Kennedy remarked on the poverty of the Cherokee people during his travels to their country in early 1968. He was particularly moved by the severity and degradation of their living conditions that he witnessed during his visit. In her 1993 book, *Mankiller: A Chief and her People*, Wilma Mankiller stated that she had reason to hope as Kennedy spoke out about the issues so important to her and many other Native Americans. He stated that the federal government's failure to help and the ongoing treatment of Native Americans was "… a national tragedy and a national disgrace."[9] Kennedy's assassination in June 1968, following so closely after Martin Luther King Jr. was assassinated on April 4, 1968, stunned the nation. These tragic events happened in a short period of time, and the American public felt the negative effects of both, which also served to highlight the fact that the "balance" so integral to Native American lives was off, as both Dr. King and Kennedy were fierce supporters of civil rights for Native Americans, as well as African Americans. That imbalance was further displayed during the demonstrations outside the August 26-29, 1968 Democratic convention in Chicago. The unrest in the country was palatable from the years of fighting the Vietnam War and also reeling from the assassinations of Kennedy and Dr. King.

Employment Assistance Program

The national relocation of Native Americans that began during the 1950s under the Eisenhower administration gradually morphed into employment assistance, which provided for on-the-job training, apprenticeship and adult vocational training, as well as financial help and advice for individuals or families to help them adjust to their new jobs and environments. In many ways, what the relocation program did not achieve, the employment assistance program did. The Bureau of Indian Affairs (BIA) estimated that 200,000 Indians moved to metropolitan areas by

1967-68. These skills took people to new locations to fill jobs, thus assimilating them into the American population. Once at their new locations, usually in major metropolitan areas across the country from their homes, some of the people, but not all, were taught practical experience in day-to-day living such as managing money and establishing a bank account, visiting post offices and service agencies, shopping for clothing, food and other necessities, riding a bus or buying a car.

Wilma Mankiller relates the challenges faced by her family from their relocation. The BIA usually provided an apartment for the newly relocated people, but none were available when they arrived in San Francisco from Oklahoma in 1956. The family of nine was put up in a hotel in a district of the city notorious for prostitutes and homeless people. They had never experienced neon lights or sirens. The sights, sounds and experiences of the city were frightening. Mankiller said she refused to get on an elevator after seeing people get on, the door close and the next time it opened, different people got off.[10]

To paraphrase Mankiller's experience: After two weeks in the hotel, the BIA found them a small apartment where they lived for a year. It was difficult for Natives to find jobs, but Mankiller's dad was able to find a job in a rope factory making $42.00 a week, which fortunately was within walking distance from the apartment. Her older brother, Don, worked in the same factory; both men working grueling hours. Together their pay barely covered the essentials, but a year later and with careful budgeting, they were able to move to a small three-bedroom house. Although the government relocation program was to provide some job training, none was provided to either man. New experiences meant learning how to use a party line phone which included listening for a tone prior to dialing and knowing everyone else on the line could listen in to your conversation. The pay that Mankiller's dad and brother brought home would not handle nonessentials or luxuries, so they wore hand-me-down clothes and shopped at secondhand stores. Many people eventually succumbed to the pressures and returned to their Native homes, preferring to reconnect with their Indian values and culture.[11] Mankiller wrote, "I have met many Native people from different tribes who were relocated from remote tribal communities. They discovered, as we did, that the 'better life' the BIA had promised ... was, in reality, life in a tough, urban ghetto."[12]

Political Prisoners in Their Own Land

For the past two centuries, Native Americans have been political prisoners in a land that originally was theirs. Just as the American colonists protested British taxation without representation in 1773 when they dumped chests of tea in Boston Harbor, Native Americans experienced frustration at their "imprisonment" at the hands of the U.S. government, which resulted in growing Native American activism. Their political imprisonment started in the early days of the republic with the removal and forced marches many tribes experienced; Natives being rounded up and placed on reservations; their religion, language and government forbidden by the federal government; and new federal programs continuing into the 20th century with allotment, termination and relocation – all with the goal of overcoming the "Indian problem." American presidents and political leaders made speeches which provided some hope, but Native people needed actual beneficial changes to their lives which included less intrusion by the government. The previously quoted words of President Johnson and those of Jefferson Keel (Chickasaw), 20th President of National Congress of American Indians, in his State of the Indian Address below give a glimpse into the situation of Native Americans:

> We stand at the beginning of a new era for Indian Country and for tribal relations with the United States. Previous eras were defined by what the federal government chose to do: the Indian removal period when tribes were forcibly removed from their homelands to reservations, the reorganization and termination era, the allotment era, even the recent promise of the self-determination era. But this new era is defined by what we, as Indian nations, choose to do for ourselves. [13]

The government's relocation program brought Native

people to the San Francisco Bay Area from many different tribes. This coalescing of people resulted in an energizing of pride in their histories and cultures. Native Americans actively supported King and participated in the August 1963 March on Washington. The civil rights movement inspired Native people and the Native American Rights Fund (NARF), which is still active today, was patterned after the Legal Defense and Education Fund of the National Association for the Advancement of Colored People (NAACP).

From the speeches and writings of Dr. King, he consistently advanced the idea of social justice, equality and civil rights of all people, not just those of his own race. John Echohawk, a member of the Pawnee Tribe and executive director of NARF, said that thanks to Dr. King, "The principle of tribal sovereignty was one that captured our imaginations, and we saw great potential in enforcing this legal right in the political climate of the 1960s."[14]

Significant Legislative Actions

Several significant pieces of national legislation occurred in the mid-to-late 1960s. The Economic Opportunity Act of 1965 allowed an autonomy to Native Americans that they had not experienced for many years. They were finally able to bypass the BIA "... while they planned, developed, and implemented their own social, educational, and economic initiatives."[15] This was followed by self-determination and economic development not allowed under BIA management.

Another significant piece of legislation was derived from the speeches of various public figures who spoke out in defense of Native Americans, which increased publicity and public awareness. This, in turn, brought about the 1968 Indian Civil Rights Act (ICRA), called the Indian Bill of Rights. Native Americans were guaranteed many of the civil rights they had fought for – rights as simple as free speech, press and assembly; protection from self-incrimination; protection from double jeopardy and equal protection under the law, among others.[16]

Native Americans are citizens of two nations: their individual tribes and the United States. As such, the bill "...

protect[s] individual Indians from arbitrary and unjust actions of tribal governments."[17] Mankiller wrote that the act "… brought further federal intervention into tribal governments and courts."[18] Once again, legislation meant to help Natives oftentimes worked to their detriment. They both gained and lost through this legislation.

U.S. Indian Legacy Addressed

As the 37th President of the United States, Richard Nixon served from January 20, 1969 until his resignation on August 9, 1974. During that time, he made several significant speeches addressing the legacy between the United States and the Native Americans and made recommendations to Congress of changes to be implemented. In an unplanned trip to the Lincoln Memorial at 4:40 a.m on May 9th, 1970, Nixon spoke with some of the antiwar protestors trying to draw them out by finding common ground they could discuss. The president explained the plight of minorities in the U.S. He then highlighted the injustices that had been done to the Blacks and Native Americans. "We took a proud and independent race and virtually destroyed them. We have to find ways to bring them back into decent lives in this country."[19]

Even as a presidential candidate, Nixon gave recognition to this idea in a September 1968 campaign speech to the National Congress of American Indians when he said, "American society can allow many different cultures to flourish in harmony, and we must provide an opportunity for those Indians wishing to do so to lead a useful and prosperous life in an Indian environment."[20]

Along with more specific proposals for legislation, President Nixon's Special Message to Congress on Indian Affairs, July 8, 1970, affirmed the historic relationship between the federal government and Native Americans and allowed for Indian communities to choose to take over control and operation of federally funded Indian programs. Nixon stated: "The time has come to break decisively with the past and to create conditions for a new era in which the Indian future is determined by Indian acts and Indian decisions."[21]

Alcatraz Island Occupied – A Pivotal Event

Alcatraz Island has a long history among Native Americans of the West Coast region. Their oral history can be traced back 10,000 years when the island "… was used as a place of isolation and ostracization for tribal members who had violated a tribal law or taboo."[22] Other Natives used Alcatraz for hunting or a place to hide from the Spanish. In an effort to symbolically claim the island for Native Americans,[23] an ultimately unsuccessful four-hour Native American occupation of Alcatraz in 1964 was nonetheless significant with demands including "…the use of the island for a cultural center and an Indian university…"[24] This protest was an awakening for many Native Americans, and the subsequent years saw other protests and the formation of national Native political groups.

The political environment was different in 1969, as protest and change were coming, and Native Americans took up Robert Kennedy's idealism with a renewal of energy and purpose.[25] Alcatraz became the focus for many. The protestors were mostly college students who were members of coastal tribes, as well as those who had been relocated from the reservations. More than 20 tribes were represented in the November 1969 occupation of Alcatraz, and they took the name "Indians of All Tribes."[26] Mankiller, later the Principal Chief of the Cherokee Nation of Oklahoma, wrote that she became an activist as a result of her participation in the Alcatraz occupation.

The demands of these protestors were the same as the earlier 1964 group with one addition – they wanted a museum on the island, as well as an Indian university and cultural center. Like the Sioux treaty of 1868, many treaties between Native Americans and the American government have a clause that promises "… to return all retired, abandoned, or out-of-use federal lands to the Native peoples from whom they were acquired."[27] In their 1969, *"Proclamation to the Great White Father and All His People*, the [protestors offered to] … purchase Alcatraz Island for twenty-four dollars ($24) in glass beads and red cloth, a precedent set by the white man's purchase of a similar island about 300 years ago."[28]

At first the government demanded they leave the island,

but it became apparent when greater numbers of protestors arrived – at one time as many as 1,000 – which they intended to stay. As their numbers increased, they organized with everyone assigned a job, from sanitation to cooking to childcare, with decisions by unanimous consent, per Native custom. In response, the federal government shut off electricity to the island and towed the freshwater barges – the only source of water to the island – thus denying them that access.

The protestors were not deterred. Support for them came from many directions: water, food including dried meat and salmon from some, prayer and song from others. Even public figures showed support, including well-known television and film visitors like "…. Anthony Quinn, Jane Fonda, Jonathan Winters, Ed Ames, and Merv Griffin. Candice Bergen brought her sleeping bag and spent a night on the floor of the clinic."[29]

Alternate solutions were proposed by the government, but by mid-1970, they were at a standstill in negotiations. "On June 10, 1971, armed federal marshals, FBI agents, and Special Forces police swarmed the island … The occupation was over…."[30] But the protestors underlying goal of awakening the American public to the struggles of Native Americans worked. President Nixon rescinded the Indian termination policy and "… introduced 22 pieces of legislation to support and expand Indian self-determination:"[31]

> Occupied lands near Davis California would become home to a Native American university. The occupation of Bureau of Indian Affairs offices in Washington, D.C. would lead to the hiring of Native Americans to work in the federal agency that had such a great effect on their lives.
>
> Alcatraz may have been lost, but the occupation gave birth to a political movement which continues to today.[32]

Native Education

In the 1970s, the U.S. Department of the Interior

contracted Dr. S. Lyman Tyler, Professor of History of the University of Utah, to write *A History of Indian Policy*. He was chosen for this task because of the extensive research he had previously conducted in the area of Indian policy. The book provides material from the colonial period through June 30, 1972 and documents the increase in Indian youth completing higher education. Because of this increase in interest, Native educators supported the efforts "... to document the history and culture of Native American groups from their own point of view."[33] Tyler states that to bring change, the following must be understood:

> It is not just the Indian who has learned from us, there is much to be learned from him – the values inherent in group identity: respect for nature; the right of men to participate in the institutions that affect their lives; and that no policy or program, regardless of how well intended will succeed without his approval.[34]

During this period, four Native institutions were brought together as a consortium to help students from federally recognized Native American tribes attain undergraduate and graduate degrees. Haskell Indian Junior College in Lawrence, Kansas, founded as a residential boarding school in 1884, is now Haskell Indian Nations University. The second institution is Southwestern Indian Polytechnic Institute in Albuquerque, New Mexico. The third is the Institute of American Indian Arts located in Santa Fe, New Mexico, and the fourth is Chilocco Indian School which is located between Arkansas City, Kansas and Ponca City, Oklahoma. The original four institutions are now part of a consortium made up of 37 tribal colleges and universities all funded through the Bureau of Indian Education and cover all areas of education from agriculture to law, medicine and the arts. Graduates work in their Indian communities, as well as in positions throughout the United States and internationally.

In 2005, Washington State passed legislation which "strongly encouraged Washington's public schools to include the history and culture of Washington's Indigenous Nations in the state's history and social studies curriculum."[35] The material, developed in coordination between educators and the 29 federally recognized Native Nations in the state, is known as "Since Time

Immemorial" (STI) and is now being used in schools throughout the state.[36] In February 2018, the National Museum of American Indians (NMAI) in Washington, D.C. launched a national education initiative to utilize the vast storehouse of knowledge and artifacts held there. The initiative called "Native Knowledge 360°" (NK360°) provides educators the tools to teach the next generation of students – Native and non-native – a more accurate American history than previous generations learned.

Shana Brown, of Yakama and Muckleshoot descent, taught in a Seattle public school and was instrumental in developing the STI material. NMAI contacted STI developers, including Brown, about helping with NK360°. In 2019, Washington was the first state to include NK360° along with STI as part of the core curriculum. So it was that in December 2019, Brown taught an American History lesson focused on the "… cultural, nutritional and spiritual connections people have with food … talk[s] about the ties between salmon and the Indigenous people of the Pacific Northwest."[37] As the students discussed the connection between food and why it is important to their own families, Brown asked them how they would feel if the salmon disappeared. One of the children gave an insightful reply "… this would 'kill something deep down inside.'"[38] Brown said that Native students are more engaged in a curriculum that includes their history, and non-native students are benefiting from a more accurate presentation of U.S. and Native American history.

Richard Walker wrote an article for the *National Museum of American Indian Magazine* titled, "Native History is American History," stating that during the time the two educational programs were being developed and implemented, a survey was conducted which Sarah B. Shear detailed in her 2015 article, "Manifesting Destiny: Re/presentations of Indigenous peoples in K-12 U.S. History."[39] The survey analyzed the curriculum of all 50 states and then provided evidence that the materials "… overwhelmingly present Indigenous peoples in a pre-1900 context and relegate the importance and presence of Indigenous peoples to the distant past…. The United States has always been a colonial power that views Native peoples as in the way."[40]

The STI and NK360° curriculum provide the most accurate history for future teachers, leaders and policy makers, and it is available to educators nationwide. Some states now require Native history be taught in their public schools.

Opportunity and Self-Determination

President Nixon's July 1970 speech stating that it was time for Indians to determine their future was followed by a reconvening of the National Council on Indian Opportunity (NCIO) that was established by President Johnson in 1968. Under the leadership of Vice-President Spiro T. Agnew, the NCIO was reorganized with an enlarged membership of eight Indians and eight government leaders. Eight recommendations came out of the NCIO meetings – all carried significant changes in federal government to Indian relations. Two brought great hope, which was to provide Native Americans opportunity and self-determination.

The first recommendation was the "restoration of the sacred lands near Blue Lake, New Mexico, used for tribal and religious purposes by the Indians of Taos Pueblo."[41] In order to avoid any conflict of interest with different government agencies and "… to assure independent legal representation for the Indians' natural resource right"[42] an Indian Trust Council Authority was established. In December 1970, the Taos Pueblo Indians saw Nixon sign the congressional measure that returned the Blue Lake area to them.[43]

Then, in a 1971 report to Congress, President Nixon said "Let's face it. Most Americans today are simply fed up with government at all levels. They will not – and should not – continue to tolerate the gaps between promise and performance in Government."[44] Promises to the people throughout the United States were often that – just promises. People had lost faith in the government and lost respect for the leaders. Nixon recommended that power and authority be restored to Indian leaders so they could work for the benefit of their people. Although the Indian Reorganization Act of 1934 had started the process of restoring power and authority to the Indian leaders, much still needed to be done within the reservation leadership and within the Department of the Interior. Programs resulted that trained and educated Indians. Self-determination had become an integral ingredient of the Indian thinking, whether in the city or on the reservation:

> In President Nixon's State of the Union Message to the 92nd Congress, January 20, 1972, the philosophy of "Self-Determination for Indians" was again pronounced and emphasis was given to the fact that a newly reorganized Bureau of Indian Affairs, with almost all-Indian leadership, will from now on be concentrating its resources on a program of reservation economies, creating local Indian Action Teams for Manpower training, and increased contracting of education and other functions to Indian communities.[45]

Natural Resources and Water Rights

In 1908, the United States Supreme Court decided a case, *Winters vs United States* that has become known as the Winters Doctrine, which is referenced in all succeeding lawsuits questioning water rights. It reads as follows:

> Establishes that when the federal government created the Indian reservations, water rights were reserved in sufficient quantity to meet the purposes for which the reservation was established.
>
> An Indian Reservation may reserve water for future use in an amount necessary to fulfill the purpose of the reservation, with a priority dating from the treaty that established the reservation.[46]

Another recommendation of the 1968 NCIO meetings covered natural resources on tribal lands. Senate Bill S 1571, introduced in April 1971, was settled December 4, 1971. It provided Native title to surface lands and subsurface resources for 40 million acres and $462,500,000 from the US over a period of 11 years, as well as income of $500,000,000 in mineral revenues. The bill was accepted by the Alaska Federation of Natives and signed by President Nixon December 18, 1971:[47]

The early 1972 policy statements gave the protection of resources, and particularly Indian water rights, a high priority ... One requirement was to be an inventory that would assess the extent of the water rights held by Indians as a property right reserved under the Winters doctrine 'which the United States as trustee is obligated to protect.'[48]

The Colorado River is one of the principal sources of water for the Southwestern U.S. and Northern Mexico, and it provides water to areas as far away as California. The Arapahoe aquifer is one source that provides water for the area on the eastern side of the Colorado Rocky Mountains. "The Arapahoe aquifer encompasses approximately 4,700-square miles and ranges in thickness from zero to 400 feet. Its maximum depth is approximately 1,700 feet."[49] Despite the size of the aquifer, the increasing population in the territory puts great demands on the water supply. The humidity level in the region is always low even during high snow months which supports the sport of skiing; however, the snow melt which people, animals and crops are dependent upon has decreased in recent years. The increased population, combined with over 300 days of sunshine and the low humidity in the region results as a large percentage of the snow evaporates instead of melting and running into the rivers as it does in other areas of the country. All this contributes to the ever-decreasing water that is available for the region. As early as 1972, Commissioner Bruce stated, "... there is an increasing demand for water to support the economic growth of the American West. However, there is a limited supply. As a result, Indian people's reserved right to water is not very popular with other interests."[50]

The Ogallala Aquifer which is a major source of water for Native Americans of the west and the water supply for everyone (Native and non-native) are interconnected. "Courts have held that Indian tribes have 'reserved' rights in all waters that arise, on, border, traverse, or underlie their reservations. – Homelands without an adequate water supply are essentially worthless."[51] Basically, Indian water rights eclipse all other water claims. Everyone who wants to dig a well for their home, land or business is required to drill deep enough so that the well is drawing water from below the aquifer designated to support the Indians' homelands. Greater demand has required area Indians to take their case to court to again reiterate the rights given to them by treaty.

In his 2019 book, *The Uninhabitable Earth: Life After Warming*, David Wallace-Wells documents the loss of water in specific regions of the United States. "The United States won't be spared – boomtown Phoenix is, for instance, already in emergency planning mode, ... [52] We can extrapolate that loss to all as the following indicates:

> The Colorado River Basin, which serves water to seven states, lost twelve cubic miles of groundwater between 2004 and 2013; the Ogallala Aquifer in part of the Texas Panhandle lost 15 feet in a decade, and is expected to drain by 70 percent over the next fifty years in Kansas.[53]

Indian Policy Challenged: Activism Increases

Louis R. Bruce, a member of the Mohawk Indian tribe and an advocate of Indians' rights was Commissioner of Indian Affairs under President Nixon. In June of 1972, he is quoted as saying:

> Since I came to Washington in 1969, the face of Indian America has undergone some dramatic and far reaching changes. ... The will for self-determination has become a vital component of the thinking of Indian leadership and the grassroots Indian on every reservation and in every city. It is an irreversible trend, a tide in the destiny of American Indians that will eventually compel all of America ... to recognize the dignity and human rights of Indian people.[54]

There was a rise in Native American activism during the 1960s and 1970s. One major event showing that activism culminated with the occupation of the BIA headquarters in Washington, DC. Called the "Trail of Broken Treaties," a cross-country caravan started on the west coast in October 1972 and reached DC in early November. Eight Native organizations participated in the caravan, and the activists developed a "Twenty-Point Position" paper to define their demands, assert sovereignty of the Indian Nations and bring the nation's attention to the injustices still occurring. When the Nixon administration refused to meet with the protestors, over 500 participants occupied the BIA offices for about a week, during which time records, deeds and other papers were destroyed and some areas of the building were vandalized. Presidential aides then negotiated with the protest leaders and some concessions were made. This approach was followed in 1973 when activists occupied the Pine Ridge Indian Reservation for two months. Due to these and other activists' events and the resulting media coverage, "Public opinion polls revealed widespread sympathy for the Native Americans at Wounded Knee."[55] Following these events, the administration replaced Bruce as commissioner, and the BIA enacted some policy changes.

When Gerald Ford became president in 1974, termination had been the government's official policy since 1954. Nixon had stated a philosophy on self-determination, but it was Ford who signed the legislation in January 1975, which made it federal policy. At the signing, Ford stated:

> I am committed to furthering the self-determination of Indian communities … Self-determination means that you can decide the nature of your tribe's relationship with the Federal Government within the framework of the Self-Determination Act.[56]

James Earl Carter Jr, the 39th President, was sworn into office January 20, 1977 and served until 1981. Carter marked his inauguration as a "… new dedication within our Government, and a new spirit among us all. … to help shape a just and peaceful world that is truly humane."[57] In his 1977 book, *The Wit and Wisdom of Jimmy Carter*, Bill Adler quoted the president as stating, "The test of a government is not how popular it is with the powerful and privileged few but how honestly and fairly it deals with the many who must depend on it."[58] In the American Indian Religious Freedom Act of 1978, it states:

It is the fundamental right of every American, as

guaranteed by the first amendment of the Constitution, to worship as he or she pleases. ... This legislation sets forth the policy of the United States to protect and preserve the inherent right of American Indian, Eskimo, Aleut, and Native Hawaiian people to believe, express, and exercise their traditional religions. [59]

Mother Lode of Cherokee History

Archeologists found a significant amount of American Indian history, covering over 1,400 archaeological sites and spanning more than twelve thousand years. Situated along the Appalachian summit with broad floodplains of rivers, intermountain lands, coves, creeks and mountain summits, all were occupied during various cultural phases and "... they all represent the spiritual and material culture of the Cherokees as it was until replaced by the Euro-American material and economic culture in the nineteenth century."[60]

The Tennessee Valley Authority (TVA) operates in portions of Tennessee, Alabama, Mississippi, Georgia, North Carolina and Virginia. As a federally owned corporation chartered by Congress in 1933, it provides economic development to the Tennessee Valley, including navigation, flood control and electricity generation. As such, it has the power to claim land by eminent domain. In the 1960s and 1970s, TVA was planning to build Tellico Dam in Central Tennessee, which contained many of the previously identified archaeological sites and held much of the ancestral Cherokee sacred grounds.

Numerous publications and individuals spoke out regarding the Tellico Dam project:

> ... alerted the public to the fact that the Little Tennessee Valley was the 'richest archaeological section in the Appalachians.' Proof of these riches has been emerging since 1967. Acting under federal law (the Reservoir Salvage Act of 1960, the National Historic Preservation Act of 1966 and two other preservation and protection acts passed during the course of the

project), teams of archeologists from the University of Tennessee conducted surveys and excavations in the Tellico area. Funded principally by the National Park Service and TVA, this work was done to help guide land use so that cultural heritage could be preserved.[61]

Progress Versus Sacred Ground

While the first removal of the Cherokees was in 1838 with The Trail of Tears, there was a less well-known removal that occurred 104 years later in 1942 when the Army expanded Camp Gruber outside of Muskogee, Oklahoma, by condemning eighty tracts and forcing seventy Cherokee families to move. A third removal occurred in 1979 and followed the same pattern, with the building of Tellico Dam in Central Tennessee. Its construction was disputed by environmentalists, as well as the Cherokees. Yet the endangered snail darter garnered more media attention than the concerns of the Cherokees over the burial – under water – of their sacred grounds.

On September 17, 1979, the *U.S. News and World Report* quoted the mayor of Tellico Plains saying, "Indians moved off 200 years ago, Live Americans -be they black, white or red -are more important than the remains of dead Indians."[62] This small town in Tennessee was the heart of Cherokee protests as it and the surrounding area contained much of what was sacred to the Cherokee. People living in the states adjacent to Tennessee heard much about the snail darter from the environmentalists but seldom did the media report the Cherokee concerns. In Marilou Awaikta's book, *Selu: Seeking the Corn-Mother's Wisdom*, she writes:

> But the Cherokee are 'live Americans.' Their ancestors didn't just 'move off' the land. And 'the remains of dead Indians' include the rich and highly developed culture they left behind, a culture that is part of the heritage of all Americans, 'be they black, white or red.' Archeologists have established that the indigenous habitation of the Tellico area goes back twelve thousand years. The valley contains a national treasure of knowledge. How could the watchdog of the people fail for so long to pick up on an issue of such

239

magnitude?[63]

The Cherokee depended on the National Historic Preservation Act of 1966 and the U.S. Constitution to protect them in their legal fight against the government. Again, the law failed them, and on September 25, 1979, President Carter signed a law exempting Tellico Dam. Then, on October 12, the Eastern Band of Cherokee and the Cherokee Nation of Oklahoma jointly filed a suit charging "... that completion of the Tellico project would destroy sacred burial grounds, [and] 'denies Indians their religious freedom guaranteed under the First Amendment.'"[64] As in projects of this scope, some people approved of the dam and moved, some were forced to move and others stayed until the last minute, hoping it would not be built. However, larger forces were at work as TVA claimed 16,000 acres for the lake and 22,000 acres of adjoining property under eminent domain. Those skeptical of TVA's motive in claiming the 22,000 acres to "... regulate and control its industrial and recreational development as an economic draw in a job-poor area,"[65] proved correct when about half of that property was later turned over to developers for profit.

The political forces had won yet again. The sluice gates closed, and the Tennessee River flooded the Tennessee Valley forever drowning "... the spiritual and historic heartland of the Cherokee nation."[66] They had again suffered removal but this time from the historical and sacred sites that provided ties to their heritage. Awiakta wrote:

> And the federal government gave them time to save only a fraction of it. Apparently, four federal laws are not enough to protect this treasure... Why have We-the-People waited so long to listen? Or perhaps a more basic question is: 'In the fight against injustice, can anyone ever start early enough?' How much more of our resources can we afford to lose in the name of industry and energy? There has to be a limit. For there comes a point where material progress is no longer a virtue. 'Our claim,' said tribal council chairman Dan McCoy, 'deals with human rights and dignity.'"[67]

Non-Indian graves had been relocated but not the Cherokee. Only about 20% of the American Indian sacred burial sites had been excavated. The Cherokees wanted the remains of their ancestors to be reburied at sites of their choosing with the proper Cherokee ceremonies. Now they had lost 80% to the rising waters of the Tennessee River, and the rest was beyond their reach in boxes in the basements of the University of Tennessee waiting to be repatriated.[68] At least now, they knew that the sacred sites would no longer be desecrated, as they were covered by the rising waters of the Tennessee River.

> Some of the valley's rich heritage was preserved. Fort Loudon, an eighteenth-century British fort, was moved to an artificial bluff and developed into a tasteful museum. Many of the Cherokee artifacts taken from the excavations were put on display and interpreted there, as well as in the nearby Sequoyah Birth Place Museum. TVA had helped the Cherokees establish the museum on a tract of land the agency gave them, as it had promised to do. In June 1986, in the vicinity of the museum, Cherokee from the Eastern Band conducted a small private reinternment ceremony. The bones of 191 ancestors were returned to their rest in the valley that had been their home. ... Scholars began to write about Tellico. Its metaphorical significance became increasingly clear.[69]

The historic Cherokee capital city of Chota is in present-day Monroe Country, Tennessee. The townhouse site, listed on the National Register of Historic Places, was discovered during the excavation for Tellico Dam. "The area was raised above the reservoir's operating level and connected via a causeway to the mainland. The [new] Chota monument, consists of eight pillars – one for each of the seven Cherokee clans, and one for the nation."[70] A powerful Cherokee heritage, the grave of Chief Oconostota, "... was reinterred next to the monument. This site is now managed by the Eastern Band of the Cherokee."[71]

Author's Thoughts

From the arrival of the first settlers in the new world, Native Americans have been pushed from their ancestral lands with the often-expressed sentiment being, "What are we going to do about the "Indian problem?" The government experimented with different programs with Native Americans in the middle – never truly knowing where they stood. They did know the ultimate goals were to obtain their land, which was ideal for farming, and to expand the reach of the United States. In the early 1800s, land in Indian Territory was deemed worthless to the settlers and therefore perfect for the "Five Civilized Tribes," one of which was the Cherokee. Tribes were ultimately forced to surrender their lands, opening the area west of the Mississippi River from Mexico in the south to Canada in the north. Thirty-nine of these tribes now live in Oklahoma – an area promised to the five tribes for "As long as the rivers shall flow."

The occupation of the BIA offices in Washington DC, as well as Alcatraz Island and other national events, united Native American tribes in activism. These events strengthened the national Indian organizations which, in turn, supported their health and welfare, as well as legal rights. Standing together, their collective voices were heard as never before in U.S. history. The National Congress of American Indians is one such organization, and their words and actions carry weight as they speak for all the tribes rather than an individual Indian or tribe. The words of several U.S. Presidents and Presidents of the National Congress of American Indians exemplify the situation faced by Native Americans into the 21st Century:

John F. Kennedy

For a subject worked and reworked so often in novels, motion pictures, and television, American Indians remain probably the least understood and most misunderstood Americans of us all.[72]

Gerald Ford

I am committed to furthering the self-determination

of Indian communities but without terminating the special relationship between the Federal Government and the Indian people. I am strongly opposed to termination. Self-determination means that you can decide the nature of your tribe's relationship with the Federal Government within the framework of the Self-Determination Act, which I signed in January of 1975.[73]

Joe Garcia -19th President of the Nation Congress of American Indians

Strength, triumph over adversity, the will to succeed – the Indian Nations stand strong today. We are growing more self-sufficient, more economically developed, more politically active and, as always, steadfastly committed to the stewardship and defense of our home, the United States of America.[74]

The education programs, "Since Time Immemorial" and "Native Knowledge 360," first incorporated into the Seattle, Washington school curriculum are an important shift in the U.S. history being taught to both Native and non-native students. However, it will take a nationwide plan and several generations before people have a more realistic view of American history.

In 2020, COVID-19 struck the global community, killing many and changing the lives of people in different ways. In the U.S., the mantra of politicians, economists, healthcare personnel and first responders, as well as reporters and the general public became "We are all in this together." Native Americans were affected just as other Americans.

The Indian reservations saw the numbers of those infected rise precipitously along with the death toll, with the Navajo Nation suffering the greatest – the number of deaths in proportion to the population ranks the Navajo Nation third after New York and New Jersey. The Coronavirus Aid, Relief and Economic Security Act originally did not include any money for the reservations, but thankfully wiser heads got money allotted for Native Americans.

In this time of crisis, we need to focus on the promises of

the Pledge of Allegiance. The United States is one nation made up of many people – including the First Citizens of this great land, the Native Americans. Our hearts and minds must be united as one all-inclusive nation. In 2020, that does not appear to be who we are and that needs to change. Liberty and justice need to be a reality instead of a statement – starting now.

Endnotes:

1   Inaugural Address of President John F. Kennedy. Washington, D.C., January 20, 1961. https://www.jfklibrary.org. Accessed 10 May 2020.

2   Prucha, Francis Paul, editor. *Documents of United States Indian Policy 2nd Ed.* U of Nebraska P, 1990. p. 244.

3   Moquin, Wayne with Charles Van Doren, editors. *Great Documents in American Indian History.* Da Capo Press Inc, 1995. p. 237.

4   Moquin. p. 337-338.

5   Johnson, Lyndon B. "Special Message to the Congress on the Problems of the American Indian: 'The Forgotten American.'" 6 Mar 1968. *The American Presidency Project.* https://bit.ly/355a9nV. Accessed 14 Dec 2016.

6   Tyler, S. Lyman. *A History of Indian Policy.* U.S. Department of the Interior, Bureau of Indian Affairs, 1973. p. 200.

7   Tyler. p. 200.

8   Bennett, Robert L. Commissioner, Bureau of Indian Affairs. A poem quoted in "American Indians-A Special Minority," in remarks before the Institute of Race Relations, Fisk University, Nashville, TN, 29 Jun 1967. https://bit.ly/380Jo5V.

9 Mankiller. Wilma and Michael Wallis. *Mankiller: A Chief and Her People*. St Martin's Press, 1993. p. 160.

10 Mankiller. p. 71-72.

11 Mankiller. p. 72-73.

12 Mankiller. p. 73.

13 Keel, Jefferson. "9th Annual State of Indian Nations Address Remarks", *National Congress of American Indians,* 27 Jan 2011, https://bit.ly/2Sbkw22.

14 King, Martin Luther Jr. *Why We can't Wait*. Beacon Press. Boston. 1964. Ch 7, pp. 202-203.

15 Mankiller. Wilma and Michael Wallis. *Mankiller: A Chief and Her People*. St Martin's Press, 1993. p. 188.

16 Prucha, Francia Paul, editor. *Documents of United States Indian Policy. 2nd Edition*. U of Nebraska P, 1990. Civil Rights Act of 1968, Titles II-VII. pp. 249-256.

17 "1968: President Johnson signs the Indian Civil Rights Act." *Native Voices*. https://bit.ly/3oPXFbM.

18 Mankiller. Wilma and Michael Wallis. *Mankiller: A Chief and Her People.* St Martin's Press. 1993. p. 189.

19 Ahlers, Mike M. and Athena Jones. "Tape sheds light on surreal meeting between Nixon, protesters." 11 Nov 2011. https://cnn.it/3dLyEJx. Accessed 20 Oct 2020.

20 Hearings before the Subcommittee on Indian Affairs of the Committee on Interior and Insular Affairs, U.S. Senate S. 750 and H.R. 471. p 185.

21 Tyler S. Lyman. *A History of Indian Policy*. U.S. Department of the Interior, Bureau of Indian Affairs, 1973. p. 218.

22 Johnson, Troy. "We Hold the Rock: The Alcatraz Indian Occupation." *National Park Service*. https://bit.ly/3mL9u11. Accessed 8 Apr. 2020.

23 Johnson.

24 Johnson.

25 Mankiller, Wilma and Michael Wallis. *Mankiller: A Chief and Her People*. St Martin's Press, 1993. p. 161.

26 Johnson, Troy. "We Hold the Rock: The Alcatraz Indian Occupation." *National Park Service*. https://bit.ly/3mL9u11 Accessed 8 Apr. 2020.

27 Johnson.
28 "History is a Weapon: Alcatraz Proclamation and Letter"
    1969. historyisaweapon.com. 4/10/20.
29 Mankiller, Wilma and Michael Wallis. *Mankiller: A Chief
    and Her People*. St Martin's Press, 1993. p. 191.
30 Johnson, Troy. "We Hold the Rock: The Alcatraz Indian
    Occupation." *National Park Service*. https://bit.ly/3mL9u11.
    Accessed 8 Apr. 2020.
31 Unforgettable Change: 1960: American Indians Occupy
    Alcatraz." *picturethis.museumca.org*. https://bit.ly/3n7QwCr.
    Accessed 21 Mar 2020.
32 Johnson, Troy. "We Hold the Rock: The Alcatraz Indian
    Occupation." *National Park Service*. https://bit.ly/3mL9u11.
    Accessed 8 Apr. 2020.
33 Tyler, S. Lyman. *A History of Indian Policy*. U.S.
    Department of the Interior, Bureau of Indian Affairs, 1973. p.
    233.
34 Tyler. p. 227.
35 Walker, Richard. "Native History is American History:
    NMAI is Bringing Indigenous Perspectives Into the
    Classroom." *National Museum of American Indian
    Magazine*. Spring 2020, p. 29.
36 Walker. p. 28
37 Walker. pp. 28-33.
38 Walker. p. 28.
39 Walker. p. 29.
40 Walker. p. 29.
41 Tyler, S. Lyman. *A History of Indian Policy*. U.S.
    Department of the Interior, Bureau of Indian Affairs, 1973. p.
    221.
42 Tyler. p. 222.
43 Tyler. pp. 221-222.
44 Tyler. p.224.
45 Tyler. pp. 256-257.
46 United States, Supreme Court. *Winters v. United States, 207
    U.S. 564*, 6 Jan 1908. https://bit.ly/36mYbHg.
47 Tyler, S. Lyman. *A History of Indian Policy*. U.S.
    Department of the Interior, Bureau of Indian Affairs, 1973. p.
    275.

48 Tyler, S. Lyman. *A History of Indian Policy,* U.S. Department of the Interior, Bureau of Indian Affairs, 1973 "Policy Statement on Water Rights early 1972." p. 265.

49 "Aquifers: Arapahoe Aquifer." *Douglas County, Colorado.* https://bit.ly/3kGJvGh. Accessed 10 Apr 2020.

50 Tyler, S. Lyman. *A History of Indian Policy.* U.S. Department of the Interior, Bureau of Indian Affairs, 1973. "Policy Statement on Water Rights early 1972" p. 265.

51 "Public Rights in Water: The Winters Doctrine." Updated 18 Jun 2019. https://fla.st/3n4x3mn. Accessed 20 Apr 20.

52 Wallace-Wells, David. *The Uninhabitable Earth: Life After Warming.* Tim Duggan Books, 2019. p. 96.

53 Wallace-Wells. p 89.

54 Tyler, S. Lyman. *A History of Indian Policy.* U.S. Department of the Interior, Bureau of Indian Affairs, 1973. p. 255.

55 "Wounded Knee Incident." *Wikipedia: The Free Encyclopedia,* Wikimedia Foundation, https://bit.ly/3cPu64f. Accessed 15 Apr 2020.

56 Ford, Gerald R. *Public Papers of the Presidents of the United States: Gerald R. Ford, 1976-1977. Google Books.* https://bit.ly/3kLV13y. p. 670.

57 Carter, Jimmy. "Inaugural Address of Jimmy Carter." *Yale Law School, Lillian Goldman Law Library*, 20 Jan 1977, https://bit.ly/3iig5gP.

58 Carter, Jimmy. "Governor Jimmy Carter's Inaugural Address." *Jimmy Carter Library*, 12 January 1971, https://bit.ly/36lDV8M.

59 Public Law No. 95-341, The American Indian Religious Freedom Act, 92 Stat. 469, August 11, 1978, 42 U.S.C. § 1996. https://bit.ly/3kNPF8L. Accessed 1 Nov 2020.

60 Mails, Thomas E. *The Cherokee People, The Story of the Cherokees from Earliest Origins to Contemporary Times.* Marlowe & Co., 1992. p. 37.

61 Awiakta, Marilou. *Selu, Seeking the Corn-Mother's Wisdom.* Fulcrum Publishing, 1993. p. 51

62 Awiakta p. 58.

63 Awiakta. pp. 58-59.

64. Awiakta. p. 49.
65 Awiakta. p. 51.
66 Awiakta. p. 57.
67 Awiakta. p. 51.
68 Awiakta. p. 60.
69 Awiakta. p. 62.
70 "Chota (Cherokee town)." https://en.wikipedia.org/wiki/. Accessed 8 Apr 2020.
71 "Chota (Cherokee town)." https://en.wikipedia.org/wiki/. Accessed 8 Apr 2020.
72 Inaugural Address of President John F. Kennedy. Washington, D.C., January 20, 1961. https://www.jfklibrary.org. Accessed 10 May 2020.
73 Ford, President Gerald. "US Presidents in Their Own Words Concerning American Indians: Speech by President Gerald Ford." *Native News Online.net*. https://bit.ly/2U4t3oC. Accessed 18 Feb 2019.
74 Joe Garcia, President. "The Four Great Steps." *The National Congress of American Indians*, 2 Feb 2006. https://bit.ly/3l4bJM6, para. 4.

| THIRTEEN |

Modern Era in Indian Relations (1981 to 2020)

Over the last forty years, there have been presidential statements that emphasized a greater understanding and appreciation for the Native people, their culture and governments. In some cases, common sense laws have resulted from that awakening; however, a great deal remains to be done.

Ronald Reagan became the 40th President of the United States on January 20, 1981 and the first president of the modern era in Indian relations, which includes the early 21st century. In his inaugural address, Reagan called upon Americans to "begin an era of national renewal." In response to the serious problems facing the country, both foreign and domestic, he asserted his familiar campaign phrase: "… government is not the solution to our problem; government is the problem…"[1] and that has certainly been true for Native Americans throughout their interactions with the U.S.

Yet a little over a year later, Reagan spoke to the students and faculty at Moscow State University with a different message. Following the address, Reagan stated his opinion regarding the American Indian in a question-and-answer session:

> Let me tell you just a little something about the American Indian in our land. We have provided millions of acres of land for what are called preservations – or reservations, I should say. They, from the beginning, announced that they wanted to maintain their way of life, as they had always lived there in the desert and the plains and so forth. And we

249

set up these reservations, so they could have a Bureau of Indian Affairs to help take care of them. At the same time, we provided education for them – schools on the reservations. And they're free also to leave the reservations and be American citizens among the rest of us, and many do. Some still prefer, however, that way – that early way of life. And we've done everything we can to meet their demands as to how they want to live. Maybe we made a mistake. Maybe we should not have humored them in that wanting to stay in that kind of primitive lifestyle. Maybe we should have said, 'No, come join us; be citizens along with the rest of us.' As I say, many have; many have been very successful... And you'd be surprised; some of them became very wealthy because some of those reservations were overlaying great pools of oil, and you can get very rich pumping oil. And so, I don't know what their complaint might be.[2]

Reagan was inconsistent in his attitudes toward Native Americans, often speaking against them as he did in Moscow, while in the same year signing into law the Indian Gaming Regulatory Act (IGRA) which introduced "… the most massive movement of tribal economic growth in history. … IGRA has served to strengthen the inherent powers of American Indian government to determine and build their own economic futures."[3] At the same time IGRA helped the American Indians by allowing them to build their own economic futures, Indian country experienced major federal funding cuts to their social services program – another example of help received and help withdrawn.

U.S. Signs UN Genocide Resolution in 1988

The previous statements, along with the attitude of the U.S. government toward Native Americans over the past centuries, relates to the 1948 Resolution 260 titled "Convention on the Prevention and Punishment of the Crime of Genocide," discussed in Chapter 11 due to U.S. actions contrary to the resolution. This approach included the outlawing of Native languages, religion, culture and governments; moving Native

Americans from ancestral lands; forced enrollment and sale of land to whites; and failing to recognize tribes despite legal battles stretching back 169 years. The UN resolution was specifically to outlaw genocide. While President Truman signed it in 1948 making the U.S. the first nation to sign the accord, it could not become law until approved by the Senate. It languished there until 1988 because a small group of senators opposed the treaty seeing it as a threat to U.S. sovereignty.

The resolution was supported by Presidents Truman, Kennedy, Johnson, Nixon, Ford and Carter, but the Senate refused to ratify it until February 1986. Failure of the government to act opened the United States up to international criticism on the country's human rights stance. Finally, in November 1988, Reagan signed Resolution 260 into law during a campaign stop in Chicago.[4]

The resolution, as it was passed, lost much of its original significance and legal implications towards many groups of Americans – Native and others. Discussions of genocide and its implications are often controversial, with people having different views of what constitutes genocide. Per Reagan's words at the Chicago signing, "The legislation defines genocide as acting with the 'specific intent to destroy, in whole or in substantial part, a national, ethnic, racial, or religious group.'"[5]

A number of tribes throughout the country suffered forced marches, resulting in a large number of deaths during and after the trek, while many were rounded up and forced onto reservations. Some Native children were schooled close to home, but nonetheless were made to conform to white ideals. The children taken from their homes and sent to boarding schools – many of which were run by missionaries with the goal of making them Christian – had their hair cut, were required to dress as white people did and were forbidden from speaking their Native languages. The federal government outlawed Native American religions and tribal governments. All of these actions against Native Americans have been documented by U.S. government agencies over the course of U.S. history. As stated in 1992 by Robert Henry, former Oklahoma Attorney General:

What began as agreements between equal nations deteriorated over time to land seizures, land allotments, assimilation, tribal termination, and, some would say, deliberate attempts to do to Native Americans what Hitler once tried to do to the Jews.[6]

Native American Heritage Emphasized

Eight years after Reagan, George H. W. Bush became the forty-first president on January 20, 1989. Acee Agoyo of San Juan Pueblo, New Mexico, cofounder and editor-in-chief for *indianz.com*, wrote an article for *indianz.com* titled, "George H.W. Bush, 1924-2018, left lasting mark on Indian Country," in which he provides the highlights of Bush's administration on the Indians of America stating that Bush "… was the first president to issue a proclamation establishing November as National American Indian Heritage Month, now known as Native American Heritage Month."[7] In the November 14, 1990 proclamation, he emphasized the "… special relationship between the federal government and Indian tribes – despite a number of conflicts, inequities, and changes over the years – our unique government-to-government relationship has endured."[8] On March 2, 1992, as the United States prepared to celebrate Columbus' "discovery" in 1492, Bush proclaimed, the "Year of the American Indian … calling attention to the resilience of Indigenous peoples in light of repeated attempts to eradicate them over the prior 500 years."[9]

Although he served only one term as president, Bush signed 45 pieces of enduring legislation and oversaw policy that directly benefitted Indian country.[10] Some of the laws directly affected a specific tribe like the Ponca Restoration Act and the Zuni Land Conservation Act. Others were broader and delivered benefits to all Native Americans, as seen in the Indian Arts and Crafts Act, the Native American Graves Protection and Repatriation Act and the National Museum of the American Indian Act – all signed in Bush's first two years in office. In June 1991, Bush reaffirmed the positive aspect of Reagan's Indian policy. Bush's statement contained the following:

This government-to-government relation is the result of sovereign and independent tribal governments being incorporated into the fabric of our Nation, of Indian tribes becoming what our courts have come to refer to as quasi-sovereign domestic dependent nations. Over the years, the relationship has flourished, grown, and evolved into a vibrant partnership in which over 500 tribal governments stand shoulder to shoulder with the other governmental units that form our Republic.[11]

Over the centuries, some Native languages have declined in usage, while others have died out altogether. To counter the decline, Bush signed legislation in 1992 that helped restore Native languages through special programs within the tribal schools and communities. Another way of restoring and emphasizing usage is seen today as Native languages meet the language requirements in a number of tribal colleges.[12] There were two significant aspects of the law. One was to reverse "... the scattered policies of the 19th and 20th centuries that so devastated Native languages,"[13] and the second was to further encourage the teaching of Native languages to children, educators and interpreters. Proficiency in Native languages are an additional provision of the law in that their languages are now considered to fulfill foreign language entrances requirements at Native colleges and universities.[14]

Tribal Relationships with the Clinton Administration

Fifteen months after becoming president in January 1993, Bill Clinton invited Native American leaders to a meeting at the White House, the first meeting with a sitting president since 1822. Of the 556 invited leaders, 322 attended the meeting, which covered "... economic development, tribal sovereignty, health care, education and government-to-government relations."[15]

Clinton pledged to uphold the government's trust obligations to tribes, vowing to 'honor and respect tribal sovereignty.' That included federal protection of traditional religions and ceremonies... outlined three guiding principles for federal-tribal relationships. The first principle was to respect your values, your religions, your identity and your sovereignty, … The second principle called for a full partnership between the federal government and tribal nations, and the third demanded that the government 'improve the living conditions of those whom we serve.'[16]

During his two terms in office, Clinton signed several significant pieces of legislation that protected Native Americans. The tribes lacked autonomy in much of their lives, and this series of laws sought to correct that. The first was Public Law 103-263, which allowed tribes to levy taxes and administer their own law enforcement. The government admitted their inability to manage the Indian trust funds, and Public Law 103-412 turned management of the trusts over to the tribes. Then Clinton took a significant step in 1993 when he appointed Ada Deer as the first Native woman to be assistant secretary for Indian Affairs. Deer was from the Menominee Nation of Wisconsin.[17]

Several laws formalized apologies by the government to Indigenous groups. The most significant was in celebration of the 175th anniversary of the BIA. Kevin Gover, assistant secretary of Indian Affairs, spoke at the ceremony admitting the agency's part in "… the ethnic cleansing and cultural annihilation of Natives."[18] In his speech that day, Gover stated:

> I stand before you as the leader of an institution that in the past has committed acts so terrible that they infect, diminish and destroy the lives of Indian people decades later, generations later, these wrongs must be acknowledged if the healing is to begin.[19]

An executive order in 1996 addressed the need for federal protection of Indian sacred sites and for Indians to be allowed access to the sites for ceremonial use. For years, laws had prohibited Indians from using peyote and a new law "… prohibits the Drug Enforcement Agency from interfering in its growth and use for religious purposes."[20] This was a huge concession on the part of the government in recognizing peyote as part of Native American religious practices.

June 1996 saw the largest class-action lawsuit to that date – with around 500,000 plaintiffs – filed against the federal government. The U.S. Interior and Treasury departments were sued over the mismanagement of Indian trust funds. It wasn't until President Obama was in office that the case was finally settled for $3.4 billion.

On October 29, 1996, Clinton issued a proclamation regarding American Indian and Alaska Native peoples which included:

> Let us rededicate ourselves to the principle that all Americans have the tools to make the most of their God-given potential. For Indian tribes and tribal members, this means that the authority of tribal governments must be accorded the respect and support to which they are entitled under the law. It means that American Indian children and youth must be provided a solid education and the opportunity to go on to college. It means that more must be done to stimulate tribal economies, create jobs, and increase economic opportunities ... We must teach our children about our past – both the good and the bad – so that they may learn from our successes and mistakes ... [21]

Clinton's support continued when he visited the Pine Ridge Indian Reservation, in the southwest corner of South Dakota, in 1999. He became the first sitting president since Franklin D. Roosevelt to visit, and he discussed a wide range of topics with tribal leaders including economic, educational and housing opportunities. A visit to the Navajo Nation in the southwest U.S. came the following year where he stated:

> There is nothing more important to me than getting this government-to-government relationship right, but getting it right in a way that will empower you to lift yourselves and your children to fulfill your potential and your dreams... [22]

In February 2000, Clinton met with tribal leaders to announce his "Historic FY2001 Native American Initiative." In the fiscal budget for 2001, he proposed the largest increase ever for Native American initiatives. It stood at $9.4 billion, an increase of $1.2 million. Instead of the bulk of the money going to the BIA and the Department of Health and Human Service's Indian Health Services as in past years, Clinton proposed school construction repair, school renovation loan and grant programs, recruitment of 1,000 teachers, increased funding for tribal colleges, improving public safety and law enforcement, increased Indian healthcare by $230 million to $2.6 billion, plus funds to address the digital divide by encouraging Native Americans to enter science and technology training at Native colleges. Other programs were addressed to provide greater living conditions, including a housing grant to repair or replace dilapidated homes across Indian country.[23] Clinton's intentions to improve lives across Indian country were clear with his proposed budget; however, congressional approval is required of each fiscal year's budget, and considering the complexity of the federal budget process, there are no readily available figures to show how much of Clinton's proposed budget to improve Native American lives was approved.

In the last months of Clinton's administration, he signed several other pieces of legislation that opened "… development and employment opportunities on tribal lands [and encouraged] meaningful consultation and collaboration with tribal officials in the development of federal policies that have tribal implications."[24]

Indifference During Bush Presidency

On January 20, 2001, George W. Bush became the 43rd president. During the presidential race, he " … championed for states' rights, which he believed trumped the rights of tribes."[25] Whatever the situation – economic and specifically land claims made by his states' rights beliefs contradicted the U.S. constitution and federal Indian law and engendered politics of division.

Bush gave his attention to international affairs, which was highlighted by the 911 attack, the search for the perpetrators and subsequent wars, with domestic policy taking a back seat. Minorities took a secondary position, and Indians were relegated even lower as domestic concerns took a back seat to the foreign agenda. In her 2016 article for *indiancountrytoday.com*, Alysa Landry wrote "Bush's Indian policy was one of benign indifference."[26] Policies flow down from the president to the other federal departments, so meaningful Indian policy suffered neglect during the Bush years.

During the 2004 presidential campaign, Bush spoke to the UNITY convention for journalists of color when he stumbled over a question of Indian sovereignty and its meaning in the 21st century. He stated, "Tribal sovereignty means that. It's sovereign. You're a … you're a … you've been given sovereignty and you're viewed as a sovereign entity."[27] The following day, Reverend Jesse Jackson had a follow-up interview where he was asked about Bush' answer about tribal sovereignty. Jackson explained that sovereignty was a legal relationship between the Native American tribes and the federal government. He went on to say that states' rights have nothing to do with sovereignty, and the states have no legal rights to interfere with the Native nations.[28]

Then in declaring National American Indian Heritage Month on October 30, 2006, President Bush stated in Proclamation 8076:

> My Administration will continue to work on a government-to-government basis with tribal governments, honor the principles of tribal sovereignty and the right to self-determination, and help ensure America remains a land of promise for American Indians, Alaska Natives, and all our citizens.[29]

A search of Bush's presidential proclamations and executive orders found no further reference to Native Americans or Alaska Natives during the remainder of his second term in office.

Obama Hailed as Best President for Indian Country

The first African American elected to the presidency, Barack Obama, served as the 44th president from January 20, 2009 until January 20, 2017. In an article covering the Democratic National Convention in September 2012, writer Chris Casteel quoted Cherokee Principal Chief Bill John Baker: "[Obama] is the best president for Indian Country in the history of the United States. ... This president has made promises to Indian Country, and he's kept them, He is a promise keeper. And that needs to be recognized and rewarded."[30]

As a senator from Illinois and a presidential candidate in 2008, Obama visited the Crow Indian Reservation in Montana. He had already formulated an Indian policy and was committed to making a difference. Obama was adopted into the Crow Nation the day of his visit and "... promised to appoint an American Indian policy adviser to his senior staff and 'end nearly a century of mismanagement of Indian trust.'"[31]

A Tribal Nations Conference was held by Obama starting in his first year of office and continued throughout his eight years. His intent was to initiate a "lasting conversation" where the problems would be fully addressed. From that first conference came "... a presidential memorandum directing every cabinet agency to provide a plan within 90 days – and on an annual basis thereafter – detailing its consultations with tribes, plans to implement change in Indian country and regular progress reports."[32] Clinton had issued much the same order, but there had been no follow-through by the agencies. This time it was different. The annual conferences, which were widely attended by Indian and government leaders in a true nation-to-nation partnership, made sure Obama's objectives were carried out.

Alysa Landry wrote a series of 44 articles covering each of the U.S. Presidents for *indiancountrytoday.com*. As she prepared the article on the 44th president, she interviewed Kevin Washburn, who served as assistant secretary for Indian Affairs for Obama from 2012 to 2016. Landry quoted Washburn, a law profession at the University of New Mexico and a member of the Chickasaw Nation of Oklahoma, in her November 1, 2016 article:

> From the beginning, we saw that he was intellectually committed to Indian country. By the end, he was emotionally committed. I don't think we've seen that before.[33]

Landry's article, "Barack Obama: 'Emotionally and

Intellectually Committed to Indian Country," chronicles a commitment that allowed Obama to tackle some longstanding issues in Indian country:

- July 2010, Obama signed the Tribal Law and Order Act, expanding punitive authority of tribal courts and working to reduce violent crime – especially against women – in Indian country.
- December 2010, Obama signed the United Nations Declaration on the Rights of Indigenous People, reversing the United States' 2007 position and committing to honor indigenous peoples' right to exist.
- In March 2013, he signed the reauthorization of the Violence Against Women Act [originally signed by Clinton in 1994] extending to tribes unprecedented authority to prosecute non-Natives who commit crimes on Indian land.
- In June 2013,… [he] called for stricter compliance with the Indian Child Welfare Act, pushed for improvements in Indian schools and increased funding for suicide prevention programs in Indian country.
- In August 2015, Obama used his executive power to officially restore the Native name of Alaska's highest mountain peak of Mount McKinley back to Denali.[34]

These issues and others that were addressed during this eight-year period are but a few of the challenges faced by Native Americans.

Indian Relations Suffer Under President Trump

The 45th President of the United States, Donald J. Trump, came to office in January 2017. As early as February 1, 2017, it was stated "His political positions have been described by scholars and commentators as populist, protectionist, and nationalist."[35] Native Americans' lives and experiences have been negatively impacted because of his political positions. Examples of his actions follow:

Pipeline Traverses Tribal Grounds

The Dakota Access Pipeline (DAPL) was originally planned to cross the Missouri River north of Bismarck, North Dakota, but the residents of that city successfully blocked the pipeline, citing concerns that their drinking water supply could be contaminated by a leak or spill. Instead, the U.S. Army Corp of Engineers rerouted the pipeline south of Bismarck and just a half mile from Standing Rock Reservation. Without consent of the tribe, the "… pipeline runs underneath Lake Oahe that borders the Reservation and is the sole source of the Tribe's drinking water."[36] Records show 1,700 reportable pipeline incidents since 2016, indicating a very real possibility the tribe's water supply will be contaminated. Additionally, "The pipeline traverses Tribal sacred areas, burial grounds, and hunting and fishing areas – all expressly protected by treaties and reaffirmed by Congress and the courts."[37]

On Monday, July 6, 2020, "… the United States District Court for the District of Columbia ordered that the controversial 1,172-mile-long [Dakota Access] pipeline must be shut down within 30 days."[38] The order stipulated that a full environmental assessment must be made and new permits issued, a process which normally takes several years. Energy Transfer immediately filed a motion to halt this decision, and a federal appeals court overturned the ruling, allowing oil to keep flowing. Indigenous leaders and environmental groups continue working to shut the pipeline down.

Arizona Border Impacts Native Americans

This region is critical to Native Americans, and two independent articles highlight their concerns. In Brigit Katz' article written for *smithsonianmag.com* on September 20, 2019, she wrote that an environmental impact statement prepared by the National Park Service (NPS) identified 22 archaeological sites that will be impacted to some degree by the wall construction along the Arizona southern border with Mexico.[39] That same day, Shawn Simmons wrote for *archpaper.com* stating "… a 30-foot illuminated steel wall has the potential to cause irreparable damage to archaeological fragments spanning the area's 16,000 years of inhabitation."[40]

An article written by the online staff for *nativenewsonline.net* and published on January 13, 2020, provided information on a 62-mile stretch along Arizona's southern border with Mexico. In addition to the potential damage to the archaeological sites from the construction, the wall will intersect the lands of the Tohono O'odham Nation, which includes their sacred ancestral burial site within a reservation provided them by treaty.

Tohono O'odham Chairman Ned Norris, Jr. expressed his displeasure for the desecration of Native sacred sites within the Organ Pipe Cactus Biosphere Reserve to Assistant Secretary of the Interior for Indian Affairs Tara Sweeney. In a question-and-answer session after her speech to the National Congress of American Indians on February 15, 2020, tribal leaders questioned Sweeney "on the Trump administration's insensitivity to American Indian issues." [41] Norris specifically told her:

> They desecrated those human remains that were there … You have an obligation to protect sacred sites and sacred areas and religious areas for Native American people. You have failed to make sure [to protect sacred sites] … I call on you to exercise your responsibility and stop the destruction of sacred sites of Native American Communities.[42]

Indigenous People Struggle with COVID-19

When COVID-19 struck the U.S. in early 2020, President Trump, in conjunction with his medical advisors, instructed people who were not essential workers to stay home to help prevent the spread of the virus. Congress began working on the Coronavirus Aid, Relief, and Economic Security Act (CARES), during which financial help for the Native American people was blocked by the White House. In an article written by Levi Rickert of *nativenewsonline.net,* he quoted an April 1 Huff Post article which reported that the White House originally did not intend for Native tribes to receive any of the $2 trillion stimulus bill. When the bill was signed into law on March 27th, the tribes were allocated $8 billion in the CARES provisions."[43]

With a lawsuit pending against the federal government to prevent distribution of about 50% of the CARES money to the for-profit Alaska Native Corporations (ANC), the distribution of all money was held up, leaving tribes across the nation without any help from the federal government and specifically from the Indian Health Services.[44] The U.S. Department of the Treasury announced that "As of June 17, 2020 all payments … other than payment of amounts allocated to Alaska Native corporations, have been made."[45] These funds went to Native governments fighting the effects of the pandemic as other areas of the country do the same.

COVID-19 Struggles Continue for Navajo Nation

The infection and death rate have been great among the Navajo and other Indian people. Following on the heels of New York, the Navajo Nation in the southwest U.S. became a major hot spot for the COVID-19 outbreak.

To prevent the spread of the virus, medical experts emphasized the importance of frequently washing hands for a minimum of 20 seconds, which is not possible for a reservation where it is estimated that at least 15% of homes have no running water or sanitation systems, which requires them to haul water in buckets and barrels. Dig Deep is a nonprofit organization founded in 2011 and serves disadvantaged communities in the United States. They have undertaken the Navajo Water Project, recently installing 1,200-gallon water cisterns, which have to be filled by a water truck, for Navajo area homes; however, off-grid solar panels are also required to power the water pump and there aren't enough panels.

The Navajo currently pay 17 cents per gallon of water, which is many times what the average American consumer pays. "The EPA estimates the average American family uses 300 gallons of water per day."[46] If they could get 300 gallons a day and afford to pay 17 cents per gallon, the Navajo would be paying $51.00 a day for water. The 15% statistic for Navajos homes without running water compares to 12% throughout Indian

Country and 0.6% of all American homes. Some are glad "… to see the water truck, but many cannot even afford large containers and use whatever they have including pickle jars to hold the water – a precious commodity in this dry land.[47] "In a 2018 report to Congress, the Indian Health Service, which is one of the U.S. government's primary funders of tribal water and sanitation systems, said that the Navajo Nation has a backlog of more than $450 million in unfunded requests."[48] Cost and accessibility are two significant problems for the Navajo in the use of water as prevention against the virus.

In addition, several generations of Navajo often live in the same house, which also contributes to the spread of COVID-19. Some people live in trailers or even traditional eight-sided Hogan's with dirt floors. Kerosene is often used for lighting, wood for heating and about one-third of the 18,000 houses have no access to grid electricity. The federal government had a rural electrification project in the 1930s, but reservations were bypassed, and the Navajo Nation was no exception. There are only 10 full-service grocery stores in the 24,700 square mile reservation, so a round trip of 100 miles or more is required to shop, and fresh food must be used within a couple of days. [49] [50][51]

Help Comes from Several Sources

Until November 18, 2019, there was a coal-fired electric plant built on land leased from the reservation. Most of the electricity produced was sold to neighboring communities in Arizona and New Mexico, generating approximately $30-$40 million in taxes that was used to pay for Navajo social services. A plant closure would mean a loss of about 500 jobs – more than 90 percent of whom are Navajo – adding to the already 50% unemployment rate.[52]

In 2017, when the owners of the plant decided to close the plant at the end of the lease, the Navajo Nation leadership considered spending over $300 million to keep the plant running and people employed. However, this would have been a short-term fix and Jonathan Nez, who had been elected as President of the Navajo Nation in 2018, led the decision against bailing out the coal plant to save the jobs. Instead, the Nation focused on plans to offset their loss of electricity by building a solar array and battery storage plant.

To accomplish this goal, the Navajo leadership worked with Brent Isaac, a Navajo entrepreneur who grew up on the reservation and had "... spent years delivering off-grid solar to Navajo households without access to the electric grid. He teamed up with longtime friend Dan Rosen, chairman of Mosaic, a leading solar loan provider."[53] The plant now provides electricity to 13,000 homes on and off the reservation. The plan is to double the array with the goal to generate nearly as much electricity as the coal plant within five years.

The team got an additional boast when in late March 2020 they signed a $4 million financing contract and teamed with a "... largely native-owned company, Navajo Power, [that] was getting ready to build a major solar project in one of the poorest communities in America."[54] Their ultimate goal is to create well-paying jobs for the economically depressed community and to provide a reliable source of electricity for the reservation, as well as the greater western region of the U.S. Two important leaders in renewable energy, the California governor's energy czar and his manager of the solar grid, have already indicated an interest in the Navajo project as the state moves towards its goal of being powered 100 percent by renewable electricity by 2045.[55]

When the first COVID-19 relief package was being considered in Congress, Native Americans were not included in that relief until some congressional leaders made sure they were added to the list to receive financial aid. However, Native reservations were last to receive medical support. A number of articles have been written that highlight the number of Native American infections and deaths, particularly on the Navajo reservation which lacks access to running water and electricity on a large portion of the reservation. Help came from several different groups with some establishing "Go Fund Me" accounts for the benefit of the Navajo. The need was highlighted in an article "Navajo Nation Pres. Nez gets call from NY Gov. Cuomo, who offers Support" released by *nativenewsonline.net* on April 21, 2020. It stated that Governor Cuomo called President Nez to offer assistance to the Navajo Nation in their response efforts to COVID-19. New York State had reached its peak and was seeing a decline in virus cases, allowing the governor to offer some unused PPE equipment and supplies to the Navajo Nation. Cuomo served as Secretary of Housing and Urban Development when, in 1999, he joined President Clinton visiting Pine Ridge Reservation – the second largest reservation in the nation. This trip helped him understand the needs of Indian country. During Cuomo's conversation with Nez, he stated he has "… a great admiration and love for the Navajo."[56] He also has a deep appreciation of the struggles with the virus.

An act of compassion for the Irish by the Choctaws in the mid-1800s resulted in an act of compassion for the Navajo Nation and other Indian nations as they fight COVID-19. By an 1830 treaty with the Choctaws of Mississippi, the nation broke into two groups. One group of about 1,300 Choctaw remained in Mississippi, and the second moved to Oklahoma Territory. About 16 years after their relocation, the struggling Oklahoma group heard of the Great Irish Famine. Out of their few resources, they collected $170 – equivalent to about $5,000 in today's money – and sent it to a group in New York to combine with other money sent to Ireland. In 2020, the Irish heard about the plight of the Native Americans and about 24,000 donors collected approximately $820,000 in response to an online fundraiser to help buy food and supplies for families on the Navajo and Hopi reservations. As of mid-May, a total of over $4 million had been raised for the relief effort.[57]

Over a Century Later, The Fight for Recognition Continues

The Chinook Indian Nation – for whom the Chinook salmon are named, and which they cannot legally fish – has fought a legal battle for 169 years to obtain federal recognition. They live in Washington and Oregon but have no reservation or tribal lands. In ordinary circumstances that means they cannot obtain basic services guaranteed by treaties such as federally subsidized housing or building a center to preserve their culture. But 2020 was not ordinary as COVID-19 swept the U.S. Without federal recognition, the Chinook have no access to critical healthcare through the Indian Health Services and also are not eligible for help under the CARES Act.

In Montana, the Little Shell Tribe of Chippewa finally gained federal recognition in December 2019 in a battle they had waged since 1892. They learned in January 2020 that there would be no funding to help build a small clinic until October when the new U.S. fiscal year begins. Then COVID-19 resulted in great outlays of federal money for health and economic relief. Because the tribe was not federally recognized for the 2020 federal budget that began October 1, 2019, they are not currently eligible for any relief money for medical equipment or health services. Through the efforts of Montana's Governor Steve Bullock and U.S. Senator Jon Tester, the band has access to the Indian Health Services "... but the closest facilities are 102 miles in one direction and 126 in another."[58]

> In Michigan, the unrecognized tribes of Burt Lake
> Band of Ottawa and Chippewa Indians do not have a
> tribal health clinic. It is only through the generosity
> of a neighboring federally recognized tribe that the
> Burt Lake members have access to doctors.[59]

Both the Chinooks and the Little Shell tribes were briefly recognized under the Clinton administration; however, the Bureau of Indians Affairs has said that as landless tribes, they are not eligible to be recognized. Being landless is a result of the Indian Termination Act of 1953 which "... was used to end federal legal obligations under the treaties, dissolve the sovereign status of over 100 tribal nations and sell off the reservation lands where they lived."[60] Karina Brown writes in her article, "Specter of Pandemic Dire for Tribes Fighting for Federal Recognition," that Nola Parkey, the band's [Burt Lake] executive director said, "Well, it wasn't by their doing that they were a landless tribe."[61] They signed treaties in 1836 and again in 1855 ceding land to the U.S., but the Termination Act superseded those treaties. Since then, tribes have continued their fight to retain sovereignty and gain federal recognition:

> Federal recognition is not about semantics. It is the
> hinge that triggers the government's legal obligation

to hold unseeded territory in trust for tribes and to provide them with basic services guaranteed in the treaties that paved the way for the United States to exist.[62]

In an arbitrary manner, the government has banned tribes who were denied federal recognition from repetitioning their status. Some tribes apply and never hear back from the government.[63]

Author's Thoughts

For tribes – recognized and unrecognized – their history, language and culture reside in their elders and COVID-19 threatens to destroy all that remains of their identity. Without financial and medical help, they are facing irreparable personal and cultural loss.

This past year, the global community has seen the number of people infected with COVID-19 numbering in the millions. The U.S. sequestered people in their homes to help stem the infection rate, resulting in an economic recession. Summer 2020 saw the U.S. in the unenviable position as first in the world for the number of people infected with and dying from the virus. Both the infection rates and economic impact have adversely affected Blacks and Indigenous people disproportionately compared to other ethnic groups in the U.S. The mortality rate is highest for Black Americans with 66 deaths per 100,000, and Indigenous Americans are second with a rate of 43 deaths per 100,000. Native Americans have "… disproportionately high rates of disease such as diabetes, coronary heart disease, and respiratory infections that the CDC has identified will result in a higher risk of poor outcomes from COVID-19."[64] On the Navajo reservation – as on other reservations throughout the country – many of the People live in multigenerational households emphasizing a culture of helping one another. Additionally, they deal with many long-standing inadequacies such as insufficient and/or poor housing and no running water, sanitary systems or electricity in many areas of the reservation. All these things dramatically reduce their ability to socially distance and increases their potential infection rates.

A quote by Stacey Bohlen, CEO of the National Indian Health Board is particularly revealing. She is quoted by Joyce Fieden in her June 12, 2020 article, "Native Americans Need More Funding to Battle COVID-19, Lawmakers Told." Bohlen stated:

> We hear baseless stories from many quadrants of the nation about how 'dirty Indians' are causing the outbreaks or how private hospitals are refusing to accept referrals to treat our people. These same echoes came across all previous disease outbreaks that plagued our people from smallpox to HIV to H1N1.[65]

The Navajo are but one of many groups of Native Americans living on reservations across the country with conditions equaling that of some third world countries. Living conditions are horrible and services are limited. Within the Bureau of Indian Affairs, employees who work in the Department of Indian Services – which covers housing, health, education and other initiatives – deal with a tangle of overlapping government bureaucracy that is overwhelming and a change in political leadership can dramatically affect Indian policy. Only with presidents like George H.W. Bush and Barack Obama, who actively worked within the existing governmental framework in cooperation with Indian leaders, will the treaties be addressed, and Indian concerns and needs be met. Otherwise, the congressional branch will be more inclined to put forth a budget to satisfy their constituents – in other words those with the loudest voice or most active political action committees will get the money.

Native people believe that decisions they make will affect the next seven generations. The wait for recognition of Native Americans in the everyday life of this country, as well as honoring U.S. treaty obligations has encompassed over 200 years. Each president and every Congress has the opportunity to change policy for the betterment or detriment of the people, and all too often it has been to the detriment of Native people of this country. The wait must stop now.

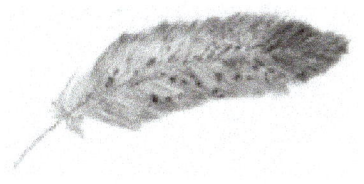

Endnotes:

1. Reagan, Ronald. "Inaugural Address of Ronald Reagan." *Reagan Library*, 20 Jan 1981. https://bit.ly/3jjT5z0.

2. Reagan, Ronald. "Address at Moscow State University, Moscow, Russia, 31 May 1988." *Miller Center*, https://bit.ly/34bGPKS. Accessed 19 May 2020.

3. Reagan, Ronald. "Reagan: A contradiction to American Indians." *nbcnews.com*. by Editorial staff Indian Country Today updated 11 Jun 2004. https://nbcnews.to/2IhbXRS.

4. Atlas, Terry. "After 40 Years, U.S. Will Join UN Treaty Outlawing Genocide." *Chicago Tribune*. 5 Nov 1988. https://bit.ly/3eCcV7c Accessed 7 Sep 2020.

5. Atlas.

6. Mankiller, Wilma. and Michael Wallis. *Mankiller: A Chief and Her People*. St Martin's Press, 1993. p 48.

7. Agoyo, Acee. "George H.W. Bush, 1924-2018, left lasting mark on Indian Country." *Indianz.com*, 4 Dec 2018. https://bit.ly/3py2HtJ. Accessed 15 May 2020.

8. Agoyo.

9. Agoyo.

10. Agoyo.

11. Prucha, Francis Paul, editor. *Documents of United States Indian Policy 3rd Ed*. U of Nebraska P, 1984. p. 335.

12. Reyhner, Jon and Edward Tennant. "Maintaining and Renewing Native Languages." *The Bilingual Research Journal,* Spring 1995, Vol 19, No 2, pp 279-304.

13. Utter, Jack. *American Indians: Answers to Today's Questions 2nd Ed. Revised and Enlarged.* U of Oklahoma P, 2001. p. 143.

14. Native American Languages Act. Summary: S. 2167 – 101st Congress (1989-1990) https://www.congress.gov/bill/101st-congress/senate-bill/2167.

15. Landry, Alysa. "Bill Clinton: Invites Tribal Leaders to White

House." *Indian Country Today*, 18 Oct 2016.
https://bit.ly/3kYAIQI. Accessed 21 May 2020.
[16] Landry.
[17] Landry.
[18] Landry.
[19] Landry.
[20] United States, Congress, House. American Indian Religious Freedom Act Amendments of 1994. https://bit.ly/346ywja. 103rd Congress, House Resolution 4230, passed 6 Oct 1994.
[21] Clinton, William. "National American Indian Heritage Month, 1996." *Federal Register,* Vol. 61, No. 213, 1 Nov 1996. Presidential Documents 56397. https://bit.ly/2G4JFta.
[22] Landry, Alysa. "Bill Clinton: Invites Tribal Leaders to White House." *Indian Country Today,* 18 Oct 2016. https://bit.ly/3kYAIQI. Accessed 21 May 2020.
[23] "President Clinton Calls for Passage of His Historic FY2001 Native American Initiative." The White House, Office of the Press Secretary, 25 Feb 2000. https://bit.ly/3mZv7vg.
[24] Landry, Alysa. "Bill Clinton: Invites Tribal Leaders to White House." *Indian Country Today,* 18 Oct 2016. https://bit.ly/3kYAIQI. Accessed 21 May 2020.
[25] Landry, Alysa. "George W. Bush: 'Actively Ignored' Indians; Struggled with Sovereignty." *Indian Country Today*, 25 Oct 2016. https://bit.ly/36rdHlD. Accessed 15 May 2020.
[26] Landry.
[27] Trahant, Mark. "Bush on Native American Issues: 'Tribal Sovereignty Means That. It's Sovereign." 10 Aug 2004. https://bit.ly/34btty9. Accessed 15 May 2020.
[28] Trahant.
[29] Bush, George. "National American Indian Heritage Month, 2006." https://bit.ly/35838Tm. Accessed 8 Nov 2020.
[30] Landry, Alysa. "Barack Obama: "Emotionally and Intellectually Committed to Indian Country." *Indian Country Today,* 1 Nov 2016. https://bit.ly/2Gl7Xii. Accessed 21 May 2020.
[31] Landry.
[32] Landry.
[33] Landry.
[34] Landry.

35 "Talk: Donald Trump/Archive 42." 1 Feb 2017.
https://bit.ly/2IjYwjP.

36 Sass, Jennifer. "Standing Rock Sioux Tribe and NRDC
Confront Federal Failures." 17 May 2019. www.nrdc.org.ss

37 Sass, Jennifer.

38 Native News Online Staff. "Judge Shuts Down Controversial
Dakota Access Pipeline Project." 6 Jul 2020.
https://bit.ly/3k98i5J.

39 Katz, Brigit. "Planned Border Wall May Threaten 22
Archaeological Sites in Arizona, N.P.R. Says." 20 Sep 2019.
smithsonianmag.com. https://bit.ly/38vGdDk.

40 Simmons, Shawn. "Border wall construction could destroy
22 archaeological sites across Arizona." 20 Sep 2019. *The
Architect's Newspaper.* https://bit.ly/36ekZas Accessed 8
Jun 2020.

41 Rickert, Levi. "Tohono O'odham Chairman Chides Indian
Affairs Leader for Desecration of Sacred Sites for Border
Wall." 14 Feb 2020. *nativenewsonline.net.*
https://bit.ly/3eIeeS3

42 Rickert.

43 Rickert, Levi. "Why the Trump Administration's Failure to
initially add tribes to $2 Trillion stimulus doesn't shock me."
11 Apr 2020. *nativenewsonline.net.* https://bit.ly/3nCjw4R.

44 Rickert, Levi. "Federal Judge Expected to Rule on
Distribution of CARE Act Funds on Monday." 27 Apr 2020.
Native News Online. https://bit.ly/3kDyDcw.

45 "Through the Coronavirus Relief Fund, the CARES Act
provides for payments to State, Local, and Tribal
governments navigating the impact of the COVID-19
outbreak." June 2020. *home.treasury.gov.*
https://bit.ly/36dYGSk.

46 "How We Use Water." *U.S. Environmental Protection
Agency.* https://bit.ly/3eICAeI. Accessed 11 Jun 2020.

47 Krol, Debra Utacia. "Navajo Nation's water shortage may be
supporting COVID-19 spread." 28 Apr 2020., *azcentral.com.*
https://bit.ly/35daq8v.

48 Krol.

49 Krol.

50   "To Build a Home: The Navajo Housing Tragedy."
      azcentral.com. https://bit.ly/2GI7PtA.
51   YouTube.com. "Step into a Hogan" 31 Aug 2016. Accessed
      through *azcentral.com.*
52   Pyper, Julia. "The Navajo Generating Station Coal Plant
      Officially Powers Down. Will Renewables Replace It?" 20
      Nov 2019. https://bit.ly/31X9YJj
53   Spector, Julian. "Developer sPower Teams Up With Navajo
      Power to Replace Coal Plant with Solar." 6 May 2020.
      https://bit.ly/36awuQ9. Accessed 24 Oct 2020.
54   Kennedy, Danny. "How the Navajo got their day in the sun."
      GreenBix. 28 May 2020. https://bit.ly/3e6jwXr. Accessed 24
      Oct 2020
55   Kennedy.
56   "Navajo Nation Pres. Nez gets call from NY Gov. Cuomo,
      who offers Support." 22 Apr 2020. Native News Online
      Staff. https://bit.ly/35OHimK
57   Hedgpeth, Dada. "The Irish are repaying a favor from 173
      years ago in Native Americans' fight against coronavirus."
      The Washington Post, 13 May 2020.
      https://wapo.st/3mxfNVK.
58   Brown, Karina. "Specter of Pandemic Dire for Tribes
      Fighting for Federal Recognition." *Courthouse News
      Service. 7 Apr 2020.* https://bit.ly/3e6ADs7.
59   Brown.
60   Brown.
61   Brown.
62   Brown.
63   Brown.
64   Frieden, Joyce. "Native Americans Need More Funding to
      Battle COVID-19, Lawmakers Told." *MedPage Today.*12
      Jun 2020. https://bit.ly/3ecgIIm
65   Frieden.

| FOURTEEN |

Concerns Continue into the 21st Century

Since the beginning of the exploration and colonization of North America, Native Americans and Alaska Natives have faced innumerable challenges in their dealings with the newcomers. Native social, economic and political concerns have been long lasting and continue into the 21st century. Some are discussed here and are indicative of the importance and numbers of issues Native Americans continue to face, as well as efforts to overcome them.

Help with Navajo Housing

One issue for the Navajo is a serious housing crisis, and an example of one group working to help comes from the U.S. Air Force. For more than 20 years, the U.S. Air Force cadets have helped the Navajo by building modular homes at the academy in Colorado Springs, Colorado. The materials are paid for by the Southwest Indian Foundation, built by the cadets and then trucked to the Navajo reservation. In this cooperative activity, sergeants assigned to the academy oversee the cadets, and the lieutenants provide instruction, and two homes are built yearly over a three-week period using mainly hand tools.[1] The cadets get hands-on experience building the homes from the ground up, which are skills that will help them in their future lives whether military or civilian. The Navajo people gain well-built homes without the cost of labor.

In fact, Matthew Silver wrote an article for *manufacturedhomepronews.com* in June 2016 highlighting Matthew Hale, who was raised on the Navajo reservation and a junior cadet at the academy at that time. Hale had the opportunity to talk with his fellow cadets during the two weeks, explaining the importance of building the houses and how much they are needed.[2] It also provided Hale an opportunity to teach his fellow cadets about the rich Navajo culture and the extreme poverty of the reservation. While many families on the reservation live in trailers because they cannot afford other housing, the cadets learned that the four-sided homes they were building would go to single men. The eight-sided hogan is traditionally for families – another aspect of their culture.[3]

Doctors Without Borders Assists Native Americans

Healthcare is another continuing problem for Native Americans. The organization Doctors Without Borders assists people dealing with medical disasters internationally. However, in April 2020, the Navajo people gained the organization's assistance through a team of nine: "… two physicians, three nurses and midwives, a water sanitation specialist, two logisticians and a health promoter."[4] Justine Coleman's article, "Doctors Without Borders in rare mission within US sends team to Navajo Nation," appeared in *thehill.com* on May 12, 2020. It highlighted the fact that it was the first time that Doctors Without Borders had responded within the U.S. and that the Navajo – who were dealing with the COVID-19 epidemic – welcomed their help. Coleman wrote that a small team was also dispatched to the Pueblos north of Albuquerque in mid-April. The plan was for the teams to remain until June.[5]

Indigenous Voting Rights

The First Citizens of this country were finally granted full citizenship in the U.S. by the Snyder Act of 1924 and with that came the right to vote; however, some western states continued to bar Native Americans from voting:

> In 1948, the Arizona Supreme Court struck down a provision of its state constitution that kept Indians from voting. Other states eventually followed suit, concluding with New Mexico in 1962, … Even with the lawful right to vote in every state, Native Americans suffered from the same mechanisms and

strategies, such as poll taxes, literacy tests, fraud and intimidation, that kept African Americans from exercising that right.[6]

With the 2013 Supreme Court ruling, states are allowed to pass their own election laws without approval of the federal government. Many of the republican-led states have used this opportunity to introduce voter ID requirements, purge voting rolls and close many polling places. This has adversely affected the poor and people living in rural areas or on a reservation. Some states require a physical address for people to register and to vote, and North Dakota will not allow tribal IDs to be used for registration unless they have a physical address. The problem is that many reservations do not have addresses as the people use P.O. boxes, often miles from their home, to get mail.[7]

In the Navajo Nation, even P.O. boxes are hard to come by. The reservation, which covers an area of 27,413 square miles, only has three post offices, and there's a waiting list to get a box, along with several generations sharing the one they were fortunate enough to get.[8] In a 2020 article written by Anna V. Smith, she recounts the stories of two people that illustrate some of the difficulties faced by those on the reservation. The first story was that of a 70-year-old Navajo woman who has to walk five miles roundtrip down a narrow, winding highway to the post office. The second was about a man who drove five hours each way to vote.[9]

Voting is so important that a group of 15 Navajo riders made a 20-mile round trip on horseback on Friday, October 20th to make their voices heard. Allie Young, a 30-year-old Navajo said, "We rode in honor of our ancestors who rode longer miles and hours just to exercise their right to vote for us, our people, our lands, Mother Earth and Father Sky, and future generations."[10]

Another issue is language. Unlike the advantage Sequoyah gave the Cherokee in the early 1800s when he provided them with a syllabary resulting in a written language, many Indigenous languages are oral, and there are no equivalent words in English. This means that a Native interpreter must be at the polling places and also means that "… mail-in ballots aren't effective or preferred by many on the reservation."[11] Anna V. Smith's article lays out a thorough indictment of the voting system as it is used against poor, Black and Indigenous people, whichincludes the following:

> Democracy is often referred to as 'The Great American Experiment' – an experiment, many often omit, built on the enslavement and extermination of people of color. Historically, the times when the experiment has been most meaningfully tested have corresponded with the times when those same people of color have challenged the status quo, forcing a reconsideration not only of who deserves a voice within the larger experiment, but who deserves to benefit from it. We are, right now, in one of those times. The resistance to the Native vote – like the resistance to the black vote, or the Latino vote – just shows how powerful that vote is, and just how much work has been done to subvert it. Today, the endurance of American democracy doesn't just hinge on shifting the lines of a district or facilitating the ability to vote. It's contingent on a willingness to acknowledge – and share – the power that stems from it.[12]

The Native American Voting Rights Act of 2018 is meant to overcome some of the challenges Native people had previously faced when trying to vote, including provisions to increase access to voter registration sites and polling locations, as well as allowing tribal ID to be used for voting ID purposes. But the Supreme Court has since ruled that North Dakota was within its state's rights to require physical addresses to register to vote. This ruling affected 69,916 eligible North Dakota voters – including 4,998 Native Americans.[13]

Abused, Missing and Murdered Indigenous Women

The issue of abused, missing and murdered Indigenous women (MMIW) has a long history in the U.S., and the issue worldwide is of such consequence that the United Nations has a permanent forum on indigenous issues including sex trafficking.

In the U.S., dealing with the issue of MMIW is compounded by federal, state and tribal law enforcement groups that are unwilling to infringe on the authority of the others. In many cases, the agents cannot or will not cross into another's "territory" to find and prosecute accused person(s); therefore, that person can cross between agencies with impunity. Even today, some laws still exist that prohibit tribal law officers from arresting a white man for crimes committed on tribal lands. The individuals are thus victimized twice over – for the crime against their persons and the lack of prosecution.

The violence against women has been addressed at various times and by countless people. It can be seen in the Violence Against Women Act (VAWA), which was originally signed by President Clinton in 1996 and reauthorized in 2000, 2005 and again when Obama signed it in March 2013. The numbers of MMIW are so staggering that websites have been established to speak out about the problem and track the numbers. Two of the groups are the Coalition to Stop Violence Against Native Women and Native Women's Wilderness. The Centers for Disease Control and Prevention tracks the statistics of MMIW – at least those that are reported. The CDC published related statistics on the *nativewomenswilderness.org* website:

> Our women are murdered at a rate 10 times higher than other ethnicities, and it's the third leading cause of death for our Women (Centers for Disease Control). The majority of these murders are committed by non-Native people on Native-owned land. Because of the lack of communication between state, local, and tribal law enforcement, it's difficult to begin the investigation process.[14]

Laws and Acts Meant to Protect MMIW

In 2016, *nativewomenwilderness.org* reported there were 5,712 known incidents of MMIW. To further highlight the problem, Senators Murkowski and Cortez Mastro hosted a Capitol Hill briefing on February 16, 2020, quoting figures from the 2016 National Institute of Justice report on American Indian and Alaska Native women, which shows 84% of them have experienced sexual violence; physical and/or psychological aggression by an intimate partner; and stalking in their lifetime.[15] The violence

Native women face isn't just on reservations; it also happens in cities where there is law enforcement. Camila Domonoske wrote an article "Police in Many U.S. Cities Fail to Track Murdered, Missing Indigenous Women," covering work two researchers, Abigail Echo-Hawk and Annita Lucchesi, did in 2018. They had contacted police departments in 71 cities across the U.S. asking them, "How many Native American women have gone missing or been murdered in a given city?"[16] About 60 percent of the police departments either did not respond or had insufficient data to even identify Native victims. The researchers also examined stories covered by the news outlets and found, "Of the 506 disappearances and murders they were able to document, the majority were never covered by any news outlet."[17]

Savanna's Act was passed in 2018 by the 115th Congress. Within the act, the National Institute of Justice relays the same disproportionately high statistics reported by *nativewomen wilderness.org*.[18] The violence is not just perpetrated by non-Indians, as there is domestic violence within Indian communities, just as there is in other communities in the United States. That said, it is a fact that one in three Native women is sexually assaulted during her life, and 67% of these assaults are perpetrated by non-natives, which was discussed in a December 2, 2019 podcast where Eric Carter-Landin talks with Cheyenne Antonio, the sex trafficking coordinator from the Eastern Navajo territory. They discussed the epidemic of missing and murdered Indigenous people in North America with a Eurocentric culture of violence rooted in the colonization of the last 500 years and that it continues to be prevalent today.[19]

Antonio stated that New Mexico has the highest number of missing and murdered Indigenous women in the U.S. When asked what the root cause might be, Antonio indicated that she feels some of the reasons are that Native people are erased from the conversation as seen in ordinary events and places like Columbus Day, Thanksgiving, city names and sports teams. Columbus Day and Thanksgiving, in actuality, highlight the early Eurocentric racism — the belief that what they did to obtain control over the People and land was justified, not the message and meaning associated with them today. And using Native American names and stereotypes, while different, is still racist, as it skews and, in many cases, erases Native culture and history.

Antonio's point was that accurate information about Native people is being erased from the conversation in ordinary events; an example is that a group of Native Americans which includes Suzan Harjo – of Hodulgee Muscogee and Cheyenne descent – and many others have been leading a fight against the Washington NFL franchise for decades. Native organizations have also been in discussions with the NFL about the use of Native symbols and names. Only in the summer of 2020 did the conversation come to the forefront when big business put pressure on the NFL to make a change did it become important to them.[20]

The Presidential Task Force on Missing and Murdered American Indians and Alaska Natives – President Trump's Executive Order 13898 known as Operation Lady Justice – is meant to address concerns regarding these missing and murdered women and children. The problem is so significant in both the U.S. and Canada that Justin Trudeau, Prime Minister of Canada, "… established the National Inquiry into Missing and Murdered Indigenous Women and Girls in September 2016."[21]

Problems Quantifying the MMIW Are Innumerable

The countless problems around the subject of missing and murdered Indigenous women and girls are almost indefinable on all levels. The numbers are difficult to quantify. Often women and girls are not reported missing for a variety of reasons. Certainly, an abuser might not speak up if someone goes missing. Those who have escaped an abusive situation do not want their whereabouts known. Law enforcement, whether on or off the reservation, will not address a missing person for a period of time in case the person has left of his or her own free will. Then, there is the problem of multiple jurisdictions and the desire to not interfere in another agency's authority. By the time the issue of a missing person is addressed, it is often too late. Whether they are missing or have been murdered, with remains seldom found, it is difficult to know definitively what happened to the person. [22][23]

Erik Ortiz wrote an article on the lack of awareness surrounding MMIW for *nbc.news.com* on July 30, 2020. Ortiz interviewed Tammy Carpenter whose daughter, Angela, who was of Hoopa and Mohave descent, was murdered two years ago in northern California. The sheriff's detective, who was not a Native American, questioned Carpenter and "... insinuated that her daughter had come from a broken home where no one had jobs and all were involved with drugs...."[24] Carpenter, understandably, was very upset over her daughter's death and the way the detective handled the situation. She strongly informed the detective that she and her two sisters had all graduated from college, that they worked, and Angela was loved:

> The perceived lack of sensitivity from law enforcement when Carter's daughter was found dead isn't unique. In the Sovereign Bodies Institute report, families described insufficient cultural awareness from law enforcement, as well as 'poor or nonexistent communication with families and survivors, chronic lack of cases brought to justice and ... past and ongoing violence perpetrated by officers.'[25]

Another issue in solving this problem is that different state and federal governments study the problem at length and make recommendations, often passing acts and laws but without adequately funding the endeavor or funding it for a limited time frame. An example of the limited time frame on the federal level can be seen in the Violence Against Women Act. Originally signed into law in 1994, it has had to be reauthorized periodically. Looking at the 113th Congress of 2013-2014 there were – in the Senate alone – 13 amendments and 44 actions on the Violence Against Women Reauthorization Act of 2013. These included word changes/clarifications to the act, title changes, new statements of the purpose, improvements to the bill, 10 roll call votes and eight related bills to the act.[26] The House of Representatives went through a similar process before it went to the president for signature. When reauthorized in 2019, there were 176 actions taken by the House.[27]

On December 5, 2019, Cherokee Principal Chief Chuck

Hoskin Jr. reported that the Oklahoma Legislature had approved an interim study on the issue of MMIW. He further said that the Department of Justice was hiring 11 coordinators to respond to the reports of MMIW across the United States. Oklahoma will have one coordinator. Hoskins continued, "The Cherokee Nation passed a law expanding our tribal VAWA law to authorize prosecution of non-Indians in domestic violence cases, taking advantage of the federal Violence Against Women Act authorizing that."[28]

In the fall of 2019, an 18-month investigative report, "A Broken Trust," aired on *newsy.com/brokentrust*, which documented the continuing problem with assaults and murders of Indian women and children. American Indian journalist Suzette Brewer (Cherokee) received the Robert F. Kennedy Journalism Award for *Newsy* for her investigation and writing of the documentary. Some of the areas she quantified included:

- There is a severe understaffing of tribal law enforcement agencies in Indian Country.
- Tribal courts are underfunded and only received less than five percent of the funding necessary.
- Congress has set limits on the maximum sentence tribal courts can impose on individuals found guilty to only one year. This includes rape. The investigative reporters uncovered exclusive records, obtained from Fort Berthold tribal prosecutor's office, that show the court on its reservation sentenced those found guilty of sexual assault to sentences of only eight days to six months.
- Funding for U.S. Attorneys, who are supposed to help prosecute major crimes in Indian Country, has gone down by more than 40 percent in the past seven years.
- The investigative reporters discovered the Montana U.S. Attorney's office declined to prosecute 64 percent of sexual assault cases across Montana reservations from 2013 to 2018.[29]

Cherokee Nation Investigators

Cherokee Nation law enforcement officers have basically had their hands tied in investigating any crimes that originate in the Nation but move beyond their jurisdiction. This has been particularly hard on them as they work the abused, sex trafficking and MMIW cases. In an article written by KenLea Henson for the Spring/Summer 2020 *Anadisgoi,* the official Cherokee Nation news, it was announced that the FBI had selected several Cherokee Nation investigators to join their task force.[30] The two officers selected have a total of 27 years working for the Cherokee marshal service and were handpicked by the FBI, which considered their work ethic, as well as their investigative work. As a result of being cross deputized; the officers will have access to resources, case files and specialized training. In Henson's article, he indicated that this is a great honor as well as a great responsibility and will allow them to cross state lines in the course of their investigations. Having the FBI partnering with them will increase their response time and ultimately help get justice for the Cherokee people.[31]

Racism Originated with Colonizers

Prior to European arrival, Native Americans had used matrilineal descent to define tribal membership. Native women participated in war among the tribes, as well as wars of their tribes against the colonizers. Some, like Nancy Ward, were given the honor of "Beloved Mother" where they sat in tribal councils, as well as the women's council, often deciding life or death for captives. It was only when the white colonizers questioned their presence during treaty negotiations that women were relegated to the background.

The issue of racism is intricately tied to the concept of blood quantum, which is itself highly subjective, and today's answers will be determined by the Indian Nation – or even the individuals within a given nation – and the federal workers who deal with Indian issues. Today's answers will differ from those of years past and will change in the future. However, it is necessary to understand where the issue is today and how important blood quantum is on a number of aspects of Indian life. And that understanding is aided by first having a basic understanding of the concept.

Ryan W. Schmidt wrote an article published January 15,

2012 for the *Journal of Anthropology* in which he stated:

> Europeans not only expropriated land and resources, but also Indian identity. ... The terms identity, ethnicity, and heritage in American Indian society are all entangled with the English conception of race, borne out of the colonial past with ideological components of exclusiveness and discreteness of group membership.[32]

Schmidt's article continued by including data from Swedish botanist Carolus Linnaeus (1707-1778) that provided scientific analysis to determine geographical human groups: Americanus, Asiaticus, Africanus and Europeaus. This worldview supported a social hierarchy accepted by Europeans that placed them in a position of prominence. This thinking then dictated the interaction between the colonizers and the Native Americans from their first encounter.[33]

In the late 1800s and early 1900s, government officials used several methods to determine blood quantum, including documents originating with the tribal census roles conducted as a result of the Allotment Act. However, a subjective method was also used by officials when they "... would mark someone potentially as 'full blood' when potentially that person was not. And that assumption was based on their appearance, on their level of cultural involvement with their community."[34]

In an attempt to limit the number of people who could qualify for tribal citizenship, the federal government instituted the "blood quantum." In its most simplistic construct blood quantum "... is the amount of 'Indian blood' that an individual possesses."[35] The Department of Interior issued a "Certified Degree of Indian Blood"[36] card, similar to a government ID card and, like driver's licenses, which are determined by the individual states, the ID card is determined by the individual "federally recognized" Indian Nation.

During allotment, government officials worked with several goals in mind. By limiting the number of people who qualified for tribal membership, there would be fewer people qualifying for land allotments, which would ultimately free up land for the settlers. At the same time, officials fixed a time frame of 25 years during which "… many full-blood American Indians could not sell their allotted land, being deemed legally incompetent by the government of the United States."[37] Even as that provided a way to protect those full-bloods termed "legally incompetent," attorneys and others found ways around this encumbrance and enabled some full-bloods to sell their allotments.[38] Some Indians, whether mixed-bloods or full-bloods, wanted to sell their land while others were tricked into selling. With Indian lands broken into individual allotments, the federal government declared, in the early 1900s, that tribal governments were no longer in effect.

It wasn't until the Meriam Report was released in 1928, which revealed the horrible living conditions on reservations, that there was public concern with Indian affairs. The report resulted in the Indian Reorganization Act of 1934, also known as the Indian Welfare Act. It was at this point that the BIA started using the term "blood quantum" in the modern sense as Americans experienced this awakened interest in Native people. American Indians, more than any other ethnic group, must constantly prove their identity.[39]

As of March 2020, 23 of the 574 federally recognized tribes determine membership by lineal descent – one is the Cherokee Nation. Although blood quantum was a white definition of "Indianness," tribes gradually accepted the definition as they sought to become a legally recognized tribal entity. Blood quantum is defined differently depending on which Native tribe is being referred to, but if it is the official requirement of a federally recognized tribe, the BIA accepts the tribe's definition as well. Information provided on *powwow.com* in a 2019 update showed that only six tribes require a blood quantum of ½, while there were 19 tribes requiring a minimum of ¼ degree blood quantum, and one is the United Keetoowah Band of Cherokee Indians of Oklahoma. Another 26 tribes require 1/8 degree, and the Eastern Band of Cherokee Indians of North Carolina is one of seven that requires 1/16 degree blood quantum.[40] This highlights the differences in tribal membership requirements within the same "historical" group of Cherokees.

These decisions have far-reaching effects for Indian people today – sometimes even whom they will marry. Adrienne Keene, whose heritage includes Cherokee, Armenian, Irish, Welsh, and German, understands the uniqueness of intermarriage between Natives and non-natives. Keene wrote an article, "Love In the Time of Blood Quantum," for *nativeappropriations.com* in April 2011 in which she provided preliminary 2010 census data that showed Native Americans have the highest rate of intermarriage. Keene then discussed the following regarding intermarriage in Native communities which aired on NPR:

> The piece focuses on a woman from the Wind River Reservation in Wyoming, and her fiancé, a Mexican-American. In her community, members must possess ¼ blood quantum for tribal enrollment, and while her children would make the cut, if they then choose to marry non-Indians, their children (her grandchildren) would no longer be tribal members.[41]

The loss of tribal membership is significant to the individual as "… it can affect child custody cases, access to free health care, education and land ownership."[42] Debra Donahue, a professor of Indian law at the University of Wyoming, stated that it has ramifications for the tribe because high rates of intermarriage decrease their blood quantum population and, with that, she quoted a post by Debbie Reese:

> Identity matters for those of us who are raised Indian. We work very hard at maintaining our nationhood and our sovereignty, and, we work to protect the integrity of our traditions from being exploited by people who don't understand them.[43]

The Re-Emergence of "Two-Spirit" People in Native Culture

Another Indian demographic being addressed is LGBTQ. In the spring of 2020, HBO had a six-part series titled "We're Here." The fourth part dealt with the place of the LGBTQ community in the area of the Navajo Reservation in the southwest U.S. The series showed that people fail to take into consideration the very real story of the lives of the LGTBQ community, the impact on their lives and that of their family and friends.[44] In Nick Estes' 2019 book, *Our History is the Future,* he wrote that from the 1970s onward, the transgender and Two-Spirit people have been among those targeted by all forms of violence. Their numbers are now included in the MMIW of Canada and the U.S, with several organizations in both countries having experts and activists working to keep the issue in front of the public.[45]

Prior to missionaries introducing Christianity, many traditional Natives appreciated the diversity among their people and believed that a person's spirit or character allowed him or her to focus on his or her individual spiritual gifts. It was these people who were looked to as religious leaders and teachers. The growing cultural pride among Native people engendered a resurgence in "red power" in the 1960s, which ushered in the gay and lesbian liberation movements.[46]

The Feather – A Symbol of High Honor

Symbols have always been significant within Native American culture and religion. Some symbols are more highly regarded in one group than another. But Native people have always held feathers in high regard, especially eagle feathers, and they are used to mark important events in their lives. There are special ceremonies regarding how to handle feathers, and their significance can be seen in the ceremony that is required if one is dropped.[47] On the blog *nativehope.org*, there is an article which provides a look into the true meaning of feathers, with emphasis on the eagle feather, to the Native American culture:

> ... it is believed that all things possess an inherent virtue, power, and wisdom. The feather, for example is a powerful symbol that signified honor and a connection between the owner, the Creator, and the bird from which the feather came. It symbolizes trust, honor, strength, wisdom, power, and freedom. It is an object that is deeply revered and a sign of high honor.[48]

Because of its cultural significance and strong medicine, eagle feathers were part of the sacred pipe offered to federal officials at the signing of a treaty.

The bald eagle became the national symbol of the United States in 1782, and when their numbers dropped, mainly due to destruction of habitat, they became federally protected in 1940. Protection followed for the golden eagle in 1962.[49] Today, the U.S. Fish and Wildlife Service oversees the laws protecting the eagles. It is illegal here for people other than Native Americans who are a member of one of the 574 federally recognized tribes, over age 18 and have a permit, to possess an eagle body, wings, feathers, feet or even eggshells:

> There are only a few ways to get hold of new eagle parts. Native Americans can apply for a seldom-granted permit to kill a bird for religious use. They can receive them as gifts or through inheritance. And they can make requests to a Denver-based repository, run by the U.S. Fish and Wildlife Service, which collects eagles that die naturally or are electrocuted by power lines, among other hazards.[50]

An article written in 2006 by Amir Efrati indicated that the number of powwows and people attending in the U.S. had, at that time, grown to almost 1,000 with the number of dancers growing from 1,000 in the mid-1990s to over 3,000.[51] Aside from the cultural aspects of the powwows, the realities of Native American life – which are not new – make the economics of the dance competitions a major consideration.[52] Based on the 2010 census, "The median income on a reservation is $29,097 compared to the national median income for Native Americans which is $40,315."[53] While the statistics provided by the Economic Policy Institute (EPI) are more recent, it still reflects a huge variation in income for Native Americans versus the total U.S. population. The EPI reported in 2017 that 32.7% of Native American children live in poverty compared to 18.4% of the total population.[54]

Dancers in the competition can get as much as $3,000 for first place, with some Indians earning their living by working the powwow circuit. There is strong motivation to win, and their regalia – which reflects items from their lives, family and tribe – is part of the judging. When participants travel to the powwows, they are required to have their feather permits with them at all times, and they must obtain another permit if planning to transport their outfits out of the country. If, for instance, a dancer goes to Canada, he or she must have a Canadian permit.[55]

The black market for feathers has grown along with the popularity of the powwows. Because of the popularity of the dances and the laws regulating the sale of feathers, Native people sometimes have to resort to the black market to obtain feathers not available on the open market. "A whole, young golden eagle sells for as much as $1,200. And a single golden eagle tail feather in mint condition can fetch more than $250."[56] As of April 2020, the Fish and Wildlife Service (fws.gov) website stated that the wait time – for a whole bird, a pair of wings and a whole tail, or a whole tail only – is three months for a bald eagle, whereas the wait time for an adult golden eagle is three years, seven months and for an immature golden eagle is seven years, six months. This long wait encourages a black market, but the penalties are severe. Know that there is another way for Native Americans to obtain the feathers legally without purchasing them. "Eagle feathers can be gifted to another enrolled member of a federally recognized tribe and passed on to children who also meet this requirement."[57] To prevent any doubt that the feathers were obtained legally, the FWS recommends that a copy of the donor's permit be kept at all times.

For these reasons, when the following caption "Rancher sentenced for killing bald eagles on Standing Rock Sioux Reservation"[58] headed an article written by Alaina Beautiful Bald Eagle on April 29, 2020, it marked an important event for Native Americans who consider the bald eagle feather a symbol of high honor, that the rancher was being held accountable.

David Meyers, age 58, is the owner of a ranch on the Standing Rock Sioux Indian Reservation in North Dakota. He was found guilty of overseeing the misapplication of a prairie dog bait which is a restricted pesticide. The six bald eagles recovered from his ranch during an EPA cleanup were confirmed to have died as a result of consuming animals that had eaten the bait. Meyer's was sentenced on April 22ⁿᵈ and "… was ordered to pay a total of $58,800 in restitution, $9,800 per eagle, a $50,000 fine, and a special assessment to the Federal Crime Victims Fund."[59] Because the charges levied against Meyers originated from several federal investigations, the tribes did not receive any of the money; however, it was a symbolic win for them.[60]

Return of the American Bison

Contrary to the western song "Oh give me a home where the buffalo roam," there have never been buffalo in North America; however, people have often used the name interchangeably for the bison. There are two types of buffalo, the water buffalo in Asia and the cape buffalo in Africa, whereas the bison have lived throughout North America for hundreds of years.[61] Jessica Heath of Flat Creek Inn in Jackson Hole, Wyoming wrote an article for the Inn's website citing estimates of the bison as high as 60 million in the 1500s, with their number reduced to 325 by 1884 as the result of intentional slaughter. The U.S. Army killed them as a way of subduing the Indians by denying an important source of food and shelter. Cattlemen killed them to prevent the bison from mingling with their herds, potentially spreading disease and eating the range grasses. Heath wrote that "Their [bison] near-extinction is a testament to the self-centeredness of 'civilized' men…"[62] The home page of the U.S. Fish and Wildlife Service states that "…. In 1910, The American Bison Society Census estimated 2,108 bison in North America (1,076 in Canada and 1,032 in the U.S.). Bison in public herds in the U.S. totaled 151."[63]

Native Americans view the bison not just as sustenance, but the large mammal has a spiritual and cultural connection to their lives. Returning the bison to their land would help the young people understand its significance. The youth have heard the stories and songs, have seen the ceremonies, but those things gain a true place in their lives and hearts when associated with the living animals.[64]

Jeremy Hance reported in *theguardian.com* that as early as 2007, the Fort Peck Reservation in northeast Montana, where the Assiniboine and Sioux tribes live, had a commercial herd but wanted to build a second herd utilizing stock from Yellowstone. The tribes had to combat the anti-bison attitudes within the Montana legislature where cattlemen fought against the bison. Bison carry the disease brucellosis, and cattlemen feared the disease could spread among their herds, "Although scientists have never recorded brucellosis jumping from bison to cattle,…"[65] The case went before the Montana supreme court before gaining approval to reintroduce Yellowstone bison to their reservation. These bison were significant because a small number that survived the 19th century slaughter lived in a remote valley in Yellowstone where they have not interbred with cattle so are more genetically pure. Approximately 23 animals from the late 1800s numbered about 4,000 animals in 2018.[66]

In addition to the cultural aspects, the bison help the environment as they graze, and their hooves aerate the soil. The prairie grasslands have experienced new growth as seeds of plants native to the area are dispersed through this natural aeration. At the same time, this has created a healthy and more balanced ecosystem benefitting many plants and animals.[67]

The added benefit resulting from the legal work done to bring the Yellowstone herd to Fort Peck was the signing, in 2016, of a Buffalo Treaty by 13 tribal nations representing reservations in the U.S. and Canada where they agreed to bring back free-ranging bison to both countries. "The Blackfoot Reservation, also in Montana, received 89 genetically pure bison from Elk Island in Canada."[68] The goal is that someday there will again be a free-ranging herd as far north as the Blood Tribe Reservation in Canada, which would make it an international herd.[69]

A May 2020 article on *nativenewsonline.net* announced a 10-year initiative of the Department of Interior.[70] Strategies to conserve the wild American bison will be considered by a working group made up of the following departments: National Park Service, U.S. Fish and Wildlife Service, Bureau of Land Management, U.S. Geological Survey and the Bureau of Indian Services. A representative of the Rosebud Reservation Economic Development stated:

We are doing something that has never been done. It shows what is possible when business, philanthropy, and government work together to create multiple bottom-line initiatives supporting the environment, people, fiscal responsibility, and Native nation building.[71]

Author's Thoughts

The challenges have changed over the years, but Native people continue to adapt to those changes, while adhering to the traditions and beliefs that have sustained them. That does not, however, mean that they are content with the status quo, and many Native people have worked their entire lifetime to make positive changes for their people.

One such individual is David Glass, a member of the White Earth Band of Ojibwe in northwest Minnesota and a leader of the National Coalition against Racism in Sports and Media, who has worked tirelessly to change team names, like the NFL Washington Redskins, as well as other NFL franchise members down to and including college and high school teams. Through the Tulsa Indian Coalition against Racism, Oneida Nation Representatives Ray Halbritter and Louis Gray, of the Osage Nation, have joined Glass as they work to educate people on the effects of using Indian names for teams, as well as the use of Indian mascots.[72]

Stephanie Fryberg is "A professor at the University of Michigan and member of the Tulalip Tribe. … [and] has spent years studying the psychological effects of Native stereotypes and logos on both Native Americans and non-Natives. She's seen precisely who gets hurt."[73] Fryberg's family has a home at the university and one on the reservation, which the family visits often to maintain and reinforce their connection with the Tulalip people. Her studies have shown:

> … that exposing Native American teenagers to Native sports mascots decreased their self-esteem, lowered the achievement-related goals they set for themselves, and diminished both their sense of community worth

and belief that their community can improve itself. ... That really gives you a sense of how powerful the imagery is. ... The only benefit to using Natives as mascots is that we have research showing that whites get a boost in self-esteem.[74]

In Chapter 12, two initiatives, Since Time Immemorial and Native Knowledge 360°, were addressed and are being used by Washington state educators. These programs present a more accurate assessment of American history, as they include Native people and cultures. In doing this, the educators have found that Native and non-native students are more engaged in history and social studies, particularly as it concerns them and the history of their state. These two programs are recognized for their historical accuracy and are available to educators nationwide, and some states now require Native history be taught in their public schools. A greater understanding of our collective history and cultures will enhance the relationships between the people of our nation.

When racism is looked at, there are specific incidents that have gained national attention. Rodney King, a Black man, was brutally beaten and arrested by four policemen – three of whom were white – in Los Angeles, California in March 1991. Despite the video recording clearly showing the altercation, the four officers were acquitted.

History provides us with teaching moments, and the 1992 Rodney King riots should have been such a moment. However, 30 years later, we still see many of the same issues with the riots and protests emerging from the recent killings of George Floyd, Eric Garner, Breonna Taylor, Ahmaud Arbery and others by police. In addition to needing to seriously address these tragedies in the present era of civil rights unrest and the call for equal treatment, it is important to note that:

> In the United States, Native Americans have the highest prevalence of fatal encounters with law enforcement of any racial or ethnic group. Yet these encounters are rarely covered in the media – for each fatal police shooting of a Native American there is an average of less than one media story.[75]

In the case of Floyd, King and so many others, there exists recordings for the world to watch. Floyd's especially is a horrific and powerful scene, and the resultant diverse protests in the U.S. and countries around the world indicate the anger at and increased awareness of racism, especially that which is systemic as it is for the Black community and for the Native people in the U.S.

To protect the Native population and businesses, the American Indian Movement (AIM) routinely patrols Native-owned businesses and neighborhoods in the Twin Cities. After the protests resulting from Floyd's death started, they had obtained a "curfew exemption" from the Minneapolis mayor's office to continue their patrols. For the majority of the night, the patrol was incident free; however, about 1:00 a.m. – without provocation or warning – the AIM patrol and Native Little Earth housing were attacked by the National Guard and Minnesota State Police with flash bang grenades and rubber bullets hitting one American Indian elder and smashing an AIM patrol vehicle's windows.[76] This is just one example of many racist and targeted attacks against Native Americans.

Today, the protests against racism feel different, in part due to participant diversity, length and breadth of the protests – maybe real change is coming. Politicians, government officials and many others are listening, from major sports owners to the diverse groups participating in the protests to the individuals who are taking different forms of action to combat it. According to news reports, more books and other media on racial injustice are being purchased and checked out from the library. At the same time, people are supporting Black businesses and donating to groups fighting racism. All of these are encouraging signs. Native Americans support those efforts, while also working to be included in positive changes for themselves.

From the start and from their ignorance and arrogance, the colonizers consistently tore the Native people and their cultures apart. This same ignorance and fear of unknown people and cultures, the unwillingness of one race to embrace a race other than their own is tearing the country apart, as this book is being written. Hopefully, the current outpouring of support for those who have experienced racism and against those who promote it will facilitate a change. It must end, not just for Native Americans, but for people of all races and cultures.

Endnotes:

1   Silver, Matthew. "Air Force Academy Cadets build Modular homes for Navajo." *manufacturedhomepronews.com.* 27 Jun 2016. https://bit.ly/3cIwMAO.

2   Silver.

3   Silver.

4   Coleman, Justine. "Doctors Without Borders in rare mission within US sends team to Navajo Nation." *The Hill.* 12 May 20. https://bit.ly/2ERmG46. Accessed 12 May 2020.

5   Coleman.

6   Library of Congress. "Voting Rights for Native Americans." https://bit.ly/2HFrsT7. Accessed 4 Aug 2020.

7   Smith, Anna V. "Report: Indigenous voters face racism and suppression." *High Country News,* 1 Jun 2020. https://bit.ly/3jdLTVf.

8   Smith.

9   Smith.

10   Native News Online Staff. "Some Navajo Nation Citizens are Voting by Horseback." *Native News Online*, 2 Nov 2020. https://bit.ly/2IXgERs.

11   Smith, Anna V. "Report: Indigenous voters face racism and suppression." *High Country News,* 1 Jun 2020. https://bit.ly/3jdLTVf.

12   Smith.

13   Native American Voting Rights Act of 2018." *Wikipedia: The Free Encyclopedia,* Wikimedia Foundation, https://bit.ly/34h6hi9. Accessed 4 Aug 2020.

14 Murdered & Missing Indigenous Women." *Native Womens Wilderness.* https://bit.ly/3n5NkYd. Accessed 29 May 2020

15 Murdered & Missing Indigenous Women." *Native Womens Wilderness.* https://bit.ly/3n5NkYd. Accessed 29 May 2020.

16 Domonoske, Camila. "Police in Many U.S. Cities Fail to Track Murdered, Missing Indigenous Women." *NPR*, 15 Nov. 2018. https://n.pr/3iivdKM. Accessed 8 Sep 2020.

17 Domonoske.

18 United States, Congress, Senate. Savanna's Act. *Congress.gov,* https://bit.ly/2Gq91Be. 115th Congress, 2nd session, Senate 1942, passed 6 Dec 2018.

19 Eric Carter-Landin talks with Cheyenne Antonio sex trafficking coordinator from Eastern Navajo territory. "True Consequences: Missing, murdered Indigenous women and Girls." 2 Dec 2019 podcast trueconsequences.com.

20 Trahant, Mark. "Washington NFL team's Standing Rock moment." 5 Jul 2020. indiancountrytoday.com.

21 "Missing and murdered Indigenous women." *Wikipedia: The Free Encyclopedia,* Wikimedia Foundation, https://bit.ly/2HL1rC5. Accessed 5 Jun 2020.

22 Ortiz, Erik. "Lack of Awareness, data hinders cases of missing and murdered Native American women, study finds." *NBC News*, 30 Jul 2020. https://nbcnews.to/3jhbI6M. Accessed 31 Jul 2020.

23 United States, Congress, House, Committee on Natural Resources, Subcommittee for Indigenous Peoples of the United States Oversight Hearing. "Reviewing the Trump Administration's Approach to the Missing and Murdered Indigenous Women (MMIW) Crisis." *U.S. Department of the Interior,* 11 Sep 2019. https://www.doi.gov/ocl/mmiw-crisis. Accessed 4 Aug 2020

24 Ortiz, Erik. "Lack of awareness, data hinders cases of missing and murdered Native American women, study finds." *NBC News*, 30 Jul 2020. https://nbcnews.to/3jhbI6M. Accessed 31 Jul 2020.

25 Ortiz.

26 United States, Congress, Senate. S.47 -Violence Against Women Reauthorization Act of 2013. 113th Congress (2013-2014), passed 7 Mar 2013. https://bit.ly/3pf38ZB

27 United States, Congress, H.R. 1585 — *Violence Against Women Reauthorization Act of 2019.* 116th Congress. (2019-2020). House report 116-21. https://bit.ly/3lqABOk.

28 Principal "Chief Chuck Hoskin Jr. "Chief Chat on MMIW." 5 Dec 2019. *Cherokee Nation Newsletter.*

29 Brewer, Suzette. "A Broken Trust Wins Robert F. Kennedy Journalism Award for Newsy. 5 Jun 2020. https://bit.ly/3lfwFAb

30 Henson, KenLea. "Building Partnerships: Cherokee Nation investigators join FBI as task force officers." *Anadisgoi, Spring/Summer 2020.* pp. 9-10.

31 Henson.

32 Schmidt, Ryan W. "American Indian Identity and Blood Quantum in the 21st Century: A Critical Review." *Hindawi: Journal of Anthropology*, 15 Jan 2012. https://bit.ly/34hjp6V.

33 Schmidt.

34 Chow, Kat. "So What Exactly is 'blood quantum'?" *Code Switch Podcast,* 9 Feb 2018. https://n.pr/36kG4BS.

35 Chow.

36 Chow.

37 Schmidt, Ryan W. "American Indian Identity and Blood Quantum in the 21st Century: A Critical Review." *Hindawi: Journal of Anthropology.* 15 Jan 2012. https://bit.ly/34hjp6V.

38 Schmidt.

39 Schmidt.

40 Hair, Josiah. "What is Blood Quantum? | Definition, Facts, Laws | Native American Indian." 27 Apr 2016, updated 24 Nov 2019. powwow.com.

41 Keene, Adrienne. "Love in the Time of Blood Quantum." *Native Appropriations*, 4 Apr 2011. https://bit.ly/33iLzit. Accessed Spring 2020.

42 Keene.

43 Reese, Dr. Debbie. "Multiracial" identity and American Indians." *American Indians in Children's Literature,* 30 Mar 2011. https://bit.ly/3p6yx0t.

44 Warren, Stephen and Johnnie Ingram, creators. *We're Here.* The Intellectual Property Corporation, HBO, Spring 2020. https://itsh.bo/3naSMIi.

45 Estes, Nick. *Our History is The Future: Standing Rock vs the*

Dakota Access Pipeline, and the Long Tradition of Indigenous Resistance. Verso, 2019. p. 31.

46 Williams, Walter L. "The 'two-spirit' people of indigenous North Americans." *The Guardian*, 11 Oct 2010. https://bit.ly/30kpb6g. Accessed 4 Jun 2020.

47 "The Feather: A symbol of high honor." *Native Hope.* https://bit.ly/3jjObCm. Accessed 2 Jun 2020.

48 The Feather

49 Efrati, Amir. "Powwows' Popularity Fuels a Black Market For Eagle Feathers." *The Wall Street Journal*, 22 Dec 2006.

50 Efrati.

51 Efrati.

52 American Indian Powwows: Commercialization." *Smithsonian Center for Folklife &Cultural Heritage.* https://s.si.edu/2EMRMcZ. Accessed 2 Aug 2020.

53 Muhammad, Dedrick Asante. Rogelio Tec and Kathy Ramirez. "Racial Wealth Snapshot: American Indians/Native Americans." *National Community Reinvestment Coalition,* 18 Nov 2019. https://bit.ly/3ijcz5u. Accessed 2 Aug 2020.

54 Wilson, Valerie. "Improved income growth for Native Americans, but lots of variation in the pace of recovery for different Asian ethnic groups." *Economic Policy Institute,* 14 Sep 2018. https://bit.ly/2GpffkQ. Accessed 2 Aug 2020.

55 Efrati. Amir. "Powwows' Popularity Fuels a Black Market For Eagle Feathers." *The Wall Street Journal*, 22 Dec 2006.

56 Efrati.

57 "How To Obtain Eagle Feathers." *The Peoples Path.* https://bit.ly/2ScMKcT. Accessed 13 Apr 2020.

58 Beautiful Bald Eagle, Alaina. "Rancher sentenced for killing bald eagles on Standing Rock Sioux Reservation." *West River Eagle.* 29 May 2020. Accessed 31 May 2020.

59 Beautiful Bald Eagle.

60 Beautiful Bald Eagle.

61 "American bison." *Wikipedia: The Free Encyclopedia,* Wikimedia Foundation, https://bit.ly/2GsE931. Accessed Jul 2020.

62 Heath, Jessica. "The Bison: from 30 million to 325 (1884) to 500,000 (today)." *Flat Creek Inn.* https://bit.ly/2Sg36BD.

63 "National Bison Range Wildlife Refuge Complex: Time Line

of the American Bison." *United States Fish and Wildlife Service,* 16 July 2020. https://bit.ly/2GldtS2.

64   Hance, Jeremy. "How Native American tribes are bringing back from brink of extinction." *The Guardian,* 12 Dec 2018 and modified 9 Sep 2019. https://bit.ly/3jhXXol. Accessed 29 Jul 2020.

65   Hance.

66   Hance.

67   Picardi, Phyllis. "Bison." *Defenders.* https://bit.ly/34bGvvE. Accessed 31 Jul 2020.

68   Picardi.

69   Hance, Jeremy. "How Native American tribes are bringing back from brink of extinction." *The Guardian,* 12 Dec 2018 and modified 9 Sep 2019. https://bit.ly/3jhXXol. Accessed 29 Jul 2020.

70   "Interior and Partners Commit to Long-Term Initiative to Conserve the American Bison." *Native News Online,* 8 May 2020. https://bit.ly/2EMR4MZ.

71   "Interior and Partners Commit to Long-Term Initiative to Conserve the American Bison." *Native News Online,* 8 May 2020. https://bit.ly/2EMR4MZ.

72   Stubbs, Roman. "As Redskins conduct name review, Native American groups say they haven't heard from team." *The Washington Post,* 7 Jul 2020. https://wapo.st/3n5iMWv.

73   Stanton, Zack. "How Native American Team Names Distort Your Psychology." *Politico,* 16 Jul 2020. https://politi.co/33htFN1.

74   Stanton.

75   Rickert, Levi. "After the Death of George Floyd, We Must Get Back to Better." *Native News Online,* 27 May 2020. https://bit.ly/3jkTHEF.

76   Rickert.

| FIFTEEN |

Promises versus Reality – In 2009 Government Held to 1800s Treaties

Do you pray for the senators, Dr. Hale?
No, I look at the senators and I pray for the country.
> Edward Everett Hale
> American Author and Unitarian clergyman
> April 3, 1822 – June 10, 1909[1]

We stand at the beginning of a new era for Indian Country and for tribal relations with the United States. Previous eras were defined by what the federal government chose to do: the Indian removal period when tribes were forcibly removed from their homelands to reservations, the reorganization and termination era, the allotment era, even the recent promise of the self-determination era. But this new era is defined by what we, as Indian nations, choose to do for ourselves.
> Jefferson Keel (Chickasaw), 20th President
> State of Indian Nations Address
> January 27, 2011[2]

The history of relations – meant to be that of nation-to-nation – between the Indian Nations and the U.S. government is littered with missteps, and Native Americans have paid and continue to pay a dear price throughout history into the present. Under the General Allotment Act of February 8, 1887 and the Curtis Act 1898, the Department of the Interior (DOI) has responsibility for tribal lands and resources which reside in trust with the federal government. It took 100 years, and the enactment of the American Indian Trust Fund Management Reform Act of 1994 before Indian tribes were able to withdraw judgment and settlement funds from DOI to manage independently. And it wasn't until 2012 that the Heath Act allowed tribes to lease their own land without the express permission of the secretary of the interior. This was a lengthy and laborious procedure, which delayed needed improvements on Indian lands. Leases of lands for "… public, religious, educational, recreational, residential, business, or agricultural purposes …"[3] would have provided much needed money for tribal governments.

Continuing Consequences of the Curtis Act

The most straightforward explanation of The Curtis Act of 1898 was that the title of all mineral rights on the allotted land, such as oil, coal, asphalt, etc., were reserved to the tribes. The money gained from the minerals was to be deposited in a trust fund maintained by the secretary of the interior and paid directly to individual Indians. Previous to the Dawes Act, money from treaties or agreements was paid to the tribe and used for the benefit of the entire tribe. Through the government's rewriting of the laws, the distribution of money was changed in two significant ways. First, through allotment, the tribal land was broken into pieces and given to individual Indians, and second, the tribal governments were dissolved. The Cherokee Nation continued to resist the stipulations of the Dawes and Curtis Acts until "… a third agreement was approved by the Cherokee on August 7, 1902, during a special election."[4] The rest of the Five Tribes acquiesced to the stipulations at that time. In order to have a Cherokee representative who could sign documents that would legally transfer title of tribal lands to individuals and be recognized by both the Cherokee people and the federal government, Chief William Charles Rogers was allowed to remain in office until his death in 1917.[5]

Treaties Are the Law of the Land

Treaties are approved by the Senate and signed into law by the president. The terms of the treaties are legally binding on all parties and are still in full force and effect today unless superseded by another treaty or amended – in this case between the U.S.

Government and the Indian Nation(s) who signed. The last treaty between the Cherokee and the U.S. was written in 1868 as an amendment to the 1866 Treaty.[6]

> I know what the misfortune of the tribes is. Their misfortune is not that they are red men, not that they are semi-civilized, not that they are a dwindling race. Their misfortune is that they hold great bodies of rich lands, which have aroused the cupidity of powerful corporations and of powerful individuals. … I greatly fear that the adoption of this provision to discontinue treaty-making is the beginning of the end in respect to Indian Lands. It is the first step in a great scheme of spoliation, in which the Indians will be plundered, corporations and individuals enriched, and the American name dishonored in history.

California Senator Eugene Casserly, 1781
Documents of American Indian Diplomacy:
Treaties, Agreements, and Conventions, 1775-1979[7]

The Power of One Person

The following provides a 21st century example of promises vs. reality, when an individual stands up for what is right for his or her people. Because of its legal precedence, the *Cobell* case will be cited for years to come.

Elouise Cobell, born Yellow Bird Woman on November 5, 1945 (died Oct 16, 2011), was a member of the Blackfoot Nation of Montana, situated on the eastern edge of Glacier National Park and about 120 miles from Great Falls. She knew the stories of "The Starvation Winter of 1883-1884 [which] took the lives of about 500 Blackfoot Indians who had been camping in the vicinity of Old Agency."[8] That year Montana had particularly brutal weather, barbed wire surrounded the Blackfoot reservation, the bison had been killed off and their supplies were black marketed by agency men – all contributing to the 555 Blackfoot (by actual count) deaths, as by spring they were reduced to eating seed potatoes and chewing the inner bark of cottonwood trees.[9] Julia Whitty wrote an article for the

September/October 2005 issue of *motherjones.com* telling of Cobell's concern for the Blackfoot people. Cobell passed the monument marking the starvation winter along Highway 89 daily as she traveled back and forth to her office.

The power of one person is demonstrated in Cobell's story. At age 18, she started asking questions of the Bureau of Indian Affairs (BIA) regarding the Individual Indian Monies (IIM) stipulated in the Dawes Act that are supposed to be paid yearly to each person who received a land allotment and carries through the generations. She was basically told that it was too complicated for her to understand, so she set about doing something about it. Whitty wrote, "Cobell became an accountant. Twelve years later, she was appointed treasurer of the Blackfoot Nation."[10] The more she learned, the more interested she became, and after talking with other Blackfoot members, she realized the following:

> … some years her fellow landowners got their checks, some years they didn't. They never received an accounting, and most (including Cobell) didn't even know, and couldn't find out, which lands exactly were theirs. Worse, some had once received payments but now no longer did, and they had no idea why. No one dared confront the BIA.[11]

In her book, *Mankiller: A Chief and Her People*, Wilma Mankiller wrote, "In 1976, when the unlawful conduct of the BIA officials came under review, a federal court said the attitude of government officials 'can only be characterized as bureaucratic imperialism.'"[12] To characterize how pervasive that attitude was, Mankiller continued "I agree with former Creek Chief Claude Box of Oklahoma, who said reforming the BIA was kind of like rotating four bald tires on an old car. The net result would be no change."[13] Elouise Cobell did not accept the status quo attitude of the BIA.

Cobell Visits Members of Blackfoot Nation

According to Whitty's article, some people Cobell visited had active oil wells on their ground but still didn't receive any money or very little. Taxes were imposed on improvements that the government never made, and people would often forfeit ownership to pay those taxes and prevent the government from withholding their IIM payments. Cobell remembered her father receiving a check for $.08. He laughed and wondered aloud about the waste of sending a payment that cost more to process than the payment itself:

> … visiting one impoverished family after another, Cobell couldn't help but notice the oil wells pumping on Blackfoot land, the thousands of heads of cattle, the rippling fields of alfalfa. The non-Indian tenants who worked these lands were living in nice houses, driving new cars, while their Blackfeet landlords were living in cold, leaky government housing, largely unemployed and undereducated. 'Why couldn't an Indian – a landholding Indian at that,' wondered Cobell, 'get a mortgage or a bank loan to start his or her own life?'[14]

As she went about her daily work, Cobell found time to help tribal members. "She founded the Blackfoot National Bank, the first national bank located on an Indian reservation and owned by a Native American tribe. In 1997, Cobell won a MacArthur genius award for her work on the bank and Native financial literacy."[15] She later stated that she had made the leap from dumb Indian to genius in one lifetime. Twenty other tribes joined the bank to form the Native American Bank based in Denver, Colorado. Cobell used $310,000 of the MacArthur award money to support a class action lawsuit against the Department of the Interior for mismanagement of the trust money.[16]

The Power of One Becomes the Power of Many

A lawsuit was filed against the United States in June 1996 by Cobell and a few other individual Indians. By the time the suit was settled, there were over 300,000 plaintiffs. The suit cited the government for its continuing inability to meet its fiduciary responsibilities:

> The case had three goals: (1) an adequate accounting of the individual Indian trust, (2) a restatement of

trust balances in conformity with the accounting rules, and (3) reform of what government officials have long conceded is a decrepit trust management system.[17]

In December 1999, *The Washington Post* reported that Secretary of the Interior Gale Norton was unable to reform the trust which was to track "... $500 million a year in royalties from 54 million acres of Indian land held in trust by the Interior Department and BIA."[18] Then in February 2002, Mary Boyle wrote an article for the Colorado Springs, Colorado *Gazette* which further stated:

> It was supposed to work this way: the government would have acted as a trustee, leasing the land and collecting royalties from oil, gas and mineral rights, and then distributing the income to Indian owners. That didn't always happen. The royalties were lost, stolen, misappropriated and in some cases not collected. Records disappeared, and officials lost track of who owned what land."[19]

The Department of the Interior was unable to meet the court's requirements and six months later, on September 17, 2002, *CBS News* reported that Norton was held in contempt of court by Judge Lamberth making her the "third Cabinet-level official to be held in contempt of court in modern history".[20]

The problems with the government's handling of the Indian accounts were first noted in 1828 when Henry Schoolcraft, an ethnographer and federal agent, wrote "... it seemed that the Indian department's fiscal affairs 'had been handled with a pitchfork... (T)here is a screw loose in the public machinery somewhere.'"[21] Dozens of scathing reports followed over the years. In 1992 – 164 years later – Schoolcraft's assessment is quoted in a congressional report which concluded, "While mismanagement of the Indian trust fund has been reported for more than a century, there is no evidence that either the Bureau or the Department of the Interior has undertaken any sustained or comprehensive effort to resolve glaring deficiencies."[22] In 1994, the Department of Interior was instructed by Congress to make a full accounting of the Indian Trust Fund. When that was not done, Cobell filed the suit.

The case carried through three administrations: Clinton, Bush and Obama. Ken Salazar was secretary of the interior when the suit finally settled. To illustrate how slow the wheels of government can turn, the following dates are important, as they delineate the gap of time before implementation:

> ... $3.4 billion settlement was reached in 2009;
> ... November 2010, Congress ratified the settlement;
> ... June 21, 2011, the Federal District Court in Washington D.C., gave it the final stamp of approval;
> ... December 2012 the first round of checks was sent out to over 300,000 beneficiaries averaging between $1,000 to $2,000 per person.[23]

Stories of Those Directly Impacted by BIA Inaction

An *Associated Press* article written by Pauline Arrillaga, "For Indians, Trust Fund Case Can Right a Century of Wrongs" printed in the *Los Angeles Times* on October 31, 1999 exemplifies the continuing fight with the government that faces many Indians today. The article tells about a 75-year-old Blackfoot Indian, Josephine Spotted Bear Wildgun, with a sixth-grade education who lives "on the southern edge of the Blackfoot Indian Reservation"[24] in the community of Heart Butte, Montana:

> Like so many other American Indian communities across the United States, Heart Butte doesn't have much. There are three churches, a school, a senior citizens center, the health department, a post office, and a volunteer fire department. Its only grocery store and gas station closed years ago. ... Josephine lives on $374.00 a month in Supplemental Security Income and whatever money her son can send home. ... When her husband died five years ago, she had to borrow $500 to pay for the funeral. ... It's difficult to conceive that this woman who struggles to buy food owns an interest in 8,718 acres of land, some leased for grazing,

most for oil and gas exploration. A computer printout of all her holdings unfurls to almost six feet in length. ...[25]

In addition, there is no set time for the checks to arrive from the BIA. It can be four to six months between checks, and the amount is just as sporadic – sometimes less than $3.00 and occasionally there will be one for $200 or $300. Native Americans cannot count on checks from the BIA to pay the bills. Josephine made sure to pay her utilities, but money for groceries was difficult to get.[26]

In Julia Whitty's 2005 article, she recounted another story that Cobell shared of 82-year-old Jim Little Bull who lived in a tiny home on the Blackfoot reservation. The house had almost no furniture and was heated by an ancient woodstove. He told of the problems he faced when his mother passed away:

> ... the government taxed her estate $7,000 for the operation and management of an irrigation system on her allotment. The problem was, although that land had been scored with ditches years before, no irrigation equipment had ever been installed, and no water other than rainfall had ever graced it. But Jim Little Bull was afraid to ask questions, worried his own Individual Indian Monies (IIM) would be withheld to pay his mother's bill. So he forfeited her land back to the government.[27]

That historic marker along Highway 89 wasn't just a story to Cobell. She understood that 500 of her people had died during the starvation winter of 1883-1884. They were discarded and forgotten by the government – but not by her.

When Cobell filed the lawsuit against the United States, it was representing all Indians "... who were land rich, [but] were living dirt-poor, without running water and electricity..."[28] The suit finally gave a voice to people like Josephine Spotted Bear Wildgun, Jim Little Bull and as a memoriam to the 500 who had starved to death. This was a fight to hold the government accountable.[29]

U.S. Government Admits Mismanagement

From 1887 to 1934 when the allotment ended, 90 million acres had passed to individual Indians or been sold. The Department of the Interior (DOI) became leasing agents for Indian lands, giving commercial rights for grazing, timber cutting, mining and use of other natural resources without obtaining the landowner's permission. The proceeds of these leases were to be held in trust, along with interest earned, by the DOI. This necessitated a general accounting of these monies, with payouts going to individual Indians on a yearly basis. Ten million acres were owned in small parcels as ownership passed along to multiple generations. By the 21st century, many land deeds had been lost or destroyed, while others were never recorded, making it difficult for the DOI to document ownership of a sliver of inherited land.[30]

Neither the records of land ownership nor of trust money and accrued interest were maintained, which makes the 1996 federal lawsuit, *Cobell v. Norton* against the Department of the Interior so effective. In response to the *Cobell* suit, the government admitted the fund had been mismanaged since its inception. "According to Cobell's forensic accountants, the government owes $176 billion to individual Indian landowners, averaging $352,000 per plaintiff ..."[31] Over 300,000 plaintiffs joined together, seeking a minimum of $10 billion dollars credited to their accounts and settled for $3.4 billion.

In addition to Cobell's forensic accountants, private accounting agencies found that the BIA used the trust money as a slush fund. Uses of the money "... included the New York City's 1975 fiscal crisis, a Chrysler bailout, and writing down part of the national debt. The most basic problem was failure to follow fundamental accounting procedures..."[32]

In 2005, when discussing the lawsuit, Cobell stated, "To those concerned that the United States can't afford a *Cobell v. Norton* settlement, she says, 'It's not your money and never was.'"[33]

Judge Lamberth – Advocate of the Indians

Royce C. Lamberth, a native of Texas, was appointed to

the bench by President Ronald Reagan in 1987 and assigned the *Cobell* lawsuit in 1996. In Stephanie Mencimer's article for *The Washington Monthly* in April 2002, she wrote that a better advocate of the Indians could not have been appointed, "Lamberth is an old-fashioned law-and-order conservative who believes that the law is the law, and he has little sympathy for those who break it."[34] Mencimer wrote that he often questioned witnesses, asking questions the lawyers wish they had thought of:

> What's amazing about Lamberth's outburst [against DOI] is not what it reveals about sloppy government, but what it reveals about the judge. Not only has Lamberth managed to stay awake during the hours of tedious testimony, but he is closely following every turn of the questioning and scrutinizing each piece of evidence along the way. He knows the material as well as any of the lawyers.[35]

In a press release dated Wednesday July 13, 2005 on *indianz.com*, Lamberth is quoted as saying:

> For those harboring hope that the stories of murder, dispossession, forced marches, assimilationist policy programs, and other incidents of cultural genocide against the Indians are merely the echoes of a horrible, bigoted government-past that has been sanitized by the good deeds of more recent history, this case serves as an appalling reminder of the evils that result when large numbers of the politically powerless are placed at the mercy of institutions engendered and controlled by a politically powerful few, ... It reminds us that even today our great democratic enterprise remains unfinished. And it reminds us, finally, that the terrible power of government, and the frailty of the restraints on the exercise of that power, are never fully revealed until government turns against the people.[36]

Stipulations of the Court Order

To comply with a court-ordered accounting of the financial and cultural records of the Indians, the Department of the Interior rented a climate-controlled, underground facility outside of Lenexa, Kansas about a half-hour southwest of Kansas City, Missouri. The circumstances surrounding the facility are documented in an article written by John Heilprin for the *Casper Star Tribune* dated May 6, 2006 and titled "They're finally going to get their accounting." Heilprin wrote:

> Seventy feet beneath the prairie, the government is filling limestone caverns – protected by guards and a bomb-sniffing dog – with truckloads of American Indians' financial and cultural records... In an irony befitting an 'Alice's Adventures in Wonderland' legal war, the government is relying on the Indian – demanded accounting – actually, it's a statistical sampling – to come up with figures that Indians claim low-ball what they are owed. The Indians who sued say now that too many records have been destroyed to come up with an accurate figure. Before 1990, the Treasury Department routinely destroyed the Indian trust's canceled checks, and court documents attest to numerous destroyed records...[37]

Heilprin described the massive project which will be ongoing (not just old documents are sent for preservation) because as Indian records are retired from the various government agencies, they are sent to be archived. To understand the scale of the Lenexa facility – it is the size of Kansas City, Missouri's football stadium, which seats over 79,000 fans.[38] It has air filters and is humidity controlled to prevent degradation of the documents. A team of accounting firms, federal contractors and government employees, along with students from nearby Haskell Indian Nation University, sort the materials. Documents and pictures are digitized and logged into the computers.

Judge Lamberth Removed from Case

U.S. District Court Judge Royce Lamberth oversaw the suit from first filing until 2006 when the following happened:

> ... the U.S. Court of Appeals for the D. C. Circuit cited Lamberth's own words to illustrate why he should be removed from the case, Cobell v.

Kempthorne, including a July 2005 opinion in which he called Interior 'a dinosaur – the morally and culturally oblivious hand-me-down of a disgracefully racist and imperialist government that should have been buried a century ago, the pathetic outpost of the indifference and anglocentrism we thought we had left behind.'[39]

The Associated Press reported in July 2006 that Lamberth was a thorn in the government's side for the many years he presided over the *Cobell* suit. After his remarks stated above, the government argued that Lamberth was "… too biased to continue with the case."[40] The U.S. Court of Appeals for the District of Columbia Circuit sided with the government lawyers, and Lamberth was removed from the case.

In 2008, Judge James Robertson was appointed the new trial judge. After reviewing the trial proceedings and documents to date, he wrote that "… complete accounting would be 'nuts'. That being the case, there had to be some other remedy for the defendants' failures."[41]

Government Loses Appeal

A two-year appeal held up the first disbursements of the 2009 settlement. Cobell died October 16, 2011 without seeing her people receive any of their long overdue money.[42] Tuesday, November 27, 2012, CNN wire staff reported the United States finalized a $3.4 billion settlement. In making the announcement that Monday, President Obama remembered Cobell for "her honorable work."

In 2009, Cobell said that "… many of those represented in the class-action suit 'subsist in the direst poverty,' and that the settlement is 'significantly less than the full amount to which the Indians are owed.'"[43] Pinning her hopes on a future when Indians would be treated more fairly, she nonetheless believed that the long process to reach a settlement was not fair.[44] In a statement quoted by the CNN wire staff on November 27, 2012, President Barack Obama said, "I welcome the final approval of the Cobell settlement agreement, clearing the way for reconciliation between the trust beneficiaries and the federal government."[45]

The agreement called for $1.5 billion to be distributed among those who were part of the lawsuit. Lest anyone believe that people received huge amounts from the settlement, the average was $1,000 to $2,000 per person. "Another $1.9 billion went into a "land consolidation program" that will allow people to sell fractions of land they own, which are silvers of once larger ancestral plots that have been divided and subdivided over generations."[46] The fractionalized land that is bought back from the voluntary sales will restore reservation land and strengthen their land base.[47]

> The buy-back program established as part of the Cobell settlement continues today and as of May 26, 2020, approximately $188 million remains, comprised of $115 million in the land purchase portion of the Fund and $73 million in the implementation portion of the Fund. Consolidated interests are immediately restored to tribal trust ownership for uses benefiting the reservation community and tribal members.[48]

Scholarships Specified in *Cobell* Settlement

In 2017, the Department of the Interior paid $12.5 million into the Cobell Scholarship Fund as the final part of the $60 million scholarship settlement of the *Cobell* suit. Indigenous Education, Inc. (IEI) located in Albuquerque, New Mexico was founded in February 2016 to administer the scholarship program.[49]

Tanya H. Lee wrote an article published on *Indian Country Today* on May 23, 2017 in which she stated, "The Cobell Scholarship Fund provides money to [Native American] full-time undergraduate and graduate students pursuing college degrees or technical training at an accredited non-profit institution of high education."[50] At the time she wrote the article, data had been provided by the Interior Department through the 2016-2017 academic year, including the summer semester, which showed the following: "... the fund has awarded more than 2,000 scholarships totaling more than $5.25 million to almost 1,000 Native American students,..." [51] Each academic year could see undergraduates awarded as much as $5,000, while graduate and doctoral students could be awarded up to $10,000.[52]

Cobell Awarded Presidential Medal of Freedom Posthumously

Julia Whitty reported in the September/October 2005 issue of *Mother Jones* that in 2002, the Blackfoot awarded Cobell warrior status, a rare honor for a woman. Cobell died in October 2011 of cancer. "In November 2016, Cobell's work on behalf of Native Americans was honored by the award of a posthumous Presidential Medal of Freedom by President Barack Obama; her son Turk Cobell accepted the award on her behalf."[53] In presenting the award, Obama stated:

> When Elouise Cobell first filed a lawsuit to recover lands and money for her people, she didn't set out to be a hero. She said, 'I just wanted... to give justice to people that didn't have it.' And her lifelong quest to address the mismanagement of American Indian lands, resources, and trust funds wasn't about special treatment, but the equal treatment at the heart of the American promise. She fought for almost 15 years – across three Presidents, seven trials, 10 appearances before a federal appeals court. All the while, she traveled the country some 40 weeks a year, telling the story of her people. And in the end, this graduate of a one-room schoolhouse became a MacArthur Genius. She is a proud daughter of Montana's Blackfeet Nation who ultimately reached a historic victory for all Native Americans. Through sheer force of will and a belief that the truth will win out, Elouise Cobell overcame the longest odds, reminding us that fighting for what is right is always worth it.[54]

American Indian Records Repository Today

The Lenexa, Kansas records facility that John Heilprin wrote about is known today as the American Indian Records

Repository (AIRR). The facility stores "Records – from as far back as the 1700s – includes trust, education and other historic Indian Affairs records."[55] From Department of Interior and Bureau of Indian Affairs official statements during the *Cobell* suit, it is known that it was impossible to account for all Indian records because many had been lost or destroyed. At that point, Lamberth ordered all existing retired records be archived at the Lenexa facility. Anyone interested in learning the scope of their work and records kept can search *doi.gov* American Indian Records Repository (AIRR). Active Indian records are held at the DOI offices, and researchers and others with interest in Indian records can access them through the National Archives and Records Administration (NARA).[56]

> The [Kansas] facility continues to receive boxes from the field as active records become inactive. A total of over 200,000 indexed boxes had been sent to AIRR for permanent storage by the end of fiscal year 2012. In the past three years, the monthly average of boxes received has been 1,157. Each standard records center box holds one cubic foot of material; one cubic foot holds approximately 2,500 sheets of paper.[57]

The AIRR facility is closed to the public but offers special access to "... authorized researchers, federal employees who are conducting the historical trust accounting, tribes, and contractors secure access to inactive records for research."[58] Because of its proximity to the AIRR facility, the students at Haskell Indian Nations University in Lawrence, Kansas receive course training at the facility in records management. As previously noted, some students and graduates then work at the facility.

A Labyrinth of Government Agencies

A large number of government agencies are involved with Native American programs and present a labyrinth to work with and through. The Native American Rights Fund, organized in 1970, is but one organization working with tribes, organizations and individuals nationwide to help work through the government's legal maze. To gain an appreciation of the agencies involved in carrying out the work of the treaties and trusts, it can help to understand, at least to a degree, the scope of their work. A 2014 document released by the Department of the Interior (DOI) stated their current responsibilities to Native Americans:

> Among their responsibilities, Interior agencies oversee $4.7 billion in trust funds derived from managing 55 million surface acres and 57 million acres of subsurface mineral estate held in trust for individual Indians, Indian tribes and Alaska Natives. Eleven million acres belong to individual Indians and 44 million acres to tribes. Interior administers more than 119,000 leases for the use of these lands, including oil, gas and mineral extraction, water and energy development, timber harvesting and grazing.[59]

Handling the trust accounts continues to be a significant task for the federal government in 2020. "According to its own statistics, the government presently holds about $5 billion in trust funds for tribes and individual Indians. The government holds 3,300 trust accounts for over 250 tribes."[60] Natural resources on Indian lands are leased and the money deposited to Individual Indian Monies (IIM) accounts, which are overseen by the Office of Trust Funds Management.[61]

Other than the DOI, these are a few of the agencies involved in Indian affairs: Bureau of Indian Education; the Indian Water Rights Office which oversees Indian water rights claims and the Office of Natural Resources Revenue and National Park Service within the DOI. Additional agencies are the Indian Gaming Commission, which is an independent agency within DOI; Indian Health Services is within the Department of Health and Human Services and Native American hunting and fishing rights fall under the U.S. Fish and Wildlife Service. The Office of Trust Funds Management oversees the American Indians and Individual Monies (IIM) accounts within the Office of the Special Trustee. This list illustrates the complexities that Native American tribes and individuals face when dealing with the DOI.[62]

Unclaimed Indian Money (IIM)

During the *Cobell* suit, the government admitted that trust accounts had been mishandled, but the additional problem continues to be lost and inaccurate records. The records of many Indians lack a physical address and even a social security number. This causes difficulties in maintaining the database for about 300,000 Native Americans in the Office of Trust Funds Management, which distributes IIM. About 47,000 possible recipients are listed as unknown because of missing critical information like married names, no contact information, unnamed heirs of deceased property owners and other issues. Some of the duties of the trustee office include overseeing annual payments, managing a Trust Beneficiary Call Center – which provides those who are missing payments a way to contact the office – handling leases and valuations of Indian lands and overseeing the Lenexa, Kansas records center.[63]

Lobbyist Bilks Tribes

In addition to having to sue the federal government for the money guaranteed by treaty, a headline in the *Colorado Springs Gazette* on July 23, 2005 read, "Lobbyist bilked tribes of millions, report says." Quoted from the *Dallas Morning News*, it showed that the Senate Committee on Indian Affairs was investigating Jack Abramoff and partner, Michael Scanlon. According to Senate documents, "The committee estimates that in 2001 alone, the two pocketed $6.5 million of $7.7 million billed to the Choctaws."[64]

A 2009 article posted by Matthew Murray to *rollcall.com* discussed the impact the Abramoff scandal had on tribal lobbying. Murray stated that the tribes felt the scandal had "unfairly tarred their community, not just Abramoff and his associates. … that the turmoil brought many tribes together."[65] The Senate Committee on Indian Affairs headed by Ben Nighthorse Campbell, a member of the Northern Cheyenne Tribe, uncovered an invoice to six tribes for $82 million in fees by Abramoff and Scanlon's firm billed for lobbying. Contrast that with the figures reported on *opensecrets.org* for lobbying work done for Indian clients in 2020. Lobbyists were paid $18,237,090 by 142 Indian clients for their annual lobbying work specifically on Indian gaming. [66] Lobbyists are active in Washington, D.C. working for many different organizations, political and non-political, and Native Americans have been candidates for their efforts. Because of these and other instances uncovered by the Senate Committee on Indian Affairs, a rigorous bidding process was established, and the lobbyists and the work they perform are more closely scrutinized.[67]

Native American Heritage Month

As President Obama proclaimed National Native American Heritage Month on November 2, 2010, he recognized the ongoing commitment of his administration in working with the First Citizens of this country stating:

> As we celebrate the contributions and heritage of Native Americans during this month, we also recommit to supporting tribal self-determination, security, and prosperity for all Native Americans. ... While we cannot erase the scourges or broken promises of our past, we will move ahead together in writing a new, brighter chapter in our joint history.[68]

History will record which administrations uphold the goal of ensuring a brighter future between the American people and the nation's First Citizens and which administrations set the goal aside for other interests.

Author's Thoughts

The House of Representatives made an arbitrary decision in 1871 to end the treaty-making process with the Indian Nations, declaring them to be "domestic dependent nations." Prior to 1871, the government utilized the treaty process to induce Native Americans to give up their lands. When agreeing to a treaty, the Indian headmen smoked a pipe – with an eagle feather to show the solemnity of the occasion – with their government counterparts. The treaties ended with white man's phrases like "As long as the moon shall rise," which Native people believed, but it was never long before more land or natural resources were desired, and the government broke the treaty. The decision to change the status of Native American tribes to domestic dependent nations forever changed the lives of the People, and it was done without their advice or consent.

Promises vs reality has been a problem throughout the relationship between the U.S. government and Native Americans. As they have in the past, the 20th and 21st centuries have seen Native Americans take their fights to the courts to obtain what is legally owed to them. Large amounts of money have been lost to them due to the government's destruction of documents and inaccurate accounting of the trust accounts. The money is theirs, and they have to fight for that, as well as the healthcare, education and many other benefits guaranteed to them by treaties that are still in "full force and effect."

A piece of paper found taped to Cobell's computer after her death reads:

> First they ignore you,
> then they laugh at you,
> then they fight you,
> then you win.[69]

In the past months, we have repeatedly heard the phrase, "We're all in this together." No matter your race or religion, whether you are a First Citizen and have been here for centuries or are a new immigrant, you are part of the rich fabric of this nation. Our diversity is what makes us strong. We need to make sure that all people in this country are afforded the rights due to them – that their voices are heard.

There are a number of ways to help our First Citizens. Some include contacting your congressperson about a Native American issue that you feel strongly about, contributing your time or donating to any of the Native organizations in your area. The Native American Rights Fund works to preserve tribal existence, protect tribal resources, promote Native American human rights and protect Native laws. Another Native organization that could use help is Saint Joseph's Indian School in Chamberlain, South Dakota, which has helped house and educate Lakota children from the surrounding reservations since its founding in 1927. Many people enjoy the National Parks and a contribution to them also benefits Native Americans as park personnel maintain Native sacred sites within the parks.

Endnotes:

1   Hale, Edward Everett. *Brainy Quote*. https://bit.ly/36zO00H
2   Keel, Jefferson. "9th Annual State of Indian Nations Address Remarks." *National Congress of American Indians,* 27 Jan 2011, https://bit.ly/2Sbkw22.
3   "Native Americans and Trusts." *Friends Committee on National Legislation.* Undated. https://bit.ly/3ncAN4z. Undated.
4   Mankiller, Wilma and Michael Wallis. *Mankiller: A Chief and Her People.* St Martin's Press, 1993. p. 138.
5   Mankiller. p. 138.
6   Kappler, Charles. Compiled and edited by. *Indian Treaties: 1778-1883.* Amereon House, 1972. pp. 996-997.
7   Deloria, Vine and Raymond J. DeMallie. *Documents of American Indian Diplomacy: Treaties, Agreements, and Conventions, 1775-1979 (Legal History of North America)"* U of Oklahoma P, Vol 1, p. 243.
8   Whitty, Julia. "Elouise Cobell's Accounting Coup." *Mother Jones,* September/October 2005, https://bit.ly/34ejSq9
9   Whitty.
10 Whitty.
11 Whitty.
12 Mankiller, Wilma and Michael Wallis. *Mankiller: A Chief and Her People.* St Martin's Press, 1993. p. 168
13 Mankiller. p. 168.
14 Whitty, Julia. "Elouise Cobell's Accounting Coup." *Mother Jones,* September/October 2005, https://bit.ly/34ejSq9.
15 Berger, Bethany R. "Elouise Cobell." https://bit.ly/2IIkkWY.

16 Whitty, Julia. "Elouise Cobell's Accounting Coup." *Mother Jones*, September/October 2005, https://bit.ly/34ejSq9.

17 Harper, Keith. "Cobel v. Norton: Redressing a Century of Malfeasance." *American Bar Association*. 1 Apr 2006. https://bit.ly/35fCnfW.

18 "Norton seeks meeting with tribes over royalities." *The Gazette*, Colorado Springs, CO 7 Dec 2001.

19 Boyle, Mary. "Norton in a historic bind." *The Gazette*, Colorado Springs, CO. 20 Feb 2020.

20 Roberts, Joel. "Interior Secretary Held in Contempt." 17 Sep 2002, *CBS News*. https://cbsn.ws/35q3yoj. Accessed 18 Sep 2002.

21 Berger, Bethany R. "Elouise Cobell." https://bit.ly/2IIkkWY. Note 13.

22 Berger. Note 14.

23 Janko, Melinda. "Elouise Cobell: A Small Measure of Justice from Issue: Summer 2013/Vol. 14 No 2." *American Indian: Magazine of Smithsonian's National Museum of The American Indian*. https://bit.ly/3lhGhdL.

24 Arrillaga, Pauline. "For Indians, Trust Fund Case Can Right a Century of Wrongs." *Los Angeles Times*. 31 Oct 1999. https://lat.ms/3eMvtBF.

25 Arrillaga.

26 Arrillaga.

27 Witty, Julia. ""Elouise Cobell's Accounting Coup." *Mother Jones*, September/October 2005, https://bit.ly/34ejSq9.

28 Janko, Melinda. "Elouise Cobell: A Small Measure of Justice from Issue: Summer 2013/Vol. 14 No 2." *American Indian: Magazine of Smithsonian's National Museum of The American Indian*. https://bit.ly/3lhGhdL.

29 Witty, Julia. ""Elouise Cobell's Accounting Coup." *Mother Jones*, September/October 2005, https://bit.ly/34ejSq9.

30 Whitty.

31 Whitty.

32 Berger, Bethany R. "Elouise Cobell." *Cobell scholar.org*. https://bit.ly/32vQgEF. Note 18.

33 Witty, Julia. ""Elouise Cobell's Accounting Coup." *Mother Jones*, September/October 2005, https://bit.ly/34ejSq9.

34 Mencimer, Stephanie. "Lone-star justice: conservatives thought Clinton-bashing Judge Royce Lamberth was on their team — until he went after the Bushies." *The Washington Monthly.* April 2002, pp. 23-30. https://bit.ly/3ePlTxZ.

35 Mencimer.

36 "Interior ordered to disclose trust fund failure." 13 Jul 2005. *Indianz.* See *Cobell v. Kempthorne.* Decided: 11 Jul 2006. https://bit.ly/36O1HZK.

37 Heilprin, John. "They're finally going to get their accounting." *Casper Star Tribune.* 6 May 2006. https://bit.ly/38thxvg

38 Heilprin.

39 Weiss, Eric M. "At U.S. Urging, Court throws Lamberth Off Indian Case." *The Washington Post.* 12 Jul 2006. https://wapo.st/3kkdZOc.

40 Weiss.

41 Berger, Bethany R. "Elouise Cobell." *Cobell scholar.org.* https://bit.ly/32vQgEF. Note 38.

42 Barnhill, Frankie. "Nearly 6,000 Idaho Natives To Receive Checks in First Round of Settlements." *Boise State Public Radio.* 12 Dec 2012. https://bit.ly/38wEGgE.

43 Courson, Paul. "U.S. offers to pay Native Americans $1.4 billion for lost funds." 8 Dec 2009. cnn.com. https://cnn.it/36lY1hL.

44 Courson.

45 Obama, Barack. "Statement of the President on the Final Approval of the Cobell Settlement." *The White House,* 26 Nov 2012. https://bit.ly/32yfFxx.

46 CNN Wire Staff. "U.S. finalizes $3.4 billion settlement with American Indians." *CNN,* 27 Nov 2012. https://cnn.it/3eKJzU8.

47 "Land Buy-Back Program for Tribal Nations." *U.S. Department of the Interior*, 31 May 2020. https://on.doi.gov/2UeGFxB.

48 "Land Buy-Back Program for Tribal Nations." *U.S. Department of the Interior*, 31 May 2020. https://on.doi.gov/2UeGFxB

49 Berger, Bethany R. "Elouise Cobell." *Cobell scholar.org.* https://bit.ly/32vQgEF. Note 38.

50 Lee, Tanya H. "Need Money for College? Cobell Scholarship Fund reaches $60 Million." *Indiancountrytoday.com,* 23 May 2017. https://bit.ly/35h4n2w.

51 Lee.

52 Lee.

53 "Elouise P. Cobell." Wikipedia: The Free Encyclopedia, Wikimedia Foundation. https://bit.ly/32xDTrS

54 Obama, Barack. "Remarks by the President at Presentation of the Presidential Medal of Freedom" *obamawhitehouse.archives.gov*, 22 Nov 2016. https://bit.ly/3eOyVM5

55 "AIRR Records." *Bureau of Trust Funds Administration: U.S. Department of the Interior,* 24 Oct 2019. https://on.doi.gov/36qzTui.

56 National Archives and Records Administration (NARA). https://www.archives.gov.

57 "AIRR Records." *Bureau of Trust Funds Administration: U.S. Department of the Interior,* 24 Oct 2019. https://on.doi.gov/36qzTui.

58 "AIRR Records."

59 "Secretary Jewell Issues Secretarial Order Affirming American Indian Trust Responsibilities." *U.S. Department of the Interior,* 20 Aug 2014. https://on.doi.gov/3pJFiFU.

60 "Hold Governments Accountable to Native Americans." *Native American Rights Fund,* undated. https://bit.ly/3kmRjNB.

61 "Reaffirmation of the Federal Trust Responsibility to Federally Recognized Indian Tribes and Individual Indian Beneficiaries." *The Secretary of the Interior,* Order No. 3335, 20 Aug 2014. https://on.doi.gov/38xHBFG.

62 Reaffirmation of the Federal Trust Responsibility to Federally...."

63 "Unclaimed Indian Moneys (IIM) and Tribal Trust Funds Search." *Bureau of Indian Affairs Indian Trust Fund,* Undated. https://bit.ly/3eMPPei.

64 "Lobbyist bilked tribes of millions, report says." *The Colorado Springs Gazette reprinted from The Dallas Morning News. 23 Jun 2005.*

65 Murray, Matthew. "Abramoff Leaves Lasting Impact on Tribal Lobbying." *www.rollcall.com*, 24 Jul 2009. https://bit.ly/2K0n5U3.

66 "Indian Gaming: Lobbying, 2020." *opensecrets.org, Center for Responsive Politics.* https://bit.ly/2GVY4rY.

67 "Indian Gaming: Lobbying, 2020."

68 Obama, Barack. "Presidential Proclamation – National Native American Heritage Month." *The White House,* 29 Oct 2010. https://bit.ly/2GXBhfq.

69 Ratledge, Mark. "The Burial of Elouise Cobell." *High Country News*, 28 Nov. 2011. https://bit.ly/2Uml6Lq.

| SIXTEEN |

21st Century Court Cases Continue the Fight

The *Cobell* case settled in 2012 for $3.4 billion is different in that the money was to have been held in a trust account – therefore never part of federal money. But, as documented in Chapter 15, it was used for several unrelated things, including corporate bailouts and reducing the federal deficit. It was the largest settlement as of this writing (2021). The Supreme Court has ruled on other Indian cases requiring the government to pay money due for the past 50 to 100 years. The following are some of the more significant cases and settlements, and they provide a look into how hard and continuously Native Americans must fight to obtain what is legally theirs.

Yankton Sioux and Santee Sioux

In 2002, the *Chicago Tribune* published an article that was reprinted in the *Colorado Springs Gazette* on December 16th titled "Payment takes 40 years." The article covers five acts of Congress that did not resolve the dispute, therefore requiring a lawsuit to reach a settlement. Forty years after the government condemned the tribes' land, an estimated 550 square miles, in order to build dams, the wrong was redressed. It was in 2002 that the government settled with nine tribes for about $625 million. Two tribes, the Yankton Sioux of southeast South Dakota and the Santee Sioux of northeast Nebraska, lost over 4,000 acres of their tribal grounds when the Missouri River covered an estimated 550 square miles in the late 1950s and 1960s. Promises made to the Yankton Sioux by the Corps of Engineers at the time the government condemned the land included moving gravesites to higher ground. Insufficient funding resulted in incomplete surveys of burial sites, and years later after a drought, the lower lake levels exposed Indian burial grounds that were never moved, which provoked deep anger among the Yankton Sioux.[1]

In a Dec. 15, 2002 article for the *Chicago Tribune*, Judith Graham quoted Michael Lawson, a historian who has researched and written extensively about the displacement. Lawson said that the rich river bottom of the Yankton Sioux was good for growing a variety of crops, including corn, hay and alfalfa, as well as gardens that produced potatoes, carrots, peas and watermelon. The bottoms also had large groves of trees that provided lumber for the Natives' needs. They had a self-sustaining way of life with abundant fish and game and playgrounds for the children. All that was lost when the land was condemned, and they were forced to leave everything behind. There were few vehicles/trucks and no way to move their few belongings. They took what they could carry when the water rose and forced them out.[2]

The displaced families fell on hard times. No longer able to live off the land and bounty of the river, they looked for the few jobs in the area. "Under the stress, social ties that had held the community together dissolved, and poverty became endemic."[3] It took 40 years for the government to compensate the tribes, and the tribal leaders told Graham that the money would be used in multiple ways to benefit the Natives as, "Both tribes intend to use the funds for schools, social services, job training and economic development."[4]

Graham's 2002 article provided additional factors driving the dam construction, which was done under 1944 congressional legislation known as the Pick-Sloan Plan. The series of dams along the Missouri River were designed to provide irrigation, generate hydropower and employment to returning World War II veterans.[5] As news and television reports showed, the melting snow and rains of 2019 proved too much for some of the dams, which burst allowing the captured water to flood thousands of acres of farmland, homes, businesses and towns along the waterway, causing millions of dollars in damage and months of untold problems for the people living in those areas.

Osage Tribe of Oklahoma

In 2011, the government agreed to pay back the $380 million owed to the Osage tribe, as a result of the Department of Interior's (DOI) accounting errors and the subsequent mismanagement of the tribe's trust account of lands and natural resources. Lenzy Krehbiel-Burton wrote an article in October 2011 for *nativetimes.com* outlining the tribe's claims made in the suit against the DOI. As in other settlements, the DOI's historic mismanagement of trust assets included the failure to provide statements of accounts and audits. The Osage Tribe received two earlier settlements totaling $331 million for claims dating back to 1972.[6]

A separate case, *Fletcher v. U.S.*, was filed by William S. Fletcher and other citizens of the Osage Nation. In the opinion and order for the case written by Gregory K. Frizzell, Chief Judge United States District Court on December 20, 2015, he outlined the following:

> In the early twentieth century, large quantities of oil and gas were discovered on lands belonging to the Osage Nation. Shortly thereafter, Congress enacted the Osage Allotment Act of 1906 … which severed the mineral estate underlying Osage lands from the surface estate, placed the mineral estate in trust, and directed the Secretary of Interior to collect and distribute royalty income every quarter to persons on the 1906 tribal membership roll.[7]

Once again, there had been a pattern in the works of Congress. Mineral deposits were found on Osage land, and Congress followed those discoveries by enacting the Osage Allotment Act of 1906. In the *Fletcher* suit, the citizens of the Osage Nation sought accounting of the oil, gas and other resources that had been extracted from their lands back to 1906. The money should have gone into individual trust accounts, not a tribal trust fund as in previous suits brought by the Osage Nation. In those cases, the government alleged that some of the documents had been lost over the years so an accurate accounting would be difficult to obtain. Jason Aamodt, attorney for Fletcher, stated that, "The results of this litigation will really be meaningful to citizens of the Osage tribe. An estimated 5,000 could see accountings for the first time in their lifetimes."[8] Two of the four original Fletcher plaintiffs – ages 71 and 95 – died prior to settlement of the case.

These cases increased interest in the tragedies surrounding the numerous deaths of Osage people in the early 1900s. For example, David Grann's book, *Killers of the Flower Moon: The Osage Murders and the Birth of the FBI,* chronicles the plot of white people to gain control of Osage land rich in oil. A white man, whose uncle was a powerful settler, married Mollie Burkhart, an Osage woman, to gain control of her family's oil wealth, which could only be gained through inheritance. Grann's research showed that Mollie's family members died under mysterious circumstances, and everyone from lawmen, prosecutors, reporters, morticians and even doctors were part of the conspiracy.[9]

Forty-One Federally Recognized Tribes Reach Settlement

In Timothy Williams' article, "U.S. Will Pay a Settlement of $1 Billion to 41 Tribes," for the *nytimes.com* in Apr 2012, he wrote that DOI settled dozens of lawsuits with tribes from Minnesota to Washington State that have over 60,000 Native citizens. The lawsuit charged that the Treasury Department and Department of the Interior "… had failed to adequately oversee concessions on Indian lands from companies that exploit a wide variety of resources, including minerals, timber, oil and gas dating back more than 100 years in some cases."[10] In making the settlement announcement, government officials stated, "About 60 other similar lawsuits by tribes against the United States have not been settled."[11] In Williams' article, he wrote that the DOI hopes to forestall future problems with the installation of their new computer system.

The money from this settlement was distributed to the tribes "… based on a formula that takes into account how much land and money the government held in trust, and the value of the concessions."[12] The tribes will decide how to use the money and various ideas have been proposed. The tribal councils, as the elected officials, will make the final decisions. Items being considered include loan programs, social services programs, reservation infrastructure construction or repair, environmental initiatives and monthly payments to members.[13]

Court Case of *Salazar v. Ramah Navajo Chapter*

The substance for this lawsuit was laid in 1975 when the Indian Self-Determination and Educational Assistance Act (ISDA) became law. Congress had two goals in mind by passing the ISDA. They wanted to offload some of the responsibility of the secretary of the interior for Indian programs, and the self-determination portion of the act allowed Native tribes to assume greater responsibility for programs on their reservations. The tribes were permitted to enter into support contracts, which previously had been administered by the federal government, and the secretary would reimburse the tribes for reasonable costs. The stipulation in the law was that: "The payment of these costs was made subject to the availability of appropriations, and Congress had imposed a statutory cap on the appropriations available to pay such costs."[14]

In 1990, the Ramah Navajo Chapter filed suit against the secretary of the interior on behalf of all Bureau of Indian Affairs (BIA) tribal contractors who had been underpaid by the secretary due to insufficient congressional appropriations. On June 18, 2012, the Supreme Court held in a 5-4 decision that the U.S. government was liable for underpayment of contracts awarded to Indian tribes from 1994 through 2001 by the BIA.[15] Justice Sonia Sotomayor wrote the majority opinion for the Supreme Court stating:

> Despite the statutory cap within the ISDA, the government must pay each tribe's support costs in full. The Court stressed that the government's contractual obligation under the ISDA should be treated like any other contract. Even if a particular agency exhausts legally available funds that were originally appropriated to satisfy a particular contract, the government is still obligated to fulfill its entire financial obligation within the contract.[16]

Cherokee Nation Benefits from Ruling

The Supreme Court then applied the *Salazar v. Ramah Navajo Chapter* ruling to cases involving contract underpayments by the Indian Health Services. An article posted on *indianz.com* dated July 15, 2014 stated that the Supreme Court awarded the Cherokee Nation $29.5 million to provide expanded and improved healthcare services. This settlement occurred only after the government did not respond to the 2005 Supreme Court ruling, and there was a change in administration. Cherokee Attorney General Todd Hembree told *indianz.com* that they were extremely pleased to reach a settlement as the Cherokee Nation had invested $100 million in building four new clinics, and the settlement would enable them to equip the centers with state-of-the-art medical devices and technology.[17]

Navajo Nation Reaches Settlement with U.S.

Sari Horwitz wrote an article in *The Washington Post* on September 24, 2014 titled "U.S. to pay Navajo Nation $554 million in largest settlement with single Indian tribe"[18] in which she reported:

> The sprawling Navajo reservation, located in parts of Arizona, Utah and New Mexico, is the largest and most populous Indian reservation, with 14 million acres of trust lands, which are leased for farming, grazing, oil, gas and other mineral extraction. The land is also leased for businesses, rights-of-way, easements and housing."[19]

This settlement covered claims against the government's mismanagement, which reached back more than 50 years. This settlement did not, however, affect the tribe's ability to pursue existing claims or future claims that arise from water rights disputes or the uranium mining that can potentially cause health issues among the tribe's people.[20]

Native American Tribes Win Suit

A *Washington Examiner* headline on September 17, 2015

read, "Native American tribes win $940 million in suit against the feds."[21] Nicole Duran wrote that the tribes had originally asked for $1 billion; however, the Obama administration settled hundreds of 25-year-old claims by 645 members regarding underpayment for contracts which the tribes managed, covering a range of services including education, police, fire and other federal services. In 2012, the Supreme Court agreed that the government did not allocate enough money to pay the contracts in full. To avoid the funding mismatch that originally sparked the lawsuits in 1990, Obama proposed in his 2016 budget "mandatory, non-discretionary funding, beginning in fiscal year 2017, for contract support costs."[22]

In Duran's article, she quoted Interior Secretary Sally Jewell who said, "Tribal self-determination and self-governance will continue to be our 'North Star' as the federal government works to assist tribes in running their own reservations and lands."[23] During the Obama administration, the president consistently emphasized cooperation between all governmental agencies and tribal governments. As a result, the Justice and Interior departments, "… have settled more than 80 similar lawsuits alleging breach of trust for federal mismanagement of their financial assets and natural resources."[24]

McGirt v. Oklahoma a Win for Indian Country

On July 9, 2020 the news quickly spread through Indian country that the U.S. Supreme Court had handed down a 5-4 ruling in favor of Jimcy McGirt that affected not only McGirt and the Muscogee Nation, with 86,100 enrolled members, and the state of Oklahoma but also sent hope throughout Indian country because of its implications. This case has legal implications for other Indian reservations and is significant for all Indian people as it reaffirms tribal sovereignty.

In writing for the majority, Justice Neil Gorsuch relied upon the laws overlaying Indian history with two major points, ultimately determining the 5-4 ruling. First, the Muscogee (Creek) reservation provided in a treaty between the U.S. government and Muscogee in 1866 had never been disestablished by the U.S. Congress. In the *Held*((b)(1) section of the ruling it states, "Once a federal reservation is established, only Congress can diminish or disestablish it. Doing so requires a clear expression of congressional intent."[25]

Because the reservation still exists, the Major Crimes Act (MCA) of 1885, provides that "… all land within the limits of any Indian reservation [falls] under the jurisdiction of the United States Government."[26] In 1971, Jimcy McGirt, a citizen of the Seminole Nation, was convicted and sentenced to life imprisonment in Oklahoma state court for rape and other sexual offenses against another Indian committed on the Muscogee reservation. He has never contested his conviction but has always contested Oklahoma's right to try him, as his crimes fall under the MCA.[27]

Sovereignty Acknowledged by Supreme Court

Amos McNac, a 77-year-old tribal medicine man and justice on the Muscogee Supreme Court, expressed his thoughts on the *McGirt* decision stating, "We experienced genocide, assimilation, colonization, and conversion policy by the government. We've survived. We still have our culture and our tradition."[28]

In the *McGirt* case, all of Eastern Oklahoma, including parts of Tulsa, is now recognized as part of the Muscogee Nation and comes under that Nation's sovereignty. Prior to the court's decision, it didn't make any difference who or where the crime was committed; it was prosecuted by the state. The significance is that the *McGirt* decision upholds promises made in treaties between the U.S. government and the Muscogee (Creek) Nation and, by extension, to treaties between the government and other tribal nations who have reservations not yet extinguished by Congress. Tribal sovereignty – long denied by state and federal officials and long fought for by all Indian people – was confirmed.[29]

Joy Expressed by Many

Nancy Deere-Turney, a citizen of the Muscogee (Creek) Nation in Oklahoma wrote an article for the *Center for Native*

American Youth on July 11th in which she stated that "… this decision affects all of us. I screamed, I laughed (in disbelief), and even shed a tear."[30] Native Americans have strongly expressed their feelings over this decision, as shown in the following examples: Joy Harjo, a Muscogee Creek citizen and poet laureate of the United States said, "It's so momentous and it's immense. It marks a possible shift. Not just for Muscogee Creek people, for all Native people."[31]

Jason Salsman, the tribe's (Muscogee) press secretary, told Jack Healy for his *nytimes.com* article:

> It made me cry. It was a powerful moment, one I wasn't ready for. It brought out emotions you didn't know would be there. It was just a promise kept. We know the history of promises that have been broken. I still get chills thinking about it.[32]

History Behind the Court's Decision

What made this Supreme Court decision so monumental was not that *McGirt's* guilty verdict was set aside as a result of this decision – federal criminal charges were filed against him in late July – but that the status of the Muscogee reservation had been upheld at the federal level. Over 47 percent of the state of Oklahoma, which covers 19 million acres on the eastern side of the state, including Tulsa, are included in the Muscogee reservation granted them in the Treaty of 1832. There are over 18 million people, Native and non-native living in this portion of the state.

In reviewing the opinion of Justice Neil Gorsuch, he said that it came down to whether McGirt "… commit[ed] his crimes in Indian Territory? Or was the crime committed on lands, as everyone seemed to assume for the past century, owned and controlled by [the] State of Oklahoma?"[33] The difference between it being state or Indian, hence federal, land makes a difference as to who can prosecute the person(s). In writing the majority opinion, Gorsuch stated:

> On the far end of the Trail of Tears was a promise. Forced to leave their ancestral lands in Georgia and Alabama, the Creek Nation received assurances that

their new lands in the West would be secure forever. In exchange for ceding 'all their land, east of the Mississippi river,' the U.S. government agreed by treaty that '[t]he Creek country west of the Mississippi shall be solemnly guaranteed to the Creek Indians.'[34]

In David K. TeSelle's article for the *National Law Review* on Aug. 5, 2020, he said that Gorsuch is a "textualist" in his construct of the law. Only Congress has the ability to change the status of a reservation and either through oversight or error, they failed to extinguish the Muscogee reservation.[35] Oklahoma attempted to argue that at least the reservation – if it ever existed – had been terminated by the laws and events since Oklahoma became a state in 1907. In the *Bostock v. Clayton Country Title VII,* an opinion written by Gorsuch on June 15, 2020, he demonstrated his textualist ideology when he wrote, "Only the written word is law, and all persons are entitled to its benefit."[36] TeSelle continued his article by providing additional comments on a textualist by writing, "To ignore the plain meaning of the words of a statute based upon matters outside the text, in Justice Gorsuch's thinking, would risk, as he stated ' … substituting stories for statutes.'"[37]

Five Tribes of Oklahoma Make Up Intertribal Council

The tribes that make up what is called "The Five Civilized Tribes" have been actively working together for the benefit of the People, protecting their sovereignty. The Cherokee, Choctaw, Chickasaw, Seminole and Muscogee founded the Intertribal Council in 1949, the oldest and largest tribal organization in America, and now represent over 750,000 Indian people nationwide.[38]

The day prior to the *McGirt* decision, Cherokee Chief Chuck Hoskin Jr. announced, via his internet communication "Chief Chat," that the Cherokee Nation hosted the Intertribal Council in their first virtual meeting. Hoskin stated:

> While each tribal government has its own unique culture and history, our five tribes share similar

issues and concerns, including how we best provide critical services – education, health care and housing – to our citizens. Working in solidarity means we can better protect our self-governance.[39]

Topics of concern not only included the pending *McGirt* Supreme Court decision and its impact, but also CARES funding and distribution, COVID-19, Native American mascots and other important items that are being discussed by state and local governments, as well as within Native communities and governments.[40]

Immediate Effects of the *McGirt v. Oklahoma* Decision

Cary Aspinwall and Graham Lee wrote a lengthy article on what this Supreme Court decision will mean for criminal justice in Indian Country and several things were noted. As an Indian reservation, the Muscogee lands, and all other Indian reservations throughout the country that have not been disestablished by Congress fall under federal jurisdiction and the Major Crimes Act (MCA), which means cases involving those like *McGirt* can only be prosecuted by the federal government in federal court.[41]

"Under federal law in Indian Country, tribes must opt in to have the death penalty as a punishment option – none of the Five Tribes has."[42] Patrick Murphy, a member of the Muscogee Nation, is on Oklahoma's death row for committing a murder of another member of the Muscogee Nation. His state conviction was overthrown by the *McGirt* decision; however, federal prosecutors indicted Murphy at the end of July, just as they did McGirt. When convicted, they will go to a federal penitentiary rather than a state jail and, if the government adheres to federal law, Murphy will be facing life in prison, not a death penalty.[43]

Legal scholars have argued for years that the MCA has led to over-incarceration of Native people in federal prisons. The figures are staggering, with Native men jailed up to four times more often than their white counterparts, while the figures for Native women are six times greater. And under federal guidelines, sentences for the same crime are much longer in federal courts than those imposed in state courts.[44] Even though sovereignty was overall a win for many reasons, it is likely some Indians will face negative consequences due to being tried federally.

McGirt Decision Causes Jurisdictional Changes

June 13, 2020 two children – members of the Cherokee Nation – died of heat exhaustion. Their father, Dustin Lee Dennis, was supposed to watch the children the June afternoon of their deaths; however, he took a nap allowing the children, three and four years old, to play in the pickup truck. That afternoon the temperature reached 90 degrees in Tulsa. Dennis was arrested by the Tulsa County prosecutors and charged with second-degree murder and felony child neglect.[45]

After the *McGirt* decision, the Oklahoma district attorney, Steve Kunzweiler, had to dismiss the charges, and he was the one who spoke with the mother about this decision. Kunzweiler recalled, "She just had this thousand-yard stare. And I didn't have any better answer. I can't do anything to help them anymore."[46] Federal prosecutors don't normally handle cases like the deaths of two children. Their focus is on human trafficking, cracking drug rings and multimillion-dollar financial crimes, but now they were being required to handle serious crimes, including murder and assault that are committed on Indian reservations. In Aspinwall and Brewer's article for *themarshallproject.org* they wrote:

> While the federal prosecutor in Tulsa says his staff is willing to pick up these cases, critics note that the Justice Department has had a long history of documented lapses in handling cases in Indian Country. For example, in the past it has declined to prosecute almost half the violent crimes committed on reservations.[47]

The immediate effect of the ruling will be major crimes previously prosecuted by the state and committed by a citizen of an Indian nation against another Indian on a reservation will be prosecuted under the MCA by a federal court. Non-natives living on an Indian reservation are not affected. If they commit a major crime, it will be prosecuted by the state, therefore nothing has changed for the non-natives.

Additional Effects to beAddressed

Gorsuch acknowledged that the *McGirt* decision would have far-reaching effects but said that the rule of law prevailed in his decision – that people need to believe that the law, not political expediency, could be depended upon in the courts.[48]

Other issues tribes, state and local governments will need to address due to the decision include tobacco and gas taxes, license plates, water rights and hunting and fishing licenses.[49] Partnerships and agreements will have to be looked at regarding gaming, which generates a significant part of Indian income, and the state has benefitted from the taxes paid on that income. Native people can contest paying taxes to Oklahoma when they live in an area where the state has no jurisdiction.[50]

Oklahoma Works to Circumvent Court Ruling

An article by Simon Romero and Graham Lee Brewer was posted on *nytimes.com* on February 20, 2020 and covered the efforts of Oklahoma's political machinery as it worked against what is seen as a challenge to the authority of the state. The *McGirt* case specifically addressed judicial authority on reservation land, and the state had been advancing other matters that go beyond the case.[51]

John Kevin Stitt is the current Republican governor of Oklahoma (as of this writing, elected 2019) and a member of the Cherokee Nation. This, however, has not led him to work for the interests of the Native population. Negotiations on a gaming compact were scheduled to expire on January 1, 2020. Stitt proposed an increase of between 13% and 25% to the exclusivity fees (taxes) on Native casinos, which were at 6%, to help the shortfall in Oklahoma's budget. Lisa Johnson Billy, a citizen of the Chickasaw Nation, stepped down from the position of Oklahoma Secretary of Native American Affairs, on December 23, 2019 "… accusing the governor of dismissing her advice and 'breaking faith' with Oklahoma's tribes."[52]

Following the *McGirt* decision, Acee Agoyo wrote an article for *indianz.com* on August 13, 2020. In addition to the taxes on gaming, the *McGirt* decision brought up a range of issues that have to be addressed between the reservation and state authorities. Efforts were made by government officials to solidify existing regulations now threatened by *McGirt* like the aforementioned casino licenses, which brought in a significant amount of income to the state. Agoyo quoted the attorney general for Oklahoma who stated:

> Oklahoma Attorney General Mike Hunter (R), who had fought the existence of the Creek Reservation at all stages of the case [*McGirt*], disclosed that he had been negotiating an agreement-in-principle that would address a wide range of regulatory, legal and business issues that weren't connected in any manner to the [*McGirt*] litigation.[53]

Federal Officials Work to Circumvent *McGirt* Decision

The case was *Worcester v. Georgia,* and the year was 1832. U.S. Supreme Court Chief Justice John Marshall announced the court's decision on this case, which was meant to strike down Georgia's law that gave non-natives the right to Cherokee land. President Jackson disagreed with the court's decision, and the Cherokee were forced from their lands and onto the 'Trail of Tears" with thousands dying:

> In the end, Andrew Jackson's story reveals the ease at which the foundation of our governmental structure can be eroded. One person, in a powerful position, deciding to challenge the political and legal norms that we've come to rely on can have a profoundly negative impact on the integrity of our legal and political system.[54]

On August 13, 2020, Acee Agoyo, Editor-in-Chief of *indianz.com*, wrote an article "Indian Country slams efforts to 'abrogate' sovereignty in wake of historic Supreme Court ruling." Agoyo reported on a letter written by Senator Jim Inhofe (R-Oklahoma) as a group the senator heads works to override the

*McGir*t ruling. It has been almost two hundred years since the *Worcester v. Georgia* ruling in support of the Cherokee that President Jackson failed to recognize. Now, the stage was set for Oklahoma and the federal government to circumvent the *McGirt v. Oklahoma* ruling, once again threating the sovereignty of the Indian nations.

Agoyo wrote that, "Sen. Jim Inhofe (R-Oklahoma), who serves as chairman of the powerful Committee on Armed Services, confirmed last week that the legislative wheels are already in motion on Capitol Hill."[55] Inhofe was putting plans in place to override or get around the *McGirt* ruling. Although he indicated that Indian people would be considered in any actions brought before the Senate, his office sent a letter to stakeholders including, "A slew of industry interests – from oil and gas developers to chicken farmers and even Walmart and American Airlines"– but no Indian tribes have been consulted or included in the proposed discussions.[56] Once again, Native people are being excluded from decisions that directly affect them.

Native American Organizations Oppose Challenges to *McGirt*

History has taught Native people to be prepared for challenges to any victories they achieve. They were proved right to be concerned about legislative challenges to *McGirt* and start preparing. Agoyo's August 13th article, which can be accessed through *indianz.com*, includes the three-page letter that was sent by eight national Native American organizations to The Honorable Jim Inhofe, with copies going to Senator James Lankford (Republican from Oklahoma) and the following members of the House of Representatives – all Republicans from Oklahoma: Kevin Hern, Markwayne Mullin, Frank Lucas, Tom Cole and Kendra Horn: "Re: Concerns about the establishment of a congressional working group undermining Tribal sovereignty and jurisdiction." The letter concludes by stating:

> We stand united in our pledge to work as partners and engage in conversations with any parties who wish to work together to ensure that the greater possibilities presented by the Court's historic

decision become realities. But we stand equally united in opposition to any rushed process that limits discussion, limits participants, and drives towards a calculated goal of passing destructive federal legislation.[57]

The letter was signed by the principal person representing the following:

- President, National Congress of American Indians
- President of the Board for the Association on American Indian Affairs
- President & CEO, The National Center for American Indian Enterprise Development
- President, Inter Tribal Association of Arizona
- Chairman Cheyenne River Sioux Tribe; Chairman Great Plains Tribal Chairmen's Association, Inc.
- President, United South and Eastern Tribes Sovereignty Protection Fund
- President, Affiliated Tribes of Northwest Indians Chairman, Midwest Alliance of Sovereign Tribes.[58]

Author's Thoughts

When I heard the *McGirt* Supreme Court decision on the morning of July 9, 2020, I celebrated with all the Native Americans who have waited so very long for recognition of their rights. In many ways, it was an admission of the trials they have endured and a recognition of their sovereignty as distinct nations within the United States. This decision specifically addressed the status of the Muscogee reservation, but it was a victory for all Native people.

The U.S. Constitution, Section 8.3 provided Congress with the power to regulate commerce with the Indian tribes. From the first treaties with the Continental Congress in 1778 until 1871, the "United States government entered into more than 500 treaties with the Native American tribes; all of these treaties have since been violated in some way or outright broken by the U.S. government, ..."[59] Breaking the treaty provisions has resulted in the lawsuits brought before the courts with some documented cases cited within this chapter – only a few of them settled and many still pending before the courts.

Although over a century late, the *McGirt* decision affirmed that the United States must stand up to its legal obligations. However belatedly, the promises behind the Trail of Tears must be honored. Justice Gorsuch concluded the "Decision of the Majority" by stating:

> The federal government promised the Creek a reservation in perpetuity. Over time, Congress has diminished that reservation. It has sometimes restricted and other times expanded the Tribe's authority. But Congress has never withdrawn the promised reservation. As a result, many of the arguments before us today follow a sadly familiar pattern. Yes, promises were made, but the price of keeping them has become too great, so now we should just cast a blind eye. We reject that thinking. If Congress wishes to withdraw its promises, it must say so. Unlawful acts, performed long enough and with sufficient vigor, are never enough to amend the law. To hold otherwise would be to elevate the most brazen and longstanding injustices over the law, both rewarding wrong and failing those in the right.[60]

We are now living in a time of great social and racial unrest and must not rely on the government to legislate changes we know are needed. When we believe one race is different from another, we fail to understand the reality that all people are created equal and that individuals can bring about great and lasting change to ensure that.

As a nation of immigrants, we must join with the Native Americans whose ancestors have long inhabited this land, so they too get the equality and opportunity guaranteed to American citizens. We can celebrate our uniqueness, join our individual stories and unite, working together for the good of one another and strengthen our nation. Decisions like *McGirt* that work to right the wrongs and illegal acts against First Americans and other citizens in our country should not be challenged or circumvented. Like

McGirt, they should be celebrated. Now we need to look hard at our history, as well as our present, to identify these issues, addressing them now, not years from now, in order to enable a more equitable future.

Endnotes:

1   *Chicago Tribune*, "Payment takes 40 years." 16 Dec 2002. *Colorado Springs Gazette.*
2   Graham, Judith. "Compensation at last for tribes that lost lands to dams." 15 Dec 2002. *Chicago Tribune*. https://bit.ly/3n8UkTY Accessed 17 Aug 2020.
3   Graham.
4   Graham.
5   Graham
6   Krehbiel-Burton, Lenzy. "Osage Nation signs agreement in trust settlement." 20 Oct 2011. *Native Times,* 20 Oct 2011. https://bit.ly/33mcSsp. Accessed 17 Aug 2020.
7   United States, District Court. "*William S. Fletcher v. The United States of America.*" Case No. 02-CV-427-GKF-PJC, 30 Dec 2015. *National Indian Law Library.* https://bit.ly/36oRh4e. Accessed 17 Aug 2020.
8   "Osage Nation beneficiaries still fighting for accounting despite setback in court." *Indianz*4 May 2017. https://www.indianz.com/News/2017/05/04/osage-nation-beneficiaries-wont-appeal t.asp#:~:text=Osage%20Nation%20beneficiaries%20still%2 0fighting%20for%20accounting%20despite%20setback%20i n%20court,Thursday%2C%20May%204&text=Citizens%20 of%20the%20Osage%20Nation,setback%20in%20their%20h istoric%20lawsuit.&text=U.S.%20have%20passed%20on%2

0without%20seeing%20the%20promised%20accounting. Accessed 17 Aug 2020. (Error in shortened link)

[9] Grann, David. *Killers of the Flower Moon: The Osage Murders and the Birth of the FBI.* Doubleday. 2017.

[10] Williams, Timothy. "U.S. Will Pay a Settlement of $1 Billion to 41 Tribes." *The New York Times,* 13 Apr 2012. https://nyti.ms/34ho6O5. Accessed 26 Jul 2020.

[11] Williams.

[12] Williams.

[13] Williams.

[14] United States, Court of Appeals for the Tenth Circuit. *Salazar v. Ramah Navajo Chapter.* Docket no. 11-551, 18 Apr 2012. *Oyez.* https://bit.ly/33iuRQ9. Accessed 25 Jul 2020.

[15] *Salazar v. Ramah Navajo Chapter.*

[16] *Salazar v. Ramah Navajo Chapter.*

[17] "HIS pays $29.5M to end contract dispute with Cheroke Nation." *Indianz,* 15 Jul 2014. https://www.indianz.com/News/2014/07/15/ihs-pays-295m-to-end-contract.asp. (Error in shortened link)

[18] Horwitz, Sari. "U.S. to pay Navajo Nation $554 million in largest settlement with single Indian tribe." *Washington Post,* 24 Sep 2014. https://wapo.st/3jkJAjb. Accessed 21 Aug 2016.

[19] Horwitz.

[20] Horwitz.

[21] Duran, Nicole. "Native American tribes win $940 million in suit against the feds." *Washington Examiner,* 17 Sep 2015. https://washex.am/3n7545y.

[22] Duran.

[23] Duran.

[24] Duran.

[25] United States, Supreme Court. McGirt v. Oklahoma. Certiorari to the Court of Criminal Appeals of Oklahoma. No. 18-9526, 9 Jul 2020. https://bit.ly/3cJwERm. Accessed 26 Aug 2020.

[26] United States, Supreme Court. *McGirt v. Oklahoma.*

[27] Millhiser, Ian. "The Supreme Court's landmark new Native American rights decision, explained." *Vox,* 10 Jul 2020.

https://bit.ly/3n4l5ZS. Accessed 11 Aug 2020.

28 Healy, Jack. "For Oklahoma Tribe, Vindication at Long Last." *New York Time,* 11 July 2020. https://nyti.ms/33jEnml.

29 Aspinwall, Cary and Graham Lee Brewer. "Indian Country. What Does That Mean for Criminal Justice There?" *The Marshall Project*, 4 Aug 2020. https://bit.ly/3kYHvKg. Accessed 9 Aug 2020

30 Deere-Turney, Nancy. "I Mvto (thank) the Supreme Court for Doing What is Right," *Center for Native American Youth,* 11 Jul 2020. https://bit.ly/33eotcS.

31 Healy, Jack. "For Oklahoma Tribe, Vindication at Long Last." *New York Times,* 11 July 2020. https://nyti.ms/33jEnml.

32 Healy.

33 TeSelle, David K. "Review of *McGirt v. Oklahoma* – How the Supreme Court and Justice Gorsuch's Revolutionary Textualism Brought America's "Trail of Tears" Promise To the Creek Nation Back From the Dead." *National Law Review*, 5 Aug 2020. https://bit.ly/34gDV7B. Accessed 10 Aug 2020.

34 Teselle.

35 Teselle.

36 Teselle.

37 Teselle.

38 Hoskin, Chuck Jr. "Chief Chat: Inter-Tribal Council utilizing technology for meeting and business." 8 July 2020. https://bit.ly/38I4SoG.

39 Hoskin.

40 Hoskin.

41 Aspinwall, Cary and Graham Lee Brewer. "Indian Country. What Does That Mean for Criminal Justice There?" *The Marshall Project*, 4 Aug 2020. https://bit.ly/3kYHvKg. Accessed 9 Aug 2020.

42 Aspinwall and Brewer.

43 Aspinwall and Brewer.

44 Aspinwall and Brewer.

45 Aspinwall and Brewer.

46 Aspinwall and Brewer.

[47] Aspinwall and Brewer.

[48] Aspinwall and Brewer.

[49] Aspinwall and Brewer.

[50] Aspinwall and Brewer.

[51] Romero, Simon and Graham Lee Brewer. "Oklahoma's Tribes United Against a Common Foe: Their Cherokee Governor." *New York Times*, 20 Feb 2020, updated 15 Jul 2020. https://nyti.ms/2GdRkFp.

[52] Romero and Brewer.

[53] Agoyo, Acee. "Indian Country slams efforts to 'abrogate' sovereignty in wake of historic Supreme Court ruling." *Indianz,* 13 Aug 2020. https://www.indianz.com/News/2020/08/13/indian-country-slams-efforts-to-abrogate.asp#:~:text=In%20a%20major%20show%20of,win%20for%20the%20first%20Americans. Accessed 15 Aug 2020. (Error in shortened link)

[54] Remembering the Time Andrew Jackson Decided to Ignore the Supreme Court In the Name of Georgia's Right to Cherokee Land." *SustainAtlanta*, 2 Apr 2015, updated 28 Jul 2016. https://bit.ly/30mvQ06. Accessed 16 Aug 2020.

[55] Agoyo, Acee. "Indian Country slams efforts to 'abrogate' sovereignty in wake of historic Supreme Court ruling." 13 Aug 2020. indianz.com. Accessed 15 Aug 2020.

[56] Agoyo.

[57] Agoyo.

[58] Agoyo.

[59] "List of United States treaties: U.S. — Native American treaties." *Wikipedia: The Free Encyclopedia,* Wikimedia Foundation, https://bit.ly/2G4rG67. Accessed 26 Jun 2020.

[60] *McGirt v. Oklahoma.* Certiorari to the Court of Criminal Appeals of Oklahoma. No. 18-9526. Decided July 9, 2020. https://bit.ly/36BsOas. Accessed 26 Aug 2020.

| SEVENTEEN |

Preserving Indian History – NAGPRA

Anthropology and archaeology are considered sciences and until faced with the 1990 Native American Graves Protection and Repatriation Act (NAGPRA) requirements, both groups considered themselves the scientific and cultural authority of the People and artifacts they were investigating. The fact that Native Americans were still living and breathing and understood the sacredness and cultural significance better than the scientists was not a consideration until NAGPRA brought Native Americans into the conversation.

The Chicago Field Museum of Natural History found itself at odds with Native Americans when the museum introduced an exhibit of "… human remains that had been excavated from burials found in an Illinois state park: Opposition to this was immediate…"[1] Consequently, the museum held a "death feast"[2] after which a group of Winnebago Indians took the remains back to their reservation for a mound burial.

Kathleen S. Fine-Dare, anthropologist and author of the book *Grave Injustice: The American Indian Repatriation Movement and NAGPRA* wrote that Native American scholars responded to the exhibit saying "Maybe we should go and excavate Christ Church Cemetery in Philadelphia or Boston, and check to see how people were doing at the time they were buried."[3] Eager to follow those thoughts with action and wanting to draw attention to the double standard for grave digging, they submitted a 1970 grant proposal in which they provided scientific justification to excavate a pioneer cemetery.[4]

Articles on repatriation written by prominent Indian scholars were printed in numerous journals.[5] This resulted is greater Native activism and culminated in a new era:

> ... Native American Graves Protection and Repatriation Act (NAGPRA), the 1990 federal repatriation law that has made a big difference in how museums and other institutions with museum-like [sic] functions deal with Native American human remains, Native American objects, Native American knowledge, and Native Americans themselves.[6]

To understand the significance of the American Indian repatriation movement and the part NAGPRA plays in that movement, it helps to know the mindset of the newcomers to the continent and their looting of Indian burial grounds, including human remains, funerary object and cultural artifacts. Cherokees experienced the desecration and looting of graves when they were forced at gunpoint from their homes and land by the Army in 1838 to start the long march to Indian Territory. Violation of Native sacred sites was commonplace.

Background: Finding and Preserving History

Many people are aware of the historical significance of the Egyptian pyramids and may have seen some of the artifacts from the pyramids in U.S. museums. Numerous archaeological sites around the world have produced historical artifacts that today are housed in museums worldwide. Due to the efforts of anthropologists and archaeologists throughout history, we have learned much about the earth and its inhabitants that otherwise would not be known. Their digging, literally and figuratively, continues to expand the scientific knowledge of our forbearers throughout the world – what they looked like, where and how they lived and the animals they utilized for survival, along with their art, tools and pottery, among other items of interest.

Beginning in July 1801 and continuing into 1805, a massive theft of Greek antiquities occurred when workers were employed to remove "... twelve or more statues, fifty-six frieze slabs, and fifteen metopes from the Parthenon"[7] plus other marble pieces from the Acropolis. This was done at the instruction of the seventh earl of Elgin in his capacity as English Ambassador. His

346

stated reason for their removal was to protect them from further damage by the Turks who, at that time, ruled the Ottoman Empire, including Greece, and to prevent the marble pieces from falling into the hands of the French. Unlike his political statements, it appears his real reason was to landscape his home with them, but dwindling fortunes forced Elgin to sell the artifacts to the British government. In researching the papers provided by Elgin from the Ottoman Turks, the British government found the documents to be invalid due to the lax policies of the Turks regarding antiquities. Thereafter called the "Elgin Marbles," the pieces became a cornerstone for the British Museum:

> Requests for the repatriation of the Elgin Marbles have been made repeatedly by the Greek government, the European Parliament, and international organization … To this day, however, British Museum officials say that the return of the Elgin Marbles is impossible. Because to do so would destroy the cultural heritage of *all mankind* …[8]

Just as protection of "old world" patrimony is important, so too is protecting sites and artifacts in the "new world," which was inhabited by man much earlier that previous estimates believed. Fen Montaigne wrote an article for the January/February 2020 *Smithsonian* magazine titled "The Fertile Shore" that discusses the discovery of archaeological sites in North and South America that are providing proof that the native people of the Americas arrived much earlier than thought. The sites provide evidence of migration possibly 5,000 years earlier than previously believed, making their arrival as much as 20,000 years ago. Of course, there is controversy among the archaeologists, but new discoveries of ancient life have been made along the Pacific coast. In an area approximately "… six feet deep and four feet square … [they] discovered more than 1,200 artifacts, mostly stone flakes, a few as old as 12,800 years old [including] rock scrapers, spear points, simple flake knives, gravers and good egg-size stones used as hammers."[9] The items are cleaned, catalogued and stored for later study and possible display at museums.

The same article by Montaigne discusses human genomes that were discovered at a dig in Montana and "Eske

Willersley, who directs the Center for Geo-Genetics at the Globe Institute at the University of Copenhagen ... pieced together a picture of the first Americans, including a 12,400-year-old boy from Montana,...."[10] These discoveries provide insights into Native ancestry – how they lived and died. With today's advances in technology and research methods, these discoveries can potentially identify the diseases that caused the death of these early people, thus providing important medical insights into different diseases and how the diseases lived and mutated, which would provide a significant boost to the scope of medical knowledge.

Although the science behind the work done by anthropologists and archaeologists was relatively young, the founding fathers of the United States and the presidents and politicians who followed them have understood the important role museums play in the recognition of the nation on the world stage. Time has shown that it was crucial then and continues to be now for our museums to highlight artifacts and discoveries from the past, as well as the accomplishments of the People. The nation was settled under the prevailing concept of Manifest Destiny, and museums have provided a visual way to demonstrate dominion over the land and its inhabitants. On February 23, 2018, Sarah E. Baires, published an article on *smithsonianmag.com* titled "White Settlers Buried the Truth about the Midwest's Mysterious Mound Cities." She documented the role that archaeologists played as they discredited the achievements of the People of North American. All this was done as the U.S. government was forcing the Native Americans from their lands. Baires wrote:

> The creation of the Myth of the Mounds parallels early American expansionist practices like the state-sanctioned removal of Native peoples from their ancestral lands to make way for the movement of "new" Americans into the Western "frontier." Part of this forced removal included the erasure of Native American ties to their cultural landscapes.[11]

Kathleen S. Fine-Dare

Fine-Dare was, until her retirement in 2018, a professor of

anthropology and gender/women's studies at Fort Lewis College in Durango, Colorado. "She continues to serve the college as Chair of the President's NAGPRA Committee and as Tribal Liaison."[12] Her extensive expertise is represented in the writing of her previously mentioned 2002 book *Grave Injustice: The American Indian Repatriation Movement and NAGPRA*. She wrote:

> My frustration over having no real "four-fielders" (i.e., anthropologists versed in all four subfields of anthropology: biological, archaeological, linguistic, and cultural) to tackle the job of meaningful consultation [on NAGPRA] and assignment of cultural affiliation pales in comparison to the frustration the tribal representatives have felt while participating in these consultations.[13]

While many people train in one, or perhaps two, of these sciences, Fine-Dare felt it is only the four-fielders who themselves felt qualified to make the repatriation judgments required of the law and that judgment should be made in coordination with the Indigenous people. To be knowledgeable in only one or two of the sciences was not enough.

Native American Graves and Repatriation Act

NAGPRA has had, and continues to have, far-reaching implications. The law states that "All federal agencies are subject to NAGPRA. All public and private museums that have received federal funds, other than the Smithsonian Institution, are subject to NAGPRA..."[14] The law required museums to complete an inventory of their collections by 1995; however, the extensive collections held by many museums resulted in extensions beyond that deadline. Although not all the items held by Harvard University's Peabody Museum of Archaeology and Ethnology were Native American, an extension was required in order to catalog the "... 8 million archaeological items just from North America, ..."[15] to determine which were/were not Native American. The Smithsonian is exempt from NAGPRA, but they "... must repatriate parts of its collection under a similar law, the National

Museum of American Indian Act."[16]

The paperwork piled up at museums as they inspected and catalogued items to determine which items fell within the law. The museums then notified the tribes that they were holding artifacts and asked whether the tribe wanted a listing. The National Park Service, under the secretary of the interior, has federal oversight of NAGPRA and thus received copies of all correspondence between the museums and the tribes. Gerald White of the Ojibwe was quoted by Willow Lawson in her 2006 article, "Indian Skeletons May Never Leave Museums," as stating, "Tribes don't have the staff, the time, the money to have people specifically assigned to these things,..."[17] The requirements of NAGPRA are infinite, and as long as artifacts continue to be found in day-to-day activities (e.g., construction of highways, plowing of fields) or through the work of scientists, there will continue to be issues for all involved in fulfilling the requirements of the law.

As with many endeavors of such significance and scope, the museums have experienced positive and negative reactions from the tribes. Native Americans have great reverence for the dead and consider burial sites sacred. Many Indigenous people have worked diligently with the museums over the years to identify, claim and repatriate the remains, funerary objects and cultural artifacts. When that has been possible, the tribe has had a private ceremony to consecrate the new reburial site. Some tribes consider DNA invasive, and there have been enough intermarriages among tribes and between tribes and the white population, that it would not provide the conclusive evidence needed on some of the older remains in the collections. And some tribes have ceased to exist. In her 2006 article, Lawson wrote:

> Further, the legislation only requires that museums use their own records to determine the collections' origin. Tribal officials say this doesn't leave room for interpretation of tribal oral history, which they say should be given more attention when weighing evidence.[18]

Other problems identified by Lawson that Native Americans and the museums are experiencing are varied and include, but are not limited to:

- Some Native groups do not want the bones of their ancestors.
- Not expecting their ancestors' graves to be desecrated, some tribes have no reburial ceremonies.
- Some Natives believe there has been spiritual contamination, and they do not want the contamination to affect their people.
- Some elders do not want to handle the bones and would rather have archaeologists or museum officials rebury the bones.[19]

In an interview conducted by John Strand of the American Alliance of Museums with James Pepper Henry in 2010, they discussed the status of NAGPRA. Henry, a member of the Kaw Nation of Oklahoma and the Muscogee Creek Nation, was at that time serving as a director and CEO of the Anchorage Museum at Rasmuson Center. He had previously worked at the Smithsonian and at the National Museum of the American Indian so was very familiar with NAGPRA, its successes and failures. During this time, he had seen a cultural shift in the museum world:

> For a long, long time ... anthropologists, scholars and curators saw themselves as the experts and the knowledge keepers of other people's cultures. ... Now people realize that it's hard to be an expert in somebody else's culture without really having a relationship with that culture.[20]

During the 20 years since NAGPRA was passed, Henry stated that "To date, almost a quarter of a million unassociated funerary object ... over 1,500 individuals ... and thousands of associated funerary and sacred objects have been returned."[21] However, Kevin Simpson quoted Chip Colwell, who was the senior curator of anthropology at the Denver Museum of Nature & Science, in an article Simpson wrote for the *Colorado Sun* on March 1, 2019. "For the fiscal year ended in September 2017, there were 185,475 sets of human remains listed in NAGPRA inventories."[22] Because of the number of human remains still in inventory and the problems identified by Lawson that exist between Native Americans and the museums regarding repatriation, many Native American remains will likely remain in museums.

Ethnology

Anthropologists study human societies and cultures through their writings, art forms and artifacts while ethnologists, a subset of anthropology, study the characteristics of various groups and the relationships within the groups. As such, the Smithsonian led early studies of Native Americans when they sent ethnologists to live with different Indian tribes. Through their daily interactions, the ethnologist was able to earn their trust and respect, learn their languages and study their customs and beliefs firsthand. It was in this way that James Mooney was trusted with the history, medicine and myths of the Cherokees, both in North Carolina and Indian Territory.

In 1879, the newly founded Bureau of American Ethnology, a part of the Smithsonian Institution, posted 22-year-old Frank Cushing to the Zuni Pueblo in an area that is today Northwest New Mexico. He was told "I want you to find out all you can about some typical tribe of Pueblo Indians ... You will probably be gone three months."[23] He took a train from Washington, D.C. to Las Vegas and traveled by mule the approximately 450 miles to the pueblo. Cushing felt a great urgency in his task because he knew the railroad was scheduled to come through that part of the territory in 1890, and he wanted to capture what was surely a disappearing way of life. The Zunis were very suspicious of his intentions, and Cushing later learned that they had considered killing him because they believed he was trying to steal their secrets. He became both a participant and an observer of the Zuni life, eventually earning their trust, and was inducted into a Zuni clan and later into the priesthood. Initial plans to be there a month stretched into five years. The products of Cushing's work were numerous "... publication[s] on Zuni religion myth, agriculture, food, and crafts..."[24] plus thousands of objects were sent to the Smithsonian and other locations.

Archaeology

In the earliest days of archaeology, people started out looking for things they could collect that could be sold. At one point, they literally sifted through approximately 60 feet of volcanic ash at Herculaneum, which was buried by an eruption of Mount Vesuvius in 79 AD.[25] Looters and black-market operators provided items to early collectors and museums. Over the years, archaeology became known as a scientific study. A methodology was developed to preserve and document items, where they were found and information about the area surrounding the site.

President Jefferson showed a particular interest in the natural history around him and demonstrated this interest when he ordered Lewis and Clark to collect plants, animals and geological specimens, as well as Native American artifacts during their mapping of the Northwest Territory. Their collections were later displayed at the Peale Museum in Philadelphia as testament of the control the nation had over the newly acquired area.[26]

Swedish Researcher Impacts Mesa Verde, Colorado

In 1890, a young Swedish researcher, Gustaf Nordenskiöld, visited the southwestern region of Colorado where he became interested in the cliff dwellers. At the time, the area was part of the Southern Ute Indian Reservation by treaty with the United States; however, it had been inhabited by many different tribes over the centuries. When Nordenskiöld visited the area, he realized that significant looting had already taken place, and he felt a sense of urgency to protect what he could. As items were recovered from the dig, he meticulously recorded "... location, time of day and photos ... liken[ed] to a frontier GPS."[27] He was considered a thief by both the Native Americans and the white residents, although for different reasons. The Native Americans realized that their cultural items, as well as the remains of their ancestors, were being removed, and the white residents saw him intruding into their black-market profiteering:

> Still, he managed to load hundreds of items onto a train and ship them east. Eventually, they wound up at the

National Museum of Finland in Helsinki, where they provided a cornerstone exhibit that fed the growing European fascination with North America's indigenous civilizations. [28]

In 1906, the United States passed the Antiquities Act which designated archeological sites on public land as important public resources. Because the National Park Service manages public lands, they are charged with "... preserv[ing] for present and future generations the historic, scientific, commemorative, and cultural values of the archaeological and historic sites and structures on these lands."[29] When President Roosevelt signed the 1906 act, it was seen as a safeguard against the haphazard digging by amateurs, as well as the purposeful looting of sites for profit.

However, by the late 1900s, estimates placed 14,500 Native American bodies in the hands of various government agencies including: "... the National Park Service, the Bureau of Land Management, and the Fish and Wildlife Service,"[30] which indicates that the government was still collecting and storing bodies. In this situation, the government cannot be seen as upholding the Antiquities Act and working to protect the rights of Native Americans.

Museums

For centuries museums have provided education and inspiration with their collections of art and artifacts. Since early times, museums were predominately financed by and oftentimes owned by individuals rather than governments. The museum collections provided a method of displaying the government or individual's wealth and cultural superiority. While some museums are still privately owned, many have been bequeathed to the government.

In Fine-Dare's book, she "... examines the imperial and nation-building contexts of collecting and displaying the spoils of victory over the 'savage' inhabitants of a nation founded in Puritanism, slavery, and capitalism."[31] She suggests that the objective of exhibiting Native American cultural items, human remains and funerary objects is to show them as part of the past and, at the same time, demonstrate cultural superiority over the Indigenous people. The Smithsonian was founded in 1846 through a donation by British scientist James Smithson. Many Native American artifacts are included in the Smithsonian's collection of "... 154 million items, [with] 19 museums, 21 libraries, nine research centers,..."[32] This includes the National Museum of the American Indian (NMAI), which has three locations in Washington, D.C., Suitland, Maryland and New York City.

From the earliest days of the United States, the cultural and social interests of the colonists sought to establish the Native Americans as inferior. In April 1990, Robert E. Bieder wrote, "A Brief Historical Survey of the Expropriation of American Indian Remains." In this, he stated, "Through the measurement of crania, both personality and intelligence could be determined. This enabled polygenists [study of crania] to devise an intelligence ranking and assign non-whites to an inferior position on the scale."[33] Anthropologists did skeletal analysis to emphasize the inferiority of non-whites and "... to encourage laws to prevent race mixture."[34]

Additionally, the collection and study of bodies and body parts provided a method of dehumanizing the People – a practice mandated by the U.S. government to fill museums and provide "scientific research."[35] In 1832, "Surgeon General William A. Hammond, initially wanted Indian bodies to advance the study of infectious diseases.... The army studied dead Indian soldiers to see how modern bullets wounded the human body."[36] By 1867-68 this request had expanded to "augment the collection of Indian crania."[37] This enlarged the collections held at the Army Medical Museum, European museums and the Smithsonian based on the Smithsonian-Army museum agreement. Methodologies were expanded and fine-tuned which "... set in motion a decades-long practice of decapitating Native people, weighing their brains and shipping them as freight to Washington DC, for more 'study.'"[38] Research indicates that:

> The crania were 'harvested' from massacre sites, battlefields, prisons, schools, burial grounds (including scaffolds, caves and water, basketry and

pottery vessels) and even from hours-old graves. One officer reported waiting 'until cover of darkness' and departure of 'the grieving family' before 'I exhumed the body and decapitated the skull ...' [39]

In the late 1800s, museums started displaying "life groups" of Native Americans as a way of representing them as people of the past. They were no longer masters of their destiny, but rather "market commodities and museum objects."[40]

Museums of Special Significance

To know more about the history of Native Americans and their cultures, there are a number of museums of special significance. The National Museum of the American Indian, which is part of the Smithsonian Institution, has three locations: George Gustav Heye Center in New York City, the National Museum of the American Indian (NMAI) on the National Mall in Washington, D.C. and the Cultural Resources Center in Suitland, Maryland. For online information on the museums go to *si.edu* and click on Visit/Museums and Zoo. The link will provide location and map, days and hours of operation and exhibit information.

The Museum of the American Indian-Heye Foundation was a little-known and less-attended museum in New York that originally opened to the public in 1922 and struggled for years to remain open. Finally, in 1984, the museum leadership reached out across the U.S. with a program prospectus describing their one-million object collection. Numerous cities expressed an interest and were prepared to furnish the resources to obtain and maintain such a collection. It was at this point that New York City realized the importance of retaining the museum and of providing the facility necessary to house and display the objects. As a result, the George Gustav Heye Center opened in lower Manhattan on October 30, 1994, featuring contemporary and historical exhibits of art and artifacts by and about Native Americans with the director stating, "... ours will be an institution that explores not just objects, but the people and cultures who created, and are still creating, those objects."[41]

The National Museum of the American Indian (NMAI)

is located on the National Mall in Washington, D.C. and opened September 2004. Native people were consulted on the design and utilization of the museum which offers a "... range of exhibitions, film and video screenings, school group programs, public programs and living culture presentations throughout the year."[42] A search of the *washington.org* website provides an oversight of the NMAI structure and the collection which "... represents over 1,200 indigenous cultures and more than 12,000 years of history."[43] Due to the large numbers of artifacts, there is no way to display them all; therefore, ongoing and rotating exhibits provide a glimpse into the lives and culture of Native Americans. Designed by Native architects, the NMAI was built of limestone material and emulates "... rock formations affected by wind and water over thousands of years."[44]

The Cultural Resources Center in Suitland, Maryland is a research center that houses approximately 800,000 objects when they are not on display at NMAI. The staff maintains a library and conservation center, as well as paper and photo archives. From inception, the intent was to make the center feel more like a home than a warehouse, so it includes large windows connecting to nature and cultural symbols. It is a resource used by Native communities as well as Native and non-native researchers.

Rory Snowarrow Fausett has written extensive and legal analysis covering a 65-year period of Indigenous Americans and United States law. Fine-Dare quotes from an article "Indigenous Cultural Rights as Human Rights" written by Fausett to provide some perspective on the numbers of remains and cultural items held by various museums:

> In the United States today, an estimated 300,000 to 2 million human remains of indigenous peoples, including many remains of our South and Central American and Pacific relatives, are housed and put on display . . . the United States National Museum – Smithsonian Institution – warehouses the remains of some 18,000 of our peoples Beyond the issue of the remains of our ancestors, literally millions of our cultural objects – many of great spiritual importance and critical cultural significance to the traditional lives

and values of our peoples – lie in boxes or vaults in these institutions. The theft and unconsented collection, cataloguing, and warehousing of our cultural patrimony continues unabated. ... [45]

In a March 2019 interview by Kevin Simpson of the *Colorado Sun* with Chip Colwell, a senior curator of anthropology at the Denver Museum of Nature & Science, Colwell expressed his concerns regarding the ongoing work being done by the country's museums in conjunction with Native Americans. "It's history, but it's politics,... It's law, but it's ethics. It's science, but it's spirituality."[46]

Museum curators and anthropologists initially felt threatened by NAGPRA – feeling that the museums would be stripped of a significant portion of their collections by the requirements. However, as they continue, even today, to converse with and listen to the Native people, both sides have come to appreciate that it is an emotionally and culturally sensitive conversation for all concerned. As museum personnel learn, they are taking guidance from Native Americans on what can be displayed and the correct way of displaying the artifacts that they are retaining. The museum-going public benefits as they are now able to gain a greater understanding of the culture of the "First People" and learn that "There is a connection from the past to the present; I [James Henry] think people forget about that. They tend to disassociate things that are in a repository with living, breathing people."[47]

Repatriation

NAGPRA brings the work of the anthropologist, archaeologist and museum together to meet a common goal – that of repatriating indigenous remains, funerary objects and cultural artifacts.

In 1945, the United Nations established an agency to promote the exchange of information, ideas and culture which became the United Nations Education, Scientific, and Cultural Organization (UNESCO). The U.S., however, withdrew its membership in 1984 and did not rejoin until 2003 after reforms were instituted by UNESCO. During this time, the 1970 Convention on the Means of Prohibiting and Preventing the Illicit Import, Export and Transfer of Ownership of Cultural Property was passed to meet the "… Sustainable Development Goals defined in the United Nations 2030 Agenda."[48] Many of the developing countries had experienced illicit trafficking of cultural property and hoped that the convention would slow, if not eliminate, the losses.

In the United States, the 1970s brought an increasing awareness and "… a growing discussion regarding the general role of museums in possessing, displaying, and representing Native American cultural objects and human remains."[49] These issues were primary in panel discussions of Indian scholars during a 1971 convention in Colorado. Repatriation also became a greater point of discussion during this time. Of the collections housed throughout the United States, Douglas Preston wrote in 1989 that the Native American Rights Fund estimated there were more then 600,000 specimens. "More than 18,000 human remains were estimated to be in the Smithsonian Institution alone, 700 of which (including associated burial goods) were returned to the Larsen Bay Tribal Council of Kodiak Island, Alaska, in 1991."[50]

There are museums throughout the world that feel that it is their right to own, collect and display artifacts they have obtained no matter the country or people represented by the items. The artifacts, whether human remains, funerary objects or cultural items, "belong" to the museum. There has been a struggle to repatriate those items, which culminated in passing the NAGPRA legislation. Native Americans have contested the collecting of their patrimony and fought for "… repatriation and reburial [which] involve deeply religious, humanitarian, and human rights matters."[51] Despite their efforts, international collections, as well as "Newly discovered remains and those in public museums…"[52] fall outside the scope of NAGPRA

It wasn't until the early 1900s that Native Americans of the Mesa Verde area uncovered the documents that gave them an understanding of the scope of the looting and vandalizing that had taken place, in addition to the items sent to Europe by

Nordenskiöld. In 2019, it was announced during "A state visit by Finnish President Sauli Niiniston to the U.S. … [that] items … including 20 sets of human remains and 28 funerary objects"[53] from Nordenskiöld's visit to Mesa Verde would be repatriated to the Native Americans. "For tribes who inhabited the area over many centuries, this announcement begins to close a long-open wound."[54] The fact that a sovereign government had volunteered to make such a major gift was a significant step forward on the ideals of the 1970 Convention. The remains and funerary objects were to be accepted by the Mesa Verde Park Service, and the four tribes affected would arrange a date, place of burial and ceremonies to reflect the importance of the return of their ancestors.

In 2001, Lawson wrote for *ABCNews* stating that "… a huge truck filled with the bones of over 2,000 People left the Peabody Museum in Cambridge, Mass.,…"[55] headed for New Mexico. Lawson also stated that some members of the Pueblo of Jemez walked 80 miles to greet the truck and accompany their ancestors to a private reburial in the largest repatriation to date.[56]

Conversations between Native Americans and public museums across the nation have been initiated through NAGPRA's passage. NAGPRA will direct the repatriation efforts for the foreseeable future because as more remains are uncovered in everyday endeavors – i.e., construction of pipeline, highways, schools, etc., plowing land for crops, an occasional hiker – there will be a need to identify and repatriate them.

Author's Thoughts

Fine-Dare wrote "When Lewis and Clark remarked about the silence as they traveled past abandoned earthworks, it was because they were passing by thousands and thousands of graves, many of which would be desecrated and claimed for science, agriculture, nation building and progress as the nineteenth century unfolded."[57]

Many nations have experienced concern for the confiscation and illegal export of their cultural items. Newly emerging and independent countries have, since the 1950s, added their voices to those concerns as they have experienced the growing black market for cultural items. UNESCO put forward the 1970 Convention to promote repatriation of cultural items while also recognizing the importance of stopping or preventing illicit trafficking in those items.[58]

The passage of NAGPRA recognized the importance of protecting and the repatriation of cultural items held by museums in the United States. However, it did not have any legal standing internationally. In addition, there was no accounting for cultural items held outside the U.S. either publicly or privately. Over the years, Native Americans have discussed these issues with the U.N and the international community at large. They have asked for Indigenous governments to be recognized by the U.N.; however, the U.N. governing body is made up of people from the same countries who colonized the U.S., and those groups have repeatedly resisted recognizing Indigenous people. On September 20, 2017, an article was published on *theconversation.com* titled "Native Americans won a vital battle at UN 40 years ago– they need help again"[59] which emphasized the work Native Americans had done at the U.N. Their most recent advances had been through two U.N. committees. The first deals with the illicit trafficking of cultural property under UNESCO and the other is the Human Rights Commission. Without being recognized by the U.N. governing body, Indigenous groups cannot even attend meetings without an invitation.

Over the centuries, there have been instances of people "obtaining" Indian artifacts either for their personal collections, notoriety, profit, scientific advancement or other purposes. While most go unnoticed and/or unreported, some looting is of such significance that it eventually gains attention. Thus was the case in 2014, when the F.B.I. raided the Indiana farm of Don Miller where they ultimately discovered over 42,000 artifacts with "... approximately 500 sets of human remains, many of which are believed to have been looted from Native American burial grounds."[60] No matter the motive for removing the pieces, it causes distress and grief to the descendants, especially those Native tribes still in existence. It is a desecration of graves and other sites when bodies are stolen, funerary object taken and even pottery and other cultural items are removed, so Native Americans continue to fight for repatriation. None of us should have to worry about or experience the graves of our ancestors being looted.

Ninety-one-year-old Miller had been a Christian missionary who lived, worked and traveled to numerous countries worldwide and was known to collect things on "archaeological digs." He enjoyed inviting "... local residents, reporters and Boy Scout troops into his home to view his artifacts; however, he kept the human remains largely out of sight." [61] Miller's collection was so extensive that the F.B.I. moved the items to a large facility to safeguard and study them. Once there, they enlisted the aid of anthropologists and museum studies graduate students of the Indianapolis area in identifying and cataloging the items.

Without records of where Miller acquired the artifacts, consultation was needed with national and international experts, as well as Native American leaders. Discussions with Native leaders proved difficult in that many of them "... consider DNA testing to be invasive so without records, it is difficult to impossible to identify the remains."[62] The intent was to return the pieces without involving the public, but the task required more help than originally thought, so in 2019 the story went public, and they were finally able to repatriate more than 350 items previously unidentified.

Don Miller's story and that of the removal of the Elgin Marbles are only two among many – and likely more than will ever be known – that show the power one man had to remove cultural items from their origins. However, in the case of Elgin, the act marked a change "... of a consciously expressed sentiment in Europe that the powerful may not have the right to strip the less powerful of their heritage." [63] The science of discovery does not give anyone the right to take artifacts from the country of origin for study and display in museums or private collections, and countries have fought against this practice since the 20th century. While this has resulted in many pieces being returned to the country of origin, thus providing people with greater insight and pride into their history and culture, it is an ongoing battle.

In an ideal world, looting of cultural and sacred artifacts would not continue; however, it is a fact in today's world – as long as there is a buyer, there will be a seller. Thus, American Indian tribes have to maintain vigilance to protect their heritage, as well as work within the legal system to have their patrimony returned.

While NAGPRA worked somewhat as intended, it also had the unfortunate effect of designating areas that were formerly part of Native American reservations – which were and still are considered sacred areas – as part of the new "public land," effectively closing the sacred sites to them.

However, the conversations engendered by NAGPRA, though oftentimes difficult and always requiring careful thought and consideration by all parties, are imperative for the continued repatriation of sacred and culturally important Native American artifacts.

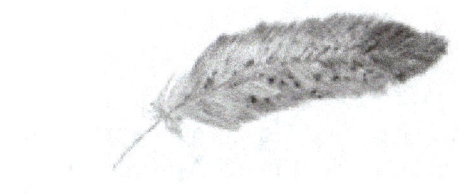

Endnotes:

[1] Fine-Dare, Kathleen S. *Grave Injustice: The American Indian Repatriation Movement and NAGPRA.* U Nebraska P. p. 77.

[2] Fine-Dare. p. 77.

[3] Fine-Dare. p. 77.

[4] Fine-Dare. p. 77.

[5] Fine-Dare. p. 77.

[6] Fine-Dare. p. 47.

[7] Fine-Dare. p. 17.

[8] Fine-Dare. p. 43.

[9] Montaigne, Fen. "The Fertile Shore" *Smithsonian Magazine,* January/February 2020. p. 34.

10   Montaigne. p. 37.

11   Baires, Sarah E. "White Settlers Buried the Truth About the Midwest's Mysterious Mound Cities." *smithsonianmag.com.* 23 Feb 2018. https://bit.ly/3oTenXt. Accessed 2 Nov 2020.

12   "About Dr. Kathleen Fine-Dare." *Fort Lewis College,* https://bit.ly/2S9Y1L0 Accessed 5 Apr 2020.

13   Fine-Dare, Kathleen S. *Grave Injustice: The American Indian Repatriation Movement and NAGPRA.* U Nebraska P, 2002. p. 166.

14   Native American Graves Protection and Repatriation Act." *National Oceanic and Atmospheric Administration.* https://bit.ly/2GoGrjX. Accessed 4 Apr 2020.

15   Willow Lawson. "Indian Skeletons May Never Leave Museums." *Abcnews.* https://abcn.ws/3jneBTG. Accessed 7 Jan 2020.

16   Lawson.

17   Lawson.

18   Lawson.

19   Lawson.

20   John Strand. "20 Years and Counting: James Pepper Henry's Multifaceted View of NAGPRA." April 4, 2020. https://bit.ly/36mnV6w. Accessed 4 Apr 2020.

21   Strand.

22   Simpson, Kevin. "To right historic wrongs, Colorado museums embraced spirit of a law that repatriated Native American artifacts and remains – largely by listening." *The Colorado Sun.* 1 Mar 2019. https://bit.ly/35xQkWG.

23   Sanjek, Roger. editor. *Fieldnotes: The Makings of Anthropology.* "The Secret Life of Fieldnotes." Cornell UP.

24   Sanjek

25   Hirst, K. Kriss. "The History of Archaeology — The First Archaeologists." *ThoughtCo.,* 15 Jan 2020. https://bit.ly/3lxrtHY. Accessed 27 Mar 2020.

26   Kathleen S. Fine-Dare. *Grave Injustice: The American Indian Repatriation Movement and NAGPRA.* U Nebraska P, 2002. p. 20 and Conn 1998: 34.

27   Kevin Simpson. "More than a century ago a European visitor

took more than 600 Native American remains and artifacts from Colorado's Mesa Verde." *Colorado Sun.* 10 Oct 2019. https://bit.ly/3n2DAhk.

28 Simpson.

29 "American Antiquities Act of 1906." *National Park Service.* 22 Jun 2017, https://bit.ly/30p0V3c.

30 Fine-Dare, Kathleen S. *Grave Injustice: The American Indian Repatriation Movement and NAGPRA.* U Nebraska P, 2002. p. 62.

31 Fine-Dare. p. 8.

32 "Smithsonian Institution." *Wikipedia: The Free Encyclopedia,* Wikimedia Foundation, https://bit.ly/2GtuusY. Accessed 28 Mar 2020.

33 Bieder, Robert E. "A Brief Historical Survey of the Expropriation of American Indian Remains." April 1990. https://bit.ly/2II3cQS, p. 5. Accessed 3 Nov 2020.

34 Bieder.

35 Fine-Dare, Kathleen S. *Grave Injustice: The American Indian Repatriation Movement and NAGPRA.* U Nebraska P, 2002. p. 32.

36 Willow Lawson. "Indian Skeletons May Never Leave Museums." *ABCNews.* https://abcn.ws/3jneBTG. Accessed 7 Jan 2020.

37 Fine-Dare, Kathleen S. *Grave Injustice: The American Indian Repatriation Movement and NAGPRA.* U Nebraska P, 2002. p. 33.

38 Fine-Dare. p. 33.

39 Fine-Dare. p. 33.

40 Fine-Dare. p. 21.

41 West, W. Richard, Founding Director National Museum of the American Indian. *"Overview: Native Peoples, The Arts and Lifeways, Fall 1994,* p 26.

42 National Museum of the American Indian." *Wikipedia: The Free Encyclopedia,* Wikimedia Foundation, https://bit.ly/3ihP2Ci. Accessed 16 Jul 2019.

43 "National Museum of the American Indian." *Washington DC,* https://bit.ly/36mKTdF. Accessed 27 Jul 2019.

44 "National Museum of the American Indian." *Washington DC,* https://bit.ly/36mKTdF. Accessed 27 Jul 2019.

45 Fine-Dare, Kathleen S. *Grave Injustice: The American Indian Repatriation Movement and NAGPRA.* U Nebraska P, 2002. p. 85.

46 Simpson, Kevin. "To right historic wrongs, Colorado museums embraced spirit of a law that repatriated Native American artifacts and remains – largely by listening." *The Colorado Sun,* 1 Mar 2019. https://bit.ly/35xQkWG.

47 Strand, John. "20 Years and Counting: James Pepper Henry's Multifaceted View of NAGPRA." April 4, 2020. https://bit.ly/36mnV6w. Accessed 4 Apr 2020.

48 United Nations, General Conference of the United Nations Educational, Scientific and Cultural Organization. "Means of Prohibiting and Preventing the Illicit Import, Export and Transfer of Ownership of Cultural Property." *unesdoc.unesco.org.* 8 Aug 1969. https://bit.ly/2G7ETeq. Accessed 4 Apr 2020.

49 "United Nations Education, Scientific, and Cultural Organization."

50 Fine-Dare, Kathleen S. *Grave Injustice: The American Indian Repatriation Movement and NAGPRA.* U Nebraska P, 2000. p. 35. And Native American Rights Fund 1991.

51 Fine-Dare. p. 8.

52 Simpson, Kevin. "More than a century ago, a European visitor took more than 600 Native American remains and artifacts from Colorado's Mesa Verde." *Colorado Sun.* 10 Oct 2019. https://bit.ly/3n2DAhk.

53 Simpson.

54 Simpson.

55 Lawson, Willow. "Indian Skeletons May Never Leave Museums" *ABCNews.*-https://abcn.ws/3jneBTG. Accessed 7 Jan 2020.

56 Lawson.

57 Fine-Dare, Kathleen S. *Grave Injustice: The American Indian Repatriation Movement and NAGPRA.* U Nebraska P,

2002. p. 51.

[58] United Nations, General Conference of the United Nations Educational, Scientific and Cultural Organization. "Means of Prohibiting and Preventing the Illicit Import, Export and Transfer of Ownership of Cultural Property." *Unesdoc.unesco.org.* 8 Aug 1969. https://bit.ly/2G7ETeq. Accessed 4 Apr 2020.

[59] Toth, Gyorgy "Native Americans won a vital battle at UN 40 years ago — they need help again." *The Conversation,* 20 Sep 2017. https://bit.ly/32K5gyO.

[60] Katz, Brigit. "The F.B.I. Is Trying to Return Thousands of Stolen Artifacts, Including Native American Burial Remains." *Smithsonian Magazine*, 4 March 2019, https://bit.ly/3kY4QM4.

[61] Katz.

[62] Katz.

[63] Fine-Dare, Kathleen S. *Grave Injustice: The American Indian Repatriation Movement and NAGPRA.* U Nebraska P, 2002. p. 43.

Author's Reflections

Resilience. Therein lies the hope for the First
Americans. After decades of physical and cultural
genocide, they keep struggling to their feet. The sacred
traditions, the wisdom of living in harmony with
nature, the reverence for things living now and past –
those things have been kept alive. But there's a
difference between life support and living, a difference
between survival and thriving, and eventually, the
lines get blurred.

Senator Byron L. Dorgan
The Girl in the Photograph[1]

Even before the signing of the Declaration of Independence, the
United States attempted to deal with what they considered the
"Indian problem." There have been a succession of acts, laws and
regulations tried over the years to take advantage of, steal from and
harm Native Americans, and despite everything, they have
survived. Their resilience is witnessed in the strength of the
People, their political systems, schools, languages and cultures
and in the overall growth of their nations.

S. Lyman Tyler recounts some in the Introduction to *A
History of Indian Policy*. They include:

The Indian Intercourse Act of 1834, which looked
toward the concentration of Indians in 'Indian
Country' west of the Mississippi and the barring of
unauthorized non-Indians from encroachment on their
lands, gave way to the Reservation System in the
1850s. Pressure to break up the tribal estates and
individualize Indian landholding developed in the
1880s and was formalized by the Allotment Act of
1887.[2]

Not until the 1920s did federal administrators publicly
admit that their policies had not accomplished the desired results

and reform of Indian affairs was demanded. In 1944, the National Congress of American Indians (NCAI) was established with the goals of protecting the land and treaty rights of Native Americans and preserving cultural values. The late 1900s brought about renewed interest in reform, which was often spearheaded by nongovernmental organizations, including The Indian Defense Association, The Native American Rights Fund, American Indian Federation, American Indian Movement and others that guard the civil and tribal rights of the many Indian Nations.

During the recent past, Native Americans have seen significant progress made in acknowledging the legal rights specified by law between the federal government and individual Indian tribes: the right to self-government, the rights as citizens and the right to protect their lands. The 2020 *McGirt v. Oklahoma* was one such significant decision. Some of this is due to lawsuits brought against the government, while at other times it is acknowledged as the humane way of treating all people. The Joint Commission of Congress on Indian Funds was aware of the situation with the trust fund when, in 1915, they issued a warning on the fraud and corruption. Other documents throughout the years made it clear that the Department of the Interior (DOI) understood the problem but seemed unable or unwilling to make a rightful accounting. Judge Royce Lamberth, who presided over the lawsuit *Cobell v. Salazar*, acknowledged the problems and forced the DOI to be accountable. Hopefully, the consolidation of Indian records in the industrial caves outside Lenexa, Kansas will continue, and Congress will maintain the mandatory, nondiscretionary funding in the federal budget as recommended by President Obama in 2016.

That said, Jack Utter addressed the issue of "Land, Resources, and Non-Gaming Economics" in his 2001 book, *American Indians: Answers to Today's Questions,* stating that the greatest resource the American Indian has is the 56,000,000 acres held in trust.[3] When the U.S. government compelled the Indians to sign the numerous treaties, the nonsubsistence resources (coal, gas, oil, gold and uranium) were not considered part of the treaty. Timber and water are also valuable resources with the western states increasingly vying for Indian water rights. Unfortunately, mismanagement by the Bureau of Indian Affairs, as exemplified in the *Cobell* lawsuit, resulted in the loss of many millions of dollars to the tribes and individual Indians.[4]

With the increased awareness of systemic racism in our country in 2021, many may not know or realize that there has been environmental racism as well. The term, environmental racism, was coined by Dr. Benjamin Chavis, Jr. in referring to a study done in 1987 "… that found a very strong correlation between race and the selection of sites for hazardous industries and waste disposal."[5] In Utter's book (2001), he provided the following definition:

> Environmental racism is generally defined as racial discrimination in environmental policy making, regulation enforcement, and waste facility siting, and also includes the exclusion of people of color from the decision-making process as well as from leadership positions in the environmental movement.[6]

In seeking profitable agreements with Indian country, the waste disposal companies offered tribes various incentives, including money and assistance programs. This was particularly prevalent in the 1990s when these companies and the federal government tried to induce Native people to allow nuclear waste sites on tribal land. The few companies and employment opportunities along with the extreme poverty on reservations meant that incentives were strong motivators to allow waste sites on Native lands, which some tribes, in desperation, agreed to. In other situations, the concerns for pollution of the land and ground water along with health concerns proved to be more important to tribes who declined to allow sites.

When it comes to discussing the wrongs done to Native Americans, it should be noted, valued and remembered that Indians of all tribes, willingly and with honor, served and died in defense of the United States during the Civil War. They served with distinction in World War I and World War II. Code talkers served in the Pacific and European theaters, with the Navajo Code Talkers being the most famous. They provided an unbreakable defense against the Nazis, saved many Allied lives and helped win the war. Native Americans continued their legacy of service in the Korean War, as well as the Vietnam War, and more recently they have served proudly in Iraq and Afghanistan. They did this out of love for this country. They are People of two realities – they are citizens of the U.S. and citizens of their tribal nations.

Wilma Mankiller highlighted the fact that Native Americans live and work in the non-Indian, modern world, while their cultures sustain them throughout any adversity they face. Elected as the first woman deputy chief in Cherokee history, Mankiller took office in August 1983. In a 1984 speech in Denver, she stated, "Women can help turn the world right side up. We bring a more collaborative approach to government. And if we do not participate, then decisions will be made without us."[7] A collaboration between men and women, between different ethnic groups and cultural beliefs will make our democracy stronger.

Cherokee Chief Hoskins, along with Kimberly Teehee, were guests on ABC's show *Matter of Fact* hosted by Soledad O'Brien on November 10, 2019.[8] At that time, they discussed Hoskins' appointment of Teehee as a delegate-designate to the House of Representatives – a position specified in two treaties between the United States and the Cherokee people. The two treaties are the 1785 Treaty of Hopewell and the 1835 Treaty of New Echota, which ultimately forced the Cherokee to leave their homeland in the Southeastern U.S. The House has stalled for 235 years on the legislation recognizing the right of a nonvoting delegate of the Cherokee Nation to be seated. What will it take for them to recognize the rights that their predecessors wrote into law with those treaties? If recognized, Teehee's role as a First Citizen of the United States would be similar to those of representatives from Washington, D.C., Puerto Rico, American Samoa, Guam and the United States Virgin Islands.

Charles J. Kappler compiled and edited a list of all treaties spanning 1778-1883 between the federal government and the Native Nations. In 1972, Brantley Blue, Indian Claims Commissioner of Washington, D.C. wrote the forward for the reprint, which made the 1,074-page volume available to libraries and the public for the first time since the original printing in 1904. It is an invaluable resource for students of history, researchers and Native Americans working to find information about their past. As one reads through the treaties, with all the legal language, preambles, articles and witnesses for the government and the

Indians, there is evidence of the complexity and enormity of the documents.

On the government side, there were skilled negotiators often with legal training, who used words like miles, survey, directions (north to east) as examples. These men knew what they wanted – land, waterways, etc. – and had the knowledge and words to negotiate treaties against Indian representatives who usually could not speak the white man's language, and the meanings were often lost or misrepresented in the translations. The government spoke one language, while the Indians had many. Even in 2017, there were approximately 296 known Indigenous languages spoken, or formerly spoken, north of Mexico.

Kappler's compilation of the treaties makes the reader aware of the changing names of tribes as the government and the settlers pushed across the land. Some tribes no longer exist – the People, culture and languages gone for all time. Others neared extinction but over time have united their people, developed tribal governments and educated their children in their Native languages and culture. They attend trade schools and colleges, earning degrees which help strengthen their people. They are doctors, lawyers, environmentalist, educators as well as plumbers, electricians and auto mechanics. They continue to learn while embracing their past, their language and culture – things that make them who they are.

Utter provided a definition of tribe in his book, *American Indians: Answers to Today's Questions*, when he stated:

> Legally, no universal definition for the generic term 'tribe' exists in the U.S. Constitution, federal statutes, or regulations. Nonetheless, the term is specifically found in the Constitution, in hundreds of statutes, in hundreds of treaties, and in numerous regulations. In most instances, a question of a tribe's political existence can now be resolved by reference to a treaty, legislative agreement, statute, or executive order of the President 'recognizing' the tribe at some time in the past.[9]

The federal bureaucrats believed that by dispersing Native Americans into the mainstream of America, "Indian" ways would be relinquished, and they would become like other Americans. Their communal form of government, religion and way of life were ridiculed and legally outlawed. Before that, in the late 1800s, Native children were forcibly removed from their homes and sent to boarding schools. Some returned to the reservations after they were grown, but there were no jobs, they had no homes and were emotionally cut off from their families. An entire generation of children was lost to their families and tribes.

The 20th century saw an end to the government boarding school system, a recognition of Indians' contribution to the war effort and resultant citizenship. Then came the beginning of the dispersal program in the early 1950s, which was meant to relocate Native Americans from reservations to the cities primarily of the Midwest and West Coast. This was yet another program to take care of the Indian problem by assimilating them into the American population. While a number of Native Americans made their homes in their new cities, many of them eventually returned to their Native homes and land. Without the relocation program, they would never have been compelled to make this choice.

After a lecture by a Lakota author at the University of Colorado in Boulder, a question was asked that might resonate with many: "Why should I be held responsible for the plight of Native Americans."[10] The straight-forward answer is because we know the truth. "U.S. Americans benefit from past acts of dispossession, slavery and forced assimilation."[11] Because we were not alive at the time does not relieve us of the need to correct the injustice which continues today.

In Senator Byron L. Dorgan's 2019 book, *The Girl in the Photograph: The True Story of a Native American Child, Lost and Found in America*, he writes about a Native girl, Tamara, from the Standing Rock Indian Reservation. Dorgan had been Chairman of the Committee on Indian Affairs while in the Senate and read an article in *The Bismark Tribune* about a Native child who had been severely abused to the point of broken bones while in foster care at age two. It stated that it was days before social services rescued her. When removed from the home, a child was usually placed with a member of the extended family, but the article did not specify the foster care situation for Tamara. Her grandfather "… was attempting to take legal action again the Bureau of Indian Affairs for what had been done to his grandchildren."[12]

Moved by the situation and wanting to understand more, Dorgan went to North Dakota to connect with the child and her grandfather, but over time lost track of her as she moved through the foster care system. Thirty-three years after clipping and saving the article, he was able to reconnect with her, and she agreed to talk to him and use her story as an example of the numerous problems with the Indian Health Service which is within the Department of Health and Human Services, their lack of adequate funding and their lack of support of the Native people throughout the country. Since retirement, Dorgan created a nonprofit organization to help Native American youth living on Indian reservation.[13]

In light of the problems with the health service, it was a particularly memorable event in 2019 when Chief Hoskins wrote of the opening of "The largest tribal outpatient health facility in American … [which was] a transformational moment in Cherokee Nation's history."[14] He outlined the struggles the Cherokee Nation faced in getting the facility when he wrote:

> Enshrined in treaties, set forth in statutes, and embodied in court decisions is a solemn promise that, as reparation for the hardship and dispossession borne by our ancestors at the hands of the United States, this country would provide for the health and welfare of tribal citizens in perpetuity. We, as Indian nations, have struggled for decades with the United States' failures to adequately fulfill that obligation.[15]

In addition to not keeping the healthcare promise, significant negative changes were made to the environmental policy of the U.S. during the Trump administration. Some of these included the U.S. withdrawal from the Paris Agreement of 2015, easing rules for coal-burning power plants and an executive order on the Dakota Access Pipeline, which directly affects Indian tribes in the Dakotas and Iowa.

Nina Lakhani wrote an article on January 23, 2021 for *grist.org* in which she is quoted as saying, "Last week, 75 Indigenous female leaders from across the country sent a letter to the incoming administration calling on it to immediately halt fossil fuel projects which threaten their land, water, health, culture, and security. They wrote: 'No more broken promises, no more broken Treaties … We urge you to fulfill the United States promise of sovereign relations with Tribes, and your commitment to robust climate action.'"[16]

President Biden issued an executive order on his first day in office canceling the Keystone XL pipeline. First proposed in 2008, the Keystone pipeline was designed to transport approximately 830,000 barrels of tar sands oil a day from Alberta, Canada to the refineries on the Gulf Coast of Texas. Extracting oil from the tar sand is a difficult process, with steep environmental and economic costs, and the project has strong proponents both for and against. No information was known on the Biden administration's stance on other fossil fuel projects by late January 2021.

The National Environmental Policy Act of 1970 provides the guidelines for the EPA, one of which is to require an environmental impact statement on all federal projects to include archaeological surveys to determine whether the proposed actions would adversely affect the human environment. First announced in 2014, the pipeline had to be authorized by the federal government since it runs across Indian lands. However, to date (2020), an impact statement has not been done for the pipeline, and it was routed through known Native ancestral lands and sacred burial grounds of several Native tribes. This is but another example of imperialism – a policy of extending a country's power and influence through diplomacy or military force – that has been practiced against the original peoples of the Americas since the first Europeans set foot on the land. This is, in fact, yet another example of domestic racism and injustice against Native Americans.

Ironically, one way I believe to begin to capture the spirit of how Natives feel for their land, occurred in space. It's through the thoughts voiced by astronauts as they viewed the earth from the depths of space and expressed by Archibald MacLeish, an American poet and writer:

To see the earth as it truly is, small and blue and

beautiful in that eternal silence where it floats, is to see ourselves as riders on the earth together, brothers on that bright loveliness in the eternal cold – brothers who know now they are truly brothers.[17]

Regardless of our differences, we are ultimately all "brothers and sisters" on this planet. It is, therefore, critically important that we understand our history to prevent past mistakes from reoccurring. We must never forget about the destructive forces behind the invasions upon the Native Americans in order to move forward without their repetition and with reparation. As a country, we must do the hard work of understanding and taking actions to support Native Americans in order to make lasting changes. Their history and continuing struggles, specifically against treaties that have not been honored, racist acts and acculturation are more than unacceptable; it is a travesty of justice and equality to the First Americans of this country. In my heart and through my research, I believe it is time to work harder to right the wrongs that were, and still are, committed against Native Americans. This book is one way I hope to help in their fight for reparation and equality. My other hope is that this book will enlighten, create change and motivate others to join in.

Endnotes

[1] Dorgan, Senator Byron L. *The Girl in the Photograph.* Thomas Dunne Books, 2019, p. 21.

[2] Tyler, S. Lyman. United States Department of the Interior, Bureau of Indian Affairs, 1973. p. 7.

[3] Utter, Jack. *American Indians: Answers to Today's Questions 2nd Ed. Revised and Enlarged.* U of Oklahoma P, 2001. p. 218

[4] Utter. p. 218.

[5] Utter. p. 228.

[6] Utter. p. 228.

[7] Mankiller. p. 242.

[8] O'Brien, Soledad. "A nearly 200-year-old deal could put the first Cherokee Nation delegate in Congress. Will she be approved?" *Matter of Fact*, 9 Nov 2019. https://bit.ly/2GVYCNS.

[9] Utter, Jack. *American Indians: Answers to Today's Questions 2ⁿᵈ Ed.* Revised and Enlarged. U of Oklahoma P, 2001. p. 58.

[10] Dorgan, Senator Byron L. *The Girl in the Photograph.* Thomas Dunne Books, 2019. p. 6.

[11] Dorgan. p. 7.

[12] Dorgan. Introduction, p. 3.

[13] Dorgan.

[14] Hoskin, Jr., Chuck. "New Cherokee Health Center will transform health care for generations." 9 Dec 2019. *Cherokee Phoenix.* https://bit.ly/3f1GAXS.

[15] Hoskin.

[16] Lakhani, Nina. "No more broken treaties': Indigenous leaders urge Biden to shut down Dakota Access pipeline." 14 Jan 2021. https://bit.ly/3qWrQye. Accessed 26 Jan 2021.

[17] Macleish, Archibald. *New York Times*, "Riders on Earth Together, Brothers in Eternal Cold." *The New York Times,* 25 Dec 1968. https://nyti.ms/3dleeXG. Accessed 6 October 2020.

Bibliography

"1842 Slave Revolt in the Cherokee Nation." *Wikipedia: The Free Encyclopedia*, Wikimedia Foundation. https://bit.ly/355vblf. Accessed 28 Aug 2019.

"1917: American Indians volunteer for WWI."*The United States World War One Centennial Commission.* Accessed 20 Jan 2020. https://bit.ly/3l0BxZL.

1968: President Johnson signs the Indian Civil Rights Act." *Native Voices.* https://bit.ly/3oPXFbM.

"A Broken Trust Wins Robert F. Kennedy Journalism Award for Newsy." *Native News Online,* 5 Jun 2020. https://bit.ly/3jiSXQw.

"About Dr. Kathleen Fine-Dare." *Fort Lewis College,* https://bit.ly/2S9Y1L0. Accessed 5 Apr2020.

"About the Eastern Band of Cherokee Indians." *Cherokee Preservation Foundation.* https://bit.ly/2IbWcMj. Accessed 31 Jan 2017.

"About Us." *Cherokee Heritage Center*, 27 Jul 2019. https://bit.ly/3n5QLhG.

"Act of May 27, 1908: 35 Stat. 312, H.R. 151641." http://thorpe.ou.edu/treatises/statutes/Fct35.html.

Adair, James. *The History of The American Indians*. Pantianos Classics, First published in 1775.

Agoyo, Acee. "George H.W. Bush, 1924-2018, left lasting mark on Indian Country." *Indianz.com*, 4 Dec 2018. https://www.indianz.com/News/2018/12/04/george-hw-bush-19242018-left-lasting-mar.asp. Accessed 15 May 2020. (Error in shortened link)

Agoyo, Acee. "Indian Country slams efforts to 'abrogate' sovereignty in wake of historic Supreme Court ruling." *Indianz*, 13 Aug 2020. https://www.indianz.com/News/2020/08/13/indian-country-slams-efforts-to-abrogate.asp#:~:text=In%20a%20major%20show%20of,win%20for%20the%20first%20/Americans. Accessed 15 Aug 2020. (Error in shortened link)

Agoyo, Acee. "National Congress of American Indians stands strong against efforts to erode tribal sovereignty." *Indianz,* 23

Jul 2020.
https://www.indianz.com/News/2020/07/23/national-
congress-of-american-indians-st-
1.asp#:~:text=National%20Congress%20of % 20 A
merican% 20 Indians% 20 stands% 20 strong %
20against%20efforts%20to%20erode%20tribal%20sovereig
nty,Thursday%2C%20July%2023&text=The%20tribe%20a
nd%20its%20leaders,efforts%20to%20erode%20their%20s
overeignty. Accessed 15 Aug 2020. (Error in shortened link)

Ahlers,Mike M.and Athena Jones."Tape sheds light on surreal
meeting between Nixon, protesters." 11 Nov 2011.
https://cnn.it/3dLyEJx. Accessed 20 Oct 2020.

"AIRR Records." *Bureau of Trust Funds Administration: U.S.
Department of the Interior,* 24 Oct 2019.
https://on.doi.gov/36qzTui.

Alderman, Pat. *Nancy Ward / Dragging Canoe: Cherokee
Chieftainess/Cherokee-Chickamauga War Chief.* 2nd ed.,
Overmountain Press, 1978.

"American Antiquities Act of 1906." *National Park Service,* 22 Jun
2017, https://bit.ly/30p0V3c.

"American bison." *Wikipedia: The Free Encyclopedia,*
Wikimedia Foundation, https://bit.ly/2GsE931. Accessed Jul
2020.

"America 1900: The General Allotment Act." The American
Experience, *National Public Radio.*
https://www.pbs.org/wgbh/americanexperience/features/1900-
allotment-act/

American Indian Nonfiction: An Anthology of Writings, 1760-
1930s. "To the Senate and House of Representatives. John Ross
et al (1836) Southeast and Indian Territory." File Copy, National
Archives, RG 233, 25th Cong. U of Oklahoma P. 2007.

"American Indian Powwows: Commercialization." *Smithsonian
Center for Folklife & Cultural Heritage.*
https://s.si.edu/2EMRMcZ. Accessed 2 Aug 2020.

Anderson,William L,editor.*Cherokee Removal:Before and After.*
Brown Thrasher Books, U of Georgia P, 1991.

Anderson, William L., Jane L. Brown & Anne F. Rogers, edited
& annotated by. *The Payne-Butrick Papers: Volumes 1, 2, 3.* U
of Nebraska P, 2010.

Anderson, William L., Jane L. Brown & Anne F. Rogers, edited & annotated by *The Payne-Butrick Papers: Vol 4, 5, 6.* U of Nebraska P, 2010.

"Aquifers: Arapahoe Aquifer." *Douglas County, Colorado.* https://bit.ly/3kGJvGh. Accessed 10 Apr 2020.

Arrillaga, Pauline. "For Indians, Trust Fund Case Can Right a Century of Wrongs." *Los Angeles Times*, 31 Oct 1999. https://lat.ms/3eMvtBF.

Aspinwall, Cary and Graham Lee Brewer. "Indian Country. What Does That Mean for Criminal Justice There?" *The Marshall Project*, 4 Aug 2020. https://bit.ly/3kYHvKg. Accessed 9 Aug 2020.

Atlas, Terry. "After 40 Years, U.S. Will Join UN Treaty Outlawing Genocide." *Chicago Tribune,* 4 Nov 1988. https://bit.ly/3eCcV7c. Accessed 7 Sep 2020.

Awiakta, Marilou. *Selu, Seeking the Corn-Mother's Wisdom.* Fulcrum Publishing, 1993.

Baires, Sarah E. "White Settlers Buried the Truth About the Midwest's Mysterious Mound Cities." *Smithsonian Magazine.* 23 Feb 2018. https://bit.ly/3oTenXt. Accessed 2 Nov 2020.

Barnhill, Frankie. "Nearly 6,000 Idaho Natives To Receive Checks in First Round of Settlements." *Boise State Public*

Beautiful Bald Eagle, Alaina. "Rancher sentenced for killing bald eagles on Standing Rock Sioux Reservation." *West River Eagle,* 29 Apr 2020. https://bit.ly/349AIXu. Accessed 31 May 2020.

Bell, Danna. "Native Americans in the First World War and the Fight for Citizenship." *The Library of Congress,* 5 Apr 2018. https://bit.ly/31mBRud. Accessed 20 Jan 2020.

Bennett, Robert L. Commission. A poem quoted in "American Indians-A Special Minority," in remarks before the Institute of Race Relations, Fisk University, Nashville, TN, 29 June 1967. https://bit.ly/380Jo5V.

Berger, Bethany R. "Elouise Cobell." *cobellscholar.org.* https://bit.ly/2IIkkWY.

Bieder, Robert E. *A Brief Historical Survey of the Expropriation of American Indian Remains.* April 1990. https://bit.ly/2II3cQS.p.5. Accessed 3 Nov 2020.

Boyle, Mary. "Norton in a historic bind." *The Gazette*, Colorado Springs, CO. 20 Feb 2020.

Brewer, Suzette. "A Broken Trust Wins Robert F. Kennedy Journalism Award for Newsy." *Native News Online,* 5 Jun 2020. https://bit.ly/3lfwFAb.

Brown, Dee Alexander. *Bury My Heart at Hounded Knee: An Indian History of the American West.* Hampton Sides, 2009.

Brown, Karina. "Specter of Pandemic Dire for Tribes Fighting for Federal Recognition." *Courthouse News Service, 7 Apr 2020.* https:// bit.ly/3e6ADs7.

Budd, Thomas. *Good Order Established in Pennsylvania & New Jersey in America, Being a True Account of the Country; With its Produce and Commodities There Made in the Year 1685.* London, 1685.

Bush, George. "National American Indian Heritage Month, 2006." *George W. Bush White House Archives,* https://bit.ly/35838Tm. Accessed 8 Nov 2020.

Carter, Jimmy. "Governor Jimmy Carter's Inaugural Address." *Jimmy Carter Library*, 12 January 1971, https://bit.ly/36lDV8M.

Carter, Jimmy. "Inaugural Address of Jimmy Carter." *Yale Law School, Lillian Goldman Law Library*, 20 Jan 1977, https://bit.ly/3iig5gP.

Carter-Landin, Eric, host. "Missing and Murdered Indigenous Women and Girls." *True Consequences Podcast,* 2 Dec 2019. https://bit.ly/36mFKma.

"Cherokee freedmen controversy." *Wikipedia: The Free Encyclopedia*, Wikimedia Foundation, https://bit.ly/37ta9zR. Accessed 2 Sep 2019.

Chavez, Will, Assistant Editor, *Cherokee Phoenix*. "Camp Gruber Forced 2nd Removal for Cherokees." 22 Oct 2012. https://www. cherokeephoenix.org/Article/index/6717.

Chow, Kat, reporter. "Judge Rules That Cherokee Freedmen Have Right to Tribal Citizenship." 31 Aug 2017. https://n.pr/3m0F3mP.

Chow, Kat, reporter. "So What Exactly is 'blood quantum'?" *Code Switch Podcast,* 9 Feb 2018. https://n.pr/36kG4BS.

Christianson, James R. "Removal: A Foundation for the Formation of Federal Indian Policy." *Journal of Cherokee Studies*, *Vol. X, No. 2, Fall 1985.*

"Civil War Era NC." *Civil War Era North Carolina.* https://cwnc.omeka. chass.ncsu.edu. Accessed 2 Sep 2019.

Clinton, William. "Indian Sacred Sites". *Federal Register*, Vol. 61, No. 104, 29 May 1996. Presidential Documents 26771. https://bit.ly/2GbRPQc.

Clinton, William. "National American Indian Heritage Month, 1996." *Federal Register, V*ol. 61, No. 213, 1 Nov 1996. Presidential Documents 56397. https://bit.ly/2G4JFta.

CNN Wire Staff. "U.S. finalizes $3.4 billion settlement with American Indians." *CNN,* 27 Nov 2012. https://cnn.it/3eKJzU8.

Coleman, Justine. "Doctors Without Borders in rare mission within US sends team to Navajo Nation." *The Hill,* 12 May 20. https://bit.ly/2ERmG46. Accessed 12 May 2020.

"Colonel W. S. Foster to Gen. W. Scott, Nov. 24. 1838." *Journal of Cherokee Studies, Vol. IV, No. 4, Fall 1979. Commercial Appeal, November 24, 1977.* (a quote from Awaikta pg 313)

Confer, Clarissa W. *The Cherokee Nation in the Civil War.* U of Oklahoma P, 2007.

Courson, Paul. "U.S. offers to pay Native Americans $1.4 billion for lost funds." *CNN,* 8 Dec 2009. https://cnn.it/36lY1hL.

Courtney, Gary. "Seminary Hall, at Northeastern State University." *Deviant Art,* 20 Mar 2016. https://bit.ly/3lTpSfh.

Curtis, Gene. "Only in Oklahoma: State housed German POWs during WWII." *Tulsa World,* 10 Feb 2007, updated 24 Feb 2019. https://bit.ly/36aIhy7. Accessed 22 Aug 2019.

Dale, Edward Evertt and Gaston Litton. *Cherokee Cavaliers: Forty Years of Cherokee History as told in the Correspondence of the Ridge-Watie-Boudinot Family (Volume 19).* U of Oklahoma P, 1939.

"Dawes Act (1887)" *Our Documents.* https://bit.ly/3pjNVqa. Accessed 19 Dec 2019.

Debo, Angie. *And Still the Waters Run: The Betrayal of the Five Civilized Tribes.* Princeton UP, 1940.

"Declaration of Independence, 1776." *America's Founding Documents.* https://bit.ly/3lNQ6jl.

Deere-Turney, Nancy. "MVTO Supreme Court For Doing What Is Right." *Center for Native American Youth,* 11 Jul 2020. https://bit.ly/33eotcS.

de Las Casas, Bartolome'. *History of the Indies,* translated and edited by Andree Collard. Harper & Row, 1971.

Deloria, Vine and Raymond J. DeMallie. *Documents of American Indian Diplomacy: Treaties, Agreements, and Conventions, 1775-1979 (Legal History of North America)*. U of Oklahoma P, 1999.

de Tocqueville, Alexis. *Democracy in America*, edited by Richard D. Heffner. Mentor, 1956.

Diggins, John Patrick. *John Adams: The American Presidents Series.* Times Books, Henry Holt and Company, 2003.

Domonoske, Camila. "Police in Many U.S. Cities Fail to Track Murdered, Missing Indigenous Women." *NPR*, 15 Nov. 2018. https://n.pr/3iivdKM. Accessed 8 Sep 2020.

Dorgan, Senator Byron L. *The Girl in the Photograph.* Thomas Dunne Books, 2019.

Douglas County, Colorado. "Aquifers: Arapahoe Aquifer." *Douglas County, Colorado.* https://bit.ly/33f91wT. Accessed 10 Apr 2020.

Drinnon, Richard. *Facing West: The Metaphysics of Indian-Hating and Empire-Building.* U of Oklahoma P, 1997.

Driver, Alice. "Why We Need More Female Journalists at The U.S. – Mexico Border." *Worldark,* Holiday 2019.

Dyer, Thomas G. *Theodore Roosevelt and the Idea of Race.* Louisiana State U P, 1980.

Duran, Nicole. "Native American tribes win $940 million in suit against the feds." *Washington Examiner,* 17 Sep 2015. https://washex.am/3n7545y.

Eckert, Allan W. *A Dark & Bloody River: Chronicles of the Ohio River Valley.* Bantam Books, 1995.

Editorial Staff, Indian Country Today. "Reagan: A contradiction to American Indians." *NBCNews,* updated 11 Jun 2004. https:// nbcnews.to/36lFPpW. Commentary.

Editors, History.com. "Transcontinental Railroad." *History.com,* 20 Apr 2010, updated 11 Sep 2019. https://bit.ly/38f7ycY.

Efrati, Amir. "Powwows' Popularity Fuels a Black Market For Eagle Feathers." *The Wall Street Journal*, 22 Dec 2006.

Ehle, John. *Trail of Tears: The Rise and Fall of the Cherokee Nation.* Anchor Books, Doubleday, 1988.

Ellington, Charlotte. *Beloved Mother, The Story of Nancy Ward.* The Overmountain Press, 1994.

"Elouise P. Cobell." *Wikipedia: The Free Encyclopedia,* Wikimedia Foundation. https://bit.ly/32xDTrS.

Eschner, Kat. "Fearing a Smallpox Epidemic, Civil War Troops

Tried to Self-Vaccinate." *Smithsonian Magazine*, 1 May 2017. https://bit.ly/3dyK8A1.

Estes, Nick. *Our History is The Future: Standing Rock vs the Dakota Access Pipeline, and the Long Tradition of Indigenous Resistance.* Verso, 2019. Evans, E. Raymond. "Fort Marr Blockhouse: Last Evidence of America's First Concentration Camps." *Journal of Cherokee Studies, Vol. II, No. 2, Spring 1977.*

Evans, E. Raymond. "Highways to Progress: Nineteenth Century Roads in the Cherokee Nation." *Journal of Cherokee Studies, Vol. 11, No. 4, Fall 1977.*

Evarts, Jeremiah. *Cherokee Removal: The William Penn Essays and Other Writings,* edited and with an introduction by Francis Paul Prucha, U of Tennessee P, 1981. "Budget Process: Federal Budget 101." *National Priorities Project.* https://bit.ly/3673kkQ. Accessed 7 Nov 2020.

Fine-Dare, Kathleen S. *Grave Injustice: The American Indian Repatriation Movement and NAGPRA.* U of Nebraska P, 2002.

Finger, John R. "The Impact of Removal on the North Carolina Cherokees." *Cherokee Removal: Before and After,* edited by William L. Anderson, U of Georgia P, 1991.

Finger, John R. "The North Carolina Cherokees, 1838-1866: 'Traditionalism, Progressivism and the Affirmation of State Citizenship." *Journal of Cherokee Studies, Vol. V, No. 1, Spring 1980.*

Fite, Mrs. R.L. "An Illustrated Souvenir Catalog of the Cherokee National Female Seminary, Tahlequah, Indian Territory 1850 to 1906." *Journal of Cherokee Studies, vol. 10, no. 1, Spring 1985.* Museum of the Cherokee Indian, Spring 1985.

Fitzpatrick, Ellen. *History's Memory: Writing America's Past, 1880–1980.* Harvard UP, 2004.

Ford, Gerald R. *Public Papers of the Presidents of the United States: Gerald R. Ford, 1976-1977. Google Books.* https://bit.ly/3kLV13y.

Ford, President Gerald. "US Presidents in Their Own Words Concerning American Indians: Speech by President Gerald Ford." *Native News Online, 16 Feb 2019.* https://bit.ly/2U4t3oC. Accessed 18 Feb 2019.

Frieden, Joyce. "Native Americans Need More Funding to Battle COVID-19, Lawmakers Told." *MedPage Today.* 12

Jun 2020. https://bit.ly/3ecgIIm.

Gallatin, Albert. "A Synopsis of the Indian Tribes Within the United States East of the Rocky Mountains, and in the British and Russian Possessions in North America." *Transactions And Collections of the American Antiquarian Society Vol II,* Cambridge, 1836.

Garcia, Joe. "The Four Great Steps." *National Congress of American Indians,* 2 Feb 2006, https://bit.ly/3l4bJM6.

Gill, N.S. "Pliny and Mount Vesuvius." *Thoughtco.com.* Updated 10 Nov 2019. https://bit.ly/3l2vPWR. Accessed 28 Mar 2020.

Graham, Judith. "Compensation at last for tribes that lost lands to dams." *Chicago Tribune*, 15 Dec 2002. https://bit.ly/3n8UkTY. Accessed 17 Aug 2020.

Grann, David. *Killers of the Flower Moon: The Osage Murders and the Birth of the FBI.* Doubleday. 2017.

Greenspan, Jesse. "How Native American Code Talkers Pioneered a New Type of Military Intelligence." *History,* 5 Nov 2019. https:// bit.ly/35c3Ai9. Accessed 20 Jan 2020.

Gregory, Jack and Rennard Strickland. *Adventures of an Indian Boy.* Indian Heritage Association, 1972.

Hance, Jeremy. "How Native American tribes are bringing back from brink of extinction." *The Guardian,* 12 Dec 2018 and modified 9 Sep 2019. https://bit.ly/3jhXXol. Accessed 29 Jul 2020.

Hair, Josiah. "What is Blood Quantum? | Definition, Facts, Laws | NativeAmericanIndian." *PowWows,* 27 Apr 2016, updated 24 Nov 2019. https://bit.ly/2Gc6mve. Accessed 26 Jul 2020.

Hanke, Lewis. *Aristotle and the American Indians: A Study in Race Prejudice in the Modern World.* Henry Regnery Company, 1959 and Indiana UP, 1975.

Harjo, Suzan Shown. "The week of 9/11 – Native Peoples in the Society of Sorrow and Justice." *Indian Country Today,* 11 Sep 2018, https:// bit.ly/34gQn78.

Harper, Keith. "Cobel v. Norton: Redressing a Century of Malfeasance." *American Bar Association*, 1 Apr 2006. https://bit.ly/35fCnfW.

Healy, Jack. "For Oklahoma Tribe, Vindication at Long Last." *New York Times,* 11 July 2020. https://nyti.ms/33jEnml.

Hearings before the Subcommittee on Indian Affairs of the

Committee on Interior and Insular Affairs, U.S. Senate S. 750 and H.R. 471.

Heath, Jessica. "The Bison: from 30 million to 325 (1884) to 500,000 (today)." *Flat Creek Inn.* https://bit.ly/2Sg36BD.

Hedgpeth, Dada. "The Irish are repaying a favor from 173 years ago in Native Americans' fight against coronavirus." *The Washington Post,* 13 May 2020. https://wapo.st/3mxfNVK.

Heilprin, John. "They're finally going to get their accounting." *Casper Star Tribune.* 6 May 2006. https://bit.ly/38thxvg.

Hendrix, Janey B. "Redbird Smith and the Nighthawk Keetoowahs." *Journal of Cherokee Studies, Vol. VIII, No. 2, Fall 1983.*

Henson, KenLea. "Building Partnerships: Cherokee Nation investigators join FBI as task force officers." *Anadisgoi,* Spring/Summer 2020.

Hilberg, Paul. *The Destruction of the European Jews.* Quadrangle Books, 1961.

Hirst, K. Kriss. "The History of Archaeology — The First Archaeologists." *ThoughtCo.*, 15 Jan 2020. https://bit.ly/3lxrtHY. Accessed 27 Mar 2020.

"History is a Weapon: Alcatraz Proclamation and Letter." *History is a Weapon*, 1969 https://bit.ly/2ScXRCz. Accessed 10 Apr 2020.

Hofschneider, Anita. "Hawaiians, Pacific Islanders Confront High Rates of COVID-19 in Many States." *CivilBeat,* 10 May 2020, https://bit.ly/2SasJDO. Accessed 19 May 2020.

"Hold Governments Accountable to Native Americans." *Native American Rights Fund.* https://bit.ly/3kmRjNB.

Horwitz, Sari. "U.S. to pay Navajo Nation $554 million in largest settlement with single Indian tribe." *Washington Post,* 24 Sep 2014. https://wapo.st/3jkJAjb. Accessed 21 Aug 2016.

Hoskin, Jr., Chuck. "New Cherokee Health Center will transform health care for generations." 9 Dec 2019. *Cherokee Phoenix.* https://bit.ly/3f1GAXS.

Hoskin, Jr., Chuck. "Supporting state and federal efforts to address MMIW." *Cherokee Phoenix,* 14 Dec 2019. https://bit.ly/33jFxyd.

Hoskin, Jr., Chuck. "Chief Chat: Inter-Tribal Council utilizing technology for meeting and business." 8 July 2020. https://bit.ly/38I4SoG

Hoskin, Jr., Chuck. "Chief Chat: MMIW." 5 Dec 2019. *Cherokee Nation Newsletter.*

Hosmer, Brian. *Native Americans and the Legacy of Harry S. Truman.* Truman State UP, 2010. Introduction.

"How To Obtain Eagle Feathers." *The People's Path.* https://bit.ly/2ScMKcT. Accessed 13 Apr 2020.

"How We Use Water." *U.S. Environmental Protection Agency.* https://bit.ly/3eICAeI. Accessed 11 Jun 2020. "IHS pays $29.5M to end contract dispute with Cherokee Nation." *Indianz,* 15 Jul 2014. https://www.indianz.com/News/2014/07/15/ihs-pays-295m-to-end-contract.asp. (Error in the shortened link)

"Indian Arts and Crafts Act of 1990." *U.S. Department of the Interior,* https://on.doi.gov/3jlQ29Q. Accessed 14 Jul 2019.

"Indian Gaming: Lobbying, 2020." *opensecrets.org, Center for Responsive Politics.* https://bit.ly/2GVY4rY.

"Indian Health Service, Agency Overview," *U.S. Department of Health and Human Services.* 20 Feb 2020. https://www.ihs.gov/aboutihs/ overview.

"Indian Health Service, Agency Overview/About IHS.", *U.S. Department of Health and Human Services.* 20 Feb 2020. https:// www.ihs.gov/aboutihs/overview.

"Interior and Partners Commit to Long-Term Initiative to Conserve the American Bison." *Native News Online,* 8 May 2020. https://bit.ly/2EMR4MZ.

"Interior ordered to disclose trust fund failures." 13 Jul 2005. *Indianz.* See *Cobell v. Kempthorne.* Decided: 11 Jul 2006. https://bit.ly/3kOHDeV.

Isaacs, Sandra Muse. *Eastern Cherokee Stories: A Living Oral Tradition and Its Cultural Continuance.* U of Oklahoma P, 2019.

Jahoda, Gloria. *The Trail of Tears: The Story of the American Indian Removals 1813-1855.* Wings Books, 1975.

"John Winthrop describes life in Boston, 1634." *The Gilder Lehrman Institute of American History.* https://bit.ly/2GAl0wO.

Johnson, Lyndon B. "Special Message to the Congress on the Problems of the American Indian: 'The Forgotten American.' 6 Mar 1968." *The American Presidency Project.* https://bit.ly/355a9nV. Accessed 14 Dec 2016.

Johnson, Dr. Troy. "We Hold the Rock: The Alcatraz Indian

Occupation." *National Park Service*. https://bit.ly/3mL9u11. Accessed 8 Apr. 2020.

Janko, Melinda. "Elouise Cobell: A Small Measure of Justice from Issue." *American Indian: Magazine of Smithsonian's National Museum of The American Indian,* Summer 2013/Vol. 14 No 2. https://bit.ly/3lhGhdL.

Kappler, Charles J. compiler and editor. *Indian Treaties, 1778-1883.* Amereon House, 1972.

Katz, Brigit. "Planned Border Wall May Threaten 22 Archaeological Sites in Arizona, N.P.R. Says." 20 Sep 2019. *Smithsonian Magazine*. https://bit.ly/38vGdDk.

Katz, Brigit. "The F.B.I. Is Trying to Return Thousands of Stolen Artifacts, Including Native American Burial Remains." *Smithsonian Magazine*, 4 March 2019, https://bit.ly/3kY4QM4.

Keel, Jefferson. "9th Annual State of Indian Nations Address Remarks", *National Congress of American Indians,* 27 Jan 2011, https://bit.ly/2Sbkw22.

Keene, Adrienne. "Love in the Time of Blood Quantum." *Native Appropriations*, 4 Apr 2011. https://bit.ly/33iLzit. Accessed Spring 2020.

Kennedy, Danny. "How the Navajo got their day in the sun." *GreenBix,* 28 May 2020. https://bit.ly/3e6jwXr. Accessed 24 Oct 2020.

Kennedy, John F. "Inaugural Address of President John F. Kennedy." *John F. Kennedy Presidential Library and Museum*, 20 Jan 1961, https://bit.ly/33hGKWM. Accessed 10 May 2020.

King, Duane H., editor. "An Illustrated Souvenir Catalog of The Cherokee National Female Seminary." *Journal of Cherokee Studies, Volume X, No. 1, Spring 1985*. "An Illustrated Souvenir Catalog of The Cherokee National Female Seminary, Tahlequah, Indian Territory 1850 to 1906," Arranged and Printed at the Indian Print Shop.

King, Duane H., editor and E. Raymond Evans, consultant editorial. "The New York Spectator (New York, N.Y.)" *Journal of Cherokee Studies, Vol. IV, No. 2, Spring 1979,* January 3, 1832 from *The Boston Courier of Wednesday* reported on the Cherokee Missionaries.

King, Duane H. and E. Raymond Evans. "Tsali: The Man Behind

the Legend." *Journal of Cherokee Studies, Vol. IV, No. 4, Fall 1979.*

King, Duane H. and E. Raymond Evans. "Washington Attempts to Bring Justice to the Cherokees." *Journal of Cherokee Studies, Vol. IV, No. 2, Spring 1979.* Originally printed in *The Connecticut Courant, Jan 7, 1793.*

King, Dr. Martin Luther, Jr. *Why We Can't Wait.* Beacon Press, 1964. Knox, Donald. *Death March: The Survivors of Bataan.* Harcourt Brace Jovanovich, 1981.

Krauthamer, Barbara. "The Encyclopedia of Oklahoma History and Culture – Slavery." *Oklahoma Historical Society,* https://bit.ly/3ihjHiU.

Krehbiel – Burton, Lenzy. "Osage Nation signs agreement in trust settlement." *Native Times,* 20 Oct 2011. https://bit.ly/33mcSsp. Accessed 17 Aug 2020.

Krol, Debra Utacia. "Navajo Nation's water shortage may be supporting COVID-19 spread." *azcentral.com,* 28 Apr 2020. https://bit.ly/35daq8v.

"Land Buy-Back Program for Tribal Nations." *U.S. Department of the Interior*, 31 May 2020. https://www.doi.gov/buybackprogram.

"Land Patent Law and Legal Definition." *US Legal.* *https://bit.ly/38RQHNO.* Accessed 14 Jan 2020.

Landry, Alysa. "Theodore Roosevelt: 'The Only Good Indians Are the Dead Indians'." *Indian Country Today,* 28 Jun 2016. https://bit.ly/34cf8Sb. Accessed 15 May 2020.

Landry, Alysa. "George W. Bush: 'Actively Ignored' Indians; Struggled with Sovereignty." *Indian Country Today*, 25 Oct 2016. https://bit.ly/36rdHlD. Accessed 15 May 2020.

Landry, Alysa. "Bill Clinton: Invites Tribal Leaders to White House." *Indian Country Today,* 18 Oct 2016. https://bit.ly/3kYAIQI. Accessed 21 May 2020.

Landry, Alysa. "Barack Obama: "Emotionally and Intellectually Committed to Indian Country." *Indian Country Today,* 1 Nov 2016. https://bit.ly/2Gl7Xii. Accessed 21 May 2020.

Landry, Alysa. "Harry D. Truman: Beginning of Indian Termination Era." *Indian Country Today,* 16 Aug 2016. https://bit.ly/2U1MoHa. Latour, Mark Louis. *American Government and the Vision of the Democrats.* U P of

America, 2007.

Lawson, Willow. "Indian Skeletons May Never Leave Museums." *ABCNews.* https://abcn.ws/3jneBTG. Accessed 7 Jan 2020.

Lee, Tanya H. "Need Money for College? Cobell Scholarship Fund reaches $60 Million." *Indiancountrytoday.com,* 23 May 2017. https://bit.ly/35h4n2w.

"Lewis and Clark Expedition." *Wikipedia: The Free Encyclopedia,* Wikimedia Foundation, https://bit.ly/2SdkpmL. Accessed 21 Jul 2019.

Library of Congress, "Sioux Song and Dance. *Loc.gov.* https://bit.ly/3mZnV2e. Accessed 15 Jul 2019.

Library of Congress. "Voting Rights for Native Americans." https://bit.ly/2HFrsT7. Accessed 4 Aug 2020.

"List of United States treaties: U.S. – Native American treaties." *Wikipedia: The Free Encyclopedia,* Wikimedia Foundation, https:// bit.ly/2G4rG67. Accessed 26 Jun 2020.

"Lobbyist bilked tribes of millions, report says." *The Colorado Springs Gazette reprinted from The Dallas Morning News. 23 Jun 2005.*

Locklear, Patti K. "Corbett presents history of Oklahoma WWII Prison Camps." *Woodward News,* 26 Feb 2006. https://bit.ly/35457YC. Accessed 22 Aug 2019.

Lowe, Marjorie. "Let's Make It Happen W.W. Keeler and Cherokee Renewal." Originally published in *The Chronicles of Oklahoma,* Summer 1996. https://bit.ly/346c3Tm. Accessed 2 Aug 2019.

MacLeish, Archibald. "Riders on Earth Together, Brothers in Eternal Cold." *The New York Times,* 25 Dec 1968. https://nyti.ms/3dleeXG. Accessed 6 Oct 2020.

Mails, Thomas E. *The Cherokee People, The Story of the Cherokees from Earliest Origins to Contemporary Times.* Marlowe & Co., 1992.

Mankiller, Wilma. "Rebuilding the Cherokee Nation." Speech at Sweet Brian College, VA. 2 Apr 1993. http://gos.sbc.edu/m/mankiller.html.

Mankiller, Wilma and Michael Wallis. *Mankiller: A Chief and Her People.* St Martin's Press, 1993.

McCullough, David. *John Adams.* Simon & Schuster, 2001.

McLoughlin, William G. *After the Trail of Tears: The Cherokee's*

Struggle for Sovereignty 1839-1880. U of North Carolina P, 1994.

Mencimer, Stephanie. "Lone-star justice: conservatives thought Clinton-bashing Judge Royce Lamberth was on their team — until he went after the Bushies." *The Washington Monthly.* April 2002. https://bit.ly/3ePlTxZ.

Millhiser, Ian. "The Supreme Court's landmark new Native American rights decision, explained." *Vox,* 10 Jul 2020. https://bit.ly/3n4l5ZS. Accessed 11 Aug 2020.

"Missing and murdered Indigenous women." *Wikipedia: The Free Encyclopedia,* Wikimedia Foundation, https://bit.ly/2HL1rC5. Accessed 5 Jun 2020.

Montaigne, Fen. "The Fertile Shore." *Smithsonian Magazine,* January/ February 2020.

Monteith, Carmeleta L. "Literacy Among the Cherokee in the Early Nineteenth Century." *Journal of Cherokee Studies, Vol. IX, No. 2, Fall 1984.*

Moquin, Wayne and Charles Van Doren, editors. *Great Documents in American Indian History.* Da Capo Press Inc. 1995.

Mooney, James. *History, Myths, and Sacred Formulas of the Cherokees.* Bright Mountain Books, 1992.

Mooney, James and Frans M. Olbrechts. *The Swimmer Manuscript: Cherokee Sacred Formulas and Medicinal Prescriptions.* United States Government Printing Office, 1932.

Muhammad, Dedrick Asante. Rogelio Tec and Kathy Ramirez. "Racial Wealth Snapshot: American Indians/Native Americans." *National Community Reinvestment Coalition,* 18 Nov 2019. https:// bit.ly/3ijcz5u. Accessed 2 Aug 2020.

"Murdered & Missing Indigenous Women." *Native Womens Wilderness.* https://bit.ly/3n5NkYd. Accessed 29 May 2020.

Murray, Matthew. "Abramoff Leaves Lasting Impact on Tribal Lobbying." *Roll Call,* 24 Jul 2009. https://bit.ly/2K0n5U3.

Museum of the Cherokee Indian. "Cherokees Oppressed in Georgia." *Journal of Cherokee Studies, Vol. IV, No. 2, Spring 1979.* Originally published in *The Saturday Bulletin,* 19 Jun 1830.

Museum of the Cherokee Indian. "Georgia's Attack on the Missionaries." *Journal of Cherokee Studies, Vol. IV, No. 2,*

Spring 1979. Originally published in *New York Spectator,* 3 Jan 1832.

Museum of the Cherokee Indian. "The Murder of John Ridge." *Journal of Cherokee Studies, Vol. IV, No. 2, Spring 1979.* Originally published in *The Daily Albany Argus,* 2 Aug 1839. p. 109.

Museum of the Cherokee Indian. "Washington Attempts to Bring Justice to the Cherokees." *Journal of Cherokee Studies, Vol. IV, No. 2, Spring 1979.* Originally published in *The Connecticut Courant,* 7 Jan 1793.

Nagle, Rebecca. "Half the land in Oklahoma could be returned to Native Americans. It Should Be." *The Washington Post,* 28 Nov 2018. https://wapo.st/3n7yQH5.

National Archives and Records Administration (NARA). https://www. archives.gov.

"National Bison Range Wildlife Refuge Complex: Time Line of the American Bison." *United States Fish and Wildlife Service,* 16 July 2020. https://bit.ly/2GldtS2.

National Constitution Center Staff. "On this day, all Indians made United States citizens." *National Constitution Center.* 2 Jun 2020. https://bit.ly/3nyXLmm. Accessed 23 Jan 2020.

National Library of Medicine. "1968: President Johnson signs the Indian Civil Rights Act." *NLM.NIH.com.* https://bit.ly/2Sf VMWu.

"National Museum of the American Indian." *Washington DC,* https://bit.ly/36mKTdF. Accessed 27 Jul 2019.

"National Museum of the American Indian." *Wikipedia: The Free Encyclopedia,* Wikimedia Foundation, https://bit.ly/3ihP2Ci. Accessed 16 Jul 2019.

"Native American Disease and Epidemics." *Wikipedia: The Free Encyclopedia,* Wikimedia Foundation, https://bit.ly/34c5AXb. Accessed 14 Apr 2020.

"Native Americans and Trusts." *Friends Committee on National Legislation.* https://bit.ly/3ncAN4z.

"Native American Graves Protection and Repatriation Act." *National Oceanic and Atmospheric Administration.* https://bit.ly/2GoGrjX. Accessed 4 Apr 2020.

"Native American Voting Rights Act of 2018." *Wikipedia: The Free Encyclopedia,* Wikimedia Foundation, https://bit.ly/34h6hi9. Accessed 4 Aug 2020.

Native News Online Staff. "Judge Shuts Down Controversial Dakota Access Pipeline Project." *Native News Online,* 6 Jul 2020. https:// bit.ly/3k98i5J.

Native News Online Staff. "Some Navajo Nation Citizens are Voting by Horseback." Native News Online, 2 Nov 2020. https://bit.ly/2IXgERs.

Native News Online Staff. "Navajo Nation Pres. Nez gets call from NY Gov. Cuomo, who offers Support." *Native News Online,* 22 Apr 2020. https://bit.ly/35OHimK.

Neely, Sharlotte. *Snowbird Cherokees, People of Persistence.* U of Georgia P, 1991.

Nonnenmacher, Tomas. "History of the U.S. Telegraph Industry." *Economic History Association,* https://bit.ly/3lG5QFu. Accessed 8 Sep 2019.

Nuyujukian, D.S. (2017). "Sleep Duration and Diabetes Risk in American Indian and Alaska Native Participants of a Lifestyle Intervention Project." *Oxford Academic Sleep Research Society. Sleep,* Vol. 39, Issue 11, Nov 2016, Pages 1919-1926. https://bit.ly/36c86O1.

Obama, Barack. "Presidential Proclamation – National Native American Heritage Month." *Barack Obama White House Archives,* 29 Oct 2010. https://bit.ly/2GXBhfq.

Obama, Barack. "Remarks by the President at Presentation of the Presidential Medal of Freedom" *Barak Obama White House Archives,* 22 Nov 2016. https://bit.ly/3eOyVM5.

Obama, Barack. "Statement of the President on the Final Approval of the Cobell Settlement." *Barack Obama White House Archives,* 26 Nov 2012. https://bit.ly/32yfFxx.

O'Brien, Soledad. "A nearly 200-year-old deal could put the first Cherokee Nation delegate in Congress. Will she be approved?" *Matter of Fact,* 9 Nov 2019. https://bit.ly/2GVYCNS.

Oklahoma Tourism & Recreation Department. *"Oklahoma Indian Country Guide: One State – Many Nations,* 2019.

Oliver, Willard M. and Nancy E. Marion. *Killing the President: Assassinations, Attempts, and Rumored Attempts on U.S. Commander-in-Chief.* Praeger, Aug 2010.

Ortiz, Erik. "Lack of awareness, data hinders cases of missing and murdered Native American women, study finds." *NBC News,* 30 Jul 2020. https://nbcnews.to/3jhbI6M. Accessed 31 Jul

2020.

"Osage Nation beneficiaries still fighting for accounting despite setback in court." *Indianz* 4 May 2017. https://www.indianz.com/News/2017/05/04/osage-nation-beneficiaries-wont-appeal-t.asp#:~:text=Osage%20Nation%20beneficiaries%20still%20fighting%20for%20accounting%20despite%20setback%20in%20court,-Thursday%2C%20May%204&text=Citizens%20of%20the%20Osage%20Nation,setback.%20in%20their%20historic%20lawsuit.&text=U.S.%20have%20passed%20on%20without%20seeing%20the%20promised%20accounting. Accessed 17 Aug 2020. (Error in shortened link)

Perdue, Theda. *Nations Remembered: An Oral History of the Cherokees, Chickasaws, Choctaws, Creeks, and Seminoles in Oklahoma, 1865-1907.* U of Oklahoma P, 1993.

Perdue, Theda. "The Conflict Within: Cherokees and Removal." *Cherokee Removal: Before and After*, edited by William L. Anderson, U of Georgia P, 1991.

Picardi, Phyllis. "Bison." *Defenders*. https://bit.ly/34bGvvE. Accessed 31 Jul 2020.

Pierce, Earl Boyd and Rennard Strickland. *The Cherokee People*. Indian Tribal Series, 1973.

"President Clinton Calls for Passage of His Historic FY2001 Native American Initiative." The White House, Office of the Press Secretary, 25 Feb 2000. https://bit.ly/3mZv7vg.

"Presidential Oath of Office." ArtII.S1.C8. *United States Constitution*. https://bit.ly/32fR00J.

"Problems of the American Indian: Status of the Indian in American Life" *CQ Researcher, 13 Apr 1949.* https://bit.ly/3kBhnVj.

Prucha, Francis Paul, editor. *Documents of United States Indian Policy* 2nd Ed. U of Nebraska P, 1990.

Prucha, Francis Paul, editor. *Documents of United States Indian Policy* 3rd Ed. U of Nebraska P, 2000.

Prucha, Francis Paul. *The Great Father: The United States Government and the American Indians*. U of Nebraska P, 1984.

Public Law No. 95-341, The American Indian Religious Freedom

Act, 92 Stat. 469, August 11, 1978, 42 U.S.C. § 1996. https://bit.ly/3kNPF8L. Accessed 1 Nov 2020.

"Public Rights in Water: The Winters Doctrine." Updated 18 Jun 2019. https://fla.st/3n4x3mn. Accessed 20 Apr 2020.

Pyper, Julia. "The Navajo Generating Station Coal Plant Officially Powers Down. Will Renewables Replace It?" *GTM,* 20 Nov 2019. https://bit.ly/31X9YJj.

Ratledge, Mark. "The Burial of Elouise Cobell." *High Country News*, 28 Nov. 2011. https://bit.ly/2Um16Lq.

"Reaffirmation of the Federal Trust Responsibility to Federally Recognized Indian Tribes and Individual Indian Beneficiaries." *The Secretary of the Interior,* Order No. 3335, 20 Aug 2014. https:// on.doi.gov/38xHBFG.

Reagan, Ronald. "Address at Moscow State University, Moscow, Russia, 31 May 1988." *Miller Center*, https://bit.ly/34bGPKS. Accessed 19 May 2020.

Reagan, Ronald. "Inaugural Address of Ronald Reagan." *Reagan Library*, 20 Jan 1981. https://bit.ly/3jjT5z0.

Reese, Dr. Debbie. "Multiracial" identity and American Indians." *American Indians in Children's Literature,* 30 Mar 2011. https://bit.ly/3p6yx0t.

"Remembering the Time Andrew Jackson Decided to Ignore the Supreme Court In the Name of Georgia's Right to Cherokee Land." *Sustain Atlanta*, 2 Apr 2015, updated 28 Jul 2016. https://bit.ly/30mvQ06. Accessed 16 Aug 2020.

Reyhner, Jon and Edward Tennant. "Maintaining and Renewing Native Languages." *The Bilingual Research Journal,* Spring 1995, Vol 19, No 2.

Rickert, Levi. "After the Death of George Floyd, We Must Get Back to Better." *Native News Online*, 27 May 2020. https://bit.ly/3jkTHEF.

Rickert, Levi. "Federal Judge Expected to Rule on Distribution of CARE Act Funds on Monday." *Native News Online,* 26 Apr 2020. https://bit.ly/3kDyDcw.

Rickert, Levi. "Tohono O'odham Chairman Chides Indian Affairs Leader for Desecration of Sacred Sites for Border Wall." *Native News Online,* 14 Feb 2020. https://bit.ly/3eIeeS3.

Rickert, Levi. "Why the Trump Administration's Failure to initially add tribes to $2 Trillion stimulus doesn't shock me." *Native News Online,* 11 Apr 2020. https://bit.ly/3nCjw4R.

Rhodes, Eric. "Indian New Deal." *National Archives Pieces of History.* 20 November 2015. https://bit.ly/3ifmtVT.

Roberts, Joel. "Interior Secretary Held in Contempt." *CBS News,* 17 Sep 2002. https://cbsn.ws/35q3yoj. Accessed 18 Sep 2002.

Romero, Simon and Graham Lee Brewer. "Oklahoma's Tribes Unite Against a Common Foe: Their Cherokee Governor." *New York Times,* 20 Feb 2020, updated 15 Jul 2020. https://nyti.ms/2GdRkFp.

Roosevelt, Franklin D. "Speech at Fenway Park in Boston, MA." 4 Nov 1944. "US Presidents in Their Own Words Concerning American Indians." *Nativenewsonline.net,* edited by Levi Rickert. https://bit.ly/3cLS00L. Accessed 23 Jun 2018.

Ross, John. *The Papers of Chief John Ross, Vol 1, 1807-1838.* Gary E. Moulton, editor. U of Oklahoma P, 1985, pp. 458-461. https:// historymatters.gmu.edu/d/6598/.

Rothchild, Sylvia, editor. *Voices from the Holocaust.* New American Library, 1982.

Rozema, Vicki, editor. *Voices from The Trail of Tears.* John F. Blair, 2003.

Russell, Frederick H. *The Just War in the Middle Ages.* Cambridge UP, 1975.

St. Joseph's Indian School. "Wachipi – powwow – a Native American tradition." *St. Joseph's Indian School.* https://bit.ly/3cMU092. Accessed 16 Jul 2019.

Sanjek, Roger. editor. *Fieldnotes: The Makings of Anthropology.* "The Secret Life of Fieldnotes." Cornell UP, 1990.

Sass, Jennifer. "Standing Rock Sioux Tribe and NRDC Confront Federal Failures." *Natural Resources Defense Council.* 17 May 2019. https://on.nrdc.org/3cJkNCS.

Satz, Ronald N. "Rhetoric Versus Reality: The Indian Policy of Andrew Jackson." *Cherokee Removal: Before and After,* edited by William L. Anderson, U of Georgia P, 1991.

Schoolcraft, Henry R. *Personal Memoirs of a Residence of Thirty Years with the Indian Tribes on the American Frontiers.* Lippincott, Grambo, 1851.

Schmidt, Ryan W. "American Indian Identity and Blood Quantum in the 21st Century: A Critical Review." *Hindawi: Journal of Anthropology,* 15 Jan 2012. https://bit.ly/34hjp6V.

Schieb, Linda J. "Trends and Disparities in Stroke Mortality by

Region for American Indians and Alaska Natives." *American Journal of Public Health.* Supplement 3, Vol 104, No 33. https://bit.ly/38iL4If.

"Secretary Jewell Issues Secretarial Order Affirming American Indian Trust Responsibilities." *U.S. Department of the Interior,* 20 Aug 2014. https://on.doi.gov/3pJFiFU.

Silver, Matthew. "Air Force Academy Cadets build Modular homes for Navajo." *manufacturedhomepronews.com.* 27 Jun 2016. https://bit.ly/3cIwMAO.

Simpson, Kevin. "More than a century ago, a European visitor took more than 600 Native American remains and artifacts from Colorado's Mesa Verde." *Colorado Sun.* 10 Oct 2019. https://bit.ly/3n2DAhk.

Simpson, Kevin. "To right historic wrongs, Colorado museums embraced spirit of a law that repatriated Native American artifacts and remains – largely by listening." *The Colorado Sun,* 1 Mar 2019. https://bit.ly/35xQkWG.

Simmons, Shawn. "Border wall construction could destroy 22 archaeological sites across Arizona." *The Architect's Newspaper,* 20 Sep 2019. https://bit.ly/36ekZas. Accessed 8 Jun 2020.

Smith, Anna V. "Report: Indigenous voters face racism and suppression." *High Country News,* 1 Jun 2020. https://bit.ly/3jdLTVf.

Smith, Ryan P. "How Native American Slaveholders Complicate the Trail of Tears Narrative." *Smithsonian Magazine,* 6 Mar 2018. https://bit.ly/3cP2Jrg. Accessed 15 Oct 2019.

"Smithsonian Institution." *Wikipedia: The Free Encyclopedia,* Wikimedia Foundation, https://bit.ly/2GtuusY. Accessed 28 Mar 2020.

Soodalter, Ron. "The Tribes of Missouri Part 2: Things Fall Apart." *Missouri Life Magazine.* 6 Sep 2018. https://bit.ly/3nGYXVZ.

Spector, Julian. "Developers Power Teams Up With Navajo Power to Replace Coal Plant with Solar." 6 May 2020. https://bit.ly/36awuQ9. Accessed 24 Oct 2020.

Stannard, David E. *American Holocaust: The Conquest of the New World.* Oxford UP, 1992; see Russell, Frederick H. "The Just War in the Middles Ages." Cambridge UP, 1975; see Little, "'Holy War' Appeals and Western Christianity."

Stanton, Zack. "How Native American Team Names Distort Your Psychology." *Politico,* 16 Jul 2020. https://politi.co/33htFN1.

Strand, John. "20 Years and Counting: James Pepper Henry's Multifaceted View of NAGPRA." April 4, 2020. https://bit.ly/36mnV6w. Accessed 4 Apr 2020.

Strickland, Rennard and William M. Strickland. "Beyond the Trail of Tears: One Hundred Fifty Years of Cherokee Survival." *Cherokee Removal: Before and After*, edited by William L. Anderson, U of Georgia P, 1991.

Stubbs, Roman. "As Redskins conduct name review, Native American groups say they haven't heard from team." *The Washington Post,* 7 Jul 2020. https://wapo.st/3n5iMWv.

Takaki, Ronald T. *Iron Cages: Race and Culture in 19th – Century America.* Knopf, 1979.

The American Indian Religious Freedom Act, Public Law No, 95-341, 92 Stat. 469 (Aug 11, 1978) 14 Dec 2016. https://bit.ly/3kNPF8L. Accessed 1 Nov 2020.

"The Founding Meeting of NCAI: Preamble, adopted Nov 16, 1944." *The National Congress of American Indians,* https://bit.ly/38U6JGJ.

"Through the Coronavirus Relief Fund, the CARES Act providesfor payments to State, Local, and Tribal governments navigating the impact of the COVID-19 outbreak." *U.S. Department of the Treasury,* June 20. https://bit.ly/36dYGSk.

TeSelle, David K. "Review of *McGirt v. Oklahoma* – How the Supreme Court and Justice Gorsuch's Revolutionary Textualism Brought America's "Trail of Tears" Promise To the Creek Nation Back From the Dead." *National Law Review*, 5 Aug 2020. https://bit.ly/34gDV7B. Accessed 10 Aug 2020.

"Timeline 1954: President Eisenhower establishes the Indian Health Service." *Native Voices.* https://www.nlm.nih.gov/nativevoices/ timeline/490.html.

"The Cherokee Blood Law." https://bit.ly/33if2t2. Accessed 1 Feb 2017 and 30 Jul 2019.

"The Feather: A symbol of high honor." *Native Hope.* https://bit.ly/3jjObCm. Accessed 2 Jun 2020.

"The Compromise of 1850." *Anchor: A North Carolina History*

Online Resource. https://bit.ly/31eThsF.

Thomas, Sir Keith. *Man and the Natural World: Changing Attitudes in England 1500-1800*. Penguin Books, 1983.

Thornton, Russell. "The Demography of the Trail of Tears Period: A New Estimate of Cherokee Population Losses." *Cherokee Removal: Before and After*, edited by William L. Anderson, U of Georgia P, 1991.

Toth, Gyorgy. "Native Americans won a vital battle at UN 40 years ago— they need help again." *The Conversation,* 20 Sep 2017. https:// bit.ly/32K5gyO.

Trahant, Mark. "Bush on Native American Issues: 'Tribal Sovereignty Means That. It's Sovereign." 10 Aug 2004. https://bit.ly/34btty9. Accessed 15 May 2020.

Trahant, Mark. "Washington NFL team's Standing Rock moment." *Indian Country Today*, 5 Jul 2020. https://bit.ly/34azdIA.

Timeline 1954: President Eisenhower establishes the Indian Health Service." *Native Voices*. https://www.nlm.nih.gov/nativevoices/ timeline/490.html.

"Treaty of Hopewell, 1785." Article XIII. https://bit.ly/2Jxrm0O.

"Tribal Nations & the United States: An Introduction." National Congress of American Indians. www.ncai.org/about-tribes. Accessed 8 May 2019.

Turner, Alvin O. "Cherokee Outlet Opening." *Oklahoma Historical Society*. https://bit.ly/3cN9OZh.

Tyler, S. Lyman. *A History of Indian Policy*. U.S. Department of the Interior, Bureau of Indian Affairs, 1973.

"Unclaimed Indian Moneys (IIM) and Tribal Trust Funds Search." *Bureau of Indian Affairs Indian Trust Fund*. https://bit.ly/3eMPPei.

"Unforgettable Change: 1960: American Indians Occupy Alcatraz." *picturethis.museumca.org*. https://bit.ly/3n7QwCr. Accessed 21 Mar 2020.

Union of International Associations. "Genocide of indigenous peoples." *The Encyclopedia of World Problems and Human Potential*. http://encyclopedia.uia.org/en/problem/157395.

United Nations, General Assembly. Convention on the Prevention and Punishment of the Crime Of Genocide. Resolution 260 A (III) 9 Dec 1948. https://bit.ly/3ddr6ie.

United Nations, General Assembly. Genocide Treaty 2670,

ratified by Congress with restrictions Nov 1988, Ex B 91st 2nd Session. https:// bit.ly/34Jp71x.

United Nations, General Conference of the United Nations Educational, Scientific and Cultural Organization. "Means of Prohibiting and Preventing the Illicit Import, Export and Transfer of Ownership of Cultural Property." *unesdoc.unesco.org.* 8 Aug 1969. https://bit.ly/2G7ETeq. Accessed 4 Apr 2020.

United Nations Educational Scientific and Cultural Organization. "1970 Convention on the Means of Prohibiting and preventing the Illicit Import, Export and Transfer of Ownership of Cultural Property." *Unesdoc.unesco.org.* 14 Nov 1970. https://bit.ly/3jjx1Vo. Accessed 30 Mar 2020.

United States, Congress, H.R.1585 — *Violence Against Women Reauthorization Act of 2019.* 116th Congress (2019-2020). House Report 116-21. https://bit.ly/3lqABOk.

United States, Congress, House. American Indian Religious Freedom Act Amendments of 1994. https://bit.ly/346ywja. 103rd Congress, House Resolution 4230, passed 6 Oct 1994.

United States, Congress, House, Committee on Natural Resources, Subcommittee for Indigenous Peoples of the United States Oversight Hearing. "Reviewing the Trump Administration's Approach to the Missing and Murdered Indigenous Women (MMIW) Crisis." *U.S. Department of the Interior,* 11 Sep 2019. https://www.doi.gov/ocl/ mmiw-crisis. Accessed 4 Aug 2020.

United States, Congress, House. *Memorial of the Cherokee Nation to the United States Congress 28 September 1836.* 13th Congress, 2nd session– 49th Congress, 1st session. Doc. 99, vol. 5, p. 13.

United States, Congress, House Resources Committee, House Bill 3534. *Cherokee, Choctaw, and Chickasaw Nations Claims Settlement Act.* 107th Congress, 2nd session, House Report 107-632.

United States, Congress, Senate, Committee on Indian Affairs Oversight Hearing on Tribal Self Governance. "Indian Self-Determination and Education Assistance Act." *U.S. Department of the Interior,* 13 May 2008. https://on.doi.gov/3n7RgaH.

United States, Congress, Senate. *Native American Languages Act.*

101st Congress. Senate 2167 – 101st Congress.

United States, Congress, Senate. S.47 -Violence Against Women Reauthorization Act of 2013. 113th Congress (2013-2014), passed 7 Mar 2013. https://bit.ly/3pf38ZB.

United States, Congress, Senate. Savanna's Act. *Congress.gov,* 115th Congress, 2nd session, Senate 1942, passed 6 Dec 2018. https://bit.ly/2Gq91Be.

United States, Court of Appeals for the Tenth Circuit. *Salazar v. Ramah Navajo Chapter.* Docket no. 11-551, 18 Apr 2012. *Oyez.* https://bit.ly/33iuRQ9. Accessed 25 Jul 2020.

United States, District Court. *William S. Fletcher v. The United States of America,* Case No. 07-CV-427-GKF-PJC, 30 Dec 2015. *National Indian Law Library.* https://bit.ly/36oRh4e. Accessed 17 Aug 2020.

United State District Court, District of Montana, *United States v. Blackfeet Tribe of the Blackfeet Indian Reservation,* 364 F.Supp. 192, 10 Oct 1973. https://law.justia.com/cases/federal/district-courts/ F Supp/364/192/2259045/

United States, Supreme Court. *McGirt v. Oklahoma. Certiorari to the Court of Criminal Appeals of Oklahoma. No. 18-9526,* 9 Jul 2020. https://bit.ly/3cJwERm. Accessed 26 Aug 2020.

United States, Supreme Court. *Winters v. United States, 207 U.S. 564,* 6 Jan 1908. https://bit.ly/36mYbHg.

United States, Supreme Court. *Worcester v. Georgia,* 31 U.S. 515. 1832. https://supreme.justia.com/cases/federal/us/31/515/

Utter, Jack. *American Indians: Answers to Today's Questions 2nd Ed. Revised and Enlarged.* U of Oklahoma P, 2001.

Veazie, Mark. " Trends and Disparities in Heart Disease Among American Indians/Alaska Natives, 1990-2009." *American Journal Public Health.* Supplement 3, 2014, Vol 104, No S3: *S35967.* https:// bit.ly/3p6TEiY.

Walker, Richard. "Native History is American History: NMAI is Bringing Indigenous Perspectives Into the Classroom." *National Museum of American Indian Magazine.* Spring 2020.

Wallace-Wells, David. *The Uninhabitable Earth: Life After Warming.* Tim Duggan Books, 2019.

Warren, Stephen and Johnnie Ingram, creators. *We're Here.* The Intellectual Property Corporation, HBO, Spring 2020. https:// itsh.bo/3naSMIi.

Washington, George. "Letter to James Duane on September 7, 1783." *National Archives*, https://bit.ly/2TUzD0X. Accessed 19 July 2019.

Weiss, Eric M."At U.S. Urging, Court throws Lamberth Off Indian Case." *The Washington Post.* 12 Jul 2006. https://wapo.st/3kkdZOc.

West, Delno C. and August King, translation and commentary. *Libro de las Profecias of Christopher Columbus.* U of Florida, 1991.

West, W. Richard, Founding Director National Museum of the American Indian. *Overview: Native Peoples, The Arts and Lifeways, Fall 1994.*

Whitty, Julia. "Elouise Cobell's Accounting Coup." *Mother Jones,* September/October 2005, https://bit.ly/34ejSq9.

Williams, Edwin, compiler. "Jackson's Fifth Annual Message." *The Addresses and Messages of the Presidents of the United States, Inaugural, Annual, and Special, from 1789 to 1846 Vol. II."* Edward Walker, 1849.

Williams, Timothy. "U.S. Will Pay a Settlement of $1 Billion to 41 Tribes." *The New York Times,* 13 Apr 2012. https://nyti.ms/34ho6O5. Accessed 26 Jul 2020.

Williams, Walter L. "The 'two-spirit' people of indigenous North Americans." *The Guardian,* 11 Oct 2010. https://bit.ly/30kpb6g. Accessed 4 Jun 2020.

Wilms, Douglas C. "Cherokee Land Use in Georgia Before Removal." *Cherokee Removal: Before and After,* edited by William L. Anderson, U of Georgia P, 1991.

Wilson, Valerie. "Improved income growth for Native Americans, but lots of variation in the pace of recovery for different Asian ethnic groups." *Economic Policy Institute,* 14 Sep 2018. https://bit. ly/2GpffkQ. Accessed 2 Aug 2020.

Witty, Julia. "Elouise Cobell's Accounting Coup." *Mother Jones,* September/October 2005, https://bit.ly/34ejSq9.

Worcester v. Georgia, 31 U.S. 515, 6 Pet. 515.587 (1832) No. 42. Extinguishment of Indian Title to Lands in Georgia, 18th Cong. (1824).

"Wounded Knee Incident." *Wikipedia: The Free Encyclopedia,* Wikimedia Foundation, https://bit.ly/3cPu64f. Accessed 15 Apr 2020.

Zinn, Howard. *A People's History of the United States.* Harper and

Row, 1980

Acknowledgments

I want to thank my children for their love and support throughout the years. It has meant so much to see them grow into loving adults with families of their own. They are my greatest joy.

I want to extend my sincere thanks to those who have sustained me throughout the years of research and writing of this book. Words of encouragement and critique of materials were especially important by daughter, Elizabeth, and encouragement along with innumerable times of computer support by son, David. Until their deaths, husband, Roger, and daughter, Rhonda, provided unflagging support. To other family and friends, thank you for your understanding and support.

My research and writing are based on the centuries of work done by many writers and recorders of history without whom I would have not been able to accomplish this work. To those unsung people, thank you for providing insights into the lives and struggles of the First Citizens of this country.

My acknowledgments would be incomplete without expressing thanks and sincere appreciation to Max Garrison, my editor and friend. She has been a mainstay during this process. She was responsible for many dark hours when the chapters came back with her editorial critiques. But her edits caused rewrites that strengthened my work and gave a clearer voice to the story. Thank you, Max, for your hard work in bringing this work to life.

Author Biography

An awakened interest in and determination to understand Native American history beyond what was taught in the classroom prompted Patricia Streng to write this book. Understanding that history is primarily written by the victor, she spent uncountable hours researching, traveling and writing to thoroughly research centuries-old historical documents which prove the racism and genocide against Native Americans from the beginning. Her passion unfolds as she tells a story of their strength and resilience as they fight to regain what is rightfully theirs — from treaties to equal rights and opportunities. By writing the book, she hopes to encourage others to join in supporting Native Americans as they fight for justice and equality. Their cause is that of racial equity and has no geographical or ideological boundaries, and it is the author's desire that this book will help make a positive difference in the lives, not only of Native Americans, but of all people who have been victims of racism.